Academic Collective Bargaining

Academic Collective Bargaining

Edited by
ERNST BENJAMIN and MICHAEL MAUER

THE AMERICAN ASSOCIATION OF UNIVERSITY PROFESSORS
WASHINGTON, DC

THE MODERN LANGUAGE ASSOCIATION OF AMERICA
NEW YORK

2006

For information about obtaining permission to reprint material from this
book, send your request by mail (see address below), e-mail
(permissions@mla.org), or fax (646 458-0030).

Library of Congress Cataloging-in-Publication Data

Academic collective bargaining / edited by Ernst Benjamin and
    Michael Mauer.
        p. cm.
    Includes bibliographical references and index.
    ISBN-13: 978-0-87352-972-3 (pbk. : alk. paper)
    ISBN-10: 0-87352-972-3 (pbk. : alk. paper)
    1. Collective bargaining—College teachers—United States.
    I. Benjamin, Ernst, 1937– . II. Mauer, Michael. III. American
Association of University Professors. IV. Modern Language
Association of America.
LB2335.885.U6A233 2006
331.88'11378120973—dc22   2005036187

Printed on recycled paper

Published jointly by

The Modern Language Association of America
26 Broadway, New York, New York 10004
www.mla.org

The American Association of University Professors
1012 14th Street NW, Washington, DC 20005
www.aaup.org

CONTENTS

CONTINGENT FACULTY MEMBERS

GRADUATE ASSISTANTS

PART FIVE
REFLECTIONS AND PROSPECTS

PREFACE

As a professional association devoted to the concerns of its members, the Modern Language Association of America (MLA) is pleased to collaborate with the American Association of University Professors (AAUP) on this volume. The MLA has a long history of providing relevant data, analysis, and policy statements in the fields of language and literary study. Practitioners of the academic disciplines represented by the MLA need tools to assist them not only in their scholarly work but also in their role as advocates for their working conditions. To that end, we hope that this volume will provide some useful instruments for understanding academic collective bargaining in a historical and practical context. Being an informed academic citizen entails research into forms of organization and governance. Our aim in presenting the essays gathered here is, above all, to educate and inform.

The situation of the academic labor force has changed significantly over the past several decades. According to the AAUP's analysis of the United States Department of Education's recent survey of employees in institutions of higher education, contingent faculty members (both part-time and full-time non-tenure-track) now make up 65% of all faculty members in degree-granting institutions, an increase from 58% in 1995 and 43% in 1975. Since 1995, the total number of faculty members has grown from 931,706 to 1,173,556—an increase of 26%. Yet during that time the number of full-time faculty members with tenure decreased by more than 2,000. Although the number of full-time faculty members on the tenure track increased by 17%, the number of full-time faculty members not on the tenure track increased by 41% (Curtis).

The changing demographics of academic labor (that "quiet faculty makeover," in Jack H. Schuster's words) should alarm all of us, wherever we locate ourselves on the employment spectrum. The more jobs keep falling off the tenure track, the more the rights of the academic workforce must be protected. Some students and faculty members have found that unions offer advantages in the fight to establish and uphold good working conditions. While the MLA does not recommend any particular approach to academic collective bargaining, the association has gone on record endorsing the right of all academic employees—full- and part-time faculty members, graduate employees, and staff members—to engage in collective bargaining if they choose to do so (see "Membership," Resolution 3). This book aims to help academic employees learn about the kinds of choices that may be available to them.

The MLA has taken significant steps in recent years to address some of the issues that affect students and teachers in the language and literature fields. The MLA is not an accrediting body, and it has no judiciary or regulatory functions concerning faculty governance; academic organization; or other matters related to hiring, compensation, working conditions, and so forth. What we can do is share with our members advice based on research, on dialogue among members of association committees and governing bodies, on past practices and experiences, and on consensus among practitioners in the field. Many of these recommendations can be found at the MLA Web site (www.mla.org) or in *The Chair's Reference: ADE and MLA Guidelines and Committee Statements*. Among the most salient policy statements are those concerning professional ethics, class size and workload for teachers, use of part-time and full-time adjunct faculty members, minimum wage for full-time and part-time faculty members, conversion of non-tenure-track lines to tenure-track lines, and staffing ratios. The MLA is also a source of "best practices" documents that address matters such as teaching, evaluation, and scholarship; institutional support of informational technology for faculty members; and recruiting, hiring, mentoring, and evaluation of faculty members of color.

Long concerned with the academic job system, the MLA offers many ways of helping those who seek faculty positions. Attendees at the MLA Annual Convention can participate in workshops about the job search, hear updates on the current situation in academic hiring, schedule a one-on-one counseling session with an experienced department chair, and practice interviewing. The Association of Departments of English and the Association of Departments of Foreign Languages, both administered through the MLA, hold seminars for department chairs and directors of graduate studies to facilitate new thinking on various matters related to academic employment and professional development.

The growing use of part-time and non-tenure-track faculty members continues to be a focus of attention. In 1999 the MLA collected staffing information from 1,986 college and university departments of English and foreign languages in the United States and Canada; the data and analysis were subsequently released as a report (see "MLA Survey"). This survey was performed as part of a coordinated effort with the Coalition

for the Academic Workforce (CAW), a group established in 1997, of
which the MLA and the AAUP are members (see their Web site at www
.academicworkforce.org). The purposes of the CAW are to collect and
disseminate information on the use of part-time and contingent faculty
members and to assess its implications for students, parents, faculty members, and institutions; to articulate differences in the extent of changes
in the faculty within and among the various academic disciplines; to evaluate the consequences for society and the public good of changes in the
academic workforce; to identify and promote strategies for solving the
problems created by inappropriate use of part-time, adjunct, and similar
faculty appointments; and to strengthen teaching and scholarship. In addition to the MLA, several other organizations that belong to the CAW
undertook surveys of staffing in their fields. The report that resulted from
this research, "Who Is Teaching In U.S. College Classrooms? A Collaborative Study of Undergraduate Faculty, Fall 1999," offers valuable insights
into the academic job system and underscores why associations must
come together to face the problems that affect us all (see Coalition).

It is in this spirit of coming together that the AAUP and the MLA
have joined forces in publishing this volume on collective bargaining. We
invite you to consult this wealth of materials as you seek to improve
academic institutional life for yourself, your colleagues, and your students. I have observed that most problems we face are variants of issues
we have had to confront in the past. Much wisdom can be gleaned from
the hard lessons others have learned before us.

I wish to acknowledge the key role several people have played in bringing this project to fruition. Phyllis Franklin, executive director emerita of
the MLA, did not live to see this book published; she was deeply committed to the membership's interests and needs, and, with the backing of
the MLA Delegate Assembly and the Executive Council, she led on several measures, such as this one, that seek to improve the working conditions for academic employees. David G. Nicholls, director of MLA book
publications, has worked closely with colleagues at the AAUP to make
this volume a balanced, substantial contribution to our understanding
of the issues. He wishes to thank the MLA staff members Joseph Gibaldi
and Sonia Kane, for their participation in planning meetings; the joint
MLA-AAUP editorial committee, for evaluating the prospectuses for the

perspectives section, offering editorial advice, and selecting the prospectuses for development (the members of this committee were Heather Dubrow, Univ. of Wisconsin-Madison; Catherine C. Fraser, Indiana Univ.; Larry Glenn, Southern Connecticut State Univ.; and Chris McVay, Kent State Univ.); two consultant readers and the MLA's Publications Committee, for evaluation of the prospectus and the manuscript; and the AAUP's counsel, Donna Euben, for assistance in setting forth the terms of our collaboration. It has been a pleasure for all of us at the MLA to collaborate over the years with Mary Burgan, whose tenure as general secretary of the AAUP was marked by vigorous devotion to issues of academic freedom and rights. As she notes in her introduction, any kind of collective action must "engage the utmost energies of individuals." I hope you find these essays energizing and inspiring both personally and professionally.

ROSEMARY G. FEAL

MLA

WORKS CITED

The Chair's Reference: ADE and MLA Guidelines and Committee Statements. Spec. issue of *ADE Bulletin* 132 (2002): 1–118.

Coalition for the Academic Workforce. "Who Is Teaching in U.S. College Classrooms? A Collaborative Study of Undergraduate Faculty, Fall 1999." 12 Sept. 2005 <http://www.historians.org/caw>.

Curtis, John W. "Trends in Faculty Status, 1975–2003." 26 May 2005. 12 Sept. 2005 <http://www.aaup.org/research/FacStatTrends.htm>.

"Membership Ratification Vote." *MLA Newsletter* 32.3 (2000): 5.

"MLA Survey of Staffing in English and Foreign Language Departments, Fall 1999." 12 Sept. 2005 <http://www.mla.org/staffing_survey99>.

Schuster, Jack H. "The Faculty Makeover: What Does It Mean for Students?" *Exploring the Role of Contingent Instructional Staff in Undergraduate Learning.* Ed. Ernst Benjamin. New Directions for Higher Educ. 123. San Francisco: Jossey-Bass, 2003. 15–22.

United States. Dept. of Educ. Natl. Center for Educ. Statistics. *Staff in Postsecondary Institutions, Fall 2003, and Salaries of Full-Time Instructional Faculty, 2003–04.* 18 May 2005. 12 Sept. 2005 <http://nces.ed.gov/pubsearch/pubsinfo.asp?pubid=2005155>.

FOREWORD

Among all the American institutions that have undergone changes in the past twenty-five or so years, higher education has been at once a barometer for and a victim of the most troubling tendencies of American society as a whole. Higher education has grown by leaps and bounds and in complexity since the 1970s. The 1970s were a time when most college students were late-adolescent, middle-income students, salted by some veterans returning from an unpopular war. At the beginning of that decade, only 27.8% of college students were twenty-five or older. Today the proportion of older students is 39%, and many are turning to school to survive in the new war for economic survival (National Center). Meanwhile, the second wave of baby boomers has hit our campuses, and many come from homes with single parents, a language other than English, and little financial support. Institutions of higher education have had to adjust to these radical changes. Campuses that serve varied needs continue to proliferate and now compete alongside the standard array of ivied privates, flagship state universities, teachers colleges, and four-year liberal arts schools. American higher education now presents a dazzling spectrum, including universities that function almost exclusively as research institutes, comprehensive regional and municipal institutions that serve local needs (while aspiring to national recognition), vast academic medical complexes, teeming community colleges, and aggressive online and off-line for-profit enterprises. Robert Zemsky, Susan Shaman, and Maria Iannozzi have investigated student choice in our current array of offerings; they categorize these offerings under such headings as "name-brand" and "convenience." Following their model, we might compare the growth of our institutions with the growth of the American mall, whose attractions range from familiar department stores to specialized boutiques to outlets that promise the products of a Macy's or Saks at much lower prices (Zemsky, Shaman, and Iannozzi; Finn). Commercial growth has been a hallmark of recent American experience, and higher education has shared that growth and exemplified its variety.

The academy has also shared in the negatives associated with growth that takes place in impetuous and unfettered forms. With economic competition as their engine, and in some ways as their nemesis, colleges and universities have tried to meet the needs of a diverse and expectant population. However, they have rarely had the time or resources to adapt their physical and social environments to the changes. For, like our commerce-driven society, American higher education has tended to accommodate growth by ignoring the sustained commitment required for vital continuity. In the effort simply to grow, shoddy new classrooms and dormitories have been built while basic maintenance has been ignored elsewhere. Similarly, higher education has become more and more dependent on contingent faculty members while slighting recruitment and retention of the permanent, full-time faculty members on whom its early development was based. The harm to the social environment of higher education in these modern accommodations is analogous to the physical harms caused by the careless paving over of prairie and farm fields for new developments.

Amidst all the change, however, the traditional hierarchies in institutional authority and in the distribution of wealth and status in our society have not only survived but also intensified their hold. In higher education, as tenure has become more difficult to attain, many of those who have it lead professional lives that raise the envy of those without. This inequity often renders the existence of the bottom tiers invisible to the privileged ones. Because higher education is one of the most hierarchical of American enterprises, it has reflected the distance between the haves and the have-nots more clearly than any other institution. The concentration of resources and status at the top of our educational system—both for institutions and individual faculty members—mirrors the growing concentration of great wealth among a small percentage of fortunate Americans in the larger society. Moreover, the competition to gain admittance to the "best" colleges and universities is a national preoccupation akin to the preoccupation with that other gauge for power and fame in our culture—rankings of high-profile athletics.

In the context of these developments many faculty members in our colleges and universities feel the urge to better organize themselves for the good of the profession. The urge has been most strongly felt in the humanities—especially in English and the foreign languages. These fields have been most subject to deprofessionalization not only by institutional emphases on the "productive" technical and scientific disciplines but also by public demands that all study focus on job training. Further, the managerial expertise that spurred growth in America's commercial sector is now accepted as the best guide for growth in all its other sectors. And so the vaunted methods of business—such as just-in-time warehousing of goods and services, unbundling of skills into modules able to be outsourced, computerization of every possible facet of activity, niche marketing, and the encouragement of record-breaking efforts from every worker—have been assumed to be the keys to managing educational as well as commercial growth. Under such mandates, the best professor is either the strongest competitor for grants and contracts or a temporary worker who can be brought in or sent away at will. Such employment instability runs counter to the safeguards of academic independence and coherence: tenure, peer review, and shared governance. More important, this instability violates traditional norms of the educational process. In response, those faculty members who work with language, which involves the most basic and intimate of human cognitive activities, have been especially active in seeking to exert thoughtful control over the aims and methods of managerial enterprise in their institutions.

This book, or primer, on faculty organizing is founded on the continuing debates in the academy, and especially in the disciplines of English and the foreign languages, about how best to manage the changes of the last twenty-five years. These debates challenge colleagues to explore collective ideals rather than self-interest. Rather than think competitively, they hope to define a form of collective power that can assert long-term, professional interests. Inevitably, as faculty members compare the dismal prospects for most professors in the academy with the high aspirations of the past and as their sense of loss over the new environment deepens, many look to traditional ways of restoring autonomy, self-discipline, and dignity to their efforts. Since there was once a time in America when the labor movement provided such avenues for working people, it is no surprise that academics have taken a second look at unionization as a possible tool for asserting some measure of communal control and collective equity.

For those who are interested in using the methods and procedures of collective bargaining to regain lost ground and create new possibilities, this collection of essays offers technical as well as political and moral guidance. More than that, it offers the seasoned recognition of the vanities of human wishes that makes collective action effective by preparing for difficulties as well as successes. Thus the advice given is at once passionate and cautionary. The passion is shared by members of the two organizations that have sponsored the volume—the Modern Language

Association and the American Association of University Professors. Both associations believe that higher education is so essential to American values that it must not surrender the independence of its practitioners to commercial expediency—no matter how pressing are the calls for unlimited growth. The caution in this volume is also shared; it comes from the mutual realization that collective action cannot be successful if it does not engage the utmost energies of individuals. As the book's editors, Ernst Benjamin and Michael Mauer, repeat again and again, a union—like a faculty senate or a nation—will fail if it cannot create, instruct, and empower citizens.

In a larger sense, then, this book is about academic citizenship. It lays out one powerful way to encourage and structure citizenship in the academy, but its guidance on collective bargaining can be deployed for other kinds of collective academic efforts as well. For example, it calls for more vital faculty governance where collective bargaining is not the choice of faculty members or is unavailable because of state law. And so the AAUP offers this volume not only to our members and members of the MLA but also to faculty members in all disciplines and all schools who seek collegial ways to confront the problems of radical change in American higher education. For our new growth can bring new opportunities as well as new demands if we are willing to confront its problems.

MARY BURGAN

AAUP

WORKS CITED

Finn, Chester E., Jr. "Today's Academic Market Requires a New Taxonomy of Colleges." *Chronicle of Higher Education* 9 Jan. 1998. 14 Sept. 2005 <http://www.chronicle.com>.

National Center for Educational Statistics. "Table 176: Total Fall in Enrollment in Degree-Granting Institutions, by Attendance Status, Age, and Sex: Selected Years, 1970 to 2003." *Digest of Educational Statistics, 2003.* 16 Sept. 2005 <http://nces.ed.gov/programs/digest/>. Path: 2003; Chapter 3: Postsecondary Educ.; Enrollment; Table 176.

Zemsky, Robert, Susan Shaman, and Maria Iannozzi. "In Search of Strategic Perspective: A Tool for Mapping the Market in Postsecondary Education." Change Nov./Dec. (1997): 23–38.

INTRODUCTION

Academic collective bargaining is among the most controversial of the innovations that have transformed American colleges and universities since the 1960s. The essays in this book describe how academics have used collective bargaining to pursue professional standards and academic excellence as well as economic benefits. The editors recognize that many academics fear the contrary: that bargaining necessarily imports to the academy an industrial or adversarial approach that emphasizes economics to the detriment of professionalism and academic quality. We do not neglect these dangers, and we do not write to advocate collective bargaining for all faculties. But we do present the perspective of academics who have successfully used collective bargaining to enhance academic shared governance and who resist the imposition of a corporate style of management. Accordingly, as we describe how academic bargaining has fared on many campuses and explain how to organize and bargain effectively, we strive especially to assist those academics who choose collective bargaining with a view to enhancing professional standards and academic excellence.

Collegial Representation and Academic Bargaining

The American Association of University Professors has encouraged collegial efforts "to promote the standards, ideals and welfare of the profession" since 1915 (Amer. Assn., "Constitution" 285). Collective representation on campus through various forms of shared governance long preceded collective bargaining. AAUP believes that even when academic colleagues determine to adopt collective bargaining, they should use it to enhance, not diminish, shared governance ("Statement" 253). Accordingly, the policies and even many of the techniques described here may be, and often are, pursued collegially without formally certified bargaining, on campuses that have vigorous traditions of faculty governance. Where bargaining does exist, moreover, we presuppose and encourage cooperative efforts between the academic bargaining representative and collegial shared-governance committees or councils.

The universities and community colleges that predominate in higher education today are substantially more complex than the colleges that preceded them. So, too, those colleagues who share in teaching, research, and academic service are far more diverse than the faculty members who preceded them. Academic collective bargaining involves not only full- and part-time faculty members, instructional staff members, and graduate assistants but also many other staff members who contribute to the academic work of teaching and learning. These may include librarians (whom AAUP policy regards as faculty members), instructional specialists, advisers, counselors, researchers, admissions and financial-aid officers, health-care professionals, and others. (See AAUP, "Joint Statement" and "College"). The complexity of universities and community colleges has also increased the proportion of nonacademic to academic personnel; nonacademic personnel include those employees in clerical work, food and dormitory services, maintenance, public safety, finance, and administration. Many of these staff members engage in collective bargaining, and some of the issues and tactics discussed here pertain to them. This book does not, however, encompass all staff members who engage in collective bargaining in the academy. We focus on collective bargaining by staff members whose work primarily involves such academic responsibilities as teaching, research, and related educational services.

The Emergence and Scope of Academic Bargaining

Part 1 of this volume presents a historical overview of academic collective bargaining. The initial essay, "Faculty Bargaining," explores the history, scope, and impact of faculty organizing and bargaining. Collegial faculty associations through the AAUP and faculty unionism through the American Federation of Teachers (AFT) date to 1915 and 1916 respectively. But collegial advocacy, rather than unionization, prevailed in higher education for more than fifty years thereafter, until academic unions were enabled to secure formal recognition as bargaining agents under state and national labor law. In the late 1960s and early 1970s, as labor laws changed and as widespread gains in teacher and other public-sector organizing took place, faculty bargaining emerged and spread rapidly in the northeast and midwest states—New York, New Jersey, Pennsylvania, and Michigan—that permitted certification of faculty unions. Initial organizing efforts there were led by the AFT and the National Education Association (NEA). In 1972, after lengthy study and debate and after the adoption of bargaining by several AAUP chapters, the national AAUP set aside its historical opposition to faculty bargaining. Thereafter the association has vigorously pursued its long-standing principles in and through collective bargaining, as well as through traditional shared governance.

In 1970 the National Labor Relations Board (NLRB) decided that private universities were engaged in interstate commerce and therefore subject to the National Labor Relations Act (NLRA). This ruling spurred a short-lived extension of bargaining to private universities, especially through AAUP. The expansion was abruptly curtailed by the decision in *NLRB v. Yeshiva University* by the Supreme Court that deemed faculty members "managerial employees," ineligible for the protections of the NLRA (see Patrick Shaw's essay, "Prospects," in this volume). Although this decision denies faculty members the protections of the NLRA, it does not forbid bargaining. A small number of private-sector institutions continue to bargain through voluntary recognition. Public-sector bargaining, which continues to benefit from the protection of many state labor laws, has continued to grow. In fall 1998, more than 40% of faculty members, primarily in the public sector, were represented by bargaining agents (see Table 1 in my essay, "Faculty Bargaining," in this volume).

As faculty associations began to petition for recognition as bargaining agents, state legislatures and labor-relations boards began to determine the membership of the bargaining units these agents sought to represent. Some states defined faculty units that included full- and part-time faculty members plus a wide range of academic employees—some of whom had relatively little direct involvement in instruction or research. In other states, faculty members were defined to exclude not only noninstructional staff members but even some full-time instructional staff members. Faculty members with part-time or adjunct appointments were slower to organize separately, but, as they did seek representation, state policies again varied. Some states require separate part-time units, some include part-time in full-time units, and some limit the right to bargain exclusively to full-time faculty members. In the private sector, part-time faculty members tend to avoid combining with full-time faculty members, in part because private sector full-time faculty organizing has been curtailed by the Supreme Court's *Yeshiva* ruling.

Graduate assistant organizing is described by Patricia Gumport and Dan Julius in their essay, "Graduate Assistants' Bargaining." Graduate assistant unions flourished briefly in the early 1970s but remained confined to a few large public universities. Then, in the 1990s, stimulated by increased workloads and diminished prospects for faculty employment and assisted by major unions, including the AFT, United Auto Workers, and Communications Workers of America, graduate assistants renewed their efforts and achieved recognition at several large state universities. Soon afterward, following a favorable decision by the NLRB in a case involving New York University, graduate assistants began organizing at several leading private universities. In 2004, the NLRB reverted to its pre-NYU position that graduate assistants were essentially students, not employees, and thus were ineligible for protection under the NLRA. Where they do bargain, primarily under state law, graduate assistants are now generally in separate bargaining units and separate bargaining associations from faculty members at their institutions, although there are occasional instances where they are included with the faculty or share the same bargaining representative.

Academic Organizing and Bargaining

With or without bargaining, academic standards and professionalism depend on ensuring the effective organization and representation of the full- and part-time faculty members and graduate assistants who conduct the academic work of the academy. Where faculty organization and representation are weak, academic values rarely secure adequate representation through strong management. Management has too many competing "stakeholders," "constituencies," and "missions" to give priority to academic concerns. Academics also have competing interests, but where they organize and work in concert, they have the greatest ability to ensure that academic concerns achieve the priority appropriate to academic institutions. Parts 2 and 3 of this volume are intended to promote such effective academic organization and representation. Although we have divided the exposition of organizing and representation into two parts, it is important to understand that effective representation depends on recurrent organizing. Moreover, effective representation reinforces organization, whereas ineffective representation weakens and divides.

ACADEMIC ORGANIZING

As the essays in part 2 suggest, the initial impulse to organize typically reflects perceived weakness. That is why academics who are confident that they can protect academic and professional standards through their individual bargaining power or who are confident in the effectiveness of shared governance in their particular institution are less likely to pursue collective bargaining than faculty members in troubled institutions. And so bargaining is less frequently espoused by the more prestigious, and marketable, faculty members at the most prestigious institutions. This pattern is consistent with the legislative history and purpose of the NLRA, which established legal protections for concerted action only by those employees who lacked the bargaining power sufficient to balance that of their employers.

Organizers in the academy need to overcome the initial weakness and the threatened loss of prestige in which collective bargaining has its roots. Pete Seeger once sang, "Unions are for workers, but the teachers have prestige. They can feed their kids on that old noblesse oblige" (Seeger). Today, public school teachers seek to protect their profession through collective bargaining and are among the most organized of all employees. Additionally, full-time college and university faculty members, despite the continuing view of many that joining unions is unprofessional, have increasingly turned to bargaining to protect their profession. As a result, they are now more densely organized than employees in general and are as organized as other public employees. Part-time faculty members and graduate assistants, though less densely organized than full-time faculty members, are now organizing more rapidly. The essays in part 2 are intended to describe and assist these efforts.

In the first of his essays, "A Primer on Academic Union Organizing," Patrick Shaw discusses general organizing strategies and tactics in the context of the legal protections and limitations that affect faculty bargaining. His second essay, "Prospects for Full-Time Faculty Organizing at Private Universities and Colleges," focuses on the special problems of private institutions and explains the limits and possibilities for bargaining and collective representation in the light of the *Yeshiva* decision. In her essay, Iris Molotsky outlines the basics of faculty organizing regardless of whether the prospect of collective bargaining is imminent. The final essays in this section focus on the unique difficulties and opportunities both in organizing and in representing two distinctive sectors of academic appointees. My essay assesses part-time faculty members as well as full-time, non-tenure-track faculty members who also hold contingent appointments. Marcus Harvey's essay explains why graduate student assistants are employees as well and explores the significance of this tension. Both essays emphasize that the profession and the academy can benefit from successful organizing by these academics.

ACADEMIC BARGAINING

The first five essays in part 3 describe and assess basic collective bargaining organization and procedures. In "A Primer on Organizational Development," Michael Mauer presents an overview of the local bargaining association and emphasizes the need for recurrent organizing to sustain effective representation even after the victory in the collective bargaining election. In a second essay, "Making Collective Bargaining Work," he discusses typical bargaining tactics and the manner in which fundamental disagreements are resolved through negotiation, job actions or strikes, and impasse resolution procedures. In the third essay, Julius provides a management perspective on faculty bargaining. This essay is not included to achieve a balance between union and management perspectives, since this volume is explicitly weighted toward an AAUP perspective, one that Julius himself often shares. Rather, the editors believe that academic bargaining is less well understood and less successful when administrative needs and political complexities are inadequately considered.

Four specialized essays complete this section. Gregg Adler, a practicing labor attorney who represents academic unions, reviews the basic legal issues that typically arise in negotiations and offers advice on when and to what extent it is important to seek and employ legal counsel. James Semelroth completes the discussion of basic bargaining procedures with an explanation of how grievance and arbitration are used both to ensure individual rights and to protect the collective agreement. The two remaining essays in part 3 examine the principle substantive bargaining issues. In "The Collective Agreement: Economic Issues," I explore economic bargaining. In the final essay of part 3, I explore how major non-economic or professional issues are typically resolved. In both essays, I emphasize how traditional professorial principles and expectations, such as those historically endorsed by AAUP, can be and often are integrated into the collective agreement, not only by AAUP but by all academic bargaining representatives.

Despite their diversity, all those engaged in academic collective bargaining share some procedural and tactical concerns and the need to adapt bargaining to academic concerns and practices. Accordingly, personnel procedures must ensure the opportunity for collegial academic evaluation as well as individual rights. Grievance procedures similarly need to provide a role for the collegial judgment customary in the academy as well as for the independent arbitral review customary in collective bargaining. Most academic collective bargaining contracts now assume that in the academy shared governance, rather than the simple hierarchy of supervisor and employee, is as necessary to the quality of academic decision making with collective bargaining as without it.

The manner in which collegial academic judgment can be preserved alongside or incorporated into the bargaining relationship depends not only on institutional patterns and practices but also on a legal concept known as scope of bargaining. Where there is a right to collective bargaining, this right generally extends to all matters regarded as terms and conditions of employment. These terms and conditions may not necessarily entail or may exclude bargaining over academic issues such as curriculum, academic calendar, and staffing—or even the procedures for resolving such issues. Even where such academic matters are excluded, however, they remain the province of shared governance. Moreover, academic unions may bargain about the impact of these academic decisions. They may also confer with the administration, formally or informally, to work out effective shared-governance mechanisms for resolving areas that are not clear.

Although I do not explore this complex issue further in the introduction, readers of this volume need to understand that, despite the constraints and limitations that have developed out of the bargaining practices in other sectors, the adoption of collective bargaining does not necessarily foreclose the continuation of such academic practices as merit-based evaluation, peer review, and collegially based shared governance. Indeed, collective bargaining agreements may be, and, in the view of the editors, should be, constructed to ensure the continuance of these essential attributes of academic decision making.

Perspectives

Part 4 of this volume consists of essays from members of the academic community, who share their perspectives regarding their experiences with academic collective bargaining. These essays describe both the organizing and representational aspects of academic unionism. Although the authors generally support academic bargaining, several draw on their firsthand experience to offer reservations and concerns. Since most of the authors in this section have engaged in unionization through organizations not affiliated with AAUP, their essays reflect a more diverse perspective than the earlier essays do.

Narratives recounting campaigns for collective bargaining often portray struggle and strife, which labor-relations professionals refer to as war stories. Intense accounts of sometimes difficult and exciting battles and accomplishments, they often replicate the passions, or at least the commitments, that sustain the arduous tasks of organizing and representing colleagues in stressful circumstances. They therefore convey the motivations, frustrations, and satisfactions that accompany academic organizing and representation. Of course, experience tells us that effective academic representation, like good teaching, is best achieved when enthusiasm is tempered by integrity and careful reflection—which are represented in these essays as well.

The first group of essays in part 4 focuses on full-time faculty members, beginning with an overview of bargaining in the universities that constitute the Pennsylvania State System. Martin Morand and Ramelle MaCoy provide a useful introduction because of their retrospective look at the early years of bargaining; because their bargaining association has been variously affiliated to NEA, AAUP, and AFT; and because they analyze the role of state politics in bargaining at public universities. The three essays that follow emphasize later stages of bargaining. Brad Art's essay on bargaining by the Massachusetts State College Association (an affiliate of the NEA) depicts successful efforts to preserve tenure and professional standards against a concerted attack by a state board of higher education. Richard Katz and Dean Casale describe how the changing circumstances of faculty bargaining have affected Kean University in New Jersey, including a successful initiative to transform the leadership in their local AFT union and to increase its effectiveness in negotiating academic and professional issues. Roger Hatch and John Pfeiffer use their long-term experience with the NEA representative at Central Michigan University to show how attention to contract enforcement can sustain and enhance professional standards for the campus faculty.

A lack of job security and diverse responsibilities often mean that part-time and non-tenure-track faculty members face greater obstacles to organizing and bargaining than do full-time faculty members. The next three essays describe organizing among these contingent faculty members. Liesl Orenic describes how she balanced her family responsibilities and weighed the risks of her contingent status as she assisted the successful NEA efforts on behalf of part-time faculty members at Roosevelt University. The essays that follow are by Elizabeth Hoffman, a non-tenure-track lecturer at California State University, Long Beach, who is also vice president of the California Faculty Association (an affiliate of NEA, SEIU, and AAUP), and Gary W. Reichard, provost at California State University, Long Beach, and a former member of the statewide administrative negotiating team. Each offers a perspective on their sometimes collegial and sometimes adversarial efforts to develop appropriately professional policies for the CSU lecturers (who include both full- and part-time non-tenure-track appointees).

The four essays on graduate assistant organizing and representation that follow explore the extent to which graduate assistants find it necessary to organize collectively to counter increasingly corporate management styles in universities. Andrew Gross's argument for militant organizing and employee solidarity as a way to achieve basic employee rights is based on his observations during the drive for recognition and negotiation of a first contract by the Association of Graduate Student Employees (UAW) with the University of California. Jaclyn Janesk describes a graduate assistant organizing campaign at Cornell University that failed in part because the organizers did not persuade their colleagues of the need for collective representation. Though she recognizes the value of graduate assistant representation, Anna Geronimo Hausmann draws on her experience organizing health-care workers, as well as her graduate student representation experience at the State University of New York, Buffalo, to explore the obstacles and limits to effective graduate student organization. Alyssa Picard provides a useful counterpoint to each of these previous essays. She bargained on behalf of the graduate assistant union at the University of Michigan, which had been long established and is affiliated with the AFT. On the one hand, she describes a broad range of issues, including training, affirmative action, and child care, that may concern a more developed graduate assistant bargaining representative. On the other, she presents the case for why the transitory nature of graduate students' presence on a campus may strengthen rather than weaken their organizational effectiveness.

Editors' Perspective

In part 5, the editors conclude the book with brief appraisals. The essay "Reflections," by Benjamin, reviews the observations in part 4, "Perspectives," in the light of the book as a whole. This discussion highlights the substantial differences in the views expressed by the authors of the "war stories" from one another, from the editors, and from the authors of the preceding sections. Some of the divergences reflect circumstances; others signify differences of opinion regarding the tactics; strategy; and, in some instances, objectives of bargaining. Of course, the careful reader will observe similar differences of emphasis, if not of viewpoint, among all the authors of the volume.

In his concluding essay on the "prospects" for academic bargaining, Mauer speculates on the future of academic unionism. He outlines the legal, political, and economic obstacles to continued growth, as well as the grounds for optimism—especially in the opportunity collective bargaining affords academics who seek to participate more actively in shaping their futures. The editors of this volume believe that the prospects will be improved if academics come to share a better-informed understanding of academic collective bargaining.

Despite its adversarial quality, collective bargaining, like litigation, is fundamentally a method of conflict resolution. The legal obligation to bargain and the various pressures to reach an agreement can lead to orderly resolution though conciliation and compromise on issues that might otherwise remain festering sources of conflict. Legal regulation generally precludes bargaining from intruding on academic deliberation; thus bargaining may enhance shared governance by establishing ground rules. Absent the legal foundation and closure provided by bargaining, shared governance may too easily atrophy, and both faculty morale and administrative efficiency may wane. Further, procrastination, irresolution, and recurrent resentment often result from inconclusive or imposed outcomes.

Critics contend, however, that collective bargaining in the academy may sacrifice professional standards in the interest of short-term economic advantage. They assert that academic collective bargaining fosters mediocrity rather than meritocracy, that its bureaucratic rigidity displaces academic judgment, and that the conflict implied in the act of negotiating supplants collegial deliberation. Proponents of academic bargaining argue that what endangers professional welfare and standards is the displacement of academic administration by corporate-style management. Proponents view bargaining as a means to mitigate the tendencies for market concerns and managerial favoritism to displace merit, for managerial regulation to supplant academic judgment, and for intrusive management to replace collegial academic deliberation (Benjamin).

This volume does not affirm either the dire expectations of the critics or the hopes of the proponents. It concurs with Sidney Hook's observation in 1973 that the pertinent choice "is not between acceptance or rejection of the principle of collective bargaining but . . . under what form of collective bargaining can *the academic mission* best be preserved and strengthened" (13). Many critics and proponents of academic unionism do, however, share certain fundamental premises. These include respect for academic excellence and the need to preserve opportunity for the effective expression of academic judgment through peer review and shared governance. Because this volume has been designed to respect and promote these essential academic values, the editors hope we have been responsive to the concerns of doubters as well as advocates of faculty unionism.

Of course, academic bargaining, like collective bargaining in general, has a downside. It frequently reflects or engenders anger and frustration. These reactions may fuel, but may also disrupt, the organizing and negotiating processes. Academics, who are good at argument, need to learn that even the most reasonable arguments do not necessarily persuade— hence the need for concerted action to impose a cost on the adversary's refusal to listen. Long-term practitioners often find as well, however, that once serious negotiations have begun, effective collective bargaining depends less on winning arguments, or even on simple trade-offs, than on finding mutually acceptable solutions to difficult problems. So, although we have been fully mindful of the obstacles and frustrations inherent in academic or any bargaining, we have tried throughout this volume to encourage a problem-solving approach that promotes the professional standards we believe contribute to academic excellence.

ERNST BENJAMIN

WORKS CITED

American Association of University Professors. "College and University Academic and Professional Appointments." *Academe* 89.2 (2003): 105–08.

———. "Constitution of the Association." Amer. Assn., *Policy Documents* 285–90.

———. "Joint Statement on College and University Librarians." Amer. Assn., *Policy Documents* 238–39.

———. *Policy Documents and Reports.* 9th ed. Washington: AAUP, 2001.

———. "Statement on Governance for Institutions Engaged in Collective Bargaining." Amer. Assn., *Policy Documents* 253–54.

Benjamin, Ernst. "Unionization and Academic Excellence." *Unionization and Academic Excellence. Proceedings, Thirteenth Annual Conference.* NCSCBHEP. Apr. 1985. Ed. Joel M. Douglas. New York: Baruch Coll., CUNY, 1986. 23–27.

Hook, Sidney. "The Academic Mission and Collective Bargaining." *Proceedings, First Annual Conference.* NCSCBHEP. Apr. 1973. Ed. Maurice C. Benewitz. New York: Baruch Coll., CUNY. 8–17.

Seeger, Pete. "Teacher's Blues." *Gazette.* Vol. 1. Folkways, 1958.

PART ONE

OVERVIEW

Faculty Bargaining

ERNST BENJAMIN

In this essay I present an overview and assessment of the emergence, scale, and significance of collective bargaining by full- and part-time faculty members in American colleges and universities. I seek not only to describe the development of faculty bargaining but also to provide a foundation of sources, data, evidence, and analysis that support this volume's focus on the effective representation of academic and professional concerns through collective bargaining. I begin, therefore, by exploring why faculty members turned to collective bargaining at a time of increasing professionalism and then emphasize throughout and in the conclusion how bargaining has affected academic professionalism.

Factors Contributing to the Emergence of Academic Bargaining

Collective bargaining in higher education is rooted in the general growth of unionism stimulated by the New Deal legislation of the 1930s and the economic expansions of the 1950s and early 1960s. Despite the gains for industrial unions in the earlier times, faculty members did not begin to organize for collective bargaining until the late 1960s, when blue-collar unionism had peaked and public-sector bargaining surged. This delay in faculty organizing may reflect the fact that many faculty members, even those generally supportive of unionism, identified themselves as professionals rather than workers or even employees. Nonetheless, even though faculty members continue to identify with their disciplines, professional concerns proved less an obstacle than an incentive as academic unionism grew rapidly in the 1970s and more slowly thereafter.

The primary impetus for growth derived from two sources. First, many states adopted enabling legislation. Second, although in the 1950s and the 1960s the terms and conditions of higher education employment consistently improved, by the 1970s employment improvements substantially decelerated.

Enabling Legislation and Professional Organizing

The National Labor Relations Act (NLRA), also known as the Wagner Act, of 1935, along with other New Deal legislation that established a protected right to organize and bargain, spurred the growth of industrial unions but did not apply to the public sector. Moreover, this legislation was not found applicable to private-sector universities until 1970, following the emergence of enabling legislation for public-sector higher education bargaining in several states (Carr and VanEyck 3–8). In an early appraisal of the emergence of faculty bargaining, Joseph Garbarino found that the "extension to government workers, particularly at the state level, of the right to organize for collective bargaining is the most important single reason for the present form and growth of academic unions" ("Emergence" 3). His compelling evidence includes the observation that, as of summer 1972, thirty-six of thirty-seven formal faculty bargaining relationships in four-year institutions were in states that had enabling legislation (5). The Taylor Law, enacted in 1967, enabled bargaining for public employees in New York; within two years, the full- and part-time faculty members in the City University of New York (CUNY) were organized, followed soon afterward by faculty members and nonteaching professionals in the State University of New York system (SUNY). Other northeastern states quickly passed similar legislation, enabling organization of the faculties at the state colleges and universities in New Jersey, Pennsylvania, Massachusetts, Rhode Island, as well as Michigan (Lee, *Collective Bargaining* 12). At about the same time, in 1970, the National Labor Relations Board reversed its previous objections and ruled that colleges and universities were subject to the NLRA and that their employees had a right to bargain under the act (Carr and VanEyck 25–28).

Although the application of enabling legislation at the federal level removed a barrier to academic collective bargaining and even facilitated its spread, this protection does not explain why some faculty members chose to pursue collective bargaining and others did not. Certainly there were signs of pent-up demand. Kerry Grant, a long-term AAUP collective bargaining leader, provided an initial draft of this section of this essay, in which he recalled that as late as 1975, on the very day the enabling legislation became effective in Connecticut, local affiliates of both the AAUP and the American Federation of Teachers (AFT), filed with the state labor board to hold a representation election—each presenting "signature cards" of the required 30% of the state-college faculty-bargaining unit. By this time the readiness of national faculty unions to pursue bargaining opportunities was itself a factor in the spread of bargaining. Following the public-sector enabling legislation of the mid-1960s, the spread of public-sector bargaining, and especially teacher unionism, provided not only an example of professional bargaining but also crucial organizational support for faculty efforts to bring collective bargaining to the academy. Such support does not, however, explain why so many academics were eager to take advantage of their new opportunity.

Through the decades of the mid-century, American faculty members had experienced considerable improvement in their circumstances without bargaining. As Sidney Hook observed in the early 1970s:

> [T]he remarkable transformation in the history of American higher education in the last sixty years, especially in the growth of academic freedom, the recognition of tenure, and increased economic rewards, has been achieved *not* by exercise of power, *not* by strikes or threats of strike or disruption of community life, but by appealing to the validity of professional standards of scholarship, research and teaching. Progress was made by offering the evidence that these standards require conditions of freedom, security and reward. . . . Faculties today have more actual power in virtue of the recognition of their professional authority than they have ever had before in American History. (10)

If academic life had been improving and faculty members had been achieving their professional objectives without the tools of collective bargaining, what motivated the spread of academic unionism that began in the late 1960s and accelerated in the 1970s? And what motivates it to continue at a slower pace to the present? Although the issues that fostered organizing and bargaining at particular institutions often reflected local circumstances and personalities, there is general agreement that several economic and professional concerns were common to all such efforts.

ECONOMIC CONCERNS

Wages are often a spur for unionization, but the economic motivations for faculty bargaining cannot be attributed simply to issues of salary and compensation. Robert K. Carr and Daniel K. VanEyck observe that the shortage of faculty members following the rapid growth of higher education in the 1950s and 1960s, aided by the development of the AAUP salary survey and by comparative rankings, led to salary increases greater than the rate of inflation in every year from 1960–61 through 1968–69. Even as late as 1970–71, the average increase slightly exceeded the increase in the cost of living. But Carr and VanEyck also present survey data indicating that a majority of faculty members found their salaries unsatisfactory. Somewhat fewer of those faculty members who favored collective bargaining as of 1969 were dissatisfied with academic salary levels or their own salaries (42–55). More important to the long-term development of academic bargaining, faculty salaries adjusted for the cost of living peaked in 1971–72 and, in large part because of the inflation of the 1970s, began a ten-year decline from which they did not recover until thirty years later (Hamermesh 23–24).

Nonetheless, whatever dissatisfaction with compensation may have contributed to the rise of academic bargaining, bargaining did not prevent the erosion of faculty earnings in the 1970s. Moreover, as Harry A. Marmion emphasizes, even before the erosion of salary gains in the 1970s, larger faculty concerns with the future of higher-education finances and with the direction of institutional policies strongly contributed to the support for bargaining (3). Similarly, Garbarino emphasizes not only concerns about compensation but also the consequences of worsening economic factors for faculty professional opportunities and authority. Diminished increases in public funding meant diminished hiring rates despite the increasing production of PhDs. The decline in opportunities impaired mobility and, thereby, the market power of individual faculty members. Positions with tenure and research opportunities declined. Many new academics experienced pressure to take on increased teaching loads, and many found their positions less secure ("Emergence" 7–10). The economic squeeze also increased reliance on part-time faculty members, and the proportion of part-time faculty members who desired but were unable to obtain full-time positions increased (Benjamin, *Exploring*). Because these broader economic pressures not only contributed to the motivation for academic collective bargaining but also helped shape it, they require closer examination.

PROFESSIONAL AND GOVERNANCE CONCERNS

The economic contraction of the 1970s exacerbated structural problems that had been emerging over many years. Hook emphasizes that faculty members in prestigious universities were less likely to support collective bargaining than those in two-year and the lower-ranked four-year institutions. He also emphasizes the importance of divisions of interest between junior and senior faculty members (12). Indeed, his observations regarding improvements in higher education better describes the faculties of elite colleges and research institutions than those of comprehensive universities, less-well-endowed baccalaureate institutions, and community colleges. Many poorly financed two-year institutions were created to provide a less expensive postsecondary educational opportunity for the growing numbers of disproportionately low-income and minority students. Nearly two-thirds of the faculties of these institutions teach part-time (Benjamin, *Exploring* 6). Many normal schools and small private four-year colleges also became part of a rapidly growing and under-financed public system. Faculty members recruited to these institutions from large graduate universities often found heavier teaching loads, lower research expectations, fewer professional opportunities, and administrative structures closer to a principal-teacher model than to the collegial model that had prospered in the research universities and elite private liberal arts colleges during their development.

Not surprisingly, faculties in the less prestigious institutions looked to the achievements of collective bargaining in the elementary and secondary schools as a means for achieving their ends and dominated the early history of unionization in higher education. In the early 1970s, three-quarters of the institutions with recognized bargaining units were in the two-year sector of higher education (Angell 88). Most of the four-year institutions that adopted bargaining were former teachers colleges or urban public research universities. When the faculty of large state systems voted to bargain, the success of the election often reflected the militancy of the faculty from the regional four-year campuses and two-year colleges, as well as part-time faculty members and nonteaching professionals who outnumbered the more prestigious, and therefore generally less union-oriented, senior faculty members on the research campuses.

Enrollment growth in the 1970s outstripped the increases in full-time faculty appointments, producing larger class sizes and pressures for heavier teaching loads. Those new faculty members who found themselves at less prestigious institutions than those from which they had obtained their graduate degrees and to which they aspired frequently sought to bring professional standards up to the level of the graduate institutions that educated them. Equally important, as senior faculty members became less mobile, it became increasingly difficult for them to improve their salary and work conditions by moving elsewhere or by individually bargaining and threatening to move. As fewer faculty members were willing to risk giving up tenured positions, administrators desiring more flexibility sought to reduce the proportion of the faculty that held tenure. A faculty with rising aspirations thus found itself with declining mobility and tenure opportunities as administrators insisted on doing more with less. This mix of changes provided a fertile ground for organizing faculties that sought the power not only to ensure their welfare and security but also to protect and enhance professional practices.

Professional concerns were important in community colleges as well as in universities. George Angell, president of the State University College at Plattsburgh in New York as of 1973, has reported that two-year faculty members in Michigan and New York "gave as their primary reasons for organizing low salaries, unilateral decisions by trustees and administrators, lack of communication between administration and faculty, and a general feeling of being treated as high school teachers rather than as members of a college faculty" (89). He added:

> Perhaps the most telling factor leading to unionism, however, was the lack of academic freedom on some campuses. During the 1960s many campuses became centers of political activities directed against the war in Vietnam, racism and autocratic institutions of all types. Faculty members participating in political activities sometimes lost their jobs without a hearing. Angry faculties turned to collective tactics even before they organized unions to protect their constitutional rights. (90)

These observations apply as well to the four-year sector, where faculty members engaged in strikes or boycotts at Saint John's University (1966), Catholic University (1967), and San Francisco State University

(1969). These actions were the result of faculty agitation over academic freedom and governance concerns and took place before the emergence of efforts directed toward collective bargaining (Carr and VanEyck 180–82).

The 1960s and 1970s were also eras in which many institutions evolved and expanded. Teachers colleges, in particular, tended to have powerful administrations and relatively small faculties concentrated in a few disciplines. As these institutions expanded to become first general-purpose colleges and then regional universities, they established new departments and schools, populated by new faculty members who had expectations of professional independence and some measure of influence on institutional policy and practice. In contrast to the older faculty members, many of whom had experience with K-12 administrative practices and teachers' unions, this influx of junior faculty members fresh from graduate school or postdoctoral positions brought both their experience with research-university governance structures and their desire to make over their new homes in those models. Institutional growth brought the addition of sizeable numbers of mid-level administrators and support-staff members, many of whom also felt the need for collective action to achieve their goals. Some senior faculty members shared the view that it was time for change; others, along with many administrations, saw no reason to alter structures or policies. Further, the increasing size and complexity of institutions led faculty members to seek replacement of informal with formal mechanisms of governance (Garbarino, "Emergence" 10). Increasing divisions in such faculties also affected the expectations for bargaining. Younger faculty members might seek bargaining as a new route to power, but older faculty members sometimes turned to bargaining as a way to forestall a shift in power to younger colleagues allied with an "enterprising" new president (Carr and VanEyck, 57–58).

The intertwined concerns for professional welfare and academic authority raised serious issues regarding the future of the academy. Would the inclusion of nonteaching academic staff members in faculty-bargaining units detract from professional concerns (Carnegie Council, "Faculty Collective Bargaining" 8–9; Feller and Finkin 97–102)? Would bargaining shift power to less academically successful or junior faculty members? Would the increasing centralization fostered by system-wide bargaining lead to leveling at flagship campuses and a diminished concern for academic excellence (Hook 13–14; Garbarino, "State Experience" 68)?

Would the faculty's desire for procedural fairness and job security lead to the displacement of tenure and personnel policies for some more easily acquired form of job security (Hook 15; Chait)? Would the pursuit of greater authority by faculty members lead those dissatisfied with ineffective faculty senates to seek a substitute in the form of the union (Begin; Wollett 34–35)? Before I explore how these issues have been resolved, it seems best to survey the extent and organization of academic collective bargaining as it actually evolved.

Organization of Academic Bargaining

Some faculty and academic staff members, particularly in community colleges, have organized and continue to bargain independently or with the assistance of noneducational, particularly civil-service, unions. Most unionized faculty members, however, have organized and continue to bargain with the assistance of the AAUP, the AFT, or the National Education Association (NEA). In a few instances, academics have allied themselves with a different national organization or created a joint organization that includes one or more such organizations. Reliance on national organizations has predominated despite the fact that faculty representatives previously engaged in informal negotiations with campus administrators without substantial reliance on outside organizations.

Garbarino reports, for example, the results of an NEA survey in 1969–70 that found that 43% of 1,141 four-year institutions responding to a questionnaire "had arrangements whereby the governing board conferred with faculty representatives on salary or welfare." ("Experience" 13–14). He explains the shift to reliance on external organizations as follows:

> An independent internal organization finds it hard to provide the services that a full-fledged bargaining relationship requires. The resources needed for full-time staff to lobby in state capitals, to function in often lengthy and technical negotiation sessions, to undertake legal representation before administrative boards and the courts, to conduct grievance hearings and arbitrations, to press membership drives and carry on election campaigns, and to service the membership after a contract has been negotiated cannot be commanded by the institutional representative in the usual case. (15)

Garbarino's list provides a rationale for why academics turned to national organizations for assistance, but it somewhat overstates the argument. He also omits the consideration that the preexisting faculty committees and senates were not only local but also, like management-sponsored employee councils in industry, without independent funding. Further, they had been constituted for shared governance rather than for meeting the adversarial responsibilities and legal demands of formal collective bargaining (Lieberman 51–52).

National associations and their state affiliates often provided substantial outside assistance and even subsidies for local faculty groups during organizing drives. Thereafter, however, they usually supplied only technical training, information, and advice in support of campus bargaining and related activities. They rarely subsidized locals, and, to the extent they provided staff assistance, did so based on local dues revenues. Local bargaining representatives frequently use their own staff members and retain legal counsel and other expertise as needed. State organizations often provide public-relations and lobbying assistance by bringing local units together and sometimes by emphasizing the affiliations between teachers and other unionists. Such activities are even conducted by faculty members in some public institutions and systems without reliance on an external organization. (Michael Mauer discusses more fully how the different national unions and associations approach the issue of political activities in his "primer" in this volume.)

The reliance on national and state organizations, then, has most to do with their role in conducting organizing drives, assisting inexperienced faculty members in the early stages of bargaining, and providing special assistance in times of crisis. Over time, local dues more often subsidize state and national activities than the reverse. Cooperative efforts with and local dues support for national organizations are important, but effective bargaining depends primarily on local resources and organization. Bringing in the national union does not substitute for effective local organizing, and much of what unionized faculty members do can be achieved through campus organizing and resources, even without formal bargaining.

Faculty Unions and Associations

The AFT formed in 1916 as an affiliate of the American Federation of Labor. As that affiliation suggests, the AFT has traditionally stressed the bond between teachers' unions and unions throughout the labor movement. The AFT included college teachers from its earliest days and formed college locals as early as the 1930s. It established a college division in

1966, which included nearly seventy higher education locals by 1969 (Marmion 3). Although some AFT college-teacher locals began to establish formal collective bargaining without benefit of protective legislation in the 1950s, the real breakthrough for teachers occurred in New York in 1962, following a successful recognition strike (Carr and VanEyck 120–21). The AFT negotiated its first community-college contracts in Michigan (1966) and Chicago (1967) and its earliest four-year-college contracts at Bryant College of Business Administration in Rhode Island (1967) and at the United States Merchant Marine Academy (1968) (Hurd and Bloom 35, 66; Carr and VanEyck 17–18).

Tracing its roots to the mid–nineteenth century, the NEA is the oldest and largest of the three major organizations that represent faculty members (Carr and VanEyck 117–20). For most of its existence, the NEA was a professional organization that included principals as well as teachers; it only began significant engagement in teacher collective bargaining in response to AFT's initiatives in the mid-1960s. Participation by teachers in higher education bargaining followed immediately on its adoption of teacher bargaining, and the earliest reported two-year-college contracts, in 1965, were established at several NEA-affiliated junior colleges in Michigan (Hurd and Bloom 33–34). NEA state organizations in New Jersey and New York contributed to the rapid expansion of faculty bargaining thereafter. The NEA has continued to identify as an association rather than a union, and it has substantial noncollective bargaining membership, especially in K-12 public schools, in those states that prohibit or discourage teacher bargaining.

The AAUP was founded in 1915 as a professional organization exclusively for faculty members in higher education. Over the next fifty years, the association formulated policies and recommended practices to promote academic freedom, professional standards, and shared governance in colleges and universities. As higher education faculty unions formed in the late 1960s, the national AAUP, which had gradually broadened its membership, engaged in recurrent debates about whether its principles could coexist with collective bargaining. Nevertheless, local AAUP chapters began to pursue bargaining; they included Belleville Area College in Illinois (1967), Saint John's University in New York (1970), and Oakland University in Michigan (1971) (Hurd and Bloom 21, 36, 54). The national AAUP, which formally rejected participation in bargaining as late as 1966, slowly moved to a position that opined that a local

AAUP campus chapter might, in "extraordinary circumstances," become a bargaining agent. Finally, there was a formal endorsement of collective bargaining for AAUP chapters by AAUP's council in fall 1971 and by members at its annual meeting in June 1972 (Carr and VanEyck 121–27; Hutcheson 97–135). Then, in 1973, the association adopted its "Statement on Collective Bargaining," which asserts that collective bargaining properly pursued could be one means to further traditional faculty goals—including academic freedom and tenure, due process, and sound academic government (Amer. Assn. 56). The AAUP was initially successful in organizing single-campus, public, urban and regional universities and private-sector four-year campuses (Carr and VanEyck 138). But the growth of private-sector organizing was curtailed when the Supreme Court's 1980 *Yeshiva* decision denied most private faculty members the protections of the NLRA.

Scale of Bargaining

The competition among the three major faculty organizations—AAUP, AFT, and NEA—undoubtedly contributed to the rapid spread of collective bargaining in areas where the legal circumstances became and remained favorable. Garbarino found that as of June 1972, there were 158 bargaining institutions, of which 119 were two-year and 39 four-year institutions. The NEA led in the two-year sector, with 72 units compared with 38 AFT, 1 AAUP, and 10 independent affiliates. The four-year sector was more closely divided, with 11 NEA, 14 AFT, and 11 AAUP ("Emergence" 14). Twenty-five years later, the numbers are substantially greater, but the distribution is similar. In 1997, of 358 organized two-year campuses, NEA represented 197, AFT 112, and AAUP 9; 29 had local associations, and the others were represented by various other agents or combined organizations. Of 158 four-year campuses, AAUP represented 50, AFT 49, and NEA 35; 10 were independent or had other agents or were combined units (Hurd and Bloom 136).

It is more difficult to estimate the number and proportion of academics represented today. In 1998, Richard Hurd and Jennifer Bloom reported that 256,000 faculty members were included in bargaining units, of whom some 68,000 were in NEA units, 90,000 in AFT units, and 27,000 in AAUP units. About half of these were in the four-year units, where the distribution included 45,000 AFT, 25,000 NEA, and

25,000 AAUP units (139). This distribution does not include all those faculty members in combined AFT-AAUP, AFT-NEA units. Especially significant are the 18,400 California State University faculty members represented by the California Faculty Association, which is jointly affiliated with AAUP, NEA, and the Service Employees International Union (SEIU) but which appears in Hurd and Bloom only as an SEIU affiliate.

Of the 1,125 faculty bargaining units in the 1998 report, about 150 were composed primarily of part-time faculty members. These units encompassed some 76,000 members (Hurd and Bloom 85–109). The precise number of part-time faculty members represented in general faculty units that include both part- and full-time faculty members is unknown but may be estimated at 45,000 to 60,000, based on the 120,000 to 130,000 represented part-time faculty members reported in table 1. The proportion of part-time faculty members included in combined units varies from a small minority to a majority. Most stand-alone, part-time units are in community colleges, and two-thirds of these units are found in California, New York, and Washington.

Many faculty bargaining units include large numbers of professional staff members who neither hold faculty appointments nor engage in teaching. This complication makes it difficult to estimate the proportion of represented faculty members from the Hurd and Bloom data both because an unknown number of nonfaculty members are included as faculty and because an unknown number of unrepresented nonfaculty academics are excluded. The proportion of faculty members in bargaining units and bargaining associations may be better determined by using the data from the fall 1999 *National Study of Postsecondary Faculty [NSOPF]*, conducted in 1998 by the National Center for Education Statistics. These data, as presented in table 1, enable us to ensure that the same type of academics are counted.

Overall, about 41% of those full-time faculty or staff members who have primarily instructional responsibilities are in units represented by a bargaining agent. These primarily instructional faculty and staff members are only about three-fifths of the academics surveyed, however. When all faculty and academic staff members engaged in instruction are included, the proportion in a unit represented by a bargaining agent falls to 36%. Although this percentage counts many who are primarily researchers, administrators, and clinicians, it does not count those academic

TABLE 1. Participation of Faculty and Instructional Staff Members in Collective Bargaining by Type and Control of Institution, Fall 1998

	Estimated Number of Faculty and Staff Members		Member of an Association or Union That Serves as Their Legal Bargaining Agent (percentage)		Included in a Unit Represented by a Bargaining Agent but Not a Member (percentage)		Total Faculty and Staff Members Included in a Unit Represented by a Bargaining Agent (percentage)	
	All	Primarily Instructional	All	Primarily Instructional	All	Primarily Instructional	All	Primarily Instructional
Full-Time Faculty and Staff Members								
Doctoral								
Public	223,780	107,370	13.2	**16.2**	19.3	**20.9**	32.5	**37.1**
Private	67,330	29,780	6.0	**7.5**	8.9	**9.3**	14.9	**16.8**
4-Year/Comprehensive								
Public	101,530	79,860	31.2	**33.8**	20.1	**21.8**	51.3	**55.7**
Private	106,950	81,490	5.7	**6.6**	8.4	**8.7**	14.1	**15.3**
2-Year								
Public	108,540	89,760	51.0	**51.7**	14.6	**15.2**	65.6	**66.8**
Private	4,710	3,510	7.4	**10.0**	1.0	**1.3**	8.4	**11.3**
Total	**612,840**	**391,780**	**20.7**	**25.2**	**15.4**	**16.2**	**36.2**	**41.4**
Part-Time Faculty and Staff Members								
Doctoral								
Public	69,800	49,610	9.7	**11.3**	14.4	**12.9**	24.1	**24.2**
Private	37,520	27,100	7.4	**9.5**	10.1	**10.5**	17.5	**19.9**
4-Year/Comprehensive								
Public	59,490	54,090	19.1	**19.4**	17.1	**16.6**	36.3	**36.0**
Private	88,820	82,980	7.9	**8.3**	7.7	**8.0**	15.6	**16.3**
2-Year								
Public	186,160	161,850	21.4	**21.3**	16.2	**16.1**	37.6	**37.4**
Private	7,020	6,150	2.1	**1.2**	4.6	**3.6**	6.7	**4.8**
Total	**448,810**	**381,780**	**15.1**	**15.8**	**13.7**	**13.4**	**28.8**	**29.2**

Source: United States. Dept. of Educ. Natl. Center for Educ. Statistics. *National Study of Postsecondary Faculty (DAS), NSOPF:* 99. CD-ROM. Washington: US Dept. of Educ., 2001.

Note

"All" faculty and staff members includes both those who have faculty designations and engage in some activity related to credit-earning students and those who have instructional responsibilities, including advising and supervising students enrolled in for-credit instruction.

"Primarily instructional" faculty and staff members are those of the above who report that 50% or more of their time is devoted to instructional activities. The remaining faculty and staff members include those whose primary activities are administration, research, or some other activity such as clinical service.

staff or faculty members who have no instruction-related responsibilities. Since most part-time faculty and instructional staff members have primarily instructional responsibilities, the proportion of part-time faculty and staff members represented holds at about 28% by either calculation. The lower proportion of part-time than full-time faculty members represented reflects the greater difficulty in organizing part-time faculty members regardless of their relatively disadvantageous terms of employment.

Table 1 also enables us to compare representation by type of institution and to explore the proportions of represented faculty and staff members who have actually become members of the association that represents them. In public institutions, some two-thirds of full-time faculty and instructional staff members in two-year colleges are represented by unions, compared with just over half in four-year and comprehensive institutions and with about one-third in doctoral institutions. This distribution conforms to the expectation that faculty members are more likely to pursue bargaining at the less privileged institutions. Representation of part-time faculty members follows a similar pattern, but its variance is much less pronounced. Representation of full-time faculty members in private colleges and universities is substantially lower mainly because of the *Yeshiva* decision, which effectively denies most private-sector faculty members the protections of national labor law. *Yeshiva* has not, however, prevented some private-sector faculty members from successfully maintaining established bargaining relationships or, in a few instances, from establishing new ones. Overall public-sector representation of primarily instructional full-time faculty and staff members is almost 50%. Although much lower than the percentage for school teachers, this percentage is above the norm for all public employees. Despite that only 34 states have policies or legislation that enable collective bargaining in higher education, it is significant that faculty members who can bargain often choose to do so (Hurd and Bloom 149).

Data on representation are not the same as data on membership. Overall, about three-fifths of represented full-time and just over half of represented part-time faculty and instructional staff members belong to the organization that represents their bargaining unit. Conversely, an unknown number of faculty members, who are not included in bargaining units, are members of associations or unions that bargain for others or elsewhere. Again the participation of full-time faculty members in unions varies by type of public institution; membership ranges from three-quarters at two-year colleges to three-fifths at comprehensive and four-year universities to less than half at doctoral universities. The participation rate of part-time faculty members is lower than the rate for full-time faculty members in each type of institution. This lower membership is a disincentive to organizing and an obstacle to effective representation. The participation of full-time faculty members, like representation, is generally lower at those institutions where faculty members have greater individual bargaining power.

Faculty participation in bargaining organizations also varies by principal field of instruction. Table 2 lists the fields in descending order of membership in bargaining organizations. That social science and humanities faculty members have the highest participation rates (about two-thirds) and engineering the lowest (less than half) would not surprise most academic observers. The relatively low overall participation rate among faculty members in education, however, might surprise. This apparent anomaly reflects the difference between education faculty members in doctoral institutions, whose participation rate is similar to that of business faculty members, and in comprehensive institutions, where the participation of education faculty members is second only to those of social science faculty members. Business participation rates are somewhat higher than might be expected overall, but the relatively high participation and proportion in two-year colleges may offset low participation in doctoral institutions. The relatively high participation of faculty members in the health sciences reflects both the large two-year component in those fields and the inclusion of nursing and various allied health professions as well as medicine. These variances suggest that support for unionization is greater in those disciplines commonly viewed as being more liberal but also as having less attractive employment opportunities in or out of academe.

The Impact of Faculty Bargaining

Some early concerns about faculty bargaining focused more on process than outcome. Early observers feared that the inclusion of academic staff members and the enhanced influence of junior faculty members would cause basic employment concerns to displace professional concerns. Many also warned that the adversarial negotiating process and concomitant

TABLE 2. **Participation of Primarily Full-Time Faculty and Instructional Staff Members in Collective Bargaining by Principal Field of Instruction and Type and Control of Institution, Fall 1998**

	Estimated Number of Faculty and Staff Members	Proportion of Faculty and Instructional Staff Members Who are Included in a Unit Represented by a Bargaining Agent (percentage)	Proportion of Faculty and Instructional Staff Members Who are Members of Their Bargaining Agent (percentage)	Proportion of Bargaining-Unit Members Who Are Members of Their Bargaining Agent (percentage)
Social Sciences	**42,850**	**38.0**	**25.7**	**67.8**
Doctoral	15,620	31.5	13.7	41.2
4-Year/Comprehensive	20,420	34.6	27.1	78.3
2-Year	6,820	63.1	51.0	80.8
Humanities	**67,810**	**44.2**	**29.7**	**67.1**
Doctoral	21,840	37.2	22.2	59.6
4-Year/Comprehensive	29,840	37.6	21.7	57.6
2-Year	16,130	65.7	54.5	82.9
Health Sciences	**39,310**	**36.5**	**22.7**	**62.3**
Doctoral	17,720	34.4	11.7	48.1
4-Year/Comprehensive	10,300	30.8	16.6	53.9
2-Year	11,290	60.6	45.6	75.2
Fine Arts	**29,110**	**46.2**	**27.7**	**59.9**
Doctoral	9,290	40.1	17.6	43.8
4-Year/Comprehensive	14,090	39.4	20.3	51.5
2-Year	5,730	72.8	62.2	85.3
Business	**32,600**	**39.2**	**23.0**	**58.7**
Doctoral	8,750	25.7	7.8	30.4
4-Year/Comprehensive	14,010	29.6	14.4	48.7
2-Year	9,830	64.8	48.8	75.3
Natural Sciences	**76,650**	**41.4**	**23.8**	**57.4**
Doctoral	24,720	33.2	13.6	40.9
4-Year/Comprehensive	31,340	33.4	17.4	52.1
2-Year	20,590	63.4	45.7	72.1
Education	**27,930**	**43.7**	**24.5**	**56.1**
Doctoral	8,710	36.7	12.4	33.8
4-Year/Comprehensive	16,080	44.5	27.7	62.2
2-Year	3,140	59.2	42.0	70.9
Engineering	**17,420**	**41.8**	**17.4**	**41.7**
Doctoral	10,390	39.5	10.4	26.3
4-Year/Comprehensive	4,370	31.8	18.5	58.3
2-Year	2,670	67.1	43.0	64.1

Source: United States. Dept. of Educ. Natl. Center for Educ. Statistics. *National Study of Postsecondary Faculty (DAS), NSOPF: 99.* CD-ROM. Washington: US Dept. of Educ., 2001.

Note
Primarily instructional faculty and staff members are those faculty or staff members who engage in some activity in relation to credit-earning students and report that 50% or more of their time is devoted to instructional activity.

resort to strikes would disrupt and polarize academic activities. I begin, therefore, by assessing these procedural issues.

Labor law imposes a duty of fair representation that requires the bargaining agent to treat all unit members fairly, but the law does not require the agent to treat all members alike. Nor do organizational politics compel identical treatment of all members. In 1981, after more than a decade of faculty bargaining, J. Victor Baldridge and Frank R. Kemerer published the most comprehensive assessment of the effects of faculty bargaining. They found, contrary to their expectation, that junior faculty members would reap the greatest gains from faculty unions, that "faculty members are more inclined to preserve earlier status differences in contracts than to negotiate them away." They conclude, "Although generalizations are risky, both questionnaire research and contract analysis suggest that the leveling process has not yet been a major outcome of collective bargaining" (25). This remains true.

The parties involved in academic bargaining have not pursued benefits for the faculty constituency with the greatest numbers or with the lowest level of institutional support but have established diverse policies for the various subgroups. Full-time, senior faculty members may dominate promotion committees. Junior faculty members may be eligible for special summer research grants. Faculty members may be expected to publish, whereas counselors may not. Full-time faculty members generally receive rights and benefits unavailable to most part-time faculty members. Salary increases may be in dollars, not salary percentages, to the advantage of junior faculty and staff members. Or, salary increases may be based on selective criteria, like publication, that favor a minority of faculty members. Work assignments may vary by discipline and even within departments. If there is any pattern for full-time faculty members, it is that more diverse units, especially four-year and doctoral universities, are likely to negotiate more diverse policies regarding such basic concerns as compensation and workload (Rhoades 37; Benjamin, "Patterns" 63–71). Meanwhile, part-time faculty members remain systemically less well compensated and less well supported professionally (Rhoades 131–69; Benjamin, *Exploring*).

Despite the concern that bargaining would lead to an increase in adversarial relations and disruptive strikes, there have been no studies to determine whether such a result has materialized. Strikes, a few of them long and disruptive, have certainly occurred, but they have not been the norm. Drawing on the annual reports from the National Center for the Study of Collective Bargaining, Gary Rhoades found 48 faculty strikes between 1984 and 1994 (15). Many of these strikes were of brief duration, and their number is small when placed against the number of opportunities. The 48 strikes were no more than 3% or 4% of the at least 1,200 to 1,500 bargaining rounds in which I estimate 400 to 500 faculty units would have engaged during this time period.

Rhoades attributes "the limited strike action" among faculty members to contractual clauses prohibiting strikes during the term of the agreement (15–18). But differences in the legislative penalties and judicial enforcement of public-sector strike prohibitions have undoubtedly been more significant. This factor is evident, first, because faculty strikes have been more common, for example, in Michigan, where judges are slow to enjoin strikes, than in New York, where legislative penalties are draconian. Similarly, faculty bargaining agents engaged in system-wide bargaining, such as those in New York and California, have generally relied less on job actions than on legislative and public relations compared with those, such as in Michigan and Ohio, that have typically engaged in campus-based bargaining. Even within a single state, such as Pennsylvania, single-campus units have been more likely than multi-campus units to strike. Strikes have also been avoided in states, particularly Connecticut and Nebraska, that provide binding interest arbitration when negotiations reach impasse.

Moreover, mid-contract strikes are rare, and agreements not to strike during the life of an agreement are a commonplace. The contractual control of strikes is generally thought to be a beneficial feature of United States labor relations. The United States system, in contrast with that in the United Kingdom, has relied on grievance procedures rather than job actions to resolve individual grievances and disputes over contract interpretation. Baldridge and Kemerer note that members of both management and unions who responded to their survey reported that "the collective bargaining process helped channel and regulate conflict though the grievance procedure." They go on to observe, "Conflict management has long been recognized as a benefit of collective bargaining in the industrial setting, and that benefit seems to carry over into higher education"(2). In sum, despite the occasional work stoppages, collective bargaining has actually contributed to reducing campus conflict.

Bargaining Outcomes

Examination of bargaining outcomes reinforces the finding of Baldridge and Kemerer. But before reviewing the evidence regarding the effect of bargaining on shared governance, I return to the issues involved in negotiating basic terms and conditions of employment. These include compensation levels, salary distribution, and personnel policies.

COMPENSATION LEVELS

Bargaining was widely expected to bring increases in compensation. Collective bargaining has probably contributed to salary gains in community colleges, but its effects in four-year institutions are less evident. Writing about the early effects of bargaining in Michigan and New York, Angell found that "the rise in community college salaries in comparison to increases in civil service salaries, four-year college salaries, and cost of living indices from 1968 to 1971 indicates almost spectacular relative gains for community college faculties . . . caused at least in part by bargaining" (95). Similarly, Garbarino reasons that early salary gains in community colleges contributed to the decision of four-year faculty members to organize ("Emergence" 6).

The fiscal crisis of the 1970s led, however, to a sharp decline in real salaries across the public sector. Baldridge and Kemerer note that where there were some improvements in the compensation of unionized faculty members shown in studies before 1974, subsequent research suggests that these gains, except a $200 to $300 advantage in fringe benefits, had disappeared except in the private sector (6–7). Although simple comparisons of faculty salaries in unionized and nonunionized institutions generally show a union advantage, more careful studies that control for type of institution, location, and other key variables do not. A summary of salary studies published in 2004 found that "at best, faculty unions increase their members' average salaries by a very small percentage." The authors attribute this finding to the fact that faculty members who bargain in the public sector often lack a right to strike, and are often subject to legislative control of tuition and budget (Ehrenberg et al. 212). They also cite, however, a study that found a 7% to 14% salary advantage for unionized faculty members that they attribute to the atypical inclusion of community-college faculty members (294). It seems clear, therefore, that two-year-college faculty members have gained economically from collective bargaining but that gains are less clear in the case of four-year public institutions where the best-paid faculty members are those who retain individual bargaining power that enables them to vie for positions at nonunionized flagship campuses.

Part-time faculty salaries have not been systematically surveyed or studied, but they likely have benefited from bargaining. It is also likely that the failure of part-time-faculty salaries to keep pace with full-time salaries has at times released funds to fund full-time faculty salaries. Indeed the heavy dependence of community colleges on part-time faculty members surely contributes to the relative success of their full-time faculty salary bargaining. Part-time faculty members therefore face a difficult choice in determining whether they will do better economically in stand-alone units, where they have full control of their own bargaining positions, or in combined units or coalitions, where they may benefit from the greater bargaining power of the full-time faculty members but may also find their interests subordinated to those of the full-time faculty members. The increasing proportion of part-time faculty members with relatively poor compensation does not proportionately increase the salaries of full-time faculty. The lower compensation for part-timers drives down full-time faculty compensation by forcing more prospective faculty members to compete for fewer well-paid full-time faculty positions (Benjamin, *Exploring* 95–96).

Public-sector full-time faculty salaries did in fact decline in constant (inflation-adjusted) dollars as unionism spread in the 1970s, but the decline might have been greater without unionization. Variances between unionized and nonunionized campuses may have also been diminished by the spillover effect created when nonunion campus administrations increased salaries both to compete for faculty members from unionized campuses and to avoid unionization. Moreover, since the unionized four-year campuses are often those where individual faculty members have had less bargaining power than faculty members at the more prestigious campuses, the similarity of union outcomes to those on nonunion campuses may actually reflect a positive union effect compared with what would have occurred absent a union. Finally, since all the findings reflect averages, specific systems and campuses may have done substantially better or worse at various points in time. As a practical matter, however, expectations about possible compensation gains through unionization need to reflect specific circumstances, such as opportunities to affect public and legislative support through political action and institutional budgeting priorities through the bargaining process.

SALARY DISTRIBUTION

Variances in full-time and some part-time faculty salaries in four-year, comprehensive, and doctoral institutions primarily reflect discipline and rank. Many two-year institutions, however, do not offer rank and establish salary levels primarily on the basis of academic degree or equivalencies as well as professional or institutional longevity. Variations based on individual achievement, discipline, and rank tend to be greater at more prestigious and research-oriented institutions. Collective bargaining has incorporated these preexisting institutional differences in compensation from its inception (Carr and VanEyck 267). Nonetheless, in a subsequent study, Baldridge and Kemerer report "unionized institutions are less likely than non-unionized institutions to have merit pay systems." Moreover, those unionized institutions with merit pay allocate smaller dollar amounts for merit than nonunionized institutions with such pay (41).

Unless the measure of merit pay is simply unfettered administrative discretion to award salary increments, such comparisons are misleading because very little is known about how discretionary or selective salary awards are made in nonunionized institutions. The practices of nonunionized institutions often vary widely by department and even by individual decision makers. Thus, for example, in those nonunion settings in which a varying mix of peers, chairs, deans, and senior administrators allocate increases, some may choose to divide the increments into equal dollars or percentages whereas others may make decisions based on considerations ranging from careful merit assessments to outright favoritism. Consequently, in studying nonunionized institutions, outside researchers rarely know to what extent the prevalent discretionary increments are in fact merit- or even market-based.

In contrast, unionized faculty members have sought with substantial success to limit administrative discretion in setting salaries. This has been accomplished by various forms of across-the-board distribution and by some combination of negotiated criteria and peer review in the distribution of merit-, market-, and equity-based selective increments. Thus, although the discretionary increments may be fewer and smaller on collective bargaining campuses, their purpose is more clearly defined and more certainly subject to research. Based on a careful description and assessment of salary provisions, Rhoades found that two-thirds of four-year and about 20% of two-year contracts included some system of merit increments. Similarly, nearly half of the four-year agreements included specific market and equity provisions (73). Collective bargaining has certainly diminished administrative discretion regarding faculty salaries, but it has also preserved a spectrum of opportunities for academic judgment by administrators and by peers in awarding merit- , market- , and equity-based salary increments.

PERSONNEL POLICIES

Collective bargaining has encouraged the formalization of personnel policies in the academy. Baldridge and Kemerer report that a 1979 survey found, for example, that 88% of unionized campuses and only 55% of nonunion campuses had written tenure policies. Most important, they found that although bargaining had not influenced the establishment of tenure at four-year institutions (where tenure systems are generally present), 75% of unionized two-year campuses, compared with less than 50% of nonunion campuses, were likely to have tenure in some form (40). Moreover, there were no substantial differences between the responses of unionized and nonunionized campuses with tenure systems on such issues as the availability of immediate tenure at time of appointment, the similarity of criteria for tenure to criteria for promotion, the presence of a right of appeal, procedural correctness as a basis for appeal, and reasons for denial of tenure as a ground for appeal (35).

Early concerns regarding tenure had focused less on whether it would be abandoned on union campuses than on whether the opportunity for academic judgment would be sacrificed to job security attained without genuine review of competence (Hook 15–16). In a 1979 study of "rights issues" in 63 four-year and 42 two-year faculty agreements, Margaret K. Chandler and Daniel J. Julius found that probationary periods were not shortened by union contracts (*Faculty* 46). Moreover, they observed that the contracts often listed "the academic criteria to be used when evaluating faculty for promotion, appointment, nonrenewal and tenure." They note that the contract criteria were not uniform and were sometimes vague and that "the contracts said little about the emphasis or weight to be accorded in applying them." Among the criteria included were "teaching effectiveness, scholarly achievement, research, publications, advanced study, intellectual breadth, skill and promise as a teacher, devotion to the concept of liberal education," and so forth (47). These broad criteria obviously provide ample opportunity for academic judgment.

Chandler and Julius found further that many contracts incorporated a provision for academic freedom and that there was no evidence of abandonment of tenure. Four-fifths of the agreements also formally incorporated the procedures for establishing a faculty role in personnel policy decisions through faculty review committees and procedures for formulating faculty recommendations (47). Their conclusions undoubtedly understate the actual prevailing practice, since the one serious methodological weakness of the study was the decision to treat the absence of a specific contract provision as evidence of a lack of faculty involvement. It is crucial to recognize that academic collective bargaining agreements often remain silent on academic policies and practices where the prevailing practice is accepted and guaranteed either by a general past-policy clause or by codified university policies.

Formalization of procedures through a contractual agreement can contribute clarity and fairness but may be suspected of imposing rigidity. According to Barbara Lee, however, collective bargaining grievance procedures "have resulted not only in due process for all personnel decisions, but also . . . [in] the development of evaluation criteria that are fairer and more consistent than those employed prior to unionization" (*Collective Bargaining* 26). Nonetheless, Baldridge and Kemerer, noting a decline in the proportion of administrators and faculty members who believed that procedures had increased fairness, questioned whether bargaining had in fact done so. Since 78% of union chairs and 83% of union officials in their study continued to affirm that bargaining had increased fairness, contrasted to 26% of presidents at unionized campuses who did not, the judgment is clearly a matter of perspectives—faculty versus administrative (28, 39). Further, the decline in the perception that bargaining contributed to fairness was shaped not by the handling of routine issues but by the fiscal crisis and resulting program discontinuances and layoffs that occurred in the mid-1970s in states like New York and Michigan (37, 46). Similarly, the recent pressures on the academic job market might also lead to increased concern over lack of fairness in tenure decisions, despite improved procedures and more precise criteria for making them, simply because the opportunities for attaining tenure have declined and the bar for attaining tenure has been raised.

Such developments, however, also demonstrate that bargaining has not imposed excessive, or perhaps even adequate, rigidity on the faculty members who chose it. Baldridge and Kemerer report 1979 survey findings that dismissals of tenured faculty members, because of program discontinuance and faculty neglect of duties and incompetence, were twice as frequent at unionized than at nonunionized campuses. They suggest two reasons: bargaining may have been more likely at campuses with conflict before bargaining and, "perhaps more significantly, contracts spell out procedures and criteria which, while regularizing personnel decision-making, also furnish administrators with clear guidelines for making painful decisions" (43). At the same time, unionized campuses more often than nonunionized campuses provided retrenchment (layoff) protections such as recall rights, which give laid-off employees the first claim on suitable vacancies for a period of years (86% to 48% respectively), and seniority rights, which designate the order of layoffs (60% to 30%). In sum, collective bargaining campuses were more likely to have retrenchment policies, more likely to use them (32% to 20%), and twice as likely to have retrenched tenured faculty members (44). The greater use of retrenchment on unionized campuses may also reflect the more-extensive unionization of the two-year and public institutions that experienced the primary effect of the fiscal crisis of the 1970s.

Chandler and Julius found that four-year agreements more often provided a substantial faculty role in retrenchment decisions and procedures than two-year agreements (44). Similarly, Rhoades's later study found a much higher incidence of "financial exigency" protections in four-year and AAUP contracts than in others (91). Four-year contracts are also more than twice as likely to require faculty involvement in retrenchment decisions (67% to 31%) and somewhat more likely to have not only seniority or other provisions to define the order in which faculty layoffs may occur but also notice provisions (104, 109). The underlying difference is between contracts that routinely permit layoffs because of underenrollment and budget declines and those that adopt the AAUP policies requiring demonstration of financial exigency or senate involvement in academic program discontinuance. This observation is supported by Chandler and Julius's 1985 updated study, which found that AAUP contracts provided the greatest faculty authority on retrenchment issues ("By Whose Right?" 104). In either type of agreement, faculty members can be and occasionally are dismissed, but contracts may ensure not simply that dismissals are difficult but that they occur fairly and for sound reasons.

In the only systematic study of the effect of collective bargaining on part-time faculty conditions of employment, Rhoades finds relatively few effective contracts (131–71). He emphasizes the lack of protections in hiring procedures, nonreappointment, and assignments. Some of the major categories in his analysis are unlikely to reveal part-time faculty protections, however. For example, hiring provisions are rare even in full-time contracts. Layoff provisions are generally concerned with protecting full-time faculty members, not part-time faculty members, since part-time faculty members are usually subject to reappointment at the end of each term and thus do not need to be laid off. Some part-time faculty agreements do include provisions that afford greater notice of whether they will be reappointed, receive support for office hours, enjoy academic freedom, and participate in governance and other professional activities. (See, e.g., the essays in this volume by Orenic, Hoffman, and Reichard; see also Thompson.)

SHARED GOVERNANCE

Faculty bargaining has not replaced shared governance on unionized campuses. As early as 1978, in an extended discussion of governance at four-year institutions, Lee found that "[i]n contrast to earlier fears, the presence of a faculty union often strengthens the role of a faculty senate" (*Collective Bargaining* 28). Similarly, Baldridge and Kemerer, writing in 1981, explain that they had previously been "skeptical about the continued vitality of the 'dual track' arrangement, with the senate focusing on academic matters and the union on economic matters." But a review of survey data convinced them of the persistence of a dual-track concept in which unions and senates conduct different activities. They found that presidents of unionized institutions see "a slight increase in senate influence in such academic areas as admissions, degree requirements, and curriculum, while they view unions as increasing their influence over such economic matters as faculty salaries and working conditions" (19).

Just as the collective bargaining enhancements to procedural fairness in personnel matters have not ensured that faculty members will be fully protected against extreme swings in the budget cycle or the market, so the modest improvements in shared governance fall short of establishing faculty self-determination. Rhoades has offered substantial evidence that as of 1998, for example, university managers had largely retained control of such critical emerging issues as intellectual property and distance education (173–256). He found it especially telling that two-year contracts were more likely than four-year contracts to protect intellectual property (253). Protection of intellectual property is essential to academic freedom because it ensures the integrity of faculty members' work (AAUP, "Distance" 177–84). Although negotiation of such protection has increased since Rhoades's study, the issue of intellectual property highlights the limitations of bargaining effectiveness and provides a useful way to identify three key factors that affect the relation between faculty bargaining and the faculty role in shared governance.

First, the absence of intellectual property clauses in some four-year agreements is not the anomaly it may appear. Rhoades recognized that the faculties in four-year institutions are more likely than those at other institutions to have intellectual property sufficiently valuable to tempt management to seek profit from it. However, they are also, by virtue of their ability to generate such property, likely to have greater individual bargaining power and to feel less interest in or need for union protection. For example, physicians included in faculty bargaining units have generally preferred not to have the union negotiate the part of their compensation derived from medical practice. They contend that they can do better on their own, and they fear a possible union bias toward redistribution. Similarly, research faculty members with large grants have generally looked to themselves and their research colleagues, not their faculty union, for protection regarding how the institutions expended grant and overhead funds. Unions exist to protect those who have little individual market power. The absence of some professional protections in faculty contracts may, therefore, reflect the continuing strength of some faculty groups rather than weakness or erosion of influence.

Second, precisely because the dual track persists, governance issues cannot be adequately assessed through contract analysis alone. Where shared governance is strong or where, as in New Jersey, state labor law sharply restricts negotiation on academic or governance issues, faculty unions may be satisfied to leave some personnel and governance issues to the traditional shared-governance mechanisms. Even where governance practices are incorporated into the agreement, which is frequently the practice in AAUP agreements, they are usually only incorporated by reference (Lee, "Senates" 57; Baldridge and Kemerer 21). Studying those agreements where governance is referenced in contracts will not provide much evidence of specific protections. Simply stated, the persistence of shared governance means that collective agreements do not fully define the extent of faculty protections and authority.

Third, faculty members are, as Rhoades contends, "managed professionals." Although faculty members are professional employees, they are employees nonetheless. As employees, they are subjects rather than agents of managerial authority. As professionals, they provide independent academic judgment, an essential contribution to academic policymaking. The employee status explains why they need, and should have, the right to bargain collectively. Their professional responsibilities also explain why institutions need and should preserve shared governance. There is no reason either to expect or to fear that faculty bargaining will result in total faculty control. But collective bargaining has enhanced the faculty's role in establishing its own terms and conditions of employment, and it has sustained and in some respects enhanced the faculty's role in shared governance.

WORKS CITED

American Association of University Professors. "Distance Education and Intellectual Property." *Policy Documents and Reports.* 9th ed. Washington: AAUP, 2001. 177–84.

———. "Statement on Collective Bargaining." *Policy Documents and Reports.* Washington: AAUP, 1977. 56.

Angell, George W. "Two-Year College Experience." Duryea and Fisk 87–107.

Baldridge, J. Victor, Frank R. Kemerer, et al. *Assessing the Impact of Faculty Collective Bargaining.* AAHE-ERIC Higher Educ. Research Report 8. Washington: AAHE, 1981.

Begin, James P. "Collective Bargaining and Collegiality." *Proceedings, First Annual Conference.* NCSCBHEP. Apr. 1973. Ed. Maurice C. Benewitz. New York: Baruch Coll., CUNY, 1973. 109–116.

Benjamin, Ernst, ed. *Exploring the Role of Contingent Instructional Staff in Undergraduate Learning.* New Directions for Higher Education 123. San Francisco: Jossey-Bass, 2003.

———. "Patterns of Professional Evaluation and Assigned Duties in Faculty Collective Bargaining Agreements." *Higher Education Collective Bargaining during a Period of Change. Proceedings, Twenty-Second Annual Conference.* NCSCBHEP. Apr. 1994. Ed. Frank R. Annunziato and Beth H. Johnson. New York: Baruch Coll., CUNY, 1994. 63–71.

Carnegie Council on Policy Studies in Higher Education. *Faculty Bargaining in Public Higher Education: A Report and Two Essays.* San Francisco: Jossey-Bass, 1977.

————. "Faculty Collective Bargaining in Public Higher Education—Three Key Issues." Carnegie, *Faculty* 1–22.

Carr, Robert K., and Daniel K. VanEyck. *Collective Bargaining Comes to the Campus.* Washington: Amer. Council on Educ., 1973.

Chait, Richard. "Collective Bargaining and Tenure: A Collision Course." *Collective Bargaining in Higher Education. Proceedings, Third Annual Conference.* NCSCBHEP. Apr. 1975. Ed. Thomas M. Mannix. New York: Baruch Coll., CUNY, 1975. 60–67.

Chandler, Margaret K., and Daniel J. Julius. "By Whose Right? Management Rights and Governance in the Unionized Institutions." *Unionization and Academic Excellence. Proceedings, Thirteenth Annual Conference.* NCSCBHEP. Apr. 1985. Ed. Joel M. Douglas. New York: Baruch Coll., CUNY, 1986. 91–117.

————. *Faculty vs. Administration: Rights Issues in Academic Collective Bargaining.* New York: NCSCBHEP, Baruch Coll., CUNY, 1979.

Duryea, E. D., and Robert S. Fisk. *Faculty Unions and Collective Bargaining.* San Francisco: Jossey-Bass, 1973.

Ehrenberg, Ronald G., et al. "Collective Bargaining in American Higher Education." *Governing Academia.* Ed. Ronald G. Ehrenberg. Ithaca: Cornell UP, 2004. 209–32.

Elam, Stanley, and Michael H. Moskow. *Employment Relations in Higher Education.* Bloomington: Phi Beta Kappa, 1969.

Feller, David E., and Matthew W. Finkin. "Legislative Issues in Faculty Collective Bargaining." Carnegie Council, *Faculty Bargaining* 73–183.

Garbarino, Joseph W. "Emergence of Collective Bargaining." Duryea and Fisk 1–19.

————. "State Experience in Collective Bargaining." Carnegie Council, *Faculty Bargaining*, 29–72.

Hamermesh, Daniel S. "Quite Good News for Now." *Academe* 88.2 (2002): 20–29.

Hook, Sidney. "The Academic Mission and Collective Bargaining." *Proceedings, First Annual Conference.* NCSCBHEP. Apr. 1973. Ed. Maurice C. Benewitz. New York: Baruch Coll., CUNY, 1973. 8–17.

Hurd, Richard, and Jennifer Bloom, with Beth Hillman Johnson. *Directory of Faculty Contracts and Bargaining Agents in Institutions of Higher Education* 24. New York: NCSCBHEP Baruch Coll., CUNY, 1998.

Hutcheson, Philo A. *A Professional Professoriate: Unionization, Bureaucratization, and the AAUP.* Nashville: Vanderbilt UP, 2000.

Lee, Barbara A. *Collective Bargaining in Four-Year Colleges: Impact on Institutional Practice.* AAHE-ERIC Higher Educ. Research Report 5. Washington: AAHE, 1978.

————. "Contractually Protected Senates at Four-Year Colleges." *The Legal and Economic Status of Collective Bargaining in Higher Education. Proceedings, Ninth Annual Conference.* NCSCBHEP. Apr. 1981. Ed. Joel M. Douglas, New York: Baruch Coll. CUNY, 1981. 56–61.

Lieberman, Myron, "Representational Systems in Higher Education." Elam and Moskow. 40–101.

Marmion, Harry A. "Faculty Organizations in Higher Education." Elam and Moskow 1–39.

Rhoades, Gary. *Managed Professionals: Unionized Faculty and Restructuring Academic Labor.* Albany: State U of New York P, 1998.

Thompson, Karen. "Contingent Faculty and Student Learning: Welcome to the Strativersity." Benjamin, *Exploring* 41–47.

United States. Dept. of Educ. Natl. Center for Educ. Statistics. *National Study of Postsecondary Faculty (DAS), NSOPF: 99.* CD-ROM. Washington: US Dept. of Educ., 2001.

Wollett, Donald H. "Issues at Stake." Duryea and Fisk 20–43.

Graduate Assistants' Bargaining

PATRICIA J. GUMPORT and DANIEL J. JULIUS

The organizing efforts of graduate assistants have sparked concern from participants and observers alike. To characterize these concerns and place them in historical context, we begin this essay with an overview of the organizational conditions in which graduate student unionization emerged. We then examine a range of views over its appropriateness, paying particular attention to what is known about the effects on the student-mentor relationship.

Surprisingly, little has been written that synthesizes information on the institutional and demographic characteristics of the collective bargaining activities of graduate students, and even less has been written on its catalysts and consequences. To construct this narrative, we draw on the scant published literature and our own extensive case-study research from 1999 and 2002, when we conducted interviews, examined archival data, and analyzed all existing collective bargaining agreements for provisions and clauses that could potentially affect faculty-student interactions (for a full analysis see Julius and Gumport).

The Emergence and Forms of Graduate Assistant Representation

The emergence of graduate assistants' organizing to gain formal recognition as employee bargaining units must be understood in the context of the dramatic post–World War II expansion of American universities. In addition to the tremendous growth in their size and research capacity, universities accommodated surges in enrollments and degree production at both undergraduate and graduate levels, especially during the 1960s.

University infrastructures became more complex, and ensuring the inter-dependence among parts of the organization became a major set of man-agement challenges.

Predictably, this expansion was not without strain. Signs of strain became prevalent in academic workplaces, where groups began to artic-ulate their own interests and organize to protect them. Faculty collective bargaining began in earnest in the 1960s and experienced periods of heightened activity over subsequent decades. Forty years later, nearly 40% of faculty members in four-year institutions were unionized (pri-marily in the public sector). Academically related staff members and skilled craft workers became unionized in most large systems and higher education institutions (except for those in the South).

Changes in the academic workplace and momentum from faculty collective bargaining activities strengthened the willingness and ability of graduate students to unionize. In the 1970s, dismal labor-market pros-pects for emerging PhDs exacerbated graduate students' concerns about a longer time-to-degree completion. Into the 1980s and 1990s, those con-cerns became amplified because of students' higher levels of financial indebtedness, perceptions of inadequate faculty advising, and the stark realization that universities cut costs and leveraged faculty time through the cheap labor of graduate assistants, in particular teaching assistants. Thus, although these realities were in place for some time, by the end of the 1990s the discrepancies between ideals and realities came to the fore-ground on many campuses, concurrently with discussion about the qual-ity of doctoral education at the national level (Golde and Dore; Gumport, "Learning").

Throughout these decades, assistantships, along with grants and loans, became a major source of financial aid for graduate students. In fact, the number of graduate assistants increased dramatically from 160,000 in 1975 to 216,000 in 1995 (Benjamin, *Exploring* 5). By 1999–2000, of those pursuing master's degrees, 16% had assistantships, up from 9% in 1990; and of those pursuing doctoral degrees, 47% had as-sistantships, up from 29% in 1990 (United States). Only graduate stu-dents who hold positions as teaching or research assistants (or similar academic work) are eligible to unionize; other graduate students cannot argue that they are employees.

How did academic unionization emerge in these times of organiza-tional change and in the diverse conditions of assistantships? Over the past thirty years, factors outside the academy facilitated the willingness of public-sector labor boards to hear cases with a sympathetic ear and to recommend legislation, especially in states with a high percentage of unionized government employees. The first graduate student union was established in 1969 at the University of Wisconsin, Madison. Major organizing efforts occurred in the late 1960s and early 1970s in Oregon, Michigan, Wisconsin, and New York. They surged again in the late 1980s and throughout the 1990s, in states such as Massachusetts, Illinois, Iowa, and California, and more recently at private institutions such as Yale, New York University, Columbia, Brown, and Tufts.

Graduate assistants at public and private universities have different constraints on achieving formal recognition. In public universities, state labor legislation may enable them to unionize. In private universities, the National Labor Relations Board (NLRB), applying the National Labor Relations Act, deems whether graduate assistants can be recognized as employees. While earlier rulings had rejected the claim of employee status for students, in 2000 the ruling by a regional director of the NLRB that graduate assistants at New York University were employees eligible for collective bargaining encouraged private-university organizing. In 2004, however, the NLRB reverted to its earlier position, ruling that Brown University graduate assistants were students. This ruling does not forbid bargaining by graduate students in private universities, but it does relieve these institutions of the obligation to bargain (which is exactly the strategy NYU has adopted) and is likely to slow graduate assistant organizing in the private sector.

From our research, we estimated that approximately 43,000 graduate assistants were involved in organizing drives or formal collective bargaining in 2002 (United States). We include those campuses with graduate student bargaining units certified by state or federal labor boards as well as cases where graduate student local unions have been certified by a state or federal board but not formally recognized by the employer.

Industrial unions have sought to represent graduate students, most often when the full-time faculty members are not organized or when traditional higher education bargaining agents (AFT, AAUP, NEA) were not successful or did not compete with industrial unions. At New York University, Indiana University, Cornell University, the University of Iowa, and Yale University, the graduate students are not represented by traditional higher education bargaining agents. We found that 54% of graduate student unions were represented by independent agents or by industrial unions like the United Auto Workers; Communication Workers of America; and the United Electrical, Radio, and Machine Workers of America. The remaining 46% of graduate student locals were affiliated with the AFT (30%), NEA (11%), and AAUP (4% [see Julius and Gumport]).

According to our research, published literature, and media coverage, graduate students have been motivated to organize for a variety of reasons: lengthened time-to-degree completion, financial indebtedness (especially problematic for those who are starting families), and perceptions of poor working conditions based on pay and workload differentials across the disciplines. These catalysts have been characterized as economic. Yet there have been academic reasons as well, including inadequate faculty advising, poor preparation for alternative career paths, and expectations that assistantship responsibilities should take priority over the graduate students' educational pursuits.

As powerful as these catalysts may be, it is important to keep in mind that graduate students are a large and diverse population that may not readily perceive a basis for solidarity. Research assistants and teaching assistants face different responsibilities, stipend amounts, and circumstances from each other and may have divergent interests even though they may share concerns about working conditions, job security, and the absence of a forum for grievances. Moreover, negotiations and organizing drives can drag on for years because of high turnover in leadership positions, scarce resources for organizing drives, and lack of sophistication in communication and negotiation tactics. There is also the problem of attrition; as one example, the graduate assistants' union at the University of Wisconsin, Madison, estimates that it loses approximately one-quarter of its membership every year. On some campuses, it has taken ten, even fifteen, years for graduate students to achieve a collective bargaining agreement. On other campuses, relationships remain recurrently unstable. Obviously, there are structural obstacles, even when graduate students become organized and achieve official recognition.

Consequences of Graduate Student Unionization

We turn now to examine concerns about the appropriateness of graduate assistants' collective bargaining. Our research suggests that there is no conclusive evidence—although there is much ongoing speculation—

about potential harm, which parallels the concerns expressed about faculty collective bargaining when it gained momentum in the late 1960s. Most speculation focuses on the potential negative effect on graduate education (specifically, on mentor-student relationships). It also considers the additional burdens for faculty members and administrators of working within financial and procedural limitations imposed by labor agreements. The concerns tend to be characterized differently according to the perspectives of each set of actors inside the academy—senior university administrators (as employer representatives); graduate students (as employees); and the faculty members, who are often cast in the middle—whether as implementers bound by the terms to which the other parties agreed or as a group aligned closely (but silently) with either the administration or the students.

Senior administrators are often cast as steadfastly resistant to graduate students' unionizing. Academic administrators often lack extensive experience with labor-management negotiations and may not consult those who do. External legal counsel hired to manage negotiations often do not have experience with deliberative forums where academic policies are set; they may, however, have extensive experience working the opposite side of the table from unions. Particularly in the elite research universities, where the faculty members have focused on enhancing their research productivity, labor-management relations tend to be left to non-academic types who are usually not conversant with academic governance norms. Collective bargaining does pose a high risk for senior administrators in universities, where they could potentially lose essential support from powerful academic and legislative constituencies who disapprove of their management of graduate students' organizing efforts. On the other hand, formalizing a bargaining agreement can diminish outright conflict (e.g., student protests, strikes) and thereby reduce negative publicity, animus from major donors, and even anger from state legislators over the inability of campus officials to squelch students' organizing drives.

One key controversy concerns whether graduate assistants' unionizing will damage the mentor-student relationship. There are short-term and long-term elements to these concerns. For the day-to-day working relationship, there is the potential for strained communication and awkward interactions, coupled with apprehension that faculty members will be angry with students who vote for formal contract mechanisms to protect their interests. A longer range concern is that faculty members will begin to see students as employees and themselves as supervisors, thereby jeopardizing the benefits and good will that are presumed in the mentorship model. A related concern is that unionization could diminish faculty willingness to go the extra mile for students, particularly in generously giving their time or making use of professional networks to cultivate and enhance job prospects to further students' careers.

For the most part, graduate assistants do not view the faculty member as the employer; rather, the university is the employer. Some students are not even sure who the employer is: the university, college or school, department, the principal investigator, the research funders, and so on. In our research, graduate student organizers report that many predicted negative consequences of unionization have not taken place. Some organizers and students claim that their relationships with faculty members are strengthened and may even be improved because the expectations and responsibilities of the relationship between faculty members and graduate students are more clearly delineated in labor agreements. Students who are unionized also benefit from having an established avenue that addresses grievance and workload concerns and curtails favoritism by faculty members (i.e., jobs must be posted, stipends standardized, etc.). However, the student-employees are not all of one mind. Some sources report that those in the sciences tend to be opposed to unionization (see Julius and Gumport), whereas those in the arts and humanities tend to be in favor of it. Substantial differences across the disciplines in the nature of responsibilities and compensation of assistantships may fuel disputes even in long-established unions. Moreover, we learned that those student-employees who are already formally recognized in bargaining units tend to be overwhelmed with the challenges of finding new members, administering the agreement, and other internal contract administration and organizational matters.

The faculty views range from one end of the continuum to the other. Faculty members who are themselves unionized may support graduate students because they sympathize with the objectives of these unions. Conversely, faculty members may reject the organizing efforts of graduate students, viewing the unions as constraining their behavior or potentially diluting their authority in setting policy in the university. In either case, the downside to graduate student unionization for faculty members is that it potentially diminishes departmental and faculty autonomy, procedurally if not substantively. Such drawbacks, from the point of view of faculty members, may take the form of a legal mandate to consult graduate assistants on curriculum development, course offerings, and class size or standardized procedures for hiring and compensating assistants, as well as defining the work they will do as research or teaching assistants.

Those faculty members who oppose graduate student unionization are inclined not to disrupt the status quo, including traditional decision-making practices and benefit packages. There are several dimensions here. Faculty members, along with administrators, are concerned that provisions in agreements may make it difficult to terminate assistants whose performance is inadequate. Research funds may be diverted from research itself to compensation for graduate students. Perhaps more profoundly, faculty objections to graduate student unionization may stem from an attempt to safeguard the role of faculty members as mentors and educators who socialize their students into the academic profession. Particularly for faculty members who see themselves as professionals in the academy, the labor activities of graduate students may be seen as unprofessional, regardless of whether graduate students meet the definitions of employees stipulated by state and federal labor-relations statutes and boards. Faculty members who have come to see themselves as employees in large-scale organizations are more supportive of graduate students' organizing efforts.

Graduate student unionization has altered the internal fabric of universities by reshaping the procedures for academic decision making, consultative processes, and university governance. However, our data analysis pointedly suggests that unionization, in itself, has not undermined the mentoring relationship. There are, however, other factors that do undermine it. A primary one occurs when faculty members or university administrators make explicit a conceptualization of graduate students as resources for the university to use as it sees fit. This conceptualization is more evident on campuses where shared governance has deteriorated and there is already a climate of mistrust. It is also evident at public universities struggling to adapt to waves of budget cuts, as well as at private universities coping with increased budgetary demands and competition from peer institutions. These are the conditions in which the divergent interests of organizational units and groups (departments, faculty members, students, staff members) become most palpable, so that one or more of them may seek to protect those interests through any means available to them, including unionization.

For graduate students who are considering whether to organize for formal recognition as employees, there are a plethora of legitimate questions to consider. The questions are complex, calling for knowledge of university practices and procedures, as well as human resource issues. For example, should tuition benefits (waivers and discounts) be separated from deliberations over stipend amounts and workload? Third parties may become involved, usually from state governments and federal agencies, claiming a stake in the content, processes, and outcomes of negotiations over issues within the scope of bargaining.

Any of the players can make critical mistakes, which may not be evident for decades. The individuals responsible for managing the collective bargaining process will continue to shape not only the process of unionization but also others' attitudes toward it. In this respect, the skills and styles of those administrators and faculty members assigned to perform this function are extremely important. Leadership in this arena includes the ability to legitimate and institutionalize the labor-relations process, the ability to articulate labor-relations goals to reflect the desires and needs of key organizational constituencies (trustees, president, faculty members, and students), the ability to take initiative and risks while also responding effectively to unexpected situations, an understanding of power in organizations, and the skill to neutralize opponents and determine the appropriate timing for actions.

As such processes unfold, graduate students themselves often acquire skills not anticipated when they began graduate school: leading organizing efforts, initiating strategic action, determining when to negotiate and when to walk away—the most symbolic of adversarial acts. Such skills become part of their professional socialization into the academy and may motivate action among other unrepresented groups of university employees. Moreover, the organizing effort undoubtedly exposes students to senior administrators and labor-relations professionals who become deeply involved in graduate students' working lives. While the conventional wisdom is that academic change is created by powerful external forces, the graduate assistant movement for union representation is a powerful internal force for change. Graduate students who organize and become union members will surely shape the currents of organizational change in years to come.

WORKS CITED AND SUGGESTIONS FOR FURTHER READING

Altbach, Phillip. G. *Student Politics in America*. New York: McGraw, 1974.

———. "Students: Interests, Culture, and Activism." Ed. A. Levine. *Higher Learning in America: 1980–2000*. Baltimore: Johns Hopkins UP, 1993. 203–21.

Altbach, Phillip G., Robert Berdahl, and Patricia J. Gumport, eds. *American Higher Education in the Twenty-First Century*. Baltimore: Johns Hopkins UP, 1998.

American Association of University Professors. *Statement On Graduate Students*. Washington: AAUP, 1995.

Appelquist, Thomas. "Graduate Students Are Not Employees." *Chronicle of Higher Education* 18 Apr. 1997: B6.

Association of American Universities. *Report and Recommendations: Committee on Graduate Education*. Washington: Assn. of Amer. Univ., 1998.

Baldridge, J. Victor., Frank R. Kemerer, et al. *Assessing the Impact of Faculty Collective Bargaining*. AAHE-ERIC Higher Educ. Research Report 8. Washington: AAHE, 1981.

Barba, William C. "The Graduate Student Employee Union in SUNY: A History." *Journal for Higher Education Management* 10.1 (1994): 38–48.

———. "The Unionization Movement: An Analysis Of Graduate Student Employee Union Contracts. *Business Officer* 27.5 (1994): 35–45.

Benjamin, Ernst, ed. *Exploring the Role of Contingent Instructional Staff in Undergraduate Learning*. New Directions for Higher Educ. 123. San Francisco: Jossey-Bass, 2003.

———. "Over-reliance on Part-Time Faculty: An American Trend." *International Higher Education* 21 (2000): 4–6.

Council of Graduate Employee Unions. *CGEU Union Directory, 2000*. 2001. <http://www.nagps.org/NAGPS/ecc-page/unions/CGEU_Unions.html>.

Craig, Joseph. S. "Teaching Assistant Collective Bargaining at the University of Wisconsin-Madison." *Employment and Education of Teaching Assistants: Institutional Responsibilities and Responses*. Ed. N. Chism and S. Warner. Columbus: Center for Teaching Excellence, Ohio State U, 1987. 51–63.

Curtiss, John. "Roles, Rewards, and Responsibilities: Graduate Student Unionization at the University Of Michigan." *Proceedings of the Twenty-Second Annual Conference for Higher Education Collective Bargaining during a Period of Change*. New York: NCSCBHEP, Baruch Coll., CUNY, 1994. 41–46.

Directory of Faculty Contracts and Bargaining Agents in Institutions of Higher Education. New York: NCSCBHEP, Baruch Coll., CUNY, 1997.

Douglas, Joel. M. "The Impact of *NLRB vs. Yeshiva* on Faculty Unionization at Public Colleges and Universities." *Journal of Collective Negotiations* 19.1 (1990): 1–28.

Ethington, Christopher, and Anna Pisani. "The RA and TA Experience: Impediments and Benefits to Graduate Study." *Research in Higher Education* 34 (1993): 343–54.

Garbarino, Joseph W. "Academic Collective Bargaining: A Status Report." *Unions in Transition*. Ed. Seymour Martin Lipset. San Francisco: Inst. for Contemporary Studies, 1986. 101–17.

Golde, Christopher, and Thomas Dore. *At Cross Purposes: What the Experiences of Doctoral Students Reveal about Doctoral Education*. Philadelphia: Pew Charitable Trusts, 2001.

Gumport, Patricia J. "Learning Academic Labor." *Comparative Social Research* 19 (2000): 1–23.

———. "Public Universities as Academic Workplaces." *Daedalus: Journal of the American Academy of Arts and Sciences* 126.4 (1997): 113–36.

Gumport, Patricia J., and John Jennings. "Graduate Student Employees: Unresolved Challenges." *Journal of the College and University Personnel Association* 48.3–4 (1998): 35–37.

Hewitt, Gordon. "Graduate Student Unionization: A Description of Faculty Attitudes and Beliefs." Annual Forum. Assn. for Institutional Research. Seattle. June 1999.

Hickey, Michael. "Students Wage Union Fight." *Progressive* 58.5 (1994): 17–18.

Hurd, Richard. W., et al. *Directory of Faculty Contracts and Bargaining Agents in Institutions of Higher Education* 23. New York: NCSCBHEP, Baruch Coll., CUNY, 1997.

Julia, John, and Daniel Gamble. *The University of Michigan and Graduate Employees Organization: 1975–1996*. Ann Arbor: U of Michigan, 1996.

Julius, Daniel J. "The Current Status of Graduate Student Unions: An Employer's Perspective." *Collective Bargaining and Accountability in Higher Education: A Report Card*. Ed. Caesar J. Naples. New York: NCSCBHEP, Baruch Coll., CUNY, 1999. 63–81.

———. "The Status Of Faculty and Staff Unions in Colleges and Universities: 1930s–1990s." *Managing the Industrial Labor Relations Process in Higher Education*. Ed. Julius. Washington: Coll. and Univ. Personnel Assn., 1993. 1–18.

———. "Unionization in Higher Education: The Case of Academic Employees in Large Public Systems." *California Public Employee Relations* 161 (2003): 8–15.

Julius, Daniel J., and Patricia Gumport. "Graduate Student Unionization: Catalysts and Consequences." *Review of Higher Education* 26.2 (2002): 187–216.

Kagan, Dennis, et al. "The Strike at Yale." *National Center for the Study of Collective Bargaining in Higher Education and the Professions Newsletter* 13.3 (1995): 5–8.

Kumagi, John. "In a Tight Job Market, Union Activism Grows among Graduate Students." *Physics Today* 2.5 (1999): 57–60.

Ladd, Everett C., and Seymour M. Lipset. *Professors, Unions, and American Higher Education*. Berkeley: U of California P, Carnegie Commission on Higher Educ., 1973.

Leatherman, Courtney. "As Teaching Assistants Push to Unionize, Debate Grows over What They Would Gain." *Chronicle of Higher Education* 3 Oct. 1997: A12–14.

———. "The Number of New Ph.D.'s Drops for the First Time since 1985." *Chronicle of Higher Education* 9 Feb. 2000: A12.

———. "Teaching Assistants Plan Showdown over Unionization." *Chronicle of Higher Education* 13 Nov. 1998: A10–12.

———. "Union Movement at Private Colleges Awakens after a Twenty-Year Slumber." *Chronicle of Higher Education* 21 Jan. 2000: A17–20.

———. "University Of California Opens Door to Recognition of Teaching Assistants' Union." *Chronicle of Higher Education* 26 Mar. 1999: A18.

Leatherman, Courtney, and Arlene Schneider. "Teaching Assistants Strike at University of California Campuses." *Chronicle of Higher Education* 11 Dec. 1998: A19–20.

Leatherman, Courtney, and Robin Wilson. "Embittered by a Bleak Job Market: Graduate Students Take on the MLA." *Chronicle of Higher Education* 18 Dec. 1998: A10–11.

Lipset, Seymour M., ed. *Unions in Transition*. San Francisco: Inst. for Contemporary Studies, 1986.

Lockhart, Mark M. "Teaching Assistant Unions." *Proceedings, Seventeenth Annual Conference*. NCSCBHEP. Apr. 1989. New York: Baruch Coll., CUNY, 1989.

Lovitts, Barbara A., and Cary Nelson. "The Hidden Crisis in Graduate Education: Attrition from Ph.D. Programs." *Academe* 86.6 (2000): 44–50.

Nelson, Cary, ed. *Will Teach for Food: Academic Labor in Crisis*. Minneapolis: U of Minnesota P, 1997.

"NLRB Holds That Graduate Assistants Enrolled at Private Universities are Employees under the National Labor Relations Act." *Harvard Law Review* 114 (2001): 2557–77.

Palmaffy, Timothy. "Union and Man at Yale." *New Republic* 7 June 1999: 6+.

Perkinson, Robert. "Bad Marks for Yale's Labor Policies." *Progressive* 60.2 (1996): 20–21.

Rhoades, Gary, and Robert Rhoads. "The Public Discourse of U.S. Graduate Employee Unions." *Review of Higher Education* 26.2 (2002): 163–86.

Rikard, Larry, and A. H. Nye. "The Graduate Instructor Experience: Pitfalls and Possibilities." *Journal of Physical Education, Recreation and Dance* 68.5 (1997): 33–39.

Schneider, Arlene. "Graduate Students on Thirty Campuses Rally for Unions and Better Wages." *Chronicle of Higher Education* 7 Mar. 1997: A13–15.

Schuster, Jack. "The Mutation of Higher Education and Reconfiguration of the Faculty and Their Roles." *Twenty-five Years of Higher Education Collective Bargaining. Proceedings, Twenty-fifth Annual Conference*. NCSCBHEP. New York: Baruch Coll., CUNY, 1997. 6–12.

Sexton, John. "Bargaining Practices Exclude Members." *Daily Californian* [Berkeley] 8 Feb. 2000: 5+.

Sharnoff, Ellen. "Neither Fish nor Fowl: Graduate Students, Unionization and the Academy." Go to the Head of the Class: Graduate Students and Pedagogy Forum. MLA Annual Convention. Royal York Hotel, Toronto. 29 Dec. 1993.

Smallwood, Scott. "Sacred Heart Professors Lose Bid to Unionize." *Chronicle of Higher Education* 6 July 2001: A12.

————. "Success and New Hurdles for TA Unions." *Chronicle of Higher Education* 6 July 2001: A10–12.

————. "Union? No Thanks." *Chronicle of Higher Education* 17 May 2000: A12–14.

Sprague, John, and Jody D. Nyquist. "TA Supervision." *Teaching Assistant Teaching in the 1990s.* Ed. Jody D. Nyquist, Robert D. Abbott, and Donald H. Wulff. New Directions for Teaching and Learning. San Francisco: Jossey-Bass, 1989. 37–53.

Steitz, Douglas Sorrelle, and Jennifer Allyson Hunkler. "Teaching or Learning: Are Teaching Assistants Students or Employees?" *Journal of College and University Law* 24.2 (1997): 349–75.

Swoboda, Dennis, Karen Delaney, and Robert Eckstein. "The Future of Unions in Academia." *Humanity and Society* 11.2 (1987): 165–74.

United States. Dept. of Educ. Natl. Center for Educ. Statistics. *Student Financing of Graduate and First-Professional Education, 1999–2000: Profiles of Students in Selected Degree Programs and Their Use of Assistantships.* By Susan P. Choy and Sonya Geis. Washington: NCES, 2005.

Vaughn, William. "Apprentice or Employee: Graduate Students and Their Unions." *Academe* 84.6 (1998): 43–49.

Villa, Joyce Y. "Graduate Student Organizing: Examining the Issues." *Journal of the College and University Personnel Association* 42.4 (1991): 33–40.

PART TWO

ORGANIZING

A Primer on Academic Organizing

PATRICK SHAW

The legal parameters of organizing for collective bargaining are set for the private sector by the National Labor Relations Act (NLRA) and administered by a corresponding federal agency (the National Labor Relations Board, or NLRB) that has regional offices throughout the country. Public-employee bargaining laws, referred to as enabling legislation, do not cover academics in over one-third of the states (though some local jurisdictions have separate statutory frameworks for unionization). Since the particulars of public-sector statutes can vary substantially, it is not practical to cover each of them here. But since more often than not and in more particulars than fewer, the public-sector statutes are modeled on the NLRA, an outline focusing primarily on the private-sector treatment of unionization should provide a useful introduction for all those contemplating academic organizing.

Terminology

Collective bargaining is a process through which employment-related matters are negotiated with an employer on behalf of an entire group of employees (known as the "collective bargaining unit" or simply the "bargaining unit"). The collective aspect of this form of representation does not require that every member of the group be treated identically. In many sectors of our economy, including higher education, distinctions are made between identifiable, smaller groups of employees in the overall group.

The *collective bargaining representative*, sometimes termed simply the *union* or *bargaining agent*, is the specific organization authorized by the members of a bargaining unit to negotiate with their employer over employment-related matters. *Certification of representative* (or *certification*) occurs as a result of a collective bargaining election conducted under governmental auspices and in which a majority of the bargaining-unit employees who cast ballots vote to be represented by the designated collective bargaining representative. Certification establishes an array of legal rights and obligations that govern the collective bargaining relationship.

Bargaining rights also can be obtained through *voluntary recognition*, wherein an employer voluntarily recognizes a collective bargaining representative as the representative of a group of employees. This method of achieving representation rights can be accomplished by means of a prior agreement to abide by the results of an election conducted by a mutually selected third party or by a "card check" in which the employer agrees to be bound by a showing that a majority of the employees wish the designated union to serve as their representative. Where the unit members are employees protected by a labor-relations act, voluntary recognition affords the same protections as certification.

The *subjects* or *scope of bargaining* are the legally established parameters that identify what employment-related matters must be bargained. The usual formulation is the litany wages (or salaries), hours, terms and conditions of employment. These are termed *mandatory* subjects of bargaining, meaning that the parties are obliged to bargain over these subjects. Some important nonmandatory issues may be pursued indirectly by negotiating their effect on employees. For example, if the academic calendar is deemed outside the scope of bargaining, it may be possible to influence calendar decisions by pursuing salary and workload adjustments consistent with the proposed calendar change.

A second category of bargaining subjects is known as *permissive* or *nonmandatory*, which mean that the parties may agree to bargain over, but neither party may compel the other to bargain over, the subject. *Illegal subjects* of bargaining are those about which the parties may not, even with mutual consent, bargain. A closed-shop provision, stating that union membership is a condition of hire, is an example of this category.

Faculty governance provides an important illustration of the complexity of these distinctions. The most important aspects of governance were held to be permissive subjects under the NLRA during the time that law applied to faculty members. So, for example, a college would have no obligation to bargain with the faculty representative over the authority or even the existence of a faculty senate, but the parties are legally free to do so.

However, even if governance is not a mandatory subject of bargaining and there is no agreement to bargain, the effects of decisions about governance must be bargained if they relate to mandatory subjects of bargaining. Thus, the existence of a faculty senate may not be a mandatory subject of bargaining, but a proposal by an administration that every faculty member must serve in the senate on some periodic basis is mandatory.

Bargaining (or *collective bargaining* or *negotiations*) is the process, often lengthy and not always acrimonious, by which the employer and the bargaining representative achieve a collective bargaining agreement. As a matter of law, neither party can be compelled to make any particular concessions when bargaining. But both must conduct themselves in a way that demonstrates a sincere resolve to reach agreement, a legal obligation known as the duty to *bargain in good faith*. Notwithstanding the existence of established legal tests of good-faith bargaining, the remaining ambiguity is sufficient to engender frequent controversy.

The *collective bargaining agreement* (or *contract* or *CBA*) records the agreements reached by the employer and the bargaining agent as a result of their negotiations. The central benefit of collective bargaining is the achievement of a collective bargaining agreement that, like any other legal contract, is enforceable. The enforcement mechanism provided for in all but a very small fraction of collective bargaining agreements is a grievance procedure that culminates in binding arbitration.

The Organizing Process

The laws establishing collective bargaining rights also establish governmental agencies that serve as administrative and enforcement bodies. The laws and procedures that apply to the organizing process are found in both the enabling statute itself and the regulations promulgated by the agency, as well as in judicial decisions interpreting these laws or regulations or their application.

The Election Petition

Employees who seek collective representation typically identify an existing national or state union or association to assist them politically and legally in the organizing process. A fairly large number of academics, however, are represented by their own, independent associations (although local academic unions that organize on an independent basis sometimes later choose to affiliate with a national organization).

To trigger the process by which the administering agency will conduct a collective bargaining election, at least 30% of the bargaining-unit employees must signify that they wish to be represented in collective bargaining by the named representative. This requirement is known universally as the *showing of interest*. The rationale is obvious: 30% establishes a minimum level of interest in the proposition to call for the expenditure of agency resources. As a practical matter, most unions will not file an initial election petition with less than a majority showing of interest, with the threshold often set at 60% support, because some initial signatories may support holding an election but then vote against collective representation.

The most common medium by which the showing of interest is conveyed is an *authorization card*, a postcard-size form that is signed and dated by an individual employee who states the desire to be represented in collective bargaining by the representative. Petitions are also permissible. Universally, the identities of those who sign cards are confidential (i.e., the agency will not disclose the name of any card signer to the employer).

Initial Organization

In years past, the signing of a union authorization card was the first action that most nonacademic union organizers asked those in the workplace to take. Increasingly, these unions now emulate what has long been a substantially different but standard practice in AAUP union organizing. For reasons of history, culture, and ideology, in AAUP organizing drives card signing is usually not a first but a last step in a campaign to build an organization and a consciousness through which academic workers can achieve greater influence over institutional decision making. Thus the advice generally given by AAUP to union adherents on unorganized campuses is to establish or revive an AAUP chapter, identify the most pressing issue or issues, address those issues in a public way, and demonstrate the value of an organized faculty response in ameliorating unfavorable conditions and in advancing better conditions.

Tackling such a project puts into play many of the activities and dynamics characteristic of functioning unions: electing officers; designating committees to do research; publishing electronic and written communications; holding meetings and conducting surveys to take the pulse of colleagues and to address their concerns; and conducting a membership-building drive, both to solidify the fledgling organization and to build a financial base. In this context, forums on unionization and visits to campus by colleagues who already engage in collective bargaining can present a more vivid picture of what can be gained by taking the next step and forming a union.

Once the time is ripe for the card-signing phase of the campaign, the need for a coherent structure and a deliberate approach becomes even more apparent. With an organizing committee and departmental or school representatives in place, a systematic solicitation effort is launched. Lists are constructed and updated so that the key organizers can track who has been asked to sign, whether each person has in fact submitted a card, and what reactions to the union drive were expressed. During both the card-signing phase and the subsequent run-up to the election, the union organizers need to have a comprehensive list of not only those who profess support for or opposition to the union, but also the degree to which those viewpoints are "hard" or "soft." A soft card, for example, is a signatory who supports an election but will not necessarily vote in favor of a bargaining agent. Soft support may take the form of expressing probable or conditional support.

The Election Petition and Hearing

Along with the showing of interest, an election petition, on a form provided by the agency, is filed with the agency. The petition records very basic information (names, addresses, and telephone numbers of the employer and the bargaining representative); an assertion that the minimum showing of interest has been submitted; and a description of the proposed bargaining unit, which must be an "appropriate" bargaining unit. During a prescribed period of time following the filing of the petition, other unions have the opportunity to become contestants in the union election by demonstrating some lower threshold of support (generally 10% of the proposed bargaining unit).

Time is on the side of the employer who resists collective bargaining. The passage of time is often accompanied by a waning of interest on the part of the potential unit members (particularly since the union's inability to deliver union representation and the subsequent fruits of collective bargaining can easily be portrayed as indicative of the union's ineffectiveness) and by turnover that dilutes the pool of union adherents. Unfortunately, relevant law and procedure are rife with opportunities to buy time by an employer who is willing to spend the money and to suffer the unhappiness of its employees in order to lessen the prospects of a successful organizing drive.

The easiest method by which an employer can delay the election process is to contest the appropriateness of the petitioned-for bargaining unit. The consequence of a contested unit is a hearing, which is conducted by and before the agency. A unit hearing is no different than any other kind of administrative or even judicial hearing: it has a panoply of procedures and appeals. The biggest canard in all federal labor law is the statement in the NLRB's rules and regulations that a representation hearing (i.e., a unit hearing) is nonadversarial. In fact, an employer can ensure that it is the legal equivalent of trench warfare.

Issues regarding the appropriate bargaining unit can be neverending, well-founded, or frivolous. The phrase used by legal professionals, or the "term of art," to describe an appropriate bargaining unit is *community of interest*. There is a general presumption that deference will be given to the union's proposed unit if the stated unit is an appropriate unit. The determinant is not which unit is the most appropriate. Regarding faculty units, a common issue is whether department chairs belong in the bargaining unit or not (more precisely, the issue is whether chairs are supervisors and therefore excluded from a faculty unit according to the statute being used). Other concerns are whether the appropriate unit should include part-time, temporary, and visiting faculty members; academic professionals of various types; or librarians. The result depends on whether the applicable law speaks to the issue (some statutes or regulations are quite specific) and the particular circumstances in each institution (such as how similarly or differently the institution treats the subgroups). While some issues of unit configuration are legitimate, a belligerent, and even a not very resourceful, attorney for an employer can draw on a ready supply of issues for delaying the vote and for inflating the bargaining unit with no votes.

Sustaining the Organizing Effort

Academic union organizers face the formidable task of holding together support for the union when confronted with management efforts to delay the election and dilute the unit. It is necessary to fight the legal skirmishes with the advice of competent counsel and to distinguish between when a line must be drawn in the sand and when prudence dictates that modest compromises over unit composition should be made for the sake of proceeding to an election.

Equally important is to devise means to turn the administration's tactics to the union's advantage. So while an employer is doing what it can to have the labor board's mechanisms move as slowly as possible, the union can mount a public campaign about the employees' right to decide for themselves not only whether they wish to organize but also who should and should not be included in the union effort. And since key to efforts to drain the union's momentum on the legal front is the administration's ability to spend money on lawyers, the diversion of the institution's scarce resources into lawyers' pockets can be a potent organizing tool. Unions can publicly argue that such expenditures evidence skewed priorities and can use public-records laws or other legal means to document the precise dollar amounts involved. Any foot-dragging on the administration's part in releasing such information provides an opening to a publicity campaign alleging the administration is trying to hide something.

The Election Process

Not every filing of a petition for union representation requires or results in a hearing. Even in a contested case, the parties usually manage to enter into an election agreement (though this occurs far more frequently in the public sector than in the private sector). Through an election agreement or following an adjudication and an order directing an election, the terms of the election are determined. The term most prominently included is the definition of the bargaining unit, but other critical terms, such as the date, time, and location of the election, are included as well. Vigorous disagreements commonly take place over the logistics of the election (such as whether to have mail or on-site balloting or where the sites should be located), based on each party's assessment of how to facilitate (and discourage) the voting for members of groups each considers to be most (or least) sympathetic.

The Election Campaign

Once the election is set, the union's campaign to persuade doubters and shore up its supporters goes into high gear. Usually using a scale of one to five (covering the range from strong supporters to strong opponents), the union's spreadsheet needs to assess thoroughly the support of each and every eligible voter and addressing whatever questions or concerns stand in the way of a strong yes sentiment. To contact voters, some combination of methods, including office visits and phone banking, are used. A determined push is made on the eve of the election to get out the vote among all union supporters and to try one last time to convince those who are undecided or less than adamantly opposed to vote in favor of union representation.

Two to three months is a rough but reliable estimate of the amount of time between filing the election petition and the date of the election. This estimate assumes that no hearing takes place. If a hearing is required, four to six months is a more likely time frame. As a practical matter, unions try to anticipate the probable timing of an election in calculating the most propitious time to file the cards that have been collected, accounting for such factors as the dissipation of support that may occur if the election is scheduled in a subsequent academic year.

Legal Constraints

As a legal matter, certain conduct and speech by the administration or union occurring during the election campaign may be found after the fact to have interfered with the outcome of the election, and, after the usual six or nine months of investigation and litigation, a new election may be ordered. Campaign conduct or speech that may form the basis of election objections depending on their nature and severity may also be unfair labor practices.

Objectionable conduct and speech by an employer during the course of a union organizing drive include threats of job loss or other privations; promises or grants of benefits; terminating, demoting, or otherwise causing disadvantage to employees because of their union activities; and threats of physical force or violence by either party. At more than one point in the decades it has administered private-sector labor law, the NLRB has held that misrepresentations of fact or law made at a time when the other party could not rebut the misrepresentation is objectionable. But the applicable case law now holds that most questionable representations made during the course of an organizing drive—with the exception of truly egregious breaches by either party, such as forged documents—will not serve to overturn the election results. Without exception, agencies administering bargaining laws and conducting elections are especially sensitive to misuse of their own documents for campaign purposes. Thus, distributing a sample election ballot that is clearly marked "sample" is permitted, but distributing a facsimile ballot, not identified as a sample and that has an *x* marking the spot advocated by the distributing party, is objectionable.

The Election

In conducting representation elections, the administering agency has two primary objectives: maximizing participation and assuring the regularity of the conduct of the election, including the secrecy of the ballot. These objectives must also account for such practical considerations as the number of agency representatives available to assist with the running of the election and the time required for such assistance.

Thus, collective bargaining elections are usually conducted on the employer's premises, in places and at times most convenient to the bargaining-unit employees. The mechanics of the election differ little from what you are used to at your local precinct on election day: the agency representative is joined by an observer for each party in the election, a list of eligible voters is maintained at the observers' table, and voters are marked off as they receive their ballots, which they mark in the seclusion of a voting booth. Electioneering is not permitted in the voting area or in areas where voters are in line to vote. Note, however, the still small but growing trend for labor-law agencies to conduct union representation balloting by mail, an option that can raise important tactical considerations regarding turnout for particular groups, notably adjunct faculty members.

Access to voters during the course of the campaign can be a most difficult issue for bargaining representatives who seek to convey their messages. Thus, the laws or regulations of most states require the employer to submit a list of the names and addresses of the eligible voters to the union before the election (how much in advance varies). The NLRB calls this list of voters an *Excelsior* list, named after the case in which this requirement was first imposed, *Excelsior Underwear*. In full-time faculty campaigns, gaining access to the pool of voters is generally not difficult: the organizing drive leaders (and union staff members) know who the individuals are and how to make contact with them in their offices or otherwise. The difficulties of identifying and obtaining access to adjunct faculty members or graduate student employees, especially in the course of the initial organizing outreach, can be daunting because these groups have a higher rate of turnover, often do not have offices or office hours, and tend to be on campus for limited amounts of time.

Except in the occasional case where the ballots are impounded, votes in a union election are tallied immediately on the conclusion of the voting (which for large bargaining units may occur over more than one day). A tally of ballots is issued by the agency. To the credit of the profession, voter turnout in academic union elections is generally quite high. For full-time faculty members, participation rates approaching or exceeding 90 percent are the norm, exceeding the average for other categories of employees. For the collective bargaining representative to be certified, a majority of the votes must have been cast in favor of the representative; in the event of a tie between a union and the no-agent option on the ballot, the union effort fails. Where more than one union appears on the ballot, the same rules apply, with provisions for a runoff election in the event that no majority vote is achieved on the first ballot.

The parties to the election have, typically, one week in which to file objections to the conduct of the election. In addition, issues regarding the eligibility of voters whose votes were challenged by any party (or the labor agency) during the election may also need to be resolved if the number of those votes could affect the outcome of the election. If the objections are found to have merit or if the challenged ballots might be determinative of the outcome, there will be a hearing on these issues. The hearing will obviously delay the election results and could trigger a rerun election. If there are no postelection issues, or when they have been resolved, the agency issues either a *certification of results* of the election (meaning that a majority of the voters did not choose collective bargaining) or a *certification of representative*. In the certification of results, any future collective bargaining election by the same bargaining unit may not occur for at least twelve months.

Prospects for Full-Time Faculty Organizing at Private Universities and Colleges

PATRICK SHAW

Two kinds of barriers stand in the way of the successful organization of faculty members who teach at private institutions: legal and political. This chapter explores both impediments and explains why an effort to achieve bargaining rights through the procedures of the National Labor Relations Board as the sole or primary tactic is ill advised. It concludes that private-sector faculty members can more readily achieve collective bargaining by establishing, supporting, and building a faculty union that has the means to persuade the college or university administration to deal with the union as the faculty's representative without recourse to NLRB procedures.

The number of unionized faculty members in public institutions far exceeds the number in private institutions, which represent less than 10% of the total. The key variable in this enormous disparity is the law. Many states have legislation that enables faculty members in state institutions to collectively bargain. In the private sector, however, the 1980 Supreme Court decision in *NLRB v. Yeshiva University* denies most full-time faculty members in private institutions the opportunity to pursue collective bargaining under the National Labor Relations Act (NLRA), the federal law that applies to most private and not-for-profit institutions and to nearly all other private enterprises. Part-time faculty members, except those deemed "casual employees" by the NLRB, do not face the legal impediment to unionization posed by *Yeshiva* that confronts full-time faculty members. Thus, a bargaining unit defined as "all regular part-time faculty members" will be found to be appropriate. The truly hard part in organizing part-time faculty members is achieving the political support of individuals whose physical ties with the institution are attenuated and whose employment relationship is fragile.

Unionization is the legal status generally conferred through the process known as certification, a fairly recent development in the history of collective bargaining. The 1935 Wagner Act was the initial legislation of the NLRA. It was designed to protect the process of unionizing and to establish procedures for a union to become the certified collective bargaining representative for most groups of private-sector employees. Long before the Wagner Act, however, workers formed unions. They did so by pressuring employers to recognize unions as their representatives and to bargain over the terms and conditions of their employment.

In the earliest days of union activity in the United States, such activity not only lacked legal protection but also was illegal. In 1806, eight workers in Philadelphia who had engaged in a strike were found guilty of criminal conspiracy. It was only in 1842 that a court in Massachusetts held that joining a union was not a crime. Thereafter, although it was no longer illegal to join a union, the most powerful weapon that organized workers could bring to bear on their employers to gain recognition of their unions, the strike, could be enjoined with ease until 1932, when the Norris-LaGuardia Act was passed.

As a result of the *Yeshiva* decision, full-time faculty members in private institutions are restricted in the same ways as workers were before the Wagner Act: to form and join unions and to secure recognition of unions as the collective bargaining representative are not illegal actions, but neither are they protected. Since over one-third of the states are currently without comprehensive enabling legislation (that is, a statutory framework for unionization), many public-sector academicians face at least similar challenges as those confronting their full-time private-sector faculty colleagues. Thus the lessons to be drawn in this essay on private-sector unionization efforts by full-time faculty members are applicable to many in the public sector. The obstacle is even greater in those few states that expressly prohibit public-sector authorities from negotiating legally binding agreements with employee representatives. Yet in some other states, organizing to seek legislative changes offers more promise of success than currently exists at the federal level.

The Legal Framework for Organizing

Since the passage of the Wagner Act, employees in the private sector have the legally protected right to engage in collective bargaining. As expansive as this legislation's coverage is, employees in certain industries and certain categories of persons are excluded from the protection of the NLRA. For example, "supervisors" are expressly excluded from the NLRA's scope, as are "agricultural employees." Another excluded category, "managerial employees," which figures prominently in the legal discussion of private-sector faculty unionization, is a product of judicial interpretation.

The constitutional predicate by which the United States Congress exercised its authority to regulate labor relations in private industry is the commerce clause of article 1, section 8. The reach of the NLRA encompasses all interstate commerce. Until 1970 the NLRB had declined to exercise jurisdiction over not-for-profit institutions of higher education on the premise that they did not affect interstate commerce. This obvious fiction was discarded when the NLRB did finally assert its jurisdiction in this regard in *Cornell University*, a case involving not faculty members but a state-wide bargaining unit of nonprofessional and nonsupervisory employees. The first NLRB decision specifically regarding faculty members at a private institution (*C.W. Post Center of Long Island University*), was soon reinforced by a series of similar decisions.

The *Yeshiva* Problem

Nonetheless, ten years after the NLRB first asserted its jurisdiction over not-for-profit institutions of higher education, the door to unionization was all but closed for full-time faculty members at most private institutions. In a 5-to-4 decision, the United States Supreme Court held that faculty members of Yeshiva University were managerial employees and thus not eligible for collective bargaining (*NLRB v. Yeshiva University*). The procedures leading up to the decision took six years following the Yeshiva University faculty-union petition for a collective bargaining election in October 1974. The university administration opposed the election and contended that all its faculty members were managerial or supervisory employees and thus not covered by the NLRA. A hearing was held over a five-month period generating a record containing more than 4,000 pages of testimony and 200 exhibits. A three-member panel of the NLRB granted the union's petition in December 1975 and directed an election that the union won. The administration maintained its position that its faculty members were not "employees" as defined by the NLRA and refused to bargain. In 1977, the board held that the administration had illegally refused to bargain, but a year later the United States Court of Appeals for the Second Circuit denied enforcement of the board's order. Then the case moved to the Supreme Court.

The Court defined managerial employees as both the NLRB and the Court previously had done: those who "formulate and effectuate management policies by expressing and making operative the decisions of their employer" (*Yeshiva* at 682).[1] The Court refined this definition by holding that managerial employees "must exercise discretion within or even independently of established employer policy and must be aligned with management" and normally must "represent management interests by taking or recommending discretionary actions that effectively control or implement employer policy" (*Yeshiva* at 683). The Court held that the purpose of excluding managerial employees, like the purpose of excluding supervisors from the NLRA's coverage, is to assure employers of the undivided loyalty of their representatives.

Applying this proposition to the facts of the case before the Court, Justice Powell, who wrote for the majority, stated:

[T]he faculty of Yeshiva University exercise authority which in any other context unquestionably would be managerial. Their authority in academic matters is absolute. They decide what courses will be offered, when they will be scheduled, and to whom they will be taught. They debate and determine teaching methods, grading policies, and matriculation standards. They effectively decide which students will be admitted, retained, and graduated. On occasion their views have determined the size of the student body, the tuition to be charged, and the location of a school. When one considers the function of a university, it is difficult to imagine decisions more managerial than these. To the extent the industrial analogy applies, the faculty determines within each school the product to be produced, the terms upon which it will be offered, and the customers who will be served. (*Yeshiva* at 686)

Juxtaposed with this statement of the majority view is the fundamentally opposed view of Justice Brennan, who wrote for the minority:

What the Board realized—and what the Court fails to apprehend—is that whatever influence the faculty wields in university decision making is attributable solely to its collective experience as professional educators, and not to any managerial or supervisory prerogatives. Although the administration may look to the faculty for advice on matters of professional and academic concern, the faculty offers its recommendations in order to serve its own independent interest in creating the most effective environment for learning, teaching, and scholarship. And while the administration attempts to defer to the faculty's competence whenever possible, it must and does apply its own distinct perspective to those recommendations, a perspective that is based on fiscal and other managerial policies which the faculty has no part in developing. The University always retains the ultimate decision making authority . . . and the administration gives what weight and import to the faculty's collective judgment as it chooses and deems consistent with its own perception of the institution's needs and objectives. (*Yeshiva* at 697–98)

The Yeshiva faculty union argued to the Court that the faculty's authority in institutional decision making was merely advisory (an argument advanced by every faculty member and group of faculty members who have sought to distinguish their circumstances from those of the *Yeshiva* case). The Court expressly rejected this argument, noting that the "relevant consideration is effective recommendation or control rather than final authority" (*Yeshiva* at 683n17).

Significantly—because the issue will be raised by administrations seeking to prevent faculty members from voting in a collective bargaining election—the Supreme Court declined to rule on the supervisory status of the Yeshiva faculty. The Court stated,

The record shows that faculty members at Yeshiva also play a predominant role in faculty, hiring, tenure, sabbaticals, termination, and promotion. . . . These decisions clearly have both managerial and supervisory characteristics. Since we do not reach the question of supervisory status, we need not rely primarily on these features of faculty authority. (*Yeshiva* at 686n23)

The *Yeshiva* Problem Compounded

Barely a month before the Supreme Court issued its decision in *Yeshiva*, Ronald Reagan was inaugurated as president. Within the next few years, all five members of the NLRB would be Reagan appointees. The NLRB became dominated by antiunion, anti–collective bargaining partisans, which was not surprising to those who paid attention to the views of President Reagan and his coterie on matters relating to labor relations. Thus, as one would expect, the labor board interpreted and applied the *Yeshiva* decision more restrictively than that decision calls for and thus limited the ability of faculty members to engage in collective bargaining. (One should not, however, underestimate the restrictiveness of the *Yeshiva* decision on its own terms.)

In the first couple of years following *Yeshiva* and before the board became dominated by Reagan appointees, faculty members in a handful of institutions avoided a finding that they were managerial employees.[2] In the nearly twenty years that have followed, barely another handful of faculty unions have eluded *Yeshiva*'s constraints.[3] In most of the cases that followed *Yeshiva*, and in all cases in which it can fairly be said that faculty members exercised the authority expected of professional educators, the NLRB and NLRB regional directors have concluded that the faculty members were managerial employees.[4] Two of these cases warrant particular mention: one because it represents the ultimate dilemma for a faculty that pursues collective bargaining under the NLRA as a means to assert or reassert its influence over institutional policy making, academic and otherwise; the second because it represents a benchmark for evaluating the minimal level of faculty authority that will result in a finding of "managerial" status.

In *College of Osteopathic Medicine and Surgery*, the NLRB held that the faculty members were managerial employees by virtue of their effective recommendations regarding curriculum, admissions, academic standards, and faculty personnel matters such as hiring and promotions. The spectacular irony of the case is that the faculty achieved its ability to influence decisions in these areas through collective bargaining and pursuant to its collective bargaining agreement. But the board observed that the faculty's acquisition of its managerial status through collective bargaining was irrelevant to the disposition of the case. The board offered, apparently in all seriousness, this consoling observation: "If the college removes sufficient authority from its faculty members so that they revert to the status of non-managerial employees [the NLRB will] process a proffered representation petition at that time" (*College* at 298).

As described in the board's decision in *Livingstone College*, the faculty of the college, in its ability to influence college decision making, resembled the faculties of most other reputable institutions in one important respect and looked not at all like faculties at reputable institutions in another respect. The faculty participated in academic governance by having members on various standing committees and by virtue of a faculty-wide vote on recommendations proposed by these committees. Through these means, the Livingstone faculty had substantial influence regarding curriculum, degree requirements, course content and selection, graduation requirements, and other academic matters. As Justice Brennan might have said in his *Yeshiva* dissent: "This is what faculty do by virtue of their profession, not because they are managers of their institutions."

However, unlike faculties in most four-year institutions, the Livingstone faculty had no role whatsoever in the hiring, reappointing, promoting, or tenuring of their faculty colleagues or even in the construction of the procedures that guided these personnel decisions. Despite their utter lack of participation in the usual aspects of peer review, the Livingstone faculty were deemed to be managerial employees. The NLRB held as follows:

> We have found that faculty members at Livingstone College have substantial authority in formulating and effectuating policies in academic areas. Given that the business of a university is education, it is the faculty members' participation in formulating academic policy that aligns their interest with that of management and warrants our finding them to be managerial employees. (*Livingstone* at 1314)

Post-*Yeshiva* and Other Legal Battles

The *Yeshiva* Court was careful to state that its decision should not be read to exclude all faculty members from coverage by the NLRA. But the Court did opine that faculty members in mature institutions, who, like the faculty members of Yeshiva University, participate in significant ways in the academic policy making and institutional decision making, would be found to be managerial employees. In the years since, in the relatively few cases in which the status of faculty members has been litigated, the labor board and the courts have missed few opportunities to apply *Yeshiva* in a manner that severely restricts faculty bargaining.

Faculty members and the organizations that represent them in collective bargaining have for the most part come to understand the formidable barrier posed by the current state of the law and are wary of undertaking long, expensive, problematic litigation. However, occasional cases suggest the board's capacity to be accommodating to faculty bargaining, which periodically gives renewed rise to hopes that faculty bargaining rights can be secured through legal processes.

To understand the daunting obstacles that continue to present themselves to faculty members wishing to organize under the NLRA, it is necessary to expand on the representation procedures summarized in my "primer" in this volume. After the petition is filed and the regional office of the NLRB has determined that the minimum 30% showing of interest has been demonstrated, the process begins of resolving any substantive legal issues. The board conducts a representation hearing followed by the submission and consideration of briefs. The director of the regional office of the NLRB then issues a written decision, which either party can use to trigger a request for review by the NLRB in Washington, DC. If review is denied, the regional director's decision stands, and, depending on its terms, the election petition is dismissed or an election is conducted pursuant to the terms the decision. If review is granted, the NLRB will either delay the election, assuming one has been directed by the regional director, or order that the election proceed and the ballots be impounded pending its review.

But the battle—and the attendant costs and delays—is not nearly over once the employer has thus exhausted the procedural avenues permitted by the NLRA. For even if the employees have maintained their support for collective representation after this process and a majority of them vote to be represented by the petitioning organization, the employer can then refuse to bargain. The union will file an unfair-labor-practice charge with the NLRB alleging that the refusal is illegal, and the employer will defend its refusal on the basis that the decision ordering the election was in error because the decision incorrectly defined the bargaining unit. (Specifically, the argument is that the decision should have directed the dismissal of the election petition because the faculty members are managerial employees and thus cannot legally constitute an appropriate bargaining unit.)

Under board law, such a defense is not cognizable because the employer had the opportunity to raise all issues related to the bargaining unit in the representation case. So in fairly short order (months, not years), the board will find that the employer has unlawfully refused to bargain and will issue an order requiring the employer to deal with the union. But because orders of the NLRB are not self-enforcing, the NLRB must apply to the appropriate federal appellate court for enforcement of its order (or, the employer may itself initiate an appeal seeking to have the NLRB's order set aside). In this forum, the employer will once again raise its defense that the underlying decision that directed an election was flawed. This course is so frequently followed by scofflaw employers that it has its own shorthand description: "testing certification" or, more frequently, "testing cert." (of the elected bargaining representative).

In the typical case, an employer can forestall bargaining for several years by pursuing this tactic and greatly increase the chance that even a union organizing effort with great stamina will nonetheless fail to sustain the momentum needed to establish itself as the faculty bargaining representative. Two relatively recent cases in which the faculty union won the legal battle serve as cautionary tales, illustrating the practical and legal pitfalls of full-time faculty members attempting to organize within the established statutory framework.

In 1997, in *University of Great Falls*, 325 NLRB 83, and again in 2000, in *Manhattan College*, the NLRB affirmed decisions of two NLRB regional directors, which held that faculty members at neither of the involved institutions were managerial employees. Both cases were complicated by the assertion that the NLRB lacked jurisdiction because the institutions were church-operated according to the meaning of the Supreme Court's decision in *NLRB v. Catholic Bishop of Chicago*. In that case, the Supreme Court held that the NLRB's jurisdiction over teachers in church-operated schools posed a serious risk of infringing on rights guaranteed by the religion clause of the First Amendment. Although the NLRB's jurisdiction was the subject of extensive litigation in both cases, the positions of the administrations at both the University of Great Falls and Manhattan College were rejected by the NLRB. The board found that it had jurisdiction over both schools because the purpose and function of each institution is primarily secular, because faculty members are not required to submit to the religious order that sponsors the institution or to religious teachings, and because the religious order was no longer involved in the day-to-day administration of the institution. A few years later, however, the United States Court of Appeals for the District of Columbia Circuit would overrule the labor board and hold that the board did not have jurisdiction (*Univ. of Great Falls*, 278 F.3d 1335).

Elections were held in both cases. In the *Great Falls* (325 NLRB 83) case the faculty union won, 20 to 19, but no bargaining occurred since the university immediately appealed. In the legally more interesting *Manhattan College* case, the faculty union lost the election, 47 to 76.

The *Great Falls* case did not yield a close legal case on the "managerial employee" issue and has not proved to be the harbinger of major change in the law that was suggested at the time. For example, a 1998 article in the *Chronicle of Higher Education*, titled "NLRB May End Its Opposition to Unions for Private-College Professors," featured this headline: "Experts see a major shift in a ruling to allow bargaining at U. of Great Falls" (Leatherman). A strong hint that what authority the Great Falls faculty does have would fall short of that ascribed to managerial status is a description of the university's organizational chart: a president, four vice presidents, and eight deans—that's thirteen academic executives in contrast to the forty-one faculty members in the proposed bargaining unit. More important, on the substance of the university's claim of faculty managerial status, the regional director for the NLRB first found that the deans, whose authority was extensive, were managerial employees. Next, the regional director focused on the university's governance system, which consisted of various committees. The regional director noted,

> While there are several committees on which faculty comprise a minority, it is with the influence of these faculty dominated committees that I am primarily concerned in resolving the issue of [*sic*] faculty's managerial status. Decisions or recommendations made by committees only a minority of whose members consist of representatives cannot be said to be faculty decisions or recommendations. (*Univ. of Great Falls*, 325 NLRB at 95)

After surveying the work and results of those other committees whose membership includes a majority of faculty members not holding deanships, the regional director concluded:

> Even though faculty members, either through committees or as a whole, are empowered to make recommendations in many areas, the evidence is insufficient to warrant a conclusion that these recommendations effectively control or implement employer policy to an extent that would

require excluding non-dean faculty from coverage under the Act as managerial employees. I cannot conclude, on the record before me, that faculty as a whole, or even those faculty who sit on committees are aligned with management as contemplated under *Yeshiva*. (*Univ. of Great Falls*, 325 NLRB at 97)

The decision in the *Manhattan College* case dramatically pressed against the boundaries of the *Yeshiva* decision's circumscription of faculty bargaining possibilities. In the course of his eighty-one-page opinion, the NLRB regional director was required to rule on both the college's jurisdictional argument under *Catholic Bishop*, which he rejected, and its claim that its faculty members are managerial employees. On the status issue, the regional director presented this analytical framework:

In considering the Supreme Court's *Yeshiva* decision, the Board has has placed particular emphasis on faculty roles in academic spheres, finding faculty members to be managerial even when they play no major role in nonacademic decision-making. . . . To determine managerial status, therefore, the Board looks to faculty involvement in the development and administration of academic concerns and faculty participation in the formulation of academic policy. . . . Even where the faculty's control over academic matters was not absolute, but rather subject to administrative approval or veto, the Board has nevertheless found managerial status so long as the faculty's decisions were made effective most of the time. . . . A faculty's influence, or effective recommendation, in tenure, hiring, and other nonacademic matters by themselves has been held to be not determinative of managerial status. (*Manhattan College*, slip op. at 71)

Essential to the regional director's conclusion that the Manhattan College faculty members did not effectively formulate or effectuate the college's academic policy was his determination that the department chairs were supervisory employees. The facts disclosed that the faculty members were in the minority in each of the key governance committees that determined and recommended academic policy. Their minority status was determined by combining the numbers of department chairs, who were deemed supervisors, with the deans and other administrators (who were excluded from any possible bargaining unit by agreement of the parties) and, sometimes, with student representatives. For example, a key committee, the Educational Affairs Commission, was composed of eleven faculty members, eight administrators, and four students. Thus, although faculty members outnumbered administrators, they were nevertheless in the minority.

The regional director concluded:

> Thus, it cannot be said that the Faculty, rather than some amalgam of College constituencies, exercises effective control over either the work of the Senate, any of its standing commissions, or subsequent Administrative ratification of its proposals. Under these circumstances, while it is clear that the faculty has an obvious and pervasive influence on curricular and academic life at the College, their lack of majority representation on committees empowered to create academic policy militates against finding them managerial employees. (*Manhattan College*, slip op. at 75)

One can be sure that numerous college or university administrators who were determined to remain union-free immediately began considering how to assure that faculty members constitute a majority of all the key governance committees in number but not in influence.

The regional director then turned to other matters over which the faculty had clear and substantial authority:

> In contrast to the faculty's lack of majority voice in the areas of academic policy, it falls within the province of faculty-dominated committees to make recommendations regarding distinctive features of academic life such as promotion and tenure, summer grants, sabbaticals, reduced teaching loads and the hiring and retention of tenure-track personnel, among others. (*Manhattan College*, slip op. at 76)

It is worth recalling that although the Supreme Court in *Yeshiva* declined to decide whether or not the Yeshiva faculty members were supervisors, the kinds of responsibilities identified above by the regional director in the *Manhattan* case might be used to argue for the supervisory status of faculty members.

In addressing the consequences of identifying faculty authority as supervisory, the regional director first pointed to other matters over which the faculty has little or no influence (e.g., admissions, tuition, awarding financial aid, setting the academic calendar or the financial terms of their employment). The regional director held: "Moreover, the fact that the Administration has largely conferred its approval on faculty recommendations in non-academic areas cannot in and of itself establish managerial status, absent some other indication of faculty power and control" (*Manhattan College*, slip op. at 77). However, there is very slender authority for this proposition. The decision cites but two cases: *University of Great Falls* ([19-RC-13114] and even here not the board's decision but that of the regional director) and *Lewis and Clark College* ("Faculty authority in nonacademic matters is accorded less weight in determining whether faculty are managerial employees" [at 161n30]).

Evidently, the college's prime argument to the board in support of its position that the faculty members, even if not managerial employees, are supervisors focused on the faculty members' relation to other categories of college employees such as departmental secretaries, stockroom attendants, and laboratory assistants. In a footnote, the regional director rejected this argument noting that the "contention was not specifically raised at hearing and was not fully litigated" (*Manhattan College*, slip op. at 80n26). One can be certain that had the faculty union won the election at Manhattan College and had the college decided to test certification by refusing to bargain and then obtaining federal appellate review, the issue of supervisory status would have been prominent in the argument of the case.

So faculty supporters of collective bargaining at both the University of Great Falls and Manhattan College achieved successes that few of their faculty colleagues at other private institutions have been able to achieve since the *Yeshiva* decision of 1980: they actually obtained the opportunity for an NLRB-conducted election on the proposition of collective bargaining. But, as described above, in neither case has the objective of securing collective bargaining progressed any further than a vote.

To understand this failure, consider the time frames: the faculty union's petition for an election in Manhattan College was filed 28 August 1996. After the NLRB reversed the regional director's decision that *Catholic Bishop* precluded the labor board's assertion of jurisdiction, a hearing finally began on 18 March 1997; the hearing was not completed until 2 June 1998, after 33 days of testimony. Although successful in avoiding the finding that the faculty were managerial employees, the faculty union lost the eventual election 76 to 47.

In *University of Great Falls* (19-RC-13114), the regional director of the NLRB, in his decision of 20 February 1996, rejected the university's contentions that *Catholic Bishop* required the board to withhold its jurisdiction and that, even if the board was deemed to have jurisdiction, the faculty members were managerial employees so the petition must be dismissed. A mail-ballot election was held over the period from 8 March through 29 March 1996; the ballots were impounded pending the NLRB consideration of the university's request for review. The NLRB granted that review in April 1996, and, more than a year and a half later, on 8 November 1997, the NLRB affirmed the regional director's decision and direction of election. The ballots were opened and tallied, and the union won by one vote. The union was certified as the faculty collective bargaining representative on 8 January 1998.

The university, however, refused to bargain with the union, contending that the Religious Freedom Restoration Act (RFRA) applied to proceedings under the NLRA and that the board's assertion of jurisdiction over the university would violate the RFRA. In this case of first impression, *University of Great Falls*, 331 NLRB 188, the board held that the RFRA does apply to NLRB proceedings but that the board's jurisdiction does not conflict with that statute. On 21 September 2000, the University of Great Falls appealed the NLRB's recent decision to the United States Court of Appeals for the District of Columbia Circuit. In its February 2002 ruling, the appellate court did not reach the RFRA claim but did side with the university on the applicability of *Catholic Bishop*. Finding that even the act of carefully exploring whether an institution is "sufficiently religious" would itself violate the First Amendment (*Univ. of Great Falls*, 278 F.3d 1335 at 1343), the court adopted a test that allows institutions to exempt themselves from the national collective bargaining statute by virtue of doing little more than claiming a religious mission. So the final ruling left the faculty at Great Falls University outside the protections of federal labor law.

These cases typify the frustrations of faculty members who work exceedingly hard to obtain collective bargaining rights. Indeed, they confirm the post-*Yeshiva* lesson that litigating these issues is, for the petitioning union and the faculty supporters of unionization, a legal quagmire from which little good obtains. A sampler of the procedural histories of several faculty election cases illustrates the point. In one of the earliest post-*Yeshiva* cases, and in one of the few in which faculty members were held to be nonmanagerial, *Bradford College*, the union got its election a couple of years after the petition was filed but lost in a vote of 15 to 10, out of 28 eligible faculty members. The faculty union in *Ithaca College* withstood twenty-seven days of hearing on the managerial issue only to have its petition dismissed by the NLRB. In *Florida Memorial College*, the union won the collective bargaining election in 1979 and, eight years later, was successful in getting an order from the United States Court of Appeals for the Eighth Circuit. However, as far as I can determine, the union has never been able to negotiate a collective bargaining agreement with the college. In *Livingstone College*, the election petition was filed in 1980 and an election was conducted in March 1981, but the ballots were impounded pending the college's request for review. At the end of November 1987, the NLRB dismissed the petition. Finally, in one of the few cases in which faculty members won the ability to vote for collective representation, *Saint Thomas University*, the election occurred a mere two years after the petition was filed (a relatively short time for these cases), but the union lost in lopsided fashion, 30 to 13.

Yeshiva Reform?

The occasional NLRB decision holding that faculty members have the right to be collectively represented does not evince any fundamental change in the state of the law regarding faculty collective bargaining. Even a board composed of appointees determined to expand the opportunity for faculty members to bargain is constrained by the Supreme Court's decision in *Yeshiva* and by the federal appellate courts to whom college and university employers will turn in those few cases in which faculty members are deemed to be covered by the NLRA.

There are only two means by which *NLRB v. Yeshiva University* can be overturned. The first—which at best could be described as a remote possibility for the foreseeable future—would be the Supreme Court's revisiting in another case the issue of the managerial status of faculty members and reversing itself. Alternatively, and only somewhat more realistically, would be a legislative repeal. In each legislative session from 1980, when *Yeshiva* was decided, until 1994, legislation that would have reversed *Yeshiva* was introduced in the United States Congress, under AAUP auspices. Not surprisingly, the narrow issue of full-time faculty bargaining rights attracted insufficient political support to move far, and the initiative suffered the same fate as that of a number of other attempts by labor unions to reform the national bargaining statute.

The most promising chance to accomplish legislative repeal of the

Yeshiva decision took place early in President Clinton's first term, when he directed the Departments of Commerce and Labor to establish a commission to assess federal labor laws and to make recommendations for reform. The Commission on the Future of Worker-Management Relations, known as the Dunlop Commission, after its chair, John Dunlop, an economist and former secretary of labor, held hearings for an eighteen-month period and issued its recommendations in December 1994. Many positions were advocated by organized labor during the commission's hearings. The AAUP's written position advocated a rethinking of the managerial status of all professional employees; its president and general secretary testified before the commission with specific details about their own experience of being "managers" in the academy. The commission made fifteen discrete recommendations, seven of which called for legislative action. The second recommendation states in part, "we recommend . . . [u]pdating the definitions of supervisor and manager to insure that only those with full supervisory or managerial authority and responsibility are excluded from the coverage of the law" (United States xvii).

Only a month before the Dunlop Commission issued its report and recommendations, the Republican Party gained a majority in the United States House of Representatives; therewith any hope for action on the legislative recommendations of the Dunlop Commission was extinguished.

Alternative Paths

We have seen that the law applicable to faculty bargaining poses a formidable barrier to obtaining bargaining rights, and NLRB procedures allow for long delays. Even when a faculty union prevails on the *Yeshiva* issue, and such unions often do so at a great cost both in time and effort and in concentration and money, the administration usually wins the battle that counts—the political battle.

Realistically, then, those wishing to strengthen the ability of private-sector faculty members to organize are, at least in the foreseeable future, left with the need to find an alternative to the conventional means provided for by the NLRA. Although the statutory protection of the right to unionize is effectively absent for most full-time faculty members, nothing in *Yeshiva* or in any other case makes it unlawful to unionize. The key to efforts to unionize outside the law is to use the approaches that have always been essential for successful organizing: gaining and exercising political power. Bear in mind that the federal (and generally state) labor law regulating collective bargaining provides for the possibility of achieving collective bargaining rights without an agency-conducted election. An organization will be deemed to be the exclusive representative of the covered employees if it can demonstrate that it has the support of a majority of the employees and the employer recognizes the organization as the employees' representative. This means of acquiring representative status is known as voluntary recognition, which more often than not is a misnomer because the voluntariness is usually the result of strong pressure by the employees to press their employer to recognize the representative. Thus, the argument can be made that academic unions would do well to seek voluntary recognition more often.

Beginning in the Reagan era, when the NLRB's administration of the labor laws intentionally impeded the ability of employees to unionize, many unions started to organize outside the law; that is, instead of relying on the procedures of the NLRB, which are so easily abused by employers even without a complicit labor board, unions exerted the effort and perseverance required to build strong rank-and-file support and to implement campaigns to pressure the employer to recognize the union as the bargaining representative.

Campaigns mounted by faculty members and the national organizations that assist them to gain bargaining rights in private institutions should begin with the premise that the procedures of the NLRB are unavailing or that they should be invoked only as one tactic among others intended to pressure an administration into dealing with the faculty organization as the faculty representative.

The hardest question is how to establish political support among the faculty members for obtaining bargaining rights. Here is a realistic strategy for faculty members in a private institution to unionize: the faculty establishes or revives its moribund AAUP chapter and begins active consultation with national AAUP staff members. Elected chapter leaders formulate a substantive agenda that is grounded in principle and is responsive to important issues affecting the faculty and the institution. At a well-chosen time, perhaps after conducting a faculty referendum, the chapter publicly declares unionization as an organizational objective. With majority membership and at least two-thirds of the faculty supporting this goal, the chapter notifies the administration that it represents a substantial majority of the faculty members, and it proposes a process by which the administration can confirm majority status (under the auspices of a neutral person such as a priest, minister, or rabbi or a neutral organization such as the American Arbitration Association). On confirmation that the chapter represents a majority of the faculty members, the administration recognizes the chapter as the faculty bargaining representative and agrees to commence negotiations for a collective bargaining agreement. But unless the chapter has already been successful in applying sufficient pressure on the administration to acquiesce, the administration will certainly refuse the chapter's proposal.

The chapter will, of course, be reporting fully to the faculty at each step. The chapter, with full disclosure to the faculty, files an election petition with the NLRB. However, the chapter makes clear to the faculty and to the administration that if the administration uses the NLRB's procedures in ways that delay an election (including the administration's arguing that faculty members are managerial employees), it will withdraw the petition and begin taking actions to induce the administration to recognize the chapter as the bargaining representative without an election or to agree to an NLRB-conducted election.

If the chapter is not successful in convincing the administration to proceed to an election in relatively short order, it must begin to wage its battle for bargaining rights outside the law. Hard as this endeavor is, it is preferable to an expensive, exhausting, probably futile legal case. Finally—and not to be forgotten—even if a faculty union chooses the litigation route to certification and, some years later, is successful in overcoming the legal barrier, the task of maintaining or reestablishing the political strength to win the election and to achieve its bargaining objectives must still be undertaken, a task quite similar in aim and effort to obtaining bargaining rights independent of the procedures of the NLRB.

NOTES

1. The *Yeshiva* ruling quotes the Court's decision in *NLRB v. Bell Aerospace Co.,* 416 U.S. 367, 288 (1974).

2. See *Bradford College,* 261 NLRB 565 (1982); *New York Medical College,* 263 NLRB 903 (1982); *Florida Memorial College,* 263 NLRB 1248 (1982); *Loretto Heights College,* 264 NLRB 1107 (1982); *Puerto Rico Junior College,* 265 NLRB 72 (1982).

3. See *Universidad Central de Bayamon,* 273 NLRB 1110 (1984); *Cooper Union for the Advancement of Science and Art,* 273 NLRB 1768 (1985); *Kendall School of*

Design, 299 NLRB 281 (1986); *Saint Thomas University*, 298 NLRB 280 (1990); *University of Great Falls*, 325 NLRB 83 (1997); *Manhattan College*, Case No. 2-RC-21735 (college's request for review denied by the NLRB on 9 June 2000); *California School of Professional Psychology*, Case No. 32-RC-5167 (2003).

4. See *Ithaca College*, 261 NLRB 577 (1982); *Thiel College*, 261 NLRB 580 (1982); *Duquesne University*, 261 NLRB 587 (1982); *College of Osteopathic Medicine and Surgery*, 265 NLRB 295 (1982); *University of New Haven*, 267 NLRB 939 (1983); *American International College*, 282 NLRB 189 (1986); *Boston University*, 281 NLRB 798 (1986); *Livingstone College*, 286 NLRB 1308 (1987); *University of Dubuque*, 289 NLRB 349 (1988); *Lewis and Clark College*, 300 NLRB 155 (1990); *Elmira College*, 309 NLRB 942 (1992); *Sacred Heart University*, Case No. 34-RC-1876 (2001); *The Sage Colleges*, Case No. 3-RC-11040 (2001); *Manhattanville College*, Case No. 26-RC-8277 (2001); *University of Saint Francis*, Case No. 13-RC-20682 (2002).

WORKS CITED

Bradford College, 261 NLRB 565 (1982).

College of Osteopathic Medicine and Surgery, 265 NLRB 295 (1982).

Cornell University, 183 NLRB 329 (1970).

C. W. Post Center of Long Island University, 189 NLRB 904 (1971).

Florida Memorial College, 263 NLRB 1248 (1982).

Ithaca College, 261 NLRB 577 (1982).

Leatherman, Courtney. "NLRB May End Its Opposition to Unions for Private-College Professors." *Chronicle of Higher Education* 9 Jan. 1998. <http:www.chronicle.com>.

Lewis and Clark College, 300 NLRB 155 (1990).

Livingstone College, 286 NLRB 1308 (1987).

Manhattan College, Case No. 2-RC-21735 (2000).

NLRB v. Catholic Bishop of Chicago, 440 U.S. 490 (1979).

NLRB v. Yeshiva University, 444 U.S. 672 (1980).

Saint Thomas University, 298 NLRB 280 (1990).

United States. Commission on the Future of Worker-Management Relations. *Report and Recommendations: Executive Summary*. Washington: United States Dept. of Labor; United States Dept. of Commerce, 1994.

University of Great Falls, Case No. 19-RC-13114 (1996).

University of Great Falls, 325 NLRB 83 (1997).

University of Great Falls, 278 F.3d 1335 (DC Cir. 2002).

University of Great Falls, 331 NLRB 188 (31 Aug. 2000).

Faculty Representation without Collective Bargaining

IRIS MOLOTSKY

At first glance, it might seem that organizing faculty members on campuses with little or no chance for certification is not that much different from efforts culminating in a vote for representation. Indeed, there are great similarities: support must be built, issues explored, and effective communications established. Engaging significant numbers of faculty members is vital to success in both types of campaigns, and organizers use similar motivational tools to recruit and engage campus supporters. Despite their similarities, however, mobilizing for collective action on non-collective-bargaining campuses is not simply unionization without the union label.

First, the pace of non-collective-bargaining campaigns is different from those culminating in union certification. Collective bargaining campaigns have a rhythm driven by regulatory demands. Union drives unfold in distinct stages: membership building and collection of signatures for a card campaign, unit determination, and, ultimately, the election. Obviously, the timing for achieving these objectives varies greatly from campus to campus, but the election is the driving force and final objective of any campaign. Non-collective-bargaining campaigns most commonly do not have defined time lines or externally imposed phases, giving advocacy campaign organizers more latitude in determining the dynamics of the campaign. This does not mean, of course, that advocacy campaigns lack time limitations; indeed, they tend to be shorter than certification campaigns in the initial stages.

Second, there are subtle but significant differences in the way issues are framed in advocacy campaigns. Although unionization campaigns are not necessarily restricted to terms and conditions of employment, contracts most commonly limit the scope of bargaining to these issues; hence they assume a more important role in collective bargaining campaigns. Faculty members organizing for noncertification representation, although not disregarding bread-and-butter concerns, typically emphasize issues such as academic freedom, institutional governance, evaluation of administrators, and the status of adjunct faculty members and graduate students. These campaigns focus on the need to ensure the principles defining the profession, to retain a collegial model of decision making, and to maintain institutional standards. Faculty members engaging in collective action lack protection under labor law and must force change by relying on arguments and persuasion reinforced by organizational strength. Administrators and boards, like politicians, respond to numbers and constituencies, and so faculty members seeking a voice must demonstrate strength. Faculty members can further enhance their position by gaining the backing of other academic stakeholders, such as legislators and students, as well as the news media. This essay discusses the basic elements essential to faculty members engaging in advocacy organizing.

Advocacy organizing is a two-step process. The first stage is commonly initiated by a specific incident or set of circumstances that sparks an interest in organizing. If the initial collective effort is successful and a chapter is formed, the next goal must be to sustain the organization during the second stage of development and to ensure that the chapter retains its effectiveness. Building a successful campaign requires developing a number of separate, but not independent, programs directed toward engaging the faculty, demonstrating unity, and communicating issues and ideals both internally and to the general academic public. Components should include creating an executive committee with responsibilities for leadership and strategic planning and setting up committees for membership development, issue development, and communications. Legislative- and government-relations programs are also advisable, although they may not be of primary importance in the initial stages of a campaign.

We examine how to identify leaders and build membership, how to select and develop issues, and how to create an effective communications program. We also explore the complementary roles of faculty organizations and governance bodies. Ultimately, empowering faculty members rests on three essential factors: the organization's ability to address problems, its capability for effecting change, and the amount of support it commands.

Getting Started

Campaigns frequently begin with a call from a faculty member or a group of faculty members who are disturbed by actions taken—most commonly by administrators or governing boards. When I was director of membership development for the AAUP, I often received calls from chapter officers or members who perceived violations of academic freedom or governance on their campuses. These unhappy faculty members frequently formed the nucleus of the campaign and became the leaders in the efforts to organize faculty colleagues.

Groups may choose to remain independent while in the process of organizing, but it is preferable to affiliate with a national organization that has a history of working with advocacy chapters. The affiliated chapter thus gains access to the knowledge and experience of organizers as well as colleagues on other campuses who understand the dynamics of a campaign and know how to identify and present issues. The AAUP's unique role in developing academic policy and promoting professional standards has lent legitimacy and substance to arguments that might otherwise be labeled self-interest by adversaries; that is why non-collective-bargaining faculty groups are most frequently allied with the AAUP. Finally, the resources available from national organizations, including campus visits by academic leaders, strategic planning, and mailings and literature are significant assets to a fledgling organization.

Building Membership

Success in any campaign depends on building membership, but it is surprising how often this task is not given top priority. Many faculty members find it more intellectually satisfying to work on developing position papers or writing campaign literature. Soliciting membership is hard work and takes time, but putting it aside will almost always result in a failed campaign. Understanding the composition of the faculty and assessing strengths and weaknesses in disciplines, departments, and schools is a necessary first step in the development of a membership plan. It is also useful to know the names of former local activists or chapter members who might be persuaded to renew their efforts or rejoin.

While it is important to use a wide array of faculty members in membership building, accountability must reside in a designated entity, usually the membership committee. It is not a good idea to have the executive committee or chapter organizers responsible for membership. A separate committee focused solely on increasing membership is the best way to approach this task. Appoint only people who want to work on membership to this team. By doing it this way, you gain a core of committed workers, and, at the same time, more faculty members have become invested in helping the chapter succeed. Strive for diversity on this committee: think in terms of generational differences, faculty status, discipline, race and gender. This will enable you to address multiple campus issues and sidestep perceptions of elitism or cronyism.

From an early point in the campaign, it is important to gain the support of faculty members who have the trust and respect of colleagues, particularly those who have distinguished appointments or leadership positions in governance bodies. Their support is needed to attract the uncommitted and to provide cover for more vulnerable junior faculty members. A note of caution as well: faculty members with personal grievances should not be placed in prominent leadership positions. Personalization of issues polarizes rather than unites faculty members, and it is impossible to sustain a campaign based on individual problems. This, of course, does not preclude using some personal issues as vehicles for advocating a change in practices.

The membership committee designs a plan and selects goals in consultation with the chapter leadership. The group is responsible for scheduling regular meetings, charting progress in meeting targets, and reporting to the leadership. Other faculty members besides those on the committee can be involved in recruiting, but committee members should assign and supervise all membership activities. Recruiting plans are usually determined along departmental or disciplinary divides, but strategies vary according to circumstances. They could, for example, include objectives such as targeting contingent faculty members or new hires.

Membership and support by departments and schools must be analyzed to gauge strengths and weaknesses. It is best, although rarely possible, to have representation in all departments and schools. Organization should begin with departments and programs where positions are known and accepted by advocates and members. Additional commitments are more easily obtained when the appeal comes from a departmental colleague. It is important to gain supporters quickly in the initial stages both to build momentum internally and to create the impression of a dynamic movement for outside observers.

It may seem easy to ask colleagues to join a chapter or organization, but joining involves paying dues: many faculty members find it hard to ask colleagues for money, even if it is not for personal gain. Most faculty members can frame arguments persuasively but do not know how to obtain a commitment. One of the most important tasks of the membership committee, therefore, is to train colleagues in the art of closing the deal in recruiting. Many committees use role-playing as a means of instilling confidence in recruiters. Other valuable training exercises include development of talking points for office visits and preparation of answers for anticipated questions.

There is no substitute for personal contact through an office visit. "Hall walking" is labor-intensive and time-consuming, but nothing is more effective than one-on-one contact with colleagues. Recruiters need to be trained in how to approach colleagues, what message to deliver, and how to follow through on initial contacts. Again, this is where the benefits of affiliation with a national organization are revealed. Professional organizers can help in training and can frequently work alongside faculty members on office visits. Such partnership provides an effective one-two punch: campus colleagues respond to institutional questions while professional organizers provide an overview of related national trends. For a detailed description of how to conduct office visits, consult the AAUP booklet *Guide to the Office Visit*.

Faculty members involved in building an advocacy organization are frequently reluctant to levy dues because they believe dues will reduce participation. They survive by passing the hat or by personally underwriting activities. While understandable, this is not the prescription for building a strong organization. To be effective, a group needs resources. Visibility can be gained only if there are funds to produce professional, attractive literature. Additionally, paying dues increases a member's identity with the organization and commitment to the cause.

Issue Development

As noted above, campus problems, whether isolated or chronic, are most often the motivating factors for mounting a campaign. The difficulty of

the campaign lies in deciding how to coherently and cogently frame issues raised by such problems. Strategically, the most effective route to
follow is the high road—that is, basing organizing campaigns on professional and collegial arguments. Grounding positions in principles provides
legitimacy to faculty claims, defuses assertions of self-interest, and is most
likely to win support from the broader academic community. The AAUP
publishes a compilation of its policy statements, commonly referred to as
the "Redbook," that spans almost ninety years of experience promoting
academic freedom, shared governance, and other academic and professional standards (see *Policy Documents*). These standards, widely recognized and accepted in the academic community, often form the foundation for local campaigns. Motivation always includes an element of
self-interest, of course, but individual gains for faculty members should
not become the focus of an organizing campaign, particularly on non-
collective-bargaining campuses. The arguments for collective action
should be posed in terms of the effect proposed changes will bring to the
status of the profession.

Of course, issues vary according to institutional type and size, and
objectives are always subject to the prospects for overcoming institutional
and external constraints. But, although issues differ, they tend to fall into
several broad categories. For instance, a major area of concern for faculty
members today is the extensive use of contingent faculty members, but
the response to this problem varies depending on institutional type and
category. At research institutions, the question of part-time faculty members is closely related to the status and use of graduate teaching assistants,
whereas at smaller, independent colleges, the question may be framed in
terms of the number of part-time versus full-time faculty members, or
the shrinking number of full-time, tenured positions. In another instance,
governance problems are often especially severe at smaller institutions
that serve specific religious or ethnic communities; such institutions may
struggle for survival and therefore fear that any internal questioning undermines their missions. Many small liberal arts colleges have strong
traditions of community and collegial governance but may periodically
experience episodic strains due to financial, enrollment, or leadership
problems.

Campaigns frequently include attempts to get boards to act. It must
be remembered, however, that politically appointed (or elected) board
members at public institutions respond to different pressures than board

members at private institutions, whose tenures tend to be dependent on presidential goodwill. An extreme example of board capriciousness at a private institution occurred in fall 2003, when the board at Boston University dismissed a newly appointed president before he assumed office, an action that underlines a difference between public and private institutions. Boards are most frequently involved in presidential appointments and reviews—matters that vitally affect faculty members and frequently engulf campuses in the kind of controversy that leads to faculty organizing.

Another too frequently encountered problem is downsizing, which results in losses of jobs and programs. Instead of focusing on the number of jobs lost, however, a productive faculty campaign might focus on the implications of the cuts for the educational mission of the university and its impact on students. When faculty members' salaries have been frozen for three years, the rallying theme should not be the precarious financial condition of individual members (although this is a serious concern), but the need for parity with other institutions in order to attract and retain excellent faculty members.

Although personal vilification occurs in campus organizing, as elsewhere, it is generally and properly regarded as unseemly and inappropriate. Where possible, faculty leaders should avoid linking issues with personalities and stick to principles and procedures. Where individual leadership is itself the issue, faculty members should nevertheless be careful of facts and rhetoric.

In recent years, changes in administrations or boards frequently have resulted in policy revisions that are adverse to faculty interests. Faddish higher education theorists, preferring boardrooms to classrooms, have spent energy and resources trying to replace or retool the traditional collegial model. When boards act without consultating the faculties, senates, or other academic governing structures, they arouse antagonism and lay the groundwork for collective faculty action. The changing nature of the academic workforce has created numerous hot-button issues, including the reliance on contingent faculty members, the ambiguous status of graduate students, the restructuring of programs, and the ownership of intellectual property. While faculties may not be able to staunch diminished funding at the source of some of these issues, at a minimum they need to be outspoken in opposition to it. More important, their organizing should include efforts to find reasonable solutions.

Despite the many obstacles, faculty members have achieved significant successes in recent years. The University of Minnesota provides a notable, if somewhat special, example. As a result of problems in the academic health center, the regents brought in an outside consulting firm with a mandate to reengineer the personnel structure to enable restructuring the entire campus (see Miller; Burgan). The firm's recommendations, which included significant modifications to the tenure code, alarmed a broad range of faculty members, including many of the most prominent faculty leaders. When the regents proposed to unilaterally overrule the faculty senate, an independent association launched a campaign for collective bargaining. The AAUP chapter joined in the campaign, which, although it did not achieve collective bargaining, did successfully assist the faculty senate to reverse the board's direction and limit the changes to those approved by the senate.

The campaign mobilized many faculty members and allies. Senate leaders, along with distinguished professors, spoke out against the attempt to cut institutional policies and standards to the measure of corporate operations. Favorable press coverage included sympathetic editorials and op-ed pieces that helped faculty members gain support from students, parents, and the general public. The publicity galvanized faculty members from other campuses, who lent support to their colleagues financially and through campus visits. The national AAUP had organizers on campus for the duration of the campaign, provided assistance in building membership, and helped develop positions based on enlightened professional practices.

Although the threat of collective bargaining played a significant role, including the creation of a temporary legal bar to unilateral action by the regents, much of the organizing and communications effort, as well as the actions of the faculty senate, did not specifically depend on the bargaining campaign. The key measure of success lay in the fact that, despite the lack of collective bargaining, the faculty established an effective continuing organization—in this case an AAUP chapter—with a substantially increased membership support. That traditional chapter has provided a continuing faculty voice and assisted an invigorated senate to achieve substantial improvements in faculty compensation and to maintain professional standards. The availability of the threat of collective bargaining, although somewhat unusual at major universities, is not unique. Many public universities that have so far not chosen to avail themselves of state-sanctioned bargaining opportunities do have the opportunity to use bargaining as a possibility to encourage their administrations to respect shared governance and professional standards. Moreover, since the organizational and communications activities that lead to success are not dependent on a legally protected opportunity to bargain, the deeper lesson from Minnesota is that, where there are important professional concerns at issue, an organized faculty can be effective regardless of bargaining laws and prospects.

Communications programs, to be truly successful, must target several different audiences simultaneously and deliver their messages through an array of vehicles. For example, at the beginning of a campaign, it is advisable to issue frequent brief leaflets or bulletins presenting the issues. At the same time, it is necessary to develop more in-depth position papers and arguments that can be used in meetings and debates and for recruiting members. Skillful communicators know the importance of emphasizing the points valued by their audience, and academic campaigns should follow this example by carefully designing literature to have the greatest impact on the targeted audience. This means developing multiple leaflets, posters, and position papers on the basic issues of the campaign. Internally, it is essential to inform and educate faculty members, administrators, and boards. Externally, it is important to reach out to the media, elected officials, and the general public, particularly parents. Although the messages should not misrepresent core positions, convincing campaign literature should engage interest and support through persuasion developed in accord with the audience's concerns.

The most important audience members are colleagues, for motivating and informing them is a foremost concern. Communicating occurs through personal contact, written materials, and planned activities such as rallies or debates. In the days before computers, printed newsletters were the leading internal means of conveying information. Newsletters remain the backbone of communications, but electronic distribution is faster and less expensive. Early on, chapters should establish Web sites and provide e-mail addresses that are not owned or overseen by the university. Web sites should state objectives, post articles, encourage debate, and publicize events. Good advocacy journalism sticks to the facts but shapes the story to the faculty perspective. In addition to providing news and analysis, newsletters should promote organizational objectives, achievements, and membership. For example, the headline "Membership Doubles" can convey a sense of momentum, even in cases where a chapter has gone from fifteen to thirty. Information about joining and the name of a contact person must be included in the newsletter.

A few cautionary notes about writing newsletters, print or electronic, are in order:

- Be very careful when ascribing motivation.
- Do not disparage individuals and do not air individual vendettas.
- Update Web sites frequently.
- Publish newsletters regularly.

Leafleting is an essential part of any communications campaign. Leaflets can be narrowly targeted in disciplines or schools or be aimed more broadly toward campuswide issues. In either case, covering the campus with paper creates the appearance of organizational strength and is an inexpensive way to reach the large numbers of faculty members who must be convinced. Posters serve a similar purpose and should be displayed prominently throughout the campus.

In addition to leaflets and posters, it is important to develop position papers on the professional issues driving the campaign. As discussed before, colleagues and opponents alike need to be given analyses based on facts and grounded in academic principles. Statistics, case studies, and issues placed in a national context are powerfully persuasive and can gain support inside and outside the academic community. As the campaign issues are determined, it becomes the responsibility of the communications committee to disseminate them.

Creating a public-relations component is important as well. Reporters covering education tend to have institutional contacts but rarely know faculty members or faculty concerns. Reporters should be contacted by e-mail or telephone. They should be invited to the campus to meet colleagues, perhaps at a brown-bag lunch. They must be briefed on issues. Indeed, it should be as easy for reporters to reach effective faculty spokespersons as it is for them to reach the institution's public-relations office. Sometimes faculty members are reluctant to talk to reporters, fearing they might be misquoted, but this is rarely a problem and should not become an obstacle in working with the print or electronic media.

Another aspect of public relations involves writing editorials and op-ed pieces. Knowing local newspaper and television-station policies regarding editorials increases chances for success. Faculty members whose campuses are in large, urban areas are at a slight disadvantage, because it is more difficult to place op-ed pieces in big-city newspapers, but publication can still be accomplished. Colleagues in the journalism department can be a great help with these efforts. Press releases can be useful as well. Even if they do not always generate coverage, they do add to the reporter's knowledge and help to gain recognition for the organization. Unless there is very important news or an issue creates a demand from the press, do not schedule a press conference, because they are unlikely to attract significant participation. Finally, anyone can write a letter to the editor, and those faculty members who can write short and pithy letters should be especially encouraged to do so.

Communications extends beyond the written word. As membership building continues, it becomes important to get supporters involved in activities. The sense of community created by working together reinforces commitment and provides a show of strength to opponents. Although rallies in support of faculty positions can generate enthusiasm and garner coverage, they must be carefully planned to ensure attendance. When photographers record the event for later use in newsletters and leaflets, they should be able to show a good-sized crowd. Other effective activities include debates, colloquia, and town-hall meetings. In the case of the University of Minnesota, the AAUP coordinated the efforts of visiting faculty members from campuses across the country to conduct informational workshops and to support local colleagues at meetings and protests.

State and Legislative Programs

In those states with strong higher education systems, faculty members often find it important to create a statewide faculty body to seek to influence policy. Even where one or more official statewide faculty bodies, such as statewide senates exist, it is important to create a statewide faculty advocacy group. AAUP chapters typically form state conferences, and education unions often have state organizations even in nonbargaining states as well. Faculty influence is greatly enhanced where there is a statewide leadership group, and, where possible, staff members who maintain regular contact with state educational authorities. This leadership can also provide a basis for political lobbying and public relations.

Faculty members have had a reputation for disdaining politics, preferring to leave lobbying to administrators. This probably was never true, and it certainly is not today. Policies determined at the federal and state level intrude into the classroom, ideologically and materially; faculty members have had to become part of the legislative process. Because public institutions are state-funded, it might appear that faculty members on these campuses have a greater stake in maintaining a presence in state capitals, but faculty members at private institutions need to be visible as well. Indeed, the funding difference between private and public institutions is diminishing. In an op-ed article in the *New York Times*, Stanley Fish pointed out that public funding accounts for just 25% of the university's operating costs, and in "some states the figure has dipped below 10 percent." Additionally, programs and policies imposed on public institutions are frequently adopted by their private counterparts.

Although a few large campuses (most of which are unionized) have the resources and personnel to work independently, most legislative programs are cooperative efforts. Organizations defined as charitable under tax law cannot endorse candidates (although individuals and independent political action committees can), but they can be forceful, effective advocates for higher education issues and for faculty rights. Faculties, which sometimes work cooperatively with presidential and administrative groups, can become effective players in the legislative game.

Few legislative programs involve large numbers of faculty members. Most often, a group of interested people assumes the responsibility for identifying issues and building contacts with legislators and elected officials. These faculty members are frequently social scientists, but others with policy expertise or personal political commitments and involvements also play an important role. Web sites are particularly effective tools for providing legislative information and for urging action in support or opposition to pending legislation. In addition to funding, typical issues involve scholarship money, free-speech questions, and institutional missions.

The AAUP Indiana state organization built its legislative program around gaining a faculty representative on the commission for higher education, the government agency that coordinates higher education policy in the state. After a seven-year campaign, it achieved its goal. The faculty member who spearheaded the effort, Joseph Losco, recalled that it required "lots of e-mails, phone calls, regular updates, and legislative alerts." Now, however, the faculty, in addition to the student body, has a representative at the table.

Faculty activists often stress the importance of providing visibility for elected officials. Advocacy organizations for faculty members, as charitable and educational organizations, cannot directly contribute to electoral campaign funds, but they can give awards, sponsor speeches, and provide audiences and photo opportunities, all of which generate positive press for the legislator. Office visits to elected representatives should be routine. Time spent schmoozing and building trust with members on important committees will bring future rewards. It is important to understand how the system really works and who the key players are in the political process. A veteran AAUP faculty lobbyist provided me with a useful example from Georgia, where creation-science legislation was bottled up in committee because a key legislator and the faculty lobbyist were longtime, trusted acquaintances. While some advocacy groups have formed political action committees to support candidates, because of the complex legal requirements, most non-collective-bargaining faculty groups do not choose to do this.

Quite often, individual faculty members play a formative role in educating and framing higher education issues for legislators. Another interesting case, also in Georgia, involved a study by a professor on the harmful effects of smoking (see Fischer). On the basis of the state's open-records law, the tobacco industry pressed him to reveal the names of minors he had interviewed. When the university, citing the law, released the names to industry representatives, state and national AAUP, citing academic-freedom principles, sought successfully to amend the law. The Georgia Press Association initially fought the proposed amendment, but persuasive arguments by faculty members prevailed, and the GPA agreed to the exception. Hard work, combined with sound principles and the right contacts, enabled faculty members in Georgia to retain a significant professional right. These examples illustrate the importance of an established network of contacts and a monitoring system capable of alerting faculty members to potential problems. The ability to talk directly to decision makers when problems arise is too valuable an asset to neglect.

Above, I mention the two stages involved in mobilizing faculty members—recruitment and maintenance. Legislative programs are an essential component of both elements. People considering an organization rightly ask, How will this benefit me? An effective legislative program that can point to specific achievements gives powerful reasons for joining. Equally as important, people will more likely remain committed if legislative achievements can be highlighted. Finally, and perhaps most important, legislative programs have helped faculty members promote sound practices and deflect destructive initiatives.

Faculty Governance and Advocacy Organizations

Faculty members sometimes hesitate to form advocacy groups because they fear their activities could weaken traditional faculty senates or assemblies. Actually, these organizations are complementary, and advocacy groups often strengthen the role of the faculty senate by developing and promoting coherent faculty objectives. Faculty senates are elected campus institutions with recognized rights and responsibilities, and faculty senators tend to be distinguished and respected colleagues who have accumulated wisdom about institutional life. Advocacy groups, because of their unity and commitment to specific objectives, can use the senate structure as a lever for change. Cooperation between the two provides an inside-outside strategy where the establishment faculty senate and the nonestablishment advocacy group work together to promote sound academic standards. Therefore, a primary agenda for advocacy groups should be to get colleagues elected to the senate who can then introduce and support the groups' organizational goals. Indeed, advocacy groups may hold the key to reversing the serious decline in the effectiveness of faculty governance in recent years. A combination of factors, including the proliferation of part-time and non-tenure-track faculty members, increased publication and funding demands, larger class sizes, and intensified tenure requirements, have led to a decline in faculty participation in governance. These conditions, coupled with an administrative imperative for more top-down, authoritarian management, have weakened traditional governance at many institutions. An infusion of organized faculty members working for change within traditional structures can renew faculty governance in changing times.

WORKS CITED

American Association of University Professors. *Guide to the Office Visit*. Washington: AAUP, 2004.
———. *Policy Documents and Reports*. 9th ed. Washington: AAUP, 2001.
Burgan, Mary. "Tenure and the Management of Higher Education." *Footnotes 1997.*

22 Sept. 2005 <http://www.aaup.org/publications/Footnotes/FN97/FNM BART.htm>.

Fish, Stanley. "Colleges Caught in a Vice." Editorial. *New York Times* 18 Sept. 2003, late ed.: A31.

Fischer, Paul M. "Fischer v. The Medical College of Georgia and the R. J. Reynolds Tobacco Company: A Case Study of Constraints on Research." *Academic Freedom: An Everyday Concern.* Ed. Ernst Benjamin and Donald R. Wagner. New Directions for Higher Educ. 88. San Francisco: Jossey-Bass, 1994. 33–43.

Losco, Joseph. Telephone interview. Fall, 2003.

Miller, Robert F. "How Not to Reform a Medical School." *Academe* 85.6 (1999): 47–50. 22 Sept. 2005 <http://www.aaup.org/publications/Academe/1999/99nd/ND99Mill.htm>.

Contingent Faculty Organizing and Representation

ERNST BENJAMIN

Nearly half of all faculty instructional appointments and two-thirds of those in community colleges are held by part-time faculty members. Although the various essays on full-time faculty organizing and representation in this volume apply in many respects to these part-time faculty members as well, part-time faculty organizing and representation differ sufficiently from full-time to require separate consideration. The differences do not derive primarily from varied training or responsibilities. Most part-time faculty members have graduate degrees, and teaching is the predominant responsibility of most faculty members, full-time as well as part-time. Particularly in four-year institutions, more full-time than part-time faculty members have doctoral or professional degrees and involvement in research. In two-year as well as four-year institutions, part-time instructors are less likely to have the opportunity to contribute to collegial curricular or personnel committees. But the fundamental differences between full-time and part-time faculty members are founded not on their preparation or responsibilities but on the terms and conditions of their respective appointments.

The defining characteristic of these appointments is their contingency, which derives from short-term contracts and lack of tenure eligibility. Contingency is something they have in common with some full-time, non-tenure-track faculty appointments (Amer. Assn., "Status" and *Contingent*; Benjamin, "Editor's Notes" 1–2). The differences between full-time, tenure-track appointments and non-tenure-track appointments, whether part- or full-time, are so fundamental that many observers now refer to a "bifurcated" (Gappa and Leslie, *Invisible* 2–3, 12; *Two Faculties*; Benjamin, "Reappraisal" 104–08; Rhoades 140) or "multi-tier" (Moser) system or even a "strativersity" (Thompson, "Contingent" 47), the bottom tier of which has been described by the then chancellor of the University System of Maryland as a "subfaculty" (Langenberg). Consequently, this essay applies in many respects to organizing and bargaining for the entirety of this diverse and disadvantaged stratum of full-time as well as part-time contingent appointees.

Contingent Appointments

Most part-time appointments do not differ from full-time appointments merely in being less than full-time. Only 5% of part-time appointments are tenured or tenure-eligible (Zimbler 34, table 18). These appointments generally include both the responsibilities and the rights (including tenure eligibility) of full-time faculty appointments but receive pro rata compensation based on a contractually agreed fraction of a full-time assignment. Some additional fractional-time appointments that lack tenure eligibility do include pro rata compensation.

Most part-time appointments, however, are short term, usually lasting for a single academic semester or quarter. These appointments are also typically temporary or contingent because they lack not only tenure eligibility but also any right to consideration for renewal or expectation of reappointment, even though most of the part-time appointees who hold these positions repeatedly teach the same courses in the same programs and institutions for many years. Although their remuneration is usually on a per-course or course-hour basis, part-time appointees do often teach substantial course loads; in four-year institutions, part-time faculty members often teach as many or more courses than full-time faculty members. So the activities and even the time or length of service do not so much distinguish these faculty members as their disadvantageous appointments that "are paid poorly, have little or no job security, few or no retirement health benefits, only the weakest of free speech protections, and no long term relationship or commitment to a university community or permanent faculty" (Johnson 61).

The principle institutional advantages that drive the increasing reliance on such part-time appointments include specialization, administrative flexibility or control, and cost cutting. Each of these institutional objectives helps shape the terms and conditions of part-time and full-time non-tenure-track appointments and the consequent bifurcation of the faculty.

Specialization

Specialization is the most compelling rationale for part-time appointments, although not the primary explanation for their disadvantageous terms or increasing numbers. Proponents of the view that the increased reliance on part-time appointments is essential and irreversible emphasize several ways in which part-time appointees contribute specialized expertise, experience, and knowledge. Particularly in community colleges, part-time faculty members may be professionals, such as lawyers and accountants, or even liberal arts faculty members with doctoral degrees whom the college does not need or could not afford on a full-time basis. These and other professionals may also contribute "real-world" experience and contacts. Even four-year institutions rely on part-time faculty members for practical courses in the professions and the arts (Gappa and Leslie, *Invisible* 3, 118–25). Specialization of this kind does indeed explain the need for some less than full-time appointees. It does not, however, explain why part-time faculty members, whose qualifications are often as good as or better than those of their full-time colleagues, should not hold long-term or tenured fractional-time appointments with pro rata compensation.

Part-time and full-time non-tenure-track faculty members appointed to teaching only undergraduate positions are sometimes also considered useful specialists whose dedication to teaching and teaching experience may make them as effective or even more effective than full-time faculty members, who may be preoccupied with research or institutional service responsibilities (Gappa and Leslie, *Invisible* 3, 118–20). Conversely, their lack of professional support, collegial interaction, and time for involvement in student learning may diminish their effectiveness, regardless of their commitment (Benjamin, "Reappraisal"). So, why not provide these faculty members full-time appointments or fractional-time appointments? In four-year institutions, the answer lies in part in the common argument that the faculty members appointed to teaching-only positions, even full-time positions, are not qualified for full faculty status. But why not appoint faculty members who are? Specialization may, therefore, contribute to the need for less than full-time positions, but it does not in itself account for why these positions have disproportionately disadvantageous terms and conditions of appointment.

Specialization does, however, have significant implications for organizing. Of course the diversity of academic disciplines and the faculty members attracted to them always challenge those who seek to build a unified faculty organization. But the diversity of contingent faculty members creates two further obstacles to effective organizing. Specialists who have full-time positions outside the institution are less likely to have the time, the need, or the inclination to join with other part-time faculty members to secure or participate in collective bargaining. Teaching-only specialists with full- or part-time appointments in four-year institutions, on the other hand, may have interests and pursue policies that diverge from the professional interests of the full-time, tenure-track faculty. Such conflicts of interest, with regard to matters such as tenure and research, may impair cooperation in governance representation or bargaining (Benjamin, "Reappraisal" 99–101).

Flexibility and Control

The managerial effort to enhance flexibility and control of institutional staffing probably contributes most to the noneconomic terms, if not the numbers, of contingent appointments (Rhoades 131–71). Administrators certainly require some flexibility to adapt staffing to off-campus instruction, unexpected variations in enrollment and budget, changes in student preferences, and experiments with new courses or curricula. These needs are often exacerbated, however, by poor planning, the failure of states to provide reliable funding, and excessive adaptation to student fads. The perceived need for flexibility drives managerial resistance to providing contingent appointees with timely notice of nonreappointment or even, in some instances, timely notice of appointment and specific teaching responsibilities. It also accounts for the short-term nature of most contingent appointments (Gappa and Leslie, *Invisible*, 152).

The lack of job security afforded contingent appointees not only reduces the need for planning but also enables administrators to forego complex peer-based appointment, reappointment, and dismissal procedures. Yet these procedures are widely regarded as requisite to making sound full-time, long-term academic appointments. Fundamentally, lack of job security enhances the opportunity for direct managerial control of faculty work. Contingent faculty members are subject to administrative direction in a way that tenure-track faculty members are not. This is not to say that part-time faculty members are carefully supervised. On the contrary, they are more often unsupervised and superficially evaluated. But the lack of procedural protections extended to contingent appointees does subject them, when managers deem appropriate, to demands for conformity to programmatic directions; curricular objectives; and, sometimes, questionable grading policies. These demands, as well as even broader demands for uncritical compliance or institutional "loyalty," are imposed without being mediated or checked by the collegial committees that ordinarily have an essential role in the enforcement of academic norms. This substitution of managerial for collegial direction is sometimes, especially in community colleges, explicitly intended. Even if not intentional, however, it is an inevitable concomitant of the substitution of managerial for collegial evaluation and decision making in appointments, reappointments, and dismissal. Direct managerial control divides and weakens the faculty as a whole, contributes to the unwillingness of tenure-track faculty members to share faculty authority with non-tenure-track faculty members perceived as subject to administrative manipulation, and invites an adversarial response.

The legitimate needs for administrative flexibility cannot, in any case, explain why at least two-thirds of community college faculty members and more than half of four-year faculty members hold contingent appointments. Even the combined requirements of adapting to possible variances in budget, enrollment, innovation, and off-campus instruction simply do not require that most faculty members lack careful selection, timely notice of appointment and reappointment, academic freedom, and the reasonable degree of economic security afforded by the tenure system. The bottom-line explanation for the growing and excessive dependence on contingent faculty members is not flexibility but cost saving.

Cost Saving

Many community colleges rely on part-time faculty members for low-cost instruction. The recurrent growth in the proportion of such faculty members teaching at community colleges is rooted in the fiscal crisis of the early 1970s (Benjamin, "Faculty Response"). The proportion of part-time faculty members surged from 22% to 34% between 1970 and 1980. It grew more slowly to 39% in 1989, then surged with the recession of the early 1990s to reach 44% by the middle of the decade. With the economic recovery of the later 1990s, part-time faculty appointments leveled off, although the more expensive but flexible non-tenure-track faculty appointments surged to more than half of all new appointments each year (Schuster 18).

Part-time faculty members paid on a per-credit-hour basis reduce direct instructional costs because of their lower wages and generally non-existent fringe benefits. "Pay rates are the key to employment of part-timers" (Cohen and Brawer 86). Although no regular survey of part-time faculty salaries exists, two surveys from the late 1990s found that about half of part-time faculty members earned less than $2,500 a course and most part-time faculty members earned less than $3,000 a course (Natl. Educ. Assn., "Part-Time"). Community college part-time faculty members typically earn less. Arthur M. Cohen and Florence B. Brawer present illustrative data from California, where part-time faculty members would earn $20,000 ($2,000 a course) for teaching the ten courses for which a full-time faculty member received an annual salary of $55,590 (and an additional $10,000 in fringe benefits), and Illinois, where part-time faculty members received $1,224 a course—about one-fourth of the full-time rate (86).

"Cost-saving is a reasonable objective but it is not the same as cost-effectiveness" (Benjamin, "How Over-Reliance" 6). Judith M. Gappa and David W. Leslie, while acknowledging that the increased reliance on part-time faculty members is an adaptation to both actual and potential fiscal constraints, warn against "false economies" and emphasize that "as much as it may appear that employing part-timers who are paid low wages will save money . . . adding part-timers creates substantial hidden costs to the institution. These hidden costs are behind the concerns about whether quality can be sustained when part-time faculty are employed in substantial numbers" (*Invisible* 102). They then note that turnover and increased numbers of employees cause greater administrative burden for the full-time faculty members and department chairs and result in greater personnel-management support costs.

Of course, there are hidden savings in addition to those achieved through less than pro rata salaries and fringe benefits. In "Statement from the Conference on the Growing Use of Part-time and Adjunct Faculty," participants from ten associations including the MLA, American Historical Association, and AAUP observed:

> Part-time faculty members are less likely to have offices or telephones, or to receive remuneration for office hours. They have less access to photo-copying, computer equipment, and secretarial support. Part-time (and adjunct, non-tenure-track) faculty members are less likely to receive regular evaluation and feedback from professional colleagues or to have opportunities to interact with colleagues, serve on committees, participate in faculty governance, attend professional conferences or engage in research." (3)

Whether one considers such employment to save money or bear hidden costs, these conditions of employment have a deleterious effect on the performance of all faculty members, resulting not from poor teaching skills or lack of effort but from the lack of adequate administrative, professional, and collegial support.

The focus on hidden costs, however, overlooks the obvious but controversial economic consequence of this form of cost saving: that in a market society you get, at best, what you pay for. The contrary insistence, out of purported respect, that part-time faculty members bring and contribute as much to undergraduate instruction as do faculty members who are better remunerated and supported defies elementary economic logic. In a competitive labor market, lower compensation attracts and retains either less competitive or less committed staff. Nonetheless, contingent faculty members probably do, at least in the short run, contribute more than their institutions deserve. For, if "cheap labor" always has hidden costs, there is also one circumstance in which employers may, for a time, secure a net benefit. That circumstance is a dual or stratified labor market that systematically undercompensates lower-tier employees.

The Bifurcated Faculty

The academic labor market is not as sharply stratified as those dual labor markets based entirely on race, legal status, or gender. Many of the faculty members holding contingent appointments, including graduate students, retirees, full-time professionals, and homemakers prefer part-time appointments. Moreover, Gappa and Leslie point out that many faculty members with contingent appointments are able and well-prepared professionals—evidence, they contend, that bifurcated terms and conditions of employment do not reflect a dual labor market and are unsustainable (*Two Faculties* 21–22). Even so, the market for contingent faculty appointments offers inferior terms and conditions of employment because it selects on a basis that differs from the tenure-track faculty market in three crucial respects.

First, although many contingent appointees are well qualified, they are on average less likely to have the terminal degrees and publications required to compete in the four-year, tenure-track labor market. Further, contingent appointees are generally recruited in a local, rather than the national or international, labor market; they thus do not undergo the highly competitive, peer-based selection procedures applied to tenure-track appointments (Gappa and Leslie, *Invisible*; Benjamin, "Reappraisal"). Even two-year colleges often cast a wider net and demand greater qualifications or experience in the search to fill full-time, tenure-eligible positions. In narrowly economic terms, then, the inferior compensation provided contingent faculty appointees corresponds in part to the lesser investment of these appointees in the human capital and achievements that bring higher rewards on the labor market. Nonetheless, as Gappa and Leslie correctly observe, it is "the widespread use of casual, inconsistent, and potentially exp[l]oitive employment practices—and not the qualifications or motivations of part-timers themselves—that most seriouslythreatens academic quality" (*Two Faculties* 16). Moreover, the selection of less-qualified faculty members costs the institutions and the profession opportunities not only to appoint better-qualified faculty members but also to encourage faculty members to pursue the achievements required to compete for first-tier positions.

Second, time commitment most powerfully differentiates part-time from full-time faculty members. This is particularly true in community colleges where part-time faculty qualifications are often similar to and sometimes greater than those of full-time faculty members. Part-time faculty members, who often lack offices and often are not paid for office hours, can scarcely be faulted for not keeping office hours. But the lack of time commitment also reflects competing obligations. Only one-third of part-time faculty members report that their part-time position is their primary employment and even fewer (22%) report that it is their only employment (Natl. Educ. Assn., "Part-Time Faculty"). Moreover, part-time faculty members reported that the income they received from the institution at which they held their part-time position accounted for only about one-fourth (or $12,426 of $46,124) of their total earned income (Zimbler 47, table 31). Data from an earlier survey show that nearly half of all part-time faculty members surveyed had other full-time employment (Benjamin, "Variations" 55). Many part-time faculty members also received from other employers the health benefits and retirement contributions not provided by their part-time positions. To some extent, then, the additional employers of part-time faculty members subsidize this sector of the academic labor market. The academic cost of this subsidy is, however, reflected in the fact that part-time faculty members devote less time to instruction and other involvement with students each class hour than do full-time faculty members (Benjamin, "Reappraisal" 86–88).

The third, more complex, set of factors that differentiates the market for contingent faculty members is that presupposed by the arguments of faculty associations and observers that contingent faculty members are abused and exploited (Johnson; Gottfried and Zabel; Moser; Bradley; Thompson, "Recognizing"; Tritelli). These factors are the market "imperfections" or impediments that enable management to offer and cause faculty members to accept terms and conditions of employment inferior to those that would be required in a truly free market.

That the contingent faculty members consist disproportionately of women suggests that the availability of contingent appointees reflects in some measure the sort of discrimination that classically underlies a dual labor market (Lomperis; Thompson, "Alchemy"). Between 1976 and 1995, even as the female proportion of all faculties increased from 27% to 40%, female part-time faculty members increased from 33% to 47% and female non-tenure-track appointees 34% to 45%. Thus, in 1995, when 57% of all faculty members held part-time or non-tenure-track appointments, two-thirds (66.4%) of female but only half (51%) of male faculty members held these appointments (Benjamin, "Disparities"). The reasons for these continuing disparities range from overt discrimination to differences in achievements but include disadvantages such as the disproportionate family responsibilities that often limit women to local labor markets, the generally lower levels of women's salaries, and the more limited alternative employment opportunities available to women. Further, and contrary to expectation, women holding part-time appointments are more, rather than less, likely than men to state that they would prefer full-time appointments (Benjamin, "Variations" 56).

The apparent long-term surplus of doctoral graduates in the humanities and the periodic surplus of doctoral production in the social and natural sciences also shapes the market for contingent appointments. Part-time faculty members in the liberal arts are generally less likely than those in vocational areas to have other full-time positions and more likely to say they hold part-time positions because full-time positions were not available (Benjamin, "Variations" 55–56). In overly simple market terms, these surplus doctoral graduates enable colleges and universities to recruit such faculty members to contingent appointments.

Conversely and fundamentally, however, universities and colleges create the surplus. First, the universities that rely on graduate assistants to teach lower-division students need large PhD programs that encourage possibly excessive doctoral-degree production. Second, the decisions of colleges and universities to employ non-PhDs, including graduate assistants, for lower-division instruction contribute to the shortage of tenure-track positions. In the 1950s and 1960s, the expansion of public higher education included conversion of teaching-only faculty members and institutions to teacher-scholar appointments on the one hand and to research-oriented institutions on the other. In contrast, since the fiscal crisis of the early 1970s, the expansion of community colleges and the increased reliance on contingent faculty members in four-year institutions have been used to shift the balance back toward less-expensive teaching-only positions and to relegate such appointments to second-tier terms and conditions of employment. Moreover, the availability of those part-time faculty members who have alternative full-time employment increases the competition and lowers the compensation required to fill these positions.

Whatever its causes, the bifurcated system of faculty employment disadvantages women and employs many non-PhDs to teach at substandard rates in contingent appointments. Furthermore, it forces many PhDs to choose either those contingent appointments for which they are not deemed overqualified or nonacademic employment. Although it may be that only a substantial minority of part-time and non-tenure-track faculty members are so constrained, the plight of these faculty members and their energy and skill contribute both leadership and moral purpose to the growing movement to unionize contingent faculty members. From this perspective, contingent-faculty unionization is not only concerned with the practical effort to improve the terms and conditions of contingent faculty members but also fuels a broader campaign to unite faculty members and students to resist the corporatization of the universities and to achieve a broad social-justice agenda (Gottfried and Zabel; Schell; Moser).

Contingent Faculty Organizing

Bifurcation not only fuels the faculty's effort to unite but also confronts all faculty members with the daunting prospect of a two-front war with both an increasingly powerful administration and one another. Plainly, the terms and conditions of employment for the contingent faculty members makes their challenge the greatest. Contingent-faculty organizing strategies, and often even tactics, depend on whether or to what extent contingent faculty members fight or unite with their comparatively advantaged faculty competitors or colleagues.

The Strategic Challenge: Faculty Unity

Administrators as well as faculty organizations call for the faculty to unite, but their calls are more likely to divide. Donald N. Langenberg suggests, for example, that the distinguishing characteristics of the "sub-faculty" would "simply be a fact of life, not a problem, were it not for the propensity of our status conscious regular faculty, and hence our institutions, to think of them and to treat them as if they were lesser species" (43). Mutual respect would certainly benefit both organizing and institutions, but it cannot be achieved without effective recognition of the need to improve the terms and conditions of employment afforded contingent appointees.

Gappa and Leslie do recognize the need to increase the support afforded to contingent faculty members as well as "to integrate part-time faculty into the academic community as full partners enjoying the respect and regard of their colleagues" (12). But they blame the current bifurcation on the tenured faculty members, who they term the "major advocates" (3) and "beneficiaries" (2) of the bifurcated system: "the low costs and heavy undergraduate teaching loads of the have-nots help make possible the continuation of a tenure system that protects the jobs and perquisites of the haves. Because tenured faculty benefit directly and personally from this bifurcation of the academic profession, they have a vested interest in maintaining it" (*Invisible* 2).

This argument understandably infuriates many faculty members who point to the obvious fact that boards and administrators, not faculty members tenured or otherwise, establish salary-rates, define the terms of employment, and allocate positions. Nonetheless, even an advocate of faculty professional authority, after summarizing national AAUP, AFT, and NEA statements strongly supporting part-time faculty members, notes that his findings regarding the treatment of part-time faculty appointees in (mostly two-year) collective agreements negotiated by full-time faculty members "might be read as confirming [the] view that "full-time faculty seek to protect their professional position(s)." He then observes that management "shares much of the responsibility for part-time faculty's conditions of employment" (Rhoades 138–40, 168). Any serious strategy to unite part-time and full-time faculty members must recognize and respond constructively to the genuine conflicts of interest arising from the bifurcation of appointment practices.

A faculty perspective on unity must be premised on commitment to mutual improvement of professional standards and not, as Gappa and Leslie repeatedly imply, on further erosion of the tenure system (*Invisible* 2; *Two Faculties* 22). The AAUP, AFT, and NEA each recommend policies that seek both to reverse the excessive reliance on contingent positions by restoring full-time lines and to improve substantially the terms and conditions of the remaining contingent appointments (Amer. Assn., *Contingent*; Amer. Federation, "Standards"; Natl. Educ. Assn., "Policy"). The disciplinary associations participating in the Coalition on the Academic Workforce have endorsed a similar statement ("Statement").

These statements are premised on the strategic understanding that the deficient terms and conditions of contingent appointments do not support but actually diminish the professional well-being of the full-time, tenure-track faculty. Many faculty members, full- and part-time, lack this strategic perspective because, at the local level and at particular times, budget limitations force trade-offs between faculty groups. However, at the systemwide level and over time, the disproportionate increase in contingent positions has increased the competition for the dwindling number of tenure-track positions and contributed to the alleged PhD glut. This increased competition has enabled employers to offer less compensation for the more desirable positions and helps explain why inflation-adjusted full-time faculty mean salaries have not increased since 1972 and median full-time salaries have actually declined.

The difference between the profession-wide and local situation points to an important difference between tactics and strategy. Tactically, full-time faculty members may need to concede that budget limitations at a particular time require them to accept somewhat lower increases to fund catch-up increases for part-time faculty members. Tactical considerations may provide a rationale for full-time faculty members to persuade contingent faculty colleagues to accept less than a fully proportional role in faculty governance to the extent that their contingent appointments limit their time and make them unduly subject to administrative manipulation. But the fundamental faculty strategy should be that any compromises should contribute to the recurrent joint effort to improve the professional terms and conditions of all faculty members.

Organizational Strategy and Tactics

Effective representation of contingent faculty members requires the involvement and leadership of contingent faculty members. The organizational form of that participation may vary with circumstances. Contingent faculty members participate in national and state faculty-bargaining organizations and in disciplinary societies as members; in caucuses and committees; and, less frequently, in leadership roles. Contingent faculty members have also formed an independent national organization, the Coalition of Contingent Academic Labor (COCAL), which includes several urban coalitions (Gottfried and Zabel 213; Schell). Part-time faculty members have formed effective independent state-level associations such as the California Part-Time Faculty Association and the Washington Part-Time Faculty Association (Schell). At the campus level, contingent appointees are sometimes included in comprehensive faculty units, where they may have designated representation and caucuses, establish independent units, and sometimes may themselves be divided between full- and part-time units or units that include long-term but not short-term part-time faculty members.

Where legal constraints or preexisting organization do not foreclose choice, contingent faculty activists understandably disagree regarding the best choice or combination of choices among these alternative approaches. Scott Smallwood provides a useful sampling of views in his article "United We Stand? Part-Time Professors Are Forming Unions but Many Are Wondering If Teaming up With Full-Timers Would Be Better."

Gary Rhoades has shown that many combined units have not adequately represented part-time faculty members in the past. A recent AFT publication, on the other hand, offers impressive accounts of significant recent legislative and bargaining successes (Amer. Federation, "Marching toward Equity"). These accounts also, however, implicitly confirm previous shortcomings and, too often, stress what has been accomplished for contingent faculty members rather than acknowledge the substantial role of part-time faculty associations or caucuses, particularly in Washington and California (see Schell; Jacoby).

The important debates are those not between but within bargaining agents. Contingent faculty members recently achieved major gains in the California State University System, where the California Faculty Association is affiliated with NEA, Service Employees International Union, and AAUP, and in the City University of New York, where part-time faculty members formed an independent caucus (CUNY Adjuncts Unite) to work within and alongside the Professional Staff Congress (a joint AFT and AAUP affiliate). In both cases, new union leadership emerged with the support of contingent faculty activists and placed renewed emphasis on contingent faculty issues (Hoffman and Hess; Smallwood).

In some instances, particularly at private universities lacking full-time unions (including Roosevelt University, which is described later in this volume), part-time faculty members have successfully organized and bargained independently. In others, they bargain in separate units but alongside and sometimes allied to full-time units. Karen Thompson, a longtime leader of the AAUP part-time unit at Rutgers that parallels a combined full-time faculty and graduate employee unit, reasons that part-time faculty members need resources and allies, including the full-time faculty ("Alchemy"). Keith Hoeller, a longtime leader of part-time faculty members in the state of Washington who, like Thompson, has served as a member of AAUP's Committee on Contingent Faculty and the Profession, contends that equal partnership requires proportional representation in leadership positions and split bargaining units that enable part-time faculty members to bargain their own agreements (B17). Chris Storer, a leader of the California part-time faculty who also has served as a member of the AAUP committee, claims that "being together at the bargaining table can unify faculty members against administration efforts" (qtd. in Smallwood). These differences among AAUP colleagues are significant, but they are also tactical, not strategic. Time, circumstances, and personality will affect when and how contingent and tenure-line faculty members fight or unite, but they must in the end ally, or they will fail.

Organizing Tactics

Contingent faculty members, regardless of whether they compete, ally, or join with full-time, tenure-track cohorts, must offer substantial leadership and support for organizing to be successful. Tactical decisions on forming alliances and on how to initiate and pursue an organizing campaign need to proceed with the objective of deepening and broadening this leadership and support. Excessive reliance on an outside agent or allies, however well intentioned, diminishes the active participation and influence of contingent faculty members on organizational and bargaining outcomes, which, in turn, further diminishes support.

The tactics of part-time faculty organizing are, in some respects, the reverse of those in organizing tenure-track faculty members. The dispersion of part-time faculty members may make it more difficult to collect authorization cards than to win an election. Mail ballots are thus essential to ensuring a large turnout of part-time faculty voters. This stands in contrast to the on-site turnout for full-time faculty members, which often exceeds 90%. Although the dispersion of contingent faculty members is compounded by their lack of involvement in collegial and institutional governance, this disenfranchisement is in itself a potentially significant campaign issue. Moreover, in contrast to the tenure-track faculty, contingent faculty members do not fear the loss of existing governance opportunities.

Contingent faculty organizing generally begins by focusing on policy issues in select departments in the humanities and social sciences. Contingent faculty members in these departments are likely to be more motivated because they have lower incomes, less outside employment, and less access to healthcare or other benefits. Organizing, however, often begins with departmental-level issues, such as persuading a chair to provide better notice of appointments, more assurance of reappointment, and improved access to departmental facilities and colleagues. Success in these projects can build support and morale; obstacles or defeats may lead to the recognition that broader efforts are required. Organizers, however, need to recognize that, absent an unusual institutional crisis, it is necessary to build slowly and carefully toward larger objectives and toward using more militant action because those faculty members not yet involved are likely to be more conservative than even weak supporters.

Of those part-time faculty members included in the National Study of Postsecondary Faculty, 85% state that they are satisfied with their jobs overall, despite their inequitable terms and conditions of employment. On the other hand, about half are dissatisfied with specific attributes, such as opportunities for advancement and benefits and salaries; more than one-third are dissatisfied by their (lack of) job security. Dissatisfaction is predictably greatest in the humanities, closely followed by the social sciences, especially in two-year institutions (Conley, 50–53, table 48). Specific campuses may, of course, have different attitudinal distributions, and organizers may find formal or informal surveys and interviews useful. Nonetheless, these national data indicate both why organizing often begins in humanities or social science departments and why careful planning may be required to reach beyond them.

The ephemeral nature of many contingent faculty appointments, that course listings often identify such faculty members as "staff" rather than by name, and that many teach at night and off campus increase the difficulty of communicating with them. Names may be obtained from sympathetic faculty members or administrators. Contingent faculty colleagues may be approached at campus events, orientations, or after classes. But organizers whose own positions are insecure may reasonably be reluctant to request names from administrators or post their own names and numbers as contacts on bulletin boards, in publications, on Web sites, and in e-mails. Although those engaged in organizing activities may claim legal protection, dismissal of organizers is common in the American workplace, and contingent faculty members are especially vulnerable. Thus, an organizer with an off-campus affiliation may be useful for providing a public face in the initial organizing phase, technical support and resources, and legal backup if administrative retaliation occurs. But outside organization and organizers cannot substitute for contingent-faculty self-organization.

Many contingent faculty members are already in combined full-time and part-time bargaining units whose predominantly full-time leadership seems inadequately responsive to contingent faculty concerns. Before challenging the leadership head-on, contingent faculty activists may find it useful to participate more in their association and to attempt to win support and build alliances. Where this approach does not prove effective, it may be useful to contact contingent faculty activists elsewhere for ideas and support, to develop an internal caucus around one or more specific contingent faculty issues, or even to seek support from a possible alternative bargaining agent. Such activities, which may divide and weaken the union, should not be undertaken lightly; but, as some of the previous examples indicate, full-time-led units cannot be relied on to speak adequately for contingent faculty members who do not actively speak for themselves.

That said, contingent faculty activists need resources, technical assistance, and allies. Involvement with a national coalition like COCAL and a state or national faculty bargaining agent can provide the assistance and help necessary to achieve long-term faculty unity as well.

Collective Bargaining

Part-time faculty members have gained significant improvements on campus through academic governance procedures and, at the state level, legislation. But formal collective bargaining is the most common and effective way in which contingent appointees have successfully improved their collective terms and conditions of work. As with organizing, much that can be said of bargaining for contingent faculty is encompassed in the other essays in this volume. This essay focuses only on a few distinctive issues founded on two premises. Part-time faculty members should receive pro rata compensation and both full- and part-time contingent faculty members are entitled to terms of employment consistent with academic freedom and the effective performance of their professional responsibilities.

Economic Bargaining

Faculty representatives generally agree that part-time faculty members should receive pro rata salary and benefits (Amer. Assn., *Contingent*; Amer. Federation, "Standards"; Natl. Educ. Assn., "Policy"; "Statement"). This goal is not easily achieved. Gappa and Leslie found only one institution with such a policy (*Invisible* 158) and themselves advocate only "equitable compensation" for the work performed (*Two Faculties* 23). Moreover, in view of the complexity of faculty responsibilities, neither the formula nor the base for pro rata compensation is easily defined or negotiated. Nonetheless, institutions commonly have formulas that express nonteaching responsibilities, such as advising and curricula development in class-hour equivalences, and may apply similar reasoning to develop salary equivalencies. Although administrators may argue that the base for the pro rata computation should not be the average full-time salary, the base can be reasonably established as average salaries of those faculty members with similar qualifications who are engaged in similar levels and types of instruction.

Salary level is a further problem. Because part-time faculty salaries based on course hours are seldom adjusted for inflation and frequently contain no seniority or rank-equivalency increments, they tend to lag far behind full-time salaries. So even if pro rata salaries are not initially achieved, combined units need to seek—and bargainers need to achieve—catch-up increments for the part-time faculty as a whole. Individual increases linked to experience and qualifications would also improve overall salary levels. In practice, significant increases are often tied to increased responsibilities such as office hours or attendance at orientations and workshops. Unless these activities were previously performed with compensation or pay rates were already pro rata, adjustments based on new work obligations are only real improvements to the extent that the increased pay rate exceeds the increased fraction of work time.

The absence of benefits, especially health benefits, is the most serious deficiency in part-time faculty compensation, and it is a source of dissatisfaction for 54% of these faculty members (Conley, table 53). Some states and some institutions do permit part-time faculty members to participate in group health and pension programs and contribute on a pro rata basis. Although these benefits are fundamental and should be vigorously pursued where absent, part-time faculty representatives should also bear in mind that many part-time faculty members receive these benefits from other full-time jobs or from the benefit plans of spouses or (more rarely) partners. Support for these benefits may thus be narrower than for equivalent salary dollars, but this also reduces the prospective cost to the employer.

Professional Issues

Although contingency is a defining characteristic of part-time appointments, nearly two-thirds of these appointees report that they are satisfied with their job security—substantially more than the half who are satisfied with their opportunities for promotion (Conley, tables 50, 51). The relative lack of concern for job security among part-time faculty members probably reflects that half have other full-time appointments. Full-time, non-tenure-track faculty members express similar levels of satisfaction with their job security, perhaps because many do not wish to compete for tenure and because, in many institutions, non-tenure-track faculty members are routinely reappointed. The substantial minority of contingent faculty appointees who do seek improved job security must seek to persuade their colleagues, as well as their administrations, that this protection is essential to academic freedom and professional performance of their responsibilities.

In bargaining, many contingent faculty members do seek timely notice of nonreappointment or appointment. Contingent faculty members also seek preference for reappointment, extended contracts, and promotion opportunities based on seniority and performance evaluations. AAUP policy recommends that some part-time faculty members be eligible for tenure but also recognizes that a substantial number of part-time faculty appointees will not be tenure-eligible and should pursue and receive incremental improvements in job security such as timely notice and extended terms. Full-time, non-tenure-track faculty members, however, should in most instances have the opportunity to achieve tenure based on effective performance of their assigned responsibilities (Amer. Assn., *Contingent*).

Where tenure itself is beyond reach, contracts should ensure academic freedom by requiring that the administration demonstrate cause in a peer hearing or arbitration before dismissal or nonreappointment of long-term, full-time appointees. Agreements should also provide that the administration demonstrate adequate cause in the event that part-time or full-time faculty members are suspended during the term of their appointments.

Contingent faculty members also bargain for increased professional support and opportunities for collegial integration with the full-time, tenure-track faculty members. Professional support may include time and financial support to attend professional meetings; eligibility to apply for grants to engage in curricular development and research; and access to office space, departmental services, and technical facilities. Collegial interaction may include, for example, participation in departmental meetings, service on departmental and college committees, and governance representation.

Those part-time faculty members who seek full-time appointments may also pursue the opportunity to obtain full-time positions as they become available. In those colleges where differences between part-time and full-time faculty qualifications and responsibilities are slight, the part-time faculty appointees may seek to negotiate some form of preference based on their experience and demonstrated ability. In those colleges and universities where part-time and full-time faculty qualifications are generally more differentiated, part-time faculty appointees may seek at least assurance of the right to fair consideration for new openings.

———

I have tried in this essay to fully consider the complexities that result from the bifurcation of the faculty as well as from the diversity of contingent faculty members themselves. Organizing campaigns and negotiating teams must, of course, present a less nuanced argument. But those who plan and conduct organizing campaigns and negotiations need first to understand how these divisions may undercut their efforts and then to determine how the divisions may be overcome. The fundamental fault line is not within the faculty. It is between those who believe that institutional needs require that the terms and conditions of faculty appointments must and should continue to erode and those who recognize that "[f]ailure to extend to all faculty reasonable professional commitments compromises quality and risks the stability of the profession and integrity of our standing with the public" (AAUP, "Status" 87).

WORKS CITED

American Association of University Professors. *Contingent Appointments and the Academic Profession*. Policy Statement. Nov. 2003. 24 May 2005 <http://www.aaup.org/statements>.

———. "The Status of Non-Tenure-Track Faculty." *Policy Documents and Reports*. 9th ed. Washington: AAUP, 2001.

American Federation of Teachers. "Marching toward Equity: Curbing the Exploitation and Overuse of Part-Time and Non-tenured Faculty." Washington: AFT, 2001.

———. "Standards of Good Practice in the Employment of Part-Time/Adjunct

Faculty: A Blueprint for Raising Standards and Ensuring Financial and Professional Equity." Washington: AFT, 2002.

Benjamin, Ernst. "Disparities in the Salaries and Appointments of Academic Women and Men: An Update of a 1988 Report of Committee W on the Status of Women in the Academic Profession." *Academe* 85.1 (1999): 60–62.

———. "Editor's Notes." Benjamin, *Exploring* 1–13.

———, ed. *Exploring the Role of Contingent Instructional Staff in Undergraduate Learning.* New Directions for Higher Educ. 123. San Francisco: Jossey-Bass, 2003.

———. "A Faculty Response to the Fiscal Crisis: From Defense to Offense." *Higher Education under Fire: Politics, Economics, and the Crisis of the Humanities.* Ed. Michael Bérubé and Cary Nelson. New York: Routledge, 1995. 52–72.

———. "How Over-reliance on Contingent Appointments Diminishes Faculty Involvement in Student Learning." *Peer Review* 5.1 (2002): 4–10.

———. "Reappraisal and Implications for Policy and Research." Benjamin, *Exploring* 79–113.

———. "Variations in the Characteristics of Part-Time Faculty by General Fields of Instruction and Research." Leslie 45–59.

Bradley, Gwendolyn. "Contingent Faculty and the New Academic Labor System." *Academe* 90.1 (1994): 28–31.

Cohen, Arthur M., and Florence B. Brawer. *The American Community College.* 4th ed. San Francisco: Jossey-Bass, 2003.

Conley, Valerie Martin. "Supplemental Table Update." *National Study of Postsecondary Faculty, NSOPF: 99.* US Dept. of Educ. Natl. Center for Educ. Statistics. April 2002. Washington: US Dept. of Educ., <http://nces.ed.gov/pubsearch>.

Gappa, Judith M., and David W. Leslie. *The Invisible Faculty: Improving the Status of Part-Timers in Higher Education.* San Francisco: Jossey-Bass, 1993.

———. *Two Faculties or One? The Conundrum of Part-Timers in a Bifurcated Work Force.* New Pathways Working Paper 6. Washington: Amer. Assn. for Higher Educ., 1997.

Gottfried, Barbara, and Gary Zabel. "Social Movement Unionism and Adjunct Faculty Organizing in Boston." *Steal This University: The Rise of the Corporate University and the Academic Labor Movement.* Ed. Benjamin Johnson, Patrick Kavanagh, and Kevin Mattson. New York: Routledge, 2003. 61–80.

Hoeller, Keith. "Part-Time Faculty Members and Unions." *Chronicle of Higher Education* 28 Mar. 2003: B17.

Hoffman, Elizabeth, and John Hess. *Contingent and Faculty Organizing in CFA: 1975–2005.* 2 Aug. 2004. 15 Sept. 2005 <http://www.chicagocal.org/downloads/conference=papers/Hoffman=Hess.pdf>.

Jacoby, Daniel. "Is Washington State an Unlikely Leader? Progress on Addressing Contingent Work Issues in Academia." 24 May 2005 <http://depts.washington.edu/uwaaup/parttimejac.htm>.

Johnson, Benjamin. "The Drain-O of Higher Education: Casual Labor and University Teaching." Johnson, Kavanagh, and Mattson 61–80.

Johnson, Benjamin, Patrick Kavanagh, and Kevin Mattson, eds. *Steal This University: The Rise of the Corporate University and the Academic Labor Movement.* New York: Routledge, 2003.

Langenberg, Donald N. "The Subfaculty." Leslie 39–44.

Leslie, David. W. *The Growing Use of Part-Time Faculty: Understanding Causes and Effects.* New Directions for Higher Educ. 104. San Francisco: Jossey-Bass, 1998.

Lomperis, Ana Maria Turner. "Are Women Changing the Nature of the Academic Profession?" *Journal of Higher Education* 61.6 (1990): 643–77.

Moser, Richard. "The New Academic Labor System, Corporatization, and the Renewal of Academic Citizenship." 12 June 2001. 24 May 2005 <http://www.aaup.org/Issues/part-time/cewmose.htm>.

National Education Association Research Center. "Part-Time Faculty." *Update* 7.4 (2001). 15 Sept. 2005 <http://www2.nea.org/he/heupdate/>.

———. "NEA Higher Education Policy on Part-Time and Temporary Faculty." NEA Policy Statements 12. 24 May 2005 <http://www.nea.org/he/policy12.html>.

Rhoades, Gary. *Managed Professionals: Unionized Faculty and Restructuring Academic Labor.* Albany: State U of New York P, 1998.

Schuster, Jack. H. "The Faculty Makeover: What Does It Mean for Students?" Benjamin, *Exploring* 15–22.

Smallwood, Scott. "United We Stand? Part-Time Professors Are Forming Unions but Many Are Wondering If Teaming Up with Full-Timers Would Be Better." *Chronicle of Higher Education* 21 Feb. 2003: A10.

Schell, Eileen E. "Toward a New Labor Movement in Higher Education: Contingent Labor and Organizing for Change." *Workplace* 4.1 (2001). <http://www.louisville.edu/journal/workplace>. Path: Back Issues; June 2001 4.1.

"Statement from the Conference on the Growing Use of Part-Time and Adjunct Faculty." Sept. 1997. 24 May 2005 <http://www.aaup.org/Issues/part-time/PTCONF.HTM>.

Thompson, Karen. "Alchemy in the Academy: Moving Part-Time Faculty from Piecework to Parity." *Will Teach for Food: Academic Labor in Crisis.* Ed. Cary Nelson. Minneapolis: U of Minnesota P, 1997. 278–90.

———. "Contingent Faculty and Student Learning: Welcome to the Strativersity." Benjamin, *Exploring* 41–47.

———. "Recognizing Mutual Interests." *Academe* 78.4 (1992): 22–26.

Townsend, Robert B. "Changing Relationships, Changing Values in the American Classroom." Benjamin, *Exploring* 23–32.

Tritelli, David. "From the Editor." *Peer Review* 5.1 (2002): 3.

Zimbler, Linda J. "Background Characteristics, Work Activities, and Compensation of Faculty and Instructional Staff in Post-secondary Institutions: Fall 1998." *National Study of Postsecondary Faculty, NSOPF: 99.* US Dept. of Educ. Natl. Center for Educ. Statistics, 2001. 152.

Graduate Employee Organizing and Representation

MARCUS HARVEY

What follows is not a comprehensive treatment of graduate employee unionization; rather, this essay makes some observations on the problems that typically confront graduate employee organizations and then analyzes selected contract provisions and collective bargaining issues. The luxury of jumping in medias res is afforded by Patricia J. Gumport and Daniel J. Julius's essay, which appears earlier in this volume, and by recent literature on the "corporate" academy (Soley; Slaughter and Leslie; Smith; Bok; Kirp), the employment of contingent academic laborers (Rhoades; Baldwin and Chronister), and the phenomenon of graduate employee unionization itself (Hewitt; Rhoades and Rhoads; Julius and Gumport, "Graduate"). Several essay collections, including Cary Nelson's prescient *Will Teach for Food: Academic Labor in Crisis*, do a fine job of connecting these strands (Herman and Schmid; Johnson, Kavanagh, and Mattson; Benjamin).

The Two Cultures

When C. P. Snow coined the phrase "the two cultures," he had in mind the historical divide separating practitioners of the natural sciences from those of the literary arts. While that divide is still with us—intensified perhaps by the ever-narrowing foci of academic specialists—a more profound split in the academy exists between the idealized life of the scholar and the mundane world of work. Doubtless, James Axtell had the former in mind when writing of academe's "pleasures." The academy is, however, very much a workplace, and academics frequently find their principles and aspirations in conflict with their careers and material interests.

In negotiating the tensions between these two worlds, academics typically construct multiple self-identities, each centering on a particular aspect of their working lives—discipline, department, institution, academic rank, and so on. To borrow a phrase from sociologists, these identities might best be described as the selves we academics live by (Holstein and Gubrium). The tension between vocation and avocation is not confined to the faculty but is integral to graduate students' experiences as well (Breitzer; Lee et al.)

For American graduate students, the primary locus for peer socialization and institutional engagement has traditionally been the academic department, although one might argue that a great deal of socialization in the sciences occurs at an even finer level, in specific laboratories and research groups (Clark). The academic department is a pseudofamilial entity within which each graduate student adopts a faculty mentor. The relationship is mutualistic. Graduate students aggrandize their mentor by augmenting his or her professional capital while the mentor's reputation adds to the graduate student's own luster and shapes an emerging professional identity. The mentor steers the graduate student through the oft-turbulent waters of the department, a passage that may be made difficult, if not painful, by the mentor's own "sibling rivalries" ("internecine warfare" might be a more apt metaphor for many departments), by generational tensions or other breakdowns in the relationship between mentor and mentored, or by the outright loss of one's mentor. The whole experience is mediated by a multiplicity of other academic kinfolk with whom the adroit graduate student forges close ties to ensure his or her successful completion of the doctorate. At one time—so the legend goes—it was reasonable to expect that the freshly minted PhD would have the option of becoming an academic pater familias in his or her own right, although it is not clear that the traditional system of mentoring ever adequately equipped graduate students for careers in the professoriate (Austin).

The familial model of graduate education resonates in the antiunion claim that graduate employees are apprentices and not workers, but the complete rejection of this claim leads union supporters to liken graduate employees to marginalized and exploited workers in a vast academic factory. The reality is complicated because both views are partially correct. The graduate student, as employee, does furnish low-cost skilled labor to the university, whereas the graduate employee, as student, is bound to his or her close-knit, sometimes dysfunctional, departmental family. Moreover, the actual cost of graduate employees is not as low as one might expect, although their utility to the institution goes beyond the simple fact of their labor.

The cost savings involved in substituting the labor of graduate employees for that of other academics may—on first blush—actually appear to be negative because the graduate employee's total remuneration (stipend, fee waivers, tuition remission, employee benefits) may be considerably higher on a per-course basis than the value of the wages and benefits provided to part-time faculty members, postdocs, or other contingent academics. The added cost to the institution of the graduate employees' labor is, however, effectively lower than it appears because graduate students—whether employed or not—are a critical component in the modern research university and as such are better likened to fixed (as opposed to variable) costs. The real cost of graduate employee labor is best understood as the difference between the amount paid to all those employees and the minimum investment of resources that would have been sufficient to recruit and retain the size and quality of graduate cadre desired by the institution. Adding to the complexity of this economic equation is the fact that one component of institutional demand for graduate employees comes from another segment of the academic workforce. The faculty themselves want a skilled labor force at their disposal to perform certain critical, but less glamorous, professional tasks—repetitive laboratory work, the teaching of introductory and survey courses, data crunching, bibliographic research, and so on. To the extent that the provision of graduate employee labor makes faculty employment more attractive, the money paid to attract graduate employees can also be seen as a nonpecuniary benefit to the faculty, acting, in part, to hold down professorial wages.

It seems likely that graduate students have always been used for their labor—any economic anthropologist or cliometrician can tell you that family economies benefit from the surplus labor provided by their marginal members (the old and the young; the emeriti and the graduate student). While we are disinclined to see intrafamilial labor as exploitive, the use of marginal laborers becomes more evidently problematic when those laborers are directed by agents and authorities outside the family's orbit and control. As the use of graduate employees became routinized and systematized and as entities that were external to the department assumed oversight of the graduate employee labor force, the familial dynamic gave way to more industrial relations. True, most graduate students continued to be employed within their departments, but their labor became increasingly remote from the graduate student-mentor relationship; rather, academic personnel departments and graduate schools emerged as the graduate employee's points of contact with the institution as employer. Since individual graduate students owe little allegiance to a graduate school or personnel department, graduate employees in their dealings with institutions have little incentive to tolerate working conditions that seem unfair or unrewarding.

Indeed, the impersonal and managed nature of such employment relationships are, by their very nature, out of keeping with the professional idealization of academic culture. Moreover, the mediating role of the adviser—so effective at the departmental level—proves itself to be of little value in challenging decisions made by the larger bureaucracy. Under such circumstances, graduate employees must logically look elsewhere for leverage in their dealings with institutions. The available options are limited. Research institutions generally make some provision for graduate student self-governance, but graduate student councils invariably lack the teeth of mature faculty senates and do not command the hefty fee-driven resources available to undergraduate student governments. At the national level, a handful of organizations—the National Association of Graduate and Professional Students, in particular—offer some additional resources and support but cannot effect much change on specific campuses. What remains, then, is unionization and affiliation with national and international organizations.

In Canada, graduate employee unionization is dominated by a single union, the Canadian Union of Public Employees (CUPE), but in the United States a much larger number of international unions and national organizations have a stake in graduate employee organizing. The United Automobile, Aerospace, and Agricultural Implement Workers (UAW), the Service Employees International Union (SEIU), the American Federation of Teachers (AFT), and the American Association of University Professors (AAUP) have all participated recently in successful graduate-union recognition campaigns, and the United Electrical, Radio, and Machine Workers of America, the National Education Association (NEA), and the Communications Workers of America currently represent established graduate employee unions. The Hotel Employees and Restaurant Employees union

(HERE; now merged with another AFL-CIO affiliate, UNITE!) has stead-fastly sought recognition for Yale's graduate employees for more than a decade. Unaffiliated local unions are not unknown in higher education, but they are rarely found in graduate employee organizing: graduate em-ployees at the University of Michigan did engineer an autonomous local drive but subsequently affiliated with the AFT (see Graduate Employee Organization).

Union Recognition

The initial drive to unionize—often spurred by graduate employees in disciplines that rely on contingent labor for undergraduate teaching—may be halting in the early stages as activists cast about for an affiliate and come to an understanding of their situation vis-à-vis state laws (in the case of public institutions) and the National Labor Relations Act, or NLRA (at private universities). Some disciplinary associations provide a forum for graduate students to approach graduate employee unionization as both a subject of inquiry and a field of action. Both the Radical Caucus in English and the Modern Languages and the Graduate Student Caucus, distinct, allied organizations of the Modern Language Association, have pressed the MLA's members to support graduate assistant organizing. Similarly, the American Historical Association responded to graduate em-ployee concerns by forming the Task Force on Graduate Education, spon-soring sessions on graduate employee unionization at its annual meet-ings, and establishing the "Issues in Graduate Education" section in its newsletter, *Perspectives*.

When graduate employees decide to unionize, they cannot know for certain how administrators at their institution will respond. Indeed, re-actions range widely, from the all-out offensive waged by Yale against the Graduate Employees and Students Organization (GESO-HERE) to the tacit acceptance of the Graduate Assistants United (GAU-AAUP) at the University of Rhode Island. Even where public-sector legislation permits graduate employees to bargain, administrations such as those at the Uni-versity of California and University of Illinois often engage in protracted resistance campaigns. In the private sector, opposition has been especially intense. For a brief period between 2000 and 2004, the National Labor Relations Board (NLRB) held that graduate employee unionization was protected under federal law; however, when the political balance on the board tipped to the right, so too did the board's position on graduate employee unionization. In July 2004, the board's majority ruled that graduate employees at Brown University "are primarily students and have a primarily educational, not economic, relationship with their university"; consequently, the majority reasoned, the efforts of graduate students to unionize should not be subject to the procedures and protections of the NLRA (Brown 5). Of course, removing the legal safeguards from the process is not the same as prohibiting it outright, and it remains to be seen how the various unions involved in graduate employee organizing at private institutions will respond to the board's decision in *Brown*.

Institutions that oppose graduate-employee collective bargaining generally pursue similar strategies. Formulaic legal arguments challenging the rights of graduate employees—public and private alike—to unionize based on an either-or understanding of the distinction between students and employees usually constitute the institution's first line of defense. Those arguments go against the weight of opinion—at least in the public sector—which is now decidedly in favor of recognizing that students who work for their institution and receive wages for such work are, in fact, workers. In 2003, for example, the state Public Employee Relations Commission explicitly rejected the University of Washington's argument "that any RA [research assistant] working on their own dissertation should be excluded from the proposed bargaining unit no matter how many hours they work"("State").

The AAUP has filed several amicus briefs stating its position that "graduate student assistants, like other campus employees, should have the right to organize to bargain collectively" (Amer. Assn., "Graduate Students" 269). In those briefs, the AAUP maintained that graduate employee collective bargaining is consistent with sound academic practices and not subversive of academic freedom (Rabban and Euben; Rabban et al.). Administrators, despite the weight of evidence and opinion against their doing so, frequently challenge the legal protections and professional rationales for concerted graduate employee activity. The value of such an administrative strategy rests not necessarily on the prospect of ultimately prevailing, but rather on the savings to the institution—and the damage done to the union's momentum—that results from delay. Part and parcel with this approach are a variety of rhetorical and political stratagems used to erode support for the union: administrations may liken graduate employees to apprentices, claim that the work done by graduate employees is an exercise in pedagogy, encourage (or not discourage) the expression of antiunion sentiments by faculty members, suggest that graduate employees should feel "put upon" when visited by union activists, describe academic work as "professional" or "a calling," afford other graduate student organizations more authority and respect, portray the union as an interloper, and "find" new pots of money to augment graduate employee wages and benefits. Henrik N. Dullea's assessment of the UAW's defeat (581 to 1351, with 88.4% of the unit voting) at Cornell enumerates some of the approaches that were actually avoided by the administration at that institution and provides an interesting gloss on the "typical" antiunion campaign.

Stressing the significance of administrative action, two attorneys with the management-side law firm Proskauer Rose LLP point out that "[n]ew policies on financial aid, health insurance, teacher training, and the administration of teaching and research assistant programs can dramatically influence . . . the unionization movement" (Brill and Levy 44). Certainly, the failed spring referendum at Yale in 2003 proved that administrative strategies can take a heavy toll. To demonstrate widespread graduate employee support for unionization, GESO held a nonbinding vote on unionization (supervised by the League of Women Voters) that failed by a scant 43 votes, 651 to 694 (Lee). Over the years, Yale's administration has used both carrots and sticks to resist graduate employee unionization. Carrots have generally come in the form of substantive stipend increases, whereas the stoutest cudgel has proved to be faculty pressure on graduate employees. Although impossible to quantify, roiling the faculty seems to have been particularly effective in those departments where the close confines of the laboratory create a panoptic environment and restrict contact with union activists. More remarkable than the lost vote is the tenacity of the graduate employee union movement at Yale, which has survived for many years despite a hostile environment and significant increases in graduate employee remuneration. The recognition campaign at Yale demonstrates how the motivation of graduate employees to support unionization can turn from the material to the ideological as institutional practices lay bare the power dynamics and sociocultural imperatives underlying administrative decisions. The inverse has also proved true. The institution that is home to Skull and Bones has self-consciously cast itself as the university for the world's ruling elite, and so for Yale, no less than for GESO, the struggle over unionization has become a fight over principles rather than pragmatics (Wilhelm; Phillips-Fein).

The Faculty

In the struggle for academic hearts and minds, the faculty plays a central role. Even where the environment has not been poisoned, academic culture—with its fetishization and isolation of the individual—ill prepares faculty members to act in solidarity with graduate students. The faculty's disinclination to act politically becomes even more pronounced once it becomes apparent that solidarity may involve actual inconvenience or the sacrifice of time. Finding the professors who will be receptive to the sort of advice offered by the University of Washington faculty member Gail Stygall becomes one of the key tasks in any graduate employee union drive: "If you are a tenured faculty member and your department's TAs go out on strike, support them. Inform yourself about their issues (and yours). Voice your opinions publicly. . . . Send a check to the strike fund. . . . Walk the line with the TAs" (18–19).

Graduate employee activists can experience profound disillusionment when respected professors, noted liberals and Marxists among them, fall in line with the forces marshaling in opposition to unionization (Robin). No less remarkable to them are occasional statements in defense of the right to organize from scholars identified as old fashioned, traditional, or politically conservative. There are no reliable predictors of how individual faculty members will respond to graduate employee unionization, but it is clear that institutions will exert pressure on their faculties and that such pressure will have an effect on faculty decisions.

At New York University, for example, despite that the AAUP wrote an amicus brief in defense of the graduate employees' right to unionize, relatively few faculty members actively supported the campaign. The lone untenured professor from NYU to testify before the NLRB on behalf of the graduate employees, Joel Westheimer from the Steinhardt School of Education, was subsequently denied tenure in what many saw as an egregious case of institutional reprisal (Westheimer 123–37). Although the faculty members could not have known with certainty how NYU would respond to their activism, one wonders whether the failure of other untenured faculty members to speak out in favor of the graduate employees might not be more a reflection of a chilled environment than of ideological homogeneity. Westheimer himself won a favorable settlement from NYU and joined the faculty at the University of Ottawa (Keys).

In an article published in the *Radical History Review*, two graduate employee veterans of the UAW's struggle at NYU identified the "language and ideology of academic exceptionalism" as part of the problem facing would-be academic unionists. The article reflects its authors' disappointment that more NYU faculty members had not seen through and denounced the administration's antiunion campaigns and cynical deployments of "academic freedom" and "shared governance" (Bender and Kinkela 10–12). It is too easy to dismiss the hesitancy of faculty members to embrace graduate-employee collective bargaining as a species of false consciousness. Back in 1922, Upton Sinclair lambasted professors for failing to understand that "[t]he formula, 'In union there is strength,' applies to brain workers precisely as to hand workers" (454). Today Sinclair would be proud. Union density is much higher among the faculty members than it is in America's workforce as a whole. Moreover, academia is the one, if not the only, job site where employees have not surrendered control of the shop floor. The Faustian bargain struck by labor in the postwar years—in which unions traded away worker authority for money—is one of the fundamental reasons why American labor is so weak compared with its counterparts in the other industrialized nations. Postwar managers better understood where labor relations were heading and saw "control, both of corporate policies and shop-floor conditions," as "the new frontiers of labor-management rivalry" (Zieger 226). As much as any other group of workers, academics have fought to maintain control of policies and conditions in their workplace, and they have been generally more successful than their industrial counterparts.

If faculty members are, therefore, suspicious of industrial unions in the academy, their skepticism may not be for all the wrong reasons. Since deciding (in 1972) to support the unionization of its chapters, the AAUP has maintained that shared governance and academic freedom can be reinforced by collective bargaining (Hutcheson; AAUP, "Collective Bargaining," "Academic Government"). Even as they turn to industrial modes of advocacy, graduate employee unionists should not overlook the fact that professionalism and unionism are compatible. Moreover, the degree of faculty support for graduate employee unionization is greater than many realize. Over the course of the UAW campaign, the AAUP chapter at NYU grew as a sizeable minority of faculty members sought a platform from which they could back the unionization effort. At Rutgers, faculty members and graduate employees have long coexisted in the same bargaining unit. That relationship—albeit unusual—has afforded Rutgers's graduate employees strong contractual protections and competitive remuneration. In 2002, the AAUP faculty union at the University of Rhode Island assisted graduate employees at that institution to unionize, which they did with an overwhelming margin of victory (190 to 20 in a bargaining unit of almost 600). The rationale behind the faculty's action (and, perhaps, the administration's quiescence) was the likelihood that unionization would drive up graduate employee wages, pressure the legislature to devote more resources to graduate education, and make the institution more competitive in recruiting new graduate students.

Organizational Hurdles

Graduate employee unions have a high rate of member turnover within their bargaining units. On its face, bargaining-unit churning is a function of the institution's graduate completion rate; however, a number of additional factors make graduate employee units even more volatile—at least in terms of active membership—than the graduation rate alone would indicate. In the career of any given graduate employee, there are periods of time during which he or she is not employed (summers, semesters spent on research trips, periods supported by fellowships) but is still connected to the institution and to union colleagues. Maintaining an accurate roster in such circumstances becomes impracticable and tactically undesirable; consequently, the union typically carries more members than are actually paying dues at any given moment. In addition to those completing their PhDs, unit churning is exacerbated by the actions of at least three other groups of employees. Many new graduate students will quit their programs before degree completion. Some graduate students will leave the institution after completing only their master's degree. Many PhD candidates will exhaust their funding allocation before finishing their degree requirements and will lapse out of the bargaining unit while still enrolled at the institution.

Although graduate unions must race to socialize and recruit new employees as quickly as possible, institutions where new employees make up a majority of the bargaining unit will find it exceedingly difficult to maintain organizational momentum without constant infusions of resources and assistance from their affiliates. The problem for the United Faculty of Florida at Florida Agricultural and Mechanical University has been maintaining a viable chapter at an institution where most graduate students are enrolled in master's programs and are only at the institution for a year or two. Even at institutions focused on the PhD, the churning of senior graduate students (whether they complete their degrees or run up against institutionally imposed time limits on funding eligibility) disproportionately affects the union's leadership cadre, which is likely to rely on the activism of seasoned graduate employees. Consequently, graduate employee unions are well advised to diversify their leadership as much as possible and to build redundancy (copresidencies, multiple vice presidents, large bargaining teams, and stewards' councils) into their governing structures.

At the University of Florida (UF), a change in the institutional processing of tuition waivers eliminated one of the union's key recruiting moments in a stroke. For years, all graduate assistants had been required to process their waivers in person, and this had afforded the union an ideal moment to make contact with practically every member of the bargaining unit at the beginning of the academic year. After the university discontinued this practice, the GAU (GAU-UF)—which subsists in a right-to-work state—saw its numbers dwindle. Just as important, the union's leadership group shrank until it became a subset of the English department's graduate employees. The first step out of this morass was to establish a copresidency structure, in which the presidents would be drawn—de facto if not de jure—from different departments. The next major step was to establish an expansive steward system and cultivate departmental representatives. The third step was to negotiate release-time positions so that union leaders would be assured of sufficient time and resources to do union work while remaining members of the bargaining unit (Thompson 119). In this way, the union was able to rebuild, but it could have saved itself a great deal of trouble had it implemented such reforms before the crisis struck.

Although every graduate employee union confronts the problem of membership turnover, mature units with agency-fee or fair-share provisions (see Adler's essay in this volume) in their agreements have a more manageable situation on their hands than those that do not. First, they have the resources to buy out member activists or to employ staff members and can, therefore, conduct more-intensive recruiting campaigns than would be possible without such resources. Second, agency-fee provisions fundamentally alter the economic calculus of individual employees considering whether or not they will join the union. The organizations most affected by membership turnover are those in right-to-work states (where everything from striking to agency fee may be off limits to public-sector employees) and those with ongoing recognition campaigns. In such circumstances, organizers must compensate for their structural weaknesses with ingenuity and tenacity. Take Yale, where graduate employee organizing has deep roots (GESO's precursor, TA Solidarity, began organizing and wresting concessions from Yale in the 1987–1988 academic year). Of necessity, GESO has proved itself to be highly innovative. Affiliating with HERE, in an act of solidarity that was symbolic as well as practical, GESO experimented with concerted action in its 1995 grade strike, documented the magnitude of Yale's contingent academic employment practices, and forged ties with other local unions and organizing drives. Moreover, GESO has earned a reputation for taking principled positions on a host of academic issues and maintains a high level of internal communication (Wolff; Robin and Stephens; GESO, "Casual," GESO, Home Page).

Along with sponsoring contact between activists and other employees and informing members about broader issues of social justice and academic freedom, graduate employee unions can have considerable social value for local members. A union can significantly lessen the isolation that is part and parcel of the graduate experience by simultaneously fashioning itself as a labor-advocacy organization, a force for social justice, and a broad-based academic social club. The union's social-club function mirrors the historic role of the union hall, where workers met, ate, drank, danced, forged friendships, and cultivated romances. As graduate employee happy hours and socials at institutions like the University of Florida and University of Oregon attest, the work of the union is not hindered by having fun. Such activities give union leaders a chance to identify and cultivate fresh talent.

Bargaining units tend to rely on the institutional memory of a handful of longtime activists—a critical problem in graduate employee units. The only certain thing in this line of work is that such leaders will soon be gone. Graduate-employee unions not only must engage in constant leadership recruitment and training but also must document and archive their organizations' activities, decisions, and processes in a manner that is easily followed by those who will come next. New leaders frequently lack union experience and may not even know what questions to ask of outgoing leaders. One of the greatest gifts that an activist can leave to the local is an information map for his or her successors. Graduate-employee unions ought also to make provisions for on-the-job training in key roles. Much work can, and should, be accomplished by committee, but some tasks must be performed by an individual (such as a chief negotiator, grievance officer, chief steward, treasurer, etc.). At the University of Florida, where reopener negotiations and short contract cycles lead to annual bargaining, the following year's chief negotiator generally acts as an understudy to the union's current chief negotiator so that the bargaining team is assured of leadership continuity. For wealthier unions, such continuity may be provided by staff members, but the reliance on staff members is double-edged, and unit members must strike an acceptable balance between continuity on the one hand and member control on the other.

Collective Bargaining

As several graduate-employee unions have discovered, first-contract fights are critical because they establish the framework for subsequent contract development. Graduate-employee unions should resist the temptation to accept large pay increases rather than strengthened rights, benefits, and authority in their first agreement. Among the items of anti-union propaganda that happen to be true is that campus-based unionization is no guarantor of higher wages. Of course, some administrators can put a misleading spin on this fact by alleging that unions are not effective instruments for change. A more accurate interpretation is that campus remuneration tends to follow broader market trends; as collective bargaining has driven up the market price for some graduate students, graduate-employee unions have actually accelerated the entire industry's pay scale. In fact, nonunion shops are not contractually bound to provide other benefits, and so they are actually well positioned to outpace unionized campuses in terms of base stipends (the flashy market "sticker price" on new graduate student recruits) but typically fall short of union shops in providing other, less flashy, rights, protections, and benefits. In a sense, the compensation issue will look after itself, as competition forces institutions to leapfrog over their competitors' going rate for graduate students (unions still ought to ensure that institutions do not compress the pay of graduate employees in undervalued departments or of senior graduate employees whose mobility decreases as their in-program time increases). The real fight for the union needs to be over more deeply embedded rights and privileges. What follows is a brief commentary on selected subjects of bargaining. Bread-and-butter issues (pay, benefits, workload, contract maintenance, hiring, evaluation, leaves, and separation) have been left for another day.

Bargaining Unit Composition and Recognition Articles

Although it may seem straightforward, the recognition article in graduate employee contracts merits careful consideration: graduate employee units are complex and susceptible to erosion. Although some contracts simply reiterate the unit definition from the original certification election, it is useful to detail more closely—and in terms of function—who exactly is in, and who out, of the unit. At the University of Toronto, CUPE 3902's recognition article details both exclusions and clarifications to the unit's composition (art. 2). The recognition article covering graduate employees at the University of Massachusetts, Amherst (UMass), includes those "Fellows and Trainees whose duties and responsibilities are substantially similar" to the work of explicitly recognized unit employees and covers "any work performed for compensation" (GEO-UMass, art. 1).

Such attention to detail can be a valuable safeguard against abuse. More than a decade ago, it proved necessary to negotiate a memorandum of understanding in the contracts at the University of Florida and the University of South Florida (USF) to address the depredations of cash-starved department administrators who were requiring some graduate employees "to perform teaching duties without remuneration" (GAU-USF, memorandum). The problem lingered, and years later a department at the University of Florida was exposed for compelling its graduate students to enroll in a special course—ostensibly in pedagogy—that made them serve as graduate assistants for a semester without pay. The problem came to the attention of the union when a few graduate students from that department protested that making photocopies and performing other menial tasks did not seem like particularly meaningful pedagogical exercises.

Where such problems arise, they must be dealt with aggressively by the union. The parameters of any bargaining unit, it should be noted, are negotiable. Bargaining units can be expanded by mutual agreement of the parties: the recognition article can be altered directly, its terms might be redefined elsewhere in the contract, or the bargaining unit's composition might be clarified in a sidebar agreement. This last approach was adopted at Wayne State University, where the Graduate Employees Organizing Committee's 1999 contract includes several supplemental letters of agreement (SLA), the first of which details the inclusion in the unit of certain graduate employees "presently assigned to research and research-related activities on projects unrelated to their own courses of study" (GEOC).

The protection of employment lines is another sound strategy that unions might follow. In much the same way that tenure lines have been eroded and replaced by lower-cost contingent laborers (graduate employees included), the very success of unions in driving up total graduate employee remuneration provides institutions with an incentive to substitute cheaper labor for that of its graduate students. One of the planks put forward by the Teaching Assistants Association at the University of Wisconsin, Madison, in anticipation of bargaining deals with this issue. According to the TAA's Web site, strengthening protections against contract and casual labor would "make it more difficult for the university to turn your [teaching assistant] or [program or project assistant] position into a 'student hourly' or 'undergrad TA' job with lower pay, no benefits, and no union protections." A provision in the GEO-UMass contract goes one step further by requiring that the institution measure the extent of such labor substitutions and "provide to GEO an annual report on the use of undergraduate teaching assistants" (GEO-UMass, art. 21).

Nondiscrimination

Although most administrators would be quick to proclaim their abhorrence of discrimination, there are good reasons for establishing contractual safeguards against its specific manifestations. Where contracts provide spousal benefits, for example, one might expect institutional resistance to broad definitions of who exactly constitutes a spouse. Although nondiscrimination articles often track existing legal requirements (GTAC, art. 3), collective bargaining agreements can pick up where the polity leaves off. The cost of extending benefits and contractual protections to graduate employees is relatively low, and thus graduate-employee unions sometimes have the opportunity to bargain progressive, exemplary provisions into their nondiscrimination articles. The Graduate Teaching Fellows Federation (GTFF) in Oregon negotiated protections relating to "gender identity" and "gender expression" into their contract (GTFF, art. 8). The groundbreaking first contract inked by the UAW Local 2322 on behalf of resident assistants at the University of Massachusetts, Amherst, asserts that "measures must be taken to redress the effects of past discrimination, to eliminate present and future discrimination, and to ensure equal opportunity in the areas of hiring, upgrading, demotion or transfer, recruitment, layoff or termination, and rate of compensation"; consequently, the contract mandates "positive and aggressive affirmative action" by the parties (RA-CDA, art. 7). The graduate employee contract at the same institution goes one step further by directing funds to diversity programs and by making provisions to assess program implementation (GEO-UMass, memorandum 6).

Due Process

One ought to distinguish between academic due process and the more traditional notion of due process as it relates to the disciplining and termination of employees (Joughin). In broad terms, academic due process necessitates a high level of peer involvement in disciplinary processes and is predicated on the assumption that the professoriate ought to function largely as a self-regulating profession. Those graduate employee contracts dealing with the issue tend to track the general mechanism rather than its academic variant. The UAW's first contract with the University of California provides for notice and right of response in cases of discipline and dismissal and also makes provisions for paid investigatory leave in such cases (AGSE, art. 7). Although sometimes spelled out in a limited fashion in grievance-arbitration articles, due process language ideally ensures that the following conditions are met: both union and employee receive notification of intent to discipline, the employee has meaningful response and appeal rights, the employee must be given full information about the nature of accusations or charges leveled against him or her, discipline ought to be incremental whenever possible, and witnesses in any investigation are explicitly protected from reprisals. Most of these conditions are met by the GTFF's exemplary language on "discipline and discharge" (art. 16).

Academic Freedom

Language addressing academic freedom in graduate employee contracts ranges widely, from silence at Michigan State to generous articulations of the graduate employee's pedagogical and research prerogatives in the state of Florida's three graduate-employee unions. Although open to interpretation, the controversial terms under which the UAW and NYU resolved their dispute over union recognition included an explicit disavowal by the union of its authority over "issues involving the academic mission of the University" and acceptance of narrow limits—"wages, hours and other terms and conditions of employment"—on the scope of bargaining. Whether the union can argue successfully that academic freedom constitutes a bargainable term or condition of employment remains to be seen, but "teaching methods and supervision of courses," as well as "curricula and research programs," seem to have been placed beyond the union's reach (Wheeler).

Existing contracts with UAW locals evince considerable variation in provisions made for academic freedom. The Association of Graduate Student Employees contract expands the typical management-rights article into a more aggressive statement of "Management and Academic Rights," which reserves to the university "sole authority on all decisions involving academic matters" and removes such decisions from "the grievance or arbitration procedure or collateral suit" (AGSE, art. 17). Similarly, the GEO-UMass contract seems to curtail academic freedom by "explicitly exclud[ing] matters relating to academic policies" from the scope of bargaining (art. 1). That contract also affirms the superviser's right "to determine what is taught by graduate student employees and how that teaching is to be carried out" (art. 15). Elsewhere, however, the language of the University of Amherst's contract borrows from the AAUP's "1940 Statement of Principles on Academic Freedom and Tenure with 1970 Interpretive Comments" and guarantees to graduate employees "reasonable latitude to exercise their professional judgment within their area of expertise." That same article also extends the right "to freely express in their work environment their political beliefs and/or affiliations . . . [provided that] they should be careful not to introduce matter unrelated to their subject persistently into their teaching" (GEO-UMass, art. 21).

The problem of balancing the academic freedom of graduate employees with that of their faculty supervisers is ticklish, but not impossible. Rutgers's graduate employees enjoy—contractually, at least—precisely the same academic freedom and rights as their faculty counterparts, and they also benefit from clearly articulated procedures for accessing, emending, and deleting items from their personnel files (Rutgers Council, art. 2; art. 18). The graduate employee contract at the University of Rhode Island errs on the side of caution in curtailing the academic freedom of graduate employees who "will have reasonable latitude to exercise their judgment in deciding how best to accomplish their teaching and research in their discipline . . . [and] are entitled to freedom in the classroom in discuss[ing] their discipline." Both of these rights are conditional and "subject to the supervision of the faculty of the department and college." Drawing from the original text of the AAUP's 1940 statement, the University of Rhode Island contract asserts that graduate employees "must be careful not to introduce into their teaching controversial matters that have no relation to their subject" (art. 14). The GEO-UMass negotiators astutely integrated the more generous formulation from the revised 1970 statement into their agreement, which only prohibits graduate employees from "introduc[ing] matter unrelated to their subject *persistently* [emphasis mine] into their teaching" (art. 21).

One of the strongest affirmations of graduate employee academic freedom is also one of the oldest. Dating back to the earliest contracts between GAU and the Florida Board of Regents in the early 1980s (excepting the last sentence, which first appeared in the 1987–89 agreement), the academic-freedom article from the University of Florida is sterling:

> It is the policy of the Board and UFF-GAU to encourage graduate assistants, in fulfillment of their assigned teaching responsibilities, to give their own interpretation of instructional materials used by them—whether self-chosen or prescribed by the teaching unit—within the bounds of knowledge and methodologies appropriate to the disciplinary field, under the guidance of the employing department or unit. In fulfilling assigned research duties, graduate assistants will be encouraged to exercise creativity and sound judgment in carrying out the theoretical, conceptual, and methodological design of the research under the

guidance of the research supervisor. When the Graduate Assistant is primarily responsible for the course, the Graduate Assistant shall determine grades in accordance with University and Board policies. (GAU-UF, art. 5)

Union Rights

To safeguard the contract and serve its members effectively, the union ought to negotiate aggressively in defense of its own prerogatives and rights from the outset. Broadly speaking, union rights can be grouped as follows: communications and rights of access (office space, meeting facilities, bulletin boards, institutional e-mail and Web hosting, institutional printing and distribution of the contract to unit members, access to campus mail services), information rights (timely responses to information requests, regular reports on bargaining unit composition and contract implementation, institutional budgets and financial statements), union service provisions (release time, buy-out provisions, scheduling accommodations for union officials), agency rights (payroll deduction, fair-share requirements), and solidarity rights. This last category—sometimes called picket rights—warrants an explanation. Unlike typical graduate employee contracts in the United States, some Canadian agreements afford bargaining unit members the right to honor picket lines without penalty. Best understood as the union's equivalent to the conscientious objector, picket rights are crucial to labor solidarity. The new CUPE contract at the University of Windsor is illustrative of sound language on this issue:

> In the event that any employees of the Employer, other than those covered by this Agreement, engage in a strike or where employees in a labour dispute engage in a strike and maintain picket lines, the employees covered by this Agreement shall have the right to refuse to cross such picket lines. Failure to cross such a picket line by the members of this Union shall not be considered a violation of this Agreement, nor shall it be grounds for disciplinary action. (CUPE 4580, art. 9)

Unions that allow restrictive or punitive no-strike clauses into their contracts do so to their own long-term detriment. Unfortunately, however, such clauses are typical in American graduate employee (and faculty) contracts. Consider the GEO-University of Michigan contract's "No

Interference" article. Under the terms of that article, the union "will not cause, instigate, support or encourage, nor shall any employee take part in, any concerted action against or any concerted interference with the operations of the University." Most perniciously, this article requires the GEO to become an agent of the university in the event that bargaining unit members honor picket lines and miss work as a result; in such cases, GEO must "instruct in writing any and all employees to cease their misconduct and inform them that this misconduct is a violation of the Agreement, which subjects them to disciplinary action, including discharge" (art. 3). In the long run, every union must give solidarity to get it. Contractual provisions making such exchanges impossible ought to be at the top of every bargaining team's hit list.

Tuition and Fees

Reflecting the needs of graduate employees as students, a relatively unusual component in many graduate employee contracts are the provisions made for fee and tuition remission. Once rare, tuition waivers for graduate employees have become standard at research institutions. The University of Iowa (UI) was the last of the Big Ten schools to adopt a tuition-remission plan—perhaps because raising the cost of attending the institution allowed the administration to offset stipend increases to its graduate employees. From the union's perspective, negotiating fee remission in lieu of stipend increases does little good for union coffers but can significantly benefit its members. As graduate employee stipends rise so too do the tax obligations on those employees. Tuition-remission dollars go further—from the employee's point of view—because they represent a dollar-for-dollar benefit, whereas additional stipend increases are eroded by federal and state income taxes. Moreover, tuition remission can be a more politically expedient way to enhance pay when budgets are tight and legislators or governing boards insist on holding the line on employee raises. Given the fiscal crisis against which they were working, graduate employees at UI would have had a hard time bargaining for significantly higher stipends; however, the tuition package that they negotiated eliminates any further clawbacks of graduate employee wages while masking a real raise of 5%-9% (depending on assignment) to unit employees (COGS, appendix F).

A Word on Zipper and Past-Practice Clauses

Zipper clauses, designed to preclude bargaining over changes to the terms and conditions of employment while the contract is in effect, can be found in many graduate employee contracts. The GTFF's "totality of agreement" language at the University of Oregon is typical: "neither party shall be obligated to bargain collectively with respect to any subject or matter . . . even though such subject or matter may not have been within the knowledge or contemplation of the parties at the time they negotiated or signed this Agreement" (art. 27). Rather than foreclosing the possibility of negotiations during the period when a contract is in force, graduate-employee unions should negotiate provisions allowing the parties to bargain over issues that may emerge while a contract is in effect. As long as the union ensures that such mechanisms do not allow the administration to impose changes on the bargaining unit in the event that agreement cannot be reached, such contract provisions offer the union additional leverage and the administration more flexibility.

One way to accomplish such provisions is to bargain past-practice or past-policy language that stipulates that any change in terms and conditions of employment cannot be implemented unless it is first agreed to by the union. Such articles give the union leverage in negotiations and in grievance proceedings and protect the union from being put in the awkward position of having to bargain over already-implemented policies or practices. The best past-practice language of which I am aware states that "[a]ll existing personnel policies, practices, benefits and working conditions of the Institute or any portion thereof, written or unwritten, applicable to members of the bargaining unit shall be continued in effect unless in conflict with this Agreement as now existing or as amended by subsequent agreement between the parties" (FUSFAI, art. 22).

The proliferation of graduate-employee unions and new recognition campaigns in the late 1990s not only reflected the corporatization of the academy but also heightened institutional demand for graduate students. Revolutions occur when conditions improve, and the same economic factors that allowed prospective graduate students to shop aggressively for the best offer fueled enthusiasm for collective bargaining. Unlike part-time and contingent faculty members, graduate employee collective action is sheltered because institutions have a stake in retaining graduate students through the completion of their degrees. This is not to say that collective bargaining campaigns are ever easy or that the work of running an established graduate-employee union is not extremely demanding. In fact, the particular challenges facing graduate-employee activists make their unions ideal training grounds for union leaders and committed organizers.

A number of graduate employee activists are now graduating to take jobs, not in academic departments, but rather in the labor movement. And why not? Graduate employee activists typically undergo a whirlwind education in organizing and, in the short span of a graduate career, will almost certainly have been involved with contract issues, member organizing, and union management. The UAW, AFT, SEIU, HERE, NEA, and AAUP have all tapped—or, at least, optioned—the labor of graduate-employee union leaders. The American labor movement at long last has the ability to socialize, and draw on, large segments of the country's future professional class. One hopes that they will take advantage of the opportunity.

WORKS CITED

Collective Bargaining Agreements Consulted

AGSE [Association of Graduate Student Employees, UAW Local 2865]. With the Regents of the Univ. of California. 1 June 2000–30 Sept. 2003.

COGS [Campaign to Organize Graduate Students, UE Local 896]. With the State of Iowa Board of Regents, Univ. of Iowa. 1 July 2003–30 Jun. 2005.

CUPE 3902 [Canadian Union of Public Employees, Local 3902]. With the Governing Council of the Univ. of Toronto. 1 Sept. 2001–30 Apr. 2005.

CUPE 4580 [Canadian Union of Public Employees, Local 4580]. With the Univ. of Windsor. 1 Sept. 2003–31 Aug. 2004.

FUSFAI [Faculty Union San Francisco Art Inst., AAUP]. With the San Francisco Art Institute. 1 July 2002–30 June 2007.

GAU-UF [Graduate Assistants United, NEA-AFT]. With the Board of Regents, State Univ. System, Univ. of Florida. Until 7 Jan. 2003.

GAU-URI [Graduate Assistants United, AAUP]. With the Univ. of Rhode Island. 1 Sept. 2003–1 Aug. 2004.

GAU-USF [Graduate Assistants United, NEA]. With the Board of Regents, State Univ. System, Univ. of S. Florida. 30 June 1995.

GEOC [Graduate Employees Organizing Committee, AFT Local 6123]. With Wayne State Univ. 30 May 2003–20 Feb. 2006.

GEO-UMass [Graduate Employee Organization, UAW Local 2322]. With the Univ. of Mass., Amherst. 1 July 2001–30 June 2004.

GEO-UMich [Graduate Employees Organization, AFT Local 3550]. With the Regents of the Univ. of Michigan. 7 May 2002–1 Feb. 2005.

GEU [Graduate Employees Union, AFT Local]. With Michigan State Univ. 16 May 2002–15 May 2005.

GTAC [Graduate Teaching Assistants Coalition, AFT Local 4565]. With the Univ. of Kansas and the Board of Regents. 1 Oct. 2002–30 Sept. 2005.

GTFF [Graduate Teaching Fellows Federation, AFT Local 3544]. With the Univ. of Oregon. 20 May 2002–31 Mar. 2004.

RA-CDA [Resident Assistant Unit, UAW Local 2322]. With the Board of Trustees of the Univ. of Mass., 1 July 2003–30 June 2005.

Rutgers Council of AAUP Chapters [Rutgers Council, AAUP]. With Rutgers Univ. 1 July 1999–30 June 2003.

Other Sources

American Association of University Professors. "1940 Statement of Principles on Academic Freedom and Tenure with 1970 Interpretive Comments." 1940. Rev. 1970. Amer. Assn., *Policy Documents* 3–10.

———. *Policy Documents and Reports.* 9th ed. Baltimore: Johns Hopkins UP, 2001.

———. "Statement on Academic Government for Institutions Engaged in Collective Bargaining." 1988. Amer. Assn., *Policy Documents* 253–54.

———. "Statement on Collective Bargaining." 1973. Rev. 1984. Amer. Assn., *Policy Documents* 251–52.

———. "Statement on Graduate Students." 2000. Amer. Assn., *Policy Documents.* 268–70.

Austin, Ann E. "Preparing the Next Generation of Faculty: Graduate School as Socialization to the Academic Career." *Journal of Higher Education* 73 (2002): 94–122.

Axtell, James. *The Pleasures of Academe: A Celebration and Defense of Higher Education.* Lincoln: U of Nebraska P, 1998.

Baldwin, Roger G., and Jay L. Chronister. *Teaching without Tenure: Policies and Practices for a New Era.* Baltimore: Johns Hopkins UP, 2001.

Bender, Daniel E., and Dave Kinkela. "Thirty Years of Academic Labor: The Language of Antiunionism." *Radical History Review* 79 (2001): 7–13.

Benjamin, Ernst, ed. *Exploring the Role of Contingent Instructional Staff in Undergraduate Learning.* New Directions for Higher Educ. 123. San Francisco: Jossey-Bass, 2003.

Bok, Derek. *Universities in the Marketplace: The Commercialization of Higher Education.* Princeton: Princeton UP, 2003.

Breitzer, Susan Roth. "More Than Academic: Labor Consciousness and the Rise of UE Local 896-COGS." Herman and Schmid 71–90.

Brill, Edward A., and Tracey I. Levy. "Are You Prepared for Student Unionization?" *Business Officer* (2002): 41–44.

Brown University, 341 NLRB 42 (2004). <http:www.nlrb.gov/nlrb/shared_files/weekly/w2957.htm#Brown>.

Clark, Burton R., ed. *Research Foundations of Graduate Education: Germany, Britain, France, United States, Japan*. Berkeley: U of California P, 1993.

Dullea, Henrik N. "How Cornell Beat a Union by Letting TA's Vote," *Chronicle of Higher Education* 17 Jan. 2003: B16.

Graduate Employee Organization. *A Narrative History of GEO*. 28 Dec. 2003. 26 May 2005 <www.umgeo.org/index.php?module=ContentExpress&func=display &ceid=9&meid=>.

Graduate Employees and Students Organization. "Casual in Blue: Yale and the Academic Labor Market." 28 Dec. 2003. <www.yaleunions.org/geso/archive/reports.htm>.

———. Home page. 28 Dec. 2003. <www.yaleunions.org/geso/>.

Graduate Student Employee Action Coalition. *Web Site*. 21 Dec. 2003. <www.mindspring.com/%7Egseac/update.html>.

Herman, Deborah M., and Julie M. Schmid, eds. *Cogs in the Classroom Factory: The Changing Identity of Academic Labor*. Westport: Praeger, 2003.

Hewitt, Gordon J. "Graduate Student Employee Collective Bargaining and the Educational Relationship between Faculty and Graduate Students." *Journal of Collective Negotiations* 29 (2000): 153–66.

Holstein, James A., Jaber F. Gubrium. *The Self We Live By: Narrative Identity in a Postmodern World*. New York: Oxford UP, 2000.

Hutcheson, Philo A. *A Professional Professorate: Unionization, Bureaucratization, and the AAUP*. Nashville: Vanderbilt UP, 2000.

Johnson, Benjamin, Patrick Kavanagh, and Kevin Mattson, eds. *Steal This University: The Rise of the Corporate University and the Academic Labor Movement*. New York: Routledge, 2003.

Joughin, Louis. "Academic Due Process." *Law and Contemporary Problems* 28 (1963): 573–61.

Julius, Daniel J., and Patricia J. Gumport. "Graduate Student Unionization: Catalysts and Consequences." *Review of Higher Education* 26 (2003): 187–216.

Keys, Lisa. "Grad Student 'Norma Rae' Basks in Victory over NYU." *Forward* 17 May 2002. <www.forward.com/issues/2002/02.05.17/news10.html>.

Kirp, David L. *Shakespeare, Einstein, and the Bottom Line: The Marketing of Higher Education*. Cambridge: Harvard UP, 2003.

Lee, Jenny J., et al. "Tangles in the Tapestry: Cultural Barriers to Graduate Student Unionization." *Journal of Higher Education* 75 (2004): 340–61.

Lee, Shinzong. "Graduate Students Vote Down Unionization." *Yale Daily News* 1 May 2003. <www.yaledailynews.com/article.asp?AID=22877>.

Nelson, Cary, ed. *Will Teach for Food: Academic Labor in Crisis*. Minneapolis: U of Minnesota P, 1997.

Phillips-Fein, Kim. "Yale Bites Unions." *Nation* 2 July 2001. <www.ssl.thenation.com/doc.20010702&s/phillips_fein>.

Rabban, David, and Donna Euben. *Brief of Amicus Curiae American Association of University Professors in Support of Petitioner United Automobile Workers, AFL-CIO*. NYU v. UAW. *New York University* 332 NLRB 1205 (2000).

Rabban, David, et al. *Brief of Amicus Curiae American Association of University Professors in Support of Graduate Employees Together—University of Pennsylvania*. Trustees of the University of Pennsylvania, Case no. 4-RC-20353 (2002).

Rhoades, Gary. *Managed Professionals: Unionized Faculty and Restructuring Academic Labor*. Albany: State U of New York P, 1998.

Rhoades, Gary, and Robert A. Rhoads. "The Public Discourse of U.S. Graduate Employee Unions: Social Movement Identities, Ideology, and Strategies." *Review of Higher Education* 26 (2003): 163–86.

Robin, Corey. "Blacklisted and Blue: On Theory and Practice at Yale." Johnson, Kavanagh, and Mattson 107–22.

Robin, Corey, and Michelle Stephens. "Against the Grain: Organizing TAs at Yale." Nelson 44–79.

Sinclair, Upton. *The Goose-Step: A Study of American Education*. Rev. ed. Vol. 4. Girard: Haldeman-Julius, 1923.

Slaughter, Sheila, and Larry L. Leslie. *Academic Capitalism: Politics, Policies, and the Entrepreneurial University*. Baltimore: Johns Hopkins UP, 1997.

Smith, C. W. *Market Values in American Higher Education: The Pitfalls and Promises*. Lanham: Rowman, 2000.

Snow, C. P. "The Two Cultures." *The Two Cultures*. Cambridge: Rede, 1959. Rpt. Cambridge: Cambridge UP, 1993. 1–21.

Soley, Lawrence C. *Leasing the Ivory Tower: The Corporate Takeover of Academia*. Boston: South End, 1995.

"State of Washington before the Public Employment Relations Commission." 16 Dec. 2003. 23 Jan. 2005 <http: www.perc.wa.gov/databases/rep_uc/8315.htm>.

Stygall, Gail. "A Report from a Writing Program Director in the Trenches: TAs and Unionization." *Pedagogy: Critical Approaches to Teaching Literature, Language, Composition, and Culture* 3 (2003): 7–19.

Teaching Assistants Association. *Web Site*. 21 Dec. 2003. <www.taa-madison.org/platform.html>.

Thompson, James. "Unfinished Chapters: Institutional Alliances and Changing Identities in a Graduate Employee Union." Herman and Schmid 117–35.

Westheimer, Joel. "Tenure Denied: Union Busting and Anti-intellectualism in the Corporate University." Johnson, Kavanagh, and Mattson 123–37.

Wheeler, Philip A. Letter to Terrance Nolan. 1 Mar. 2001.

Wilhelm, John. "A Short History of Unionization at Yale." Nelson 35–43.

Wolff, Rick. "Why Provoke This Strike? Yale and the U.S. Economy." Nelson 124–28.

Zieger, Robert H. *The CIO, 1935–1955*. Chapel Hill: U of North Carolina P, 1995.

PART THREE

COLLECTIVE BARGAINING PROCEDURES AND POLICIES

A Primer on Organizational Development

MICHAEL MAUER

From their inception, local bargaining organizations have to consider what sort of organizational structures to establish, because the decision to move to collective bargaining is politically complex. Moreover, organizational vitality requires recurrent efforts to ensure participation and effective representation and calls for more than simply the establishment of a sound foundation. This essay looks first at the variety of organizational decisions that newly formed academic unions have had to make and then at how established organizations can use a formal process of regular self-assessment to remain dynamic.

Initial Structural Decisions

Local academic bargaining organizations function in very different environments, since unions encompass the public and private sector, two-year and four-year institutions, different types of faculty members and academic professionals, and graduate student employees. Such variety makes it impossible to present a unitary organizational model that will suit each and every academic union. But the political considerations discussed in this essay apply to all such unions, and those considerations form the prism through which the decisions about structure are made.

Service Models and Affiliation

One especially significant factor in the structural differences among academic bargaining organizations is the servicing model on which they depend. This is determined in large part by the national organization with which they affiliate. Almost all academic locals and chapters are affiliated with a national union or association and whatever state or other component organizations may exist. In a small but growing number of cases, the national affiliate is a union that has become multijurisdictional, primarily representing noneducators. Although the number of local unions that have multiple affiliations is small, these unions represent a significant force in the national landscape. The country's three largest organizations of faculty and academic professionals—those in the California State University and the State and City University of New York systems—are each affiliated with two or more national organizations.

In most cases, a decision on affiliation is made by the initiators of the unionization effort before the formal organizing drive commences (although history amply demonstrates that affiliations are subject to change thereafter). There are substantial repercussions to the choice of affiliation partners. Local AAUP chapters function with virtually complete autonomy, for example. Although limited amounts of guidance, support, training, and assistance with networking with other AAUP collective bargaining chapters are available, the lion's share of the work at the local level of AAUP collective bargaining chapters is done by those at the local level. Neither the national AAUP nor its Collective Bargaining Congress (a grouping at the national level of all unionized AAUP chapters) possesses the constitutional authority to place wayward local organizations into trusteeship. Most national unions, in contrast, can exercise greater discipline on local chapters.

Local organizations affiliated with other national groups also attain more direct political and staff connections. The National Education Association (NEA) concentrates much of its strength at the state level, employing a corps of full-time labor-relations professionals assigned to handle the servicing needs of local organizations (both its primary K–12 membership and its much smaller higher-education constituency). The American Federation of Teachers (AFT) also maintains a network of strong state organizations (which include those K–12, higher education, health care and public employees represented by AFT in that state), which may enter into varying arrangements to provide servicing to local unions. Some larger locals work out arrangements to employ their own staff in lieu of national administration. For AFL-CIO affiliated unions (including the AFT) and for those unions in the newer Change to Win Federation, there are also organizational structures that link locals with other unions at the local, state, and national levels.[1]

It should be noted that the differences in organizational structure that result from the decision on affiliation have financial implications as well and affect the degree of autonomy a chapter will have and the outreach and lobbying it will be able to do. While the three major organizations in higher education assess roughly equivalent national dues at the local level, the per capita obligations for state services vary widely; the AAUP maximum is well under fifty dollars a year, whereas other unions may require hundreds of dollars in state dues. Those locals that have substantial state dues obligations often need to negotiate special arrangements with the state or national organization when they seek to employ their own local staff members.

For those unions that do not have their servicing needs provided by a state or national affiliate, there are still the practical and political questions of whether work will be performed at the local level by paid staff members or by the union members themselves. As a practical matter, the parameters for decisions about staffing are set in part by the size of the local bargaining organization. A local union with one hundred or so members will not have the financial wherewithal to retain a full-time staff. And a union with many thousands of members can't realistically expect to get its work done without a base of paid staff members.

Some chapters adopt a strong staff model, employing an executive director imbued with significant authority. The director oversees staff specialists, who direct the various programs and activities. Such a structure offers the clear advantages of efficiency and predictability in managing work flow and the ability to draw on the expertise of career specialists in grievance and arbitration, communications, government relations, and the other areas of concentration for union work. Other chapters, although employing competent staff support, decide not to assign significant authority to staff members and, possibly, to limit the amount of work performed by them. The arguments against the strong staff model include the virtues of direct member involvement in the life of the union; the benefit of the union's remaining close to the hearts and minds of the members; and, in the case of academic unions, the view that those who directly participate in the work of the academy can best understand and direct academic representation. There are trade-offs, of course, including the reluctance of busy academics to devote the time needed for a "second job" of union work. But there are ways of dealing with the difficulty inherent in recruiting volunteers: a sufficient portion of the local union's budget can be devoted to purchasing course release time for those activists willing to step forward and take on the union's work, and it may be possible to negotiate paid time off for union officers, grievance specialists, and others who can perform the day-to-day work of the union.

Organizational Governance

Regardless of how the local union decides to divide labor and responsibility, it is important that the union's governing documents specify the authority that individuals and bodies possess. Dangers lurk when unions don't resolve at the outset who, for example, should sign checks and exercise other financial authority, which individual or individuals will make decisions about programs or the processing and arbitration of grievances, or who has the authority to initial an agreement or recommend its adoption by the members.

Although size, geography, and bargaining unit composition will shape much of a union's organizational structure, the typical academic union at the departmental or school level has designees who handle initial inquiries and provide some basic guidance and representation services. These representatives are not expected to be expert in any particular area of the union's work, but they perform a valuable function in many instances simply by serving as a conduit for communication and by making referrals to others within the union structure. In the non-academic union world, such individuals are called union stewards or shop stewards. In the academy, they are often called department, college, or unit representatives.

At the unit-wide level of bargaining, there is generally a governing board or council that includes the officers and other elected representatives. If this is a large representative board or council, it is often supplemented by an executive committee or steering committee (consisting of the executive officers and perhaps others) with authority to make certain decisions and to conduct day-to-day business between the regularly scheduled meetings of the larger board or council.

The AAUP model encourages academic unions to address a broad range of issues, including professional matters, rather than to narrowly

focus on only bread-and-butter concerns. Although NEA and AFT locals
do not always emphasize these broad issues, they have begun to pay
more attention to such issues as academic freedom and shared governance. AAUP chapters generally supplement the typical union committee
structure (addressing the basics, such as grievance representation, communications, and government relations) with other working groups
(dealing with academic freedom, junior faculty and mentoring, and so
on). One practice that has worked well for larger academic unions is to
designate individual members of the executive board as chairs of each
such committee and to draw on interested and knowledgeable members
to flesh out their composition. This encompasses the twin goals of using
the best available expertise and integrating new faces into the work of
the union. Large multicampus unions may adopt a campus-by-campus
structure of governing bodies and committees. Academic unions operating on campuses where there are nonacademic unions need to create
some liaison structure to communicate and coordinate with those other
unions.

The organizational structure of any collective bargaining chapter
needs to integrate into the overall work of the union the various groups
that constitute the bargaining unit, such as research and teaching faculty
members, full-time and part-time faculty members, faculty and academic
professionals, faculty on different campuses or at different stages in their
careers, and male and female colleagues. Sometimes this integration is
accomplished by designating positions for members from the various
groups. So, for example, some academic unions elect multiple vice presidents to represent each group. Another way to provide for a mix of
constituent groups in leadership bodies is to have candidates chosen
by a nominating committee that is mindful of the importance of this
variety. Since legal considerations may be involved when certain slots are
designated for certain categories of individuals, it is prudent to have
legal counsel review officer criteria and other basic constitutional
arrangements.

In establishing elected offices, the question of term limits is no less
vexing for academic unions than it is for the society at large; the malady
identified in this debate is real. Without formal term limits or some other
device meant to ensure turnover, bargaining organizations will not develop new leadership and will thus not remain vital. Yet too-frequent
turnover of elected officers may result in the loss of the critical skills or

information that experienced leaders have gained and an excessive dependence on staff decision making.

Dues

A final, critically important decision for collective bargaining chapters is the amount and structure of dues. During the organizing drive, and sometimes continuing into the period when a first collective bargaining agreement is negotiated, some academic unions follow the traditional union practice of not charging dues. On the other hand, AAUP chapters encourage full AAUP membership during the organizing phase and sometimes make the signing of two cards—one taking out AAUP membership and the other petitioning for a union vote—the cornerstone of the organizing drive. Once the local organization begins in earnest its job of being a labor union, it must establish a dues structure sufficient to ensure effective representation. And, although initial decisions about dues can be revisited at any time, it is far easier to begin with a dues setup that fits the long-term needs of the local organization than it is to thereafter persuade the membership to increase the dues.

The local union's dues structure must be sufficient to cover its external obligations (to a national affiliate or state or other local assessments) and to fund local activities. Setting the individual member's dues at a flat dollar amount has certain advantages of simplicity and predictability of income flow for the union. In the interest of fairness, in full-time faculty unions the dollar amount can be pegged to rank. But a dues structure that does not track differing income levels is generally perceived as less equitable overall than a dues structure based on a percentage of individual salaries. A percentage formula also institutionalizes increases in dues income for the union, enabling it to cope with inflation and other necessary increases. The local organization cannot control increases in national or state dues obligations, which generally use a formula that factors in inflation and salary averages.

Academic unions generally negotiate payroll dues deductions for those who agree to participate, although some permit direct dues payments for members who do not wish to participate in payroll deduction. Where it is legally permitted, academics have generally found it morally defensible and politically advisable to require all those who benefit from the work of the union (that is, everyone in the bargaining unit) to contribute financially to that work through a negotiated "fair share" or "agency fee" arrangement. A union beginning its organizational life without majority membership support may need to build membership and power before negotiating such an arrangement. One device that has proved successful for such chapters is to negotiate a provision that an agency fee will kick in as soon as the union demonstrates either a simple majority (or, in some instances, a supermajority) membership. The legal structure of such provisions is discussed in the essay by Gregg Adler in this volume.

Periodic Self-Assessment

After establishing the initial structure of the local bargaining organization, the union leaders and activists set about their representational work, learning as they go. Early enthusiasm is self-propelling, but stagnancy has been the death of too many long-term local unions. To maintain effective advocacy, it is necessary to take a step back from the day-to-day flurry of activity and periodically conduct an organizational self-assessment of programs and structure (which I'll call an organizational audit or inventory). Those at the forefront of a union's work have occasional opportunities to informally reexamine, individually and as a group, the operations of the union. But a deliberate approach to self-assessment is critical.

The need for a structured organizational self-examination is affirmed by considering some common perceptions of unions. One of the most frequently heard criticisms is that the union is an entity that exists separate and apart from the bargaining unit members it purports to speak for. The typical image painted of the union is that of a small, insular group of individuals holding on to their sinecures and perquisites until retirement (and thereafter, in some cases.) Certainly, the two-dimensional portrait of unions painted by their most aggressive detractors is almost always substantially distorted. At the same time, when dedicated academic union leaders take a step back, they often recognize that over time the organization and the scope of the union's work has narrowed in focus. These activists realize that, contrary to their original intent and to their continuing vision of the union as an organization that exists to serve its members, the union may have become bureaucratized over the years, to the detriment of all.

Organizational atrophy can result from the transformations that typically occur over time. During an initial union organizing drive, the activists of the nascent organization interact one-on-one with their colleagues. In almost all campaigns, one-on-one and small group discussions are the primary means by which the core group of union activists ascertains what is on the minds of faculty colleagues. In this way, the fledgling organization can design its activities to convince a majority of the faculty to vote yes in the union election. However, in the aftermath of a successful vote for unionization, and throughout the intensive process of negotiating an initial collective agreement, the organization undergoes a natural transition to a focus on the structural foundations necessary for managing change. In this stage, a finite group of activists works to get the organization up and running and to secure an initial collective bargaining agreement. Although this work requires coordination and cooperation among the elected leaders, it does not require sustained interaction with all members.

Thereafter, as the union enters into the mature phase of its organizational existence, subtle but powerful pressures militate toward transforming the structural model from one based on organizing to one based on delivery of services. Usually no one in the organizational leadership makes a conscious decision to move in this direction, but the union gradually becomes a third party in its relationship with bargaining unit members. It collects dues payments, in exchange for which it enforces the terms of the negotiated agreements and negotiates subsequent contracts. This very natural dynamic may finally cause members to view their union the way consumers view an insurance policy: they periodically pay money to an organization to purchase a measure of security and protection.

Most wise union leaders have discovered the dangers in acquiescing to such an organizational transformation. The more bargaining unit members view the union as a third party, the greater the concomitant erosion of voluntary membership and the decline in new activists. There quickly follows a drop in the level and intensity of union activity. Then it is only a matter of time before an understandable level of realism or opportunism takes hold among administrators and trustees, resulting in less and less respect for the union as a genuine voice for the faculty.

The Elements of an Organizational Inventory

Before I proceed to an examination of the nuts and bolts of conducting an organizational inventory, a word may be in order to those organizers whose experience leads them to dismiss the necessity of engaging in such a time-consuming activity. They may believe that they already understand what changes would be beneficial for the local organization. Their attitude, certainly understandable from the point of view of knowledgeable veterans of local union activity, may be that it is simple to put into effect whatever changes in structure or focus are needed to reinvigorate the union along the way.

In many instances, longtime, savvy leaders will indeed have a solid grasp of where the local organization needs to move. But for such leaders to use their understanding to decline to engage in a structured self-examination may be unwise for two reasons. First, it is certain that an honest, free-ranging inquiry will produce a richer understanding than conventional wisdom. Additionally, the path to change may not be quite as straightforward as seeing what needs to be done and then simply doing it.

Politics and personalities may need to be addressed first. Perhaps some of those already active in the leadership ranks do not yet see what is clear to rank-and-file members, who have a different vantage point. Segments of the leadership or other components of the bargaining unit may perceive themselves as not being fully integrated into the decision making and activity of the local organization. When evaluating whether to launch an organizational audit, then, leaders should bear in mind the possibility that, even if the exercise does not yield dramatically new insights for veterans, it may serve the invaluable function of educating newer members in the organization and helping forge a consensus on the agenda for the future. In other words, when weighing whether the time and effort of conducting an organizational audit is worth the expenditure of limited human and fiscal resources, leaders should consider that there is not only potential wisdom to be gained but also a salutary effect on the dynamics of the local organization.

For faculty union leaders to take the pulse of their organization, some of the following measures of organizational vitality should be taken:

- Size of the membership: Has a substantial majority of eligible unit members voluntarily joined, so that the union speaks with credibility

as the voice of the entire body? Is the percentage of members increasing or decreasing over time?

- Size of the activist base: Is an appreciable number of members more
  than just dues payers? Do the members also contribute to the work
  of the union?

- Distribution of the membership and activist base: Does the composition of the leadership reflect the diversity of the bargaining unit
  itself? Or, does underrepresentation of identifiable groups (by discipline, gender, race, tenure status, geography, etc.) undercut the
  union's claim to speak for the full range of bargaining unit interests?

- Stagnancy of membership and activist core: Do newly hired unit
  members enroll in the organization? Do both new and longtime
  members step forward to assume leadership positions?

- Scope of chapter activity: Do public profile and agenda of the organization encompass both traditional union bread-and-butter issues
  as well as professional concerns, thereby reflecting the varied interests of those in the bargaining unit?

- Level of chapter activity: Factoring in the size of the campus, severity
  of problems being addressed, and other relevant factors, how frequently is the organization active and visible? Is there a variety of
  activities that the chapter is identified with, including advocacy, informational functions, mentoring and training programs, and so
  forth?

- Connections with other entities: Does the chapter communicate with
  and, as appropriate, work cooperatively with other faculty and nonfaculty organizations on campus? Does the chapter reach out to other
  faculty and nonfaculty organizations in the community, on a statewide level, and on a national level?

- Adequacy of existing resources and structural mechanisms: Are the
  financial and human resources available to the chapter sufficient to
  accomplish what is needed? Does the existing organizational structure, including committees and decision-making bodies, generally
  suffice to get the chapter's work done? Or has the chapter turned to
  a succession of ad hoc or informal groups to deal with new tasks?

Methods of Conducting an Organizational Inventory

The more deliberate and systematic the organizational self-examination
is, the greater the reliability of the information to be gleaned from it.

Once leaders have created a checklist that addresses the issues above, the next step is to create a list of specific indicators of the local organization's health that should be evaluated. Particular emphasis should be placed on the complaints that may have been expressed over time by members, leaders, or others. Also to be considered are the particulars of any frustrations encountered by chapter leaders and staff members in reaching their goals in the past. Further, it may become clear that consensus on how to restructure the organization or modify its programs and activities cannot be achieved without first addressing the question of their reason for being. It may well be that whatever mission statement is encapsulated in the chapter constitution and bylaws no longer expresses the desires of the membership.

Although information obtained from members is indispensable in evaluating the effectiveness of the local union, the scope of the inquiry cannot be limited to members. The views of those in the bargaining unit who have not chosen to become members (whether by declining to join in an open-shop environment or by opting for a fee-payer status in an agency-fee arrangement) are an especially important target of the inquiry. But other individuals will be in a position to contribute valuable feedback about the effectiveness of the union as well, and the observations of even indirect stakeholders will help those conducting the organizational audit to understand how the union is viewed by the entire campus community.

So, although the methods used will vary from group to group, in determining how widely to cast the information-gathering net, leaders should consider the following:

- An appropriate mix of current members and activists that takes into account the potential for different perceptions and needs that may arise from differences in discipline, academic status, tenure eligibility, age, race or ethnicity, gender, and other such factors
- Those within the scope of exclusive representation provided by the union but who are not full members as well as those who are included in the bargaining unit but have a different, identifiable set of interests and concerns (such as faculty governance leaders)
- Others who are involved in the work of teaching, research, or related professional endeavors but who are outside the union's representation (including, in some cases, department chairs)
- Any staff members of the union (bearing in mind that the staff itself

may be union represented and therefore that certain protocols should govern such communications)

- Other groups of employees on campus, whether or not they are union represented.

Types of Information

The question of what types of information should be sought when conducting an organizational inventory merits consideration at the outset. In broad terms, both documentary and oral information will serve needed functions. The initial step should be to assemble existing documents that can serve as a starting point for understanding and analyzing how the organization functions at present. It is not unusual for an organization to find that its founding documents are in disorder—out of sight and out of mind. The papers to be compiled should include

- Current governing documents (constitution and bylaws) for the local organization as well as for its parent body (or bodies)
- A sample of recent minutes of meetings and reports and of similar documents generated by the local organization's leadership bodies and its committees or other component groups
- Budgetary information, including audits from past years
- Written and electronic materials used by the local organization to recruit and to set forth its positions and activities to members and others
- The current collective bargaining agreement, plus any side letters or other formal or informal understandings with the administration relating to use of contract release time, union access to campus facilities, and so on
- Policies pertaining to internal union administration, including job descriptions both for paid staff members and for officers and others in the union leadership, and protocols for union-related travel and other activities (as well as collective bargaining agreements with unions representing the local union staff, if applicable)
- Data on membership composition and historical trends.

Surveys and Focus Groups

There may well be significant value in conducting the kind of broad, written survey that is usually employed in the course of preparing for contract negotiations. Such a questionnaire, if properly constructed and carried out, provides valuable data. Moreover, it serves the positive function of alerting others to the chapter's real desire for input and its openness to making necessary changes at the conclusion of the process. Many local organizations have found, in addition, that the impressions gathered from focus groups may be even more valuable. Focus groups are essentially collective interviews, generally of between half a dozen and a dozen participants at a time, conducted by a moderator who seeks to elicit viewpoints on a preselected list of topics. Focus groups tend to work best when homogeneous groups are set up: thus a local faculty bargaining organization might choose to have one focus group consist of tenured faculty members in the hard sciences, another of junior faculty members in the humanities, and so on. The moderator facilitates discussion and reports back to those sponsoring the groups an accurate account of what is on the minds of those interviewed.

Unlike scientific survey instruments, which provide quantitative data, focus groups offer qualitative information. Both are important for academic unions in their work, but in different ways. In establishing its agenda for upcoming negotiations, for example, a union might well wish to ascertain with as much precision as possible what percentage of its members wish to increase, hold steady, or decrease the dollars going into a merit-pay program. But in evaluating why the organization does not enjoy broader or deeper support among bargaining unit members, union leaders need to learn how it is perceived by colleagues: do constituents indicate that they are lukewarm in their support of the union because they perceive it is being too strident, or do they express the view that the union is mostly ineffective? Do they dismiss the notion of becoming active in the organization because they always see nothing but the same faces doing the work? The point of this exercise, of course, is not to establish whether such impressions are accurate or not but rather to learn what perceptions are held so that the organization can consider what changes in its program or presentation might alter them.

Local bargaining organizations that wish to conduct focus groups need to determine whether to use the services of consultants to help design the protocols to be used, conduct the sessions, and report back to the organization. The conducting of focus groups is both an art and a science, and the expertise that can be brought to bear on such a project by skilled persons can be of considerable importance. In addition, the use of an outside moderator can generate credibility for the project, both internally and externally (if the results of the focus groups are used that way).

Since financial and other considerations may preclude retaining the services of consultants, leaders may consider another option: using the volunteer services of a faculty member with expertise at the institution. But an entirely reasonable alternative is for the chapter to undertake the design and conducting of focus groups using volunteers from among its ranks. With a reasonable amount of self-education and preparation, and a good dose of common sense along the way, chapter members have done a credible job of conducting focus groups on their own.[2]

Planning for Change

It is not always obvious who should begin the job of interpreting the information that has been compiled and use it to chart future directions for the organization. Perhaps it is appropriate for the main leadership body—an executive council, steering committee, or similar group—to undertake this task. But it may well be that a group should be formed specifically to take the lead in this phase of the process. Suppose, for example, that a starting point for the organizational audit is a widely shared view that the leadership body consists disproportionately of members of certain groups—senior faculty members or those in the arts and sciences. It might be counterproductive, then, to exclude the voices from underrepresented groups from discussions about reforms. It makes sense for future planning not only to put aside the question of which group has the authority to perform actions (such as initiating bylaw revisions to make structural changes) but also to include a mix of voices.

Many chapter leaders fail to understand that the process of interpreting the information collected in the organizational inventory and shaping future directions is often a difficult one. Psychology is important here. Many of the participants in an organizational review will be individuals who have toiled for years to create the organization; understandably, they may identify (and be identified) powerfully with it. It is not always easy for them to take a step back and consider dispassionately and objectively what organizational shortcomings inevitably exist. And there also may be a level of frustration to contend with from those who feel that the local union has not in the past met its obligation to include all interested individuals and important issues in its activities.

To help the participants keep personality conflicts from interfering with the analytical work they need to do, it may be prudent to secure the services of a facilitator for group discussions. Often all that is needed is to have the discussion chaired by someone other than a regular member of the body—a leader from another campus, or even a respected member from without the local leadership body might be the appropriate choice. If the services of a skilled organizational change specialist from the union's state or national organization can be obtained, so much the better.

To further minimize tensions that may make it difficult to resolve the matters at hand, it may behoove the body to work within a fairly structured agenda. Often, a SWOT analysis is used to provide a framework for discussion of organizational change; this acronym derives from the most significant categories to consider—strengths, weaknesses, opportunities, threats. These four categories can be used at the outset in what amounts to a structured brainstorming session, where the group constructs lists of where the organization is at present (that is, its strengths and weaknesses) and what can be anticipated for the future (that is, the opportunities and threats). With such lists visible to the group—literally visible on butcher block paper or chalkboards—the discussion of change tends to become more coherent and objective.

While it is true that a certain degree of formality will serve the participants well, at the same time there should be some planned informality. Often, the right conditions for a nondefensive, nonjudgmental, wide-ranging examination of the union's effectiveness are created when the discussions take place in a break from the routine. It may thus be well worth the extra time and any added expense to hold a retreat. Pleasant surroundings and time for extensive and relaxed discussion often facilitate an easier and more productive discussion. (To set the right tone, participants in such an enterprise have been known to reject the term *retreat* in favor of *advance*.)

Agenda for Change

If the range of needed information has been gathered successfully during the inventory process, the next step is to structure a sufficiently open and thoughtful deliberation by the leadership. A note of caution may be in order here. The issues agenda that is constructed during a self-study naturally and properly consists principally of areas of concern identified by bargaining unit members, but it should not become a substitute for the leaders' responsibility to plan. It is an abdication of the leadership role to simply listen to the members and then do whatever they urge. Effective organizational leaders have to survey the scene, think ahead about any external changes that are likely to affect bargaining unit members, and then formulate and suggest lines of activity to the members.

To structure the initial discussion by the appropriate leadership body, those tasked with guiding the work of the organizational audit should prepare a written report on the information collected. Such a report could include preliminary thoughts on changes to be considered. As with the earlier phase of the process, at this stage the leadership group might also wish to hold a retreat, perhaps again calling on the services of a discussion leader from outside the current leadership.

Types of Change

There are two types of changes that chapters generally consider after an organizational audit: programmatic and structural. Clearly, the content of the program should dictate the structure, since the union's day-to-day operations should be set up to maximize the effectiveness of its activities. It follows, then, that the first area of focus for deliberation is shifts in the local union's mission and agenda. This discussion should address whether to expand or contract the scope or to refocus the emphasis of the local organization's activities. For example, should more prominence be given to addressing issues of professional concern? Or would it benefit the union to approach with more vigor its economic bargaining agenda? Should the chapter concentrate on working with faculty governance or advocate more effectively for bargaining unit members' contract rights through the grievance and arbitration process? In general, the discussion should decide the proper emphasis for current issues and try to predict emerging issues, particularly in the light of the different bargaining unit constituencies.

Once the programmatic agenda for the union is formulated, the next area of inquiry is structural changes that can help the local organization pursue its goals. Financial considerations are key: Has the dues base adequately funded needed activities? Should expense-reimbursement policies be modified and levels of financial support for those doing the local organization's work be redefined? Another important set of considerations is the organizational division of labor: Does the present composition of committees, leadership bodies, paid local leaders, and volunteers (such as departmental representatives) compose the most effective means of carrying out the agreed-on work? Should protocols be set forth clarifying expectations for leaders, staff members, and others in the organization? Needless to say, whatever specific changes are considered, it is imperative to assess their effects on renewing membership participation and support.

When the organization deliberates change, it is important to keep in mind that the organizational agenda and activities do not exist in the abstract. Consider, for example, a situation where a SWOT analysis indicates that the institution's use of adjunct faculty members is of increasing importance to the members of a combined part-time and full-time faculty bargaining unit and that at present adjunct faculty members are underrepresented in the union's membership and leadership ranks. On a substantive level, this finding points toward the adoption of certain relevant issues as a key component of the local union's agenda. But it should also factor into consideration the organization's structure and mode of operations. For example, given the difference in time and availability between full-time and part-time faculty members, should the time and place of regular membership meetings be changed? Or should the notion of face-to-face meetings be reduced or even abandoned in favor of electronic or other communications? In sum, the issues to be pursued and the structural mechanisms to be put in place must be the frameworks for continuing to build a stronger organization.

From the beginning, then, organizing a collective bargaining chapter is a continuing process. A chapter that considers that process to be over once the contract is achieved does not understand the dynamics of organizational development, the inevitability of change, and the need to plan its own evolution if it is to adapt to the challenges of growth and maturity.

NOTES

1. For more information on the typical structure of unions, from the shop floor to the international level, see Mauer.
2. There are a number of useful guides to conducting focus groups, including Morgan and Krueger's *The Focus Group Kit.*

WORKS CITED

Mauer, Michael. *The Union Member's Complete Guide.* Annapolis: Union, 2001.

Morgan, David L., and Richard A. Krueger. *The Focus Group Kit.* Thousand Oaks: Sage, 1997.

Collective Bargaining

MICHAEL MAUER

The single most visible and dramatic activity undertaken by collective bargaining agents is the negotiation of contracts with an employer. Even when a resolution is achieved amicably—that is, without resort to a strike or other dramatic job action—the process demands, more than any other type of union activity, a public and sustained interplay between the core union leadership and the membership at large.

The considerable time and effort that unions put into achieving initial and subsequent collective bargaining agreements is understandable, for the union contract serves the same purpose in the workplace as that served by laws in the larger society: within the four walls of the workplace, the union contract is the binding set of rules setting forth not only what is permitted and what is prohibited but also the consequences for a breach of the rules.

In negotiating a contract, the concrete steps of bargaining are wrapped up in broader dynamics. This essay summarizes the various stages in the formal process of collective bargaining, explaining how initial contract proposals are shaped and what structure and format govern the back-and-forth that takes place at the bargaining table to shape a final agreement. But some discussion is also in order regarding the tactical measures that influence the conduct of the parties away from the bargaining table. For the collective bargaining process is in substantial measure a manifestation of power relations. While some collective bargaining relationships are considerably more enlightened than others, it is fair to assert that the quality of a negotiated academic contract settlement is more or less proportional to the strength of support for the bargaining positions advanced in the negotiations.

Preparations

Although the first formal act for the parties in the bargaining process is presentation of proposals at the bargaining table, successful local agents work dilligently to prepare for that event. An important question for both the union and the administration, (although considerably more important for the union) is, What organizational structure will best facilitate effective and successful negotiating? In addition to selecting a bargaining team, the union must decide how to constitute itself to carry out the necessary political decision making during bargaining. Of course, this decision includes communication between the membership and the union leadership and bargaining team.

Bargaining Leadership

Given the importance of the outcome of the collective bargaining process and the emotions that often come to the fore during that process, it is hardly surprising that dangers relating to the politics of bargaining may surface. There are two common pitfalls to guard against when working for a contract. The first is a bargaining team that comes to supplant the democratically elected union leadership by making the decisions that culminate in an eventual agreement. The other is a gap between the members' expectations for the final negotiated agreement and what is actually achievable.

To help guard against the first of these dangers, some academic unions choose not to include the top elected leadership on the bargaining team. This approach emphasizes the view that the negotiators are fundamentally technicians—specialists who are given tasks by the elected leadership and who go to each bargaining session mindful of the parameters that have been set. When this organizational structure is used, the bargaining team reports back to the elected leadership on a regular basis and thus understands that it has only such authority at bargaining sessions as the union leadership has ceded. Even where the chief negotiator is invested with great authority by a chapter's leaders, the local president generally does not participate directly at the table. It is important that the union have a counterpart "above the fray" who can deal with those administrative leaders, like the university president, who rarely come to the table.

Mindful of the importance of politics in the bargaining process, many academic unions also establish a bargaining council or steering committee that is distinct from both the bargaining team and the elected leadership. Quite often, this body has no formal authority and functions in an advisory capacity only. Such a group functions best politically when it embodies a cross section of the membership. It is this representative group that often recommends initial contract proposals, although the bargaining team requires some latitude to reformulate these in appropriate and realistic contract language.

Regardless of the union's bargaining structure, it is important to have organizational mechanisms that assist in keeping the members' needs and expectations in line with those of the union leadership and bargaining team. Some chapters establish a separate network of department representatives for this purpose; others expect the bargaining-council members to function in this capacity. Many unions already have in place a structure of localized representatives. Independent of the bargaining process, these members mirror the system of shop stewards found in nonacademic unions. Even with such a system, however, it may be wise to deputize a parallel network of volunteers specifically assigned to facilitate the process of bargaining. Such representatives, who serve as a link between the individual member and the union leadership and thus convey information "up" and "down," may also assist in organizing support for the bargaining team's efforts. The idea is to keep the union leadership abreast of what is on the minds of the individual members and to keep the members apprised of progress at the bargaining table. By this mechanism the leaders' bargaining-table agenda and trade-offs and the members' expectations are kept in sync.

The question of the composition of the union bargaining team has not only structural but also practical and political components. One question is whether the team is to be appointed by the local president, elected by the membership, or selected through a combination—nominated by the president (or the union's executive decision-making body), then ratified by the membership, for example. Often the membership of the team is settled at the same general meeting where the union's initial bargaining proposals are voted on. Although the seemingly democratic system of having the team elected by the entire membership may be appealing, chapters do well to consider the alternative of appointment. It is far easier to achieve the desirable balances on the bargaining team—having a mix of individuals that reflects the constituencies of the union and also possess the necessary knowledge and skills—when a unitary process is used.

Difficulties can emerge when the two bodies are not in sync, and many local organizations have found that such difficulties may be reduced when the sole elected body—the union leadership—appoints the other body to represent them at the bargaining table.

Size is another fundamental issue for bargaining-team composition. Working on a contract requires a tremendous amount of time and effort in conducting necessary strategic preparation and in gathering research as well as in engaging in face-to-face negotiations. On the one hand, teams need to be small enough to work efficiently. Chapters are also reluctant to use up the universe of activist talent that will be needed by the union to engage in the other, concomitant parts of the bargaining process. On the other hand, it is also important to establish a bargaining team large enough to permit inclusion of people who have a direct understanding of the needs of the various members in the bargaining unit. There are nuances in the interests of tenured and junior faculty members, full-time and part-time, male and female, members of different races or cultural groups, and the union benefits by making sure that the bargaining team can speak forcefully and accurately for all. There are, of course, other ways of including the needed diversity in the bargaining process. The union can, for example, choose to have nonbargaining team members contribute their expertise to particular bargaining sessions through various forms of consultation, including attendance at relevant sessions.

Proposal Development: Acquiring Information and Expertise

The mechanisms of research and drafting that many unions establish to supplement the work of the bargaining team raise practical and political considerations. There are complex topics, like retirement plans or health-care coverage, that require specialized expertise. Sometimes the bargaining team will designate some team members to compose specialized subcommittees. More often, the chapter will designate those colleagues who have the needed expertise to lend a hand, an approach that serves two purposes. First, it draws on specialized knowledge not likely to be at the disposal of bargaining-team members, and, second, it includes a wider group of regular members in the work of framing a new contract.

One component of collective bargaining that comes naturally to academics is the acquisition of needed information. Accustomed to data collection and analysis, teachers and scholars usually have little trouble grasping the importance of acquiring detailed information, from both members and the administration, before setting the agenda for negotiations and drawing up initial proposals. Savvy academic union leaders understand that, beyond the tactical uses for information, there is a strategic component. Since collective bargaining is a process of give-and-take, each party along the way makes a series of decisions based on what trade-offs are the most and least desirable. Knowing beforehand what resources are at the disposal of the administration and what decisions about allocation of resources have been made gives the union a leg up in calculating what to push for and what to trade off.

What tends to come less naturally to academic unionists is the political component of information collection. The circulation of a written survey, for example, can be a valuable device to establish the depth of support among unit members for particular items on the bargaining agenda. Written surveys (which may include electronic formats) may be combined with meetings (departmental or larger). Experienced union leaders understand that the very act of soliciting a person's views communicates that those views matter. Similarly, when it becomes apparent that differences are emerging in the union's ranks during a stage in bargaining, the leadership may convene open meetings, not so much to learn what members are thinking as to let frustrated people vent and clear the air. Obviously, meetings allow for more give-and-take than surveys do. Finally, even an objective questionnaire can be designed to educate the responders on the issue being addressed.

Determination of the needs and desires of bargaining unit members is the first step in gathering information. The second step is requesting and acquiring facts and figures from the administration, an obligation that may be imposed on the administration by contract or by any applicable bargaining law. Unions routinely submit extensive requests for documents on such matters as pay and benefits, staffing and other personnel matters (including specific individual salaries), and other budgetary and financial information. Since some combination of foot-dragging and the legitimate burdens in collecting and producing extensive data means that months may be needed to obtain important information, it behooves the union to forward its requests to the administration well in advance of the commencement of negotiations.

Information useful in setting the bargaining agenda and in formulating proposals may be obtained from other sources as well. A union considering a new fringe benefit, for example, needs to do its homework on the costs and details of the desired coverage from potential providers. Other local bargaining organizations (including unions representing other workers on the same campus) or state or national affiliates of the union can provide useful information on contract provisions already in place on other campuses. In determining the priorities for negotiations, the union needs to analyze what is broken in the old contract and must be fixed in the new one. So, for example, either by reviewing grievance files or through extensive consultation with the grievance officer of the union, consideration can be given to those sources of dissatisfaction that are not adequately addressed by the current collective bargaining agreement; necessary provisions may be lacking, or they may be covered in a less than satisfactory way.

Proposal Formulation

Once the data have been solicited, acquired, and analyzed, the union refines its bargaining agenda and drafts its proposals. Again, this phase of the process has both practical and political components. With a solid grasp of what unit members wish to see in a new contract, the union has much of what it needs to set priorities and draft specific language. But unions, at their own peril, fail to factor in the larger political considerations. For example, it is always a mistake to accede to the "tyranny of the majority" in formulating proposals. Recently, the clearest examples of this danger have occurred when rebellions by frustrated adjunct faculty members take their full-time union colleagues by surprise. These adjunct faculty members may have reached the boiling point in the course of the repeated rounds of bargaining that reflect only the interests of the full-time, tenure-eligible faculty. Other academic unionists have learned the hard way the consequences of failing to educate the membership about the importance of the union's institutional needs in the bargaining process. For example, union leaders may properly determine that attaining lost-time provisions in the contract will enable the union to be self-sustaining, but if members view that priority as merely self-serving, the resultant division in the ranks inevitably weakens the union's bargaining position. As with other parts of the bargaining process, then, the task of formulating proposals has two important features: in its technical capacity, it determines content; in accordance with its political imperative, it gains member understanding and support.

Ground Rules

Ground rules are the final preliminary to bargaining. Parties to collective bargaining generally agree on at least some of the negotiation format in advance. The matters covered may be routine, such as timing and location of sessions and the manner of recording sessions, but all the ground rules, to a greater or lesser degree, have political and strategic implications. Take, for example, the question of who may attend sessions. Employers often seek closed sessions, limiting attendance and participation to members of the bargaining teams. Unions do well to resist any such restrictions, although there are rare topics that require confidentiality. While members may seldom insist on actually sitting in on bargaining sessions, any agreement to prohibit their presence can easily be construed as the effort of a small group of insiders to preserve their prerogatives and limit accountability. Moreover, "packing" a bargaining session may be a useful union tactic both to show members the employer's recalcitrance and to send a message to the administration that the union troops are restless.

Unions are well served if they work out in advance how the union bargainers and leadership will conduct themselves inside and outside the bargaining room. Nonacademic unions tend to adopt a fairly formal approach to the face-to-face sessions, appointing the chief negotiator to do all the speaking unless another person is designated during the course of a particular session. But higher education unions recognize that such a practice can be seen as overly restrictive through the prism of freewheeling academic culture and thus often adopt a less disciplined approach to behavior at the table. As with all aspects of unionism, however, one size does not fit all. When faced with a chief negotiator for the administration who is a "hired gun" labor-law practitioner and with an administration that takes verbatim notes of all that is said, an academic union would be acting negligently if it did not exercise self-discipline in deciding who speaks for the union and when.

Statements about the progress of negotiations made outside the bargaining room are also an important consideration. Sometimes the bargaining parties agree to a ground rule containing restrictions on statements to members, the larger campus community, or the media; however, unions should be careful to resist pressure for ground rules that require any great degree of confidentiality. Given the culture of the academy, the failure of academic union leaders to apprise their members of the progress of negotiations can easily be taken as a sign that the process is not a sufficiently democratic one. Moreover, exposing administration recalcitrance to the light of day can be one of the union's greatest sources of strength in negotiations. At the same time, union leaders must be sensitive to the sometimes delicate dynamics of adversarial collective bargaining and the importance of developing and sustaining, where possible, a degree of trust. In most circumstances, then, it is nothing short of foolhardy to proclaim loudly and publicly every last detail of what has occurred during bargaining sessions. The key is to strike the right balance between keeping the members reasonably aware of progress at the table, or lack thereof, and leaving the negotiators room to maneuver.

The Bargaining Process

The scheduling and pace of negotiations is part science and part art. Although the parties commonly agree in their ground rules how often they generally will meet and for how long, practical considerations can alter the timing in large part. Factors include the availability of members of the bargaining teams and others involved in the process, travel that may be necessary in a multicampus system, the date of expiration of the current contract, and so on. So it is simply impossible to determine at the outset when each bargaining session will take place and how long it will last. Additionally, the pace and intensity of negotiations have a character of their own and tend to pick up as the process unfolds; much is unpredictable. At times, the dynamics of progress in bargaining will dictate that the parties should put in extra time. At other times, experienced negotiators recognize that they've hit a temporary logjam in the give-and-take and that a breather will allow for cooler heads to prevail.

Many tactical and strategic considerations come into play in determining the order in which the parties will tackle different bargaining topics. The conventional wisdom holds that noneconomic issues should be resolved before dollars and cents are determined. The side that has significant noneconomic proposals is often concerned that these issues will fall off the table once the economics are settled. Management is typically concerned to withhold what it regards as its final economic offer until it feels certain that the agreement is all but complete; it does not want to provide an opportunity for renewed demands. Another argument for resolving noneconomic matters first is that they should be resolved on their own merits and not traded off for financial provisions in the new contract. Such an argument must recognize, however, not only that unions may sacrifice what is termed *language* (that is, noneconomic matters) for economics but also that some academic unions may subordinate economics to language. Thus, although union negotiators often have to wage a fight well into the course of bargaining to get an initial economic proposal put on the table by the employer, sometimes the employer will attempt to preempt the union effort to enhance professional rights. It does this by offering an attractive economic package contingent on the union's dropping other demands or consenting to a long-term agreement.

Conflict and Conflict Resolution

Sometimes bargaining is conducted in an atmosphere that remains amicable throughout, and a settlement that pleases both parties is reached through the straightforward process of give-and-take at the bargaining table. Although such conditions are too rare, when a round of bargaining is conducted by reasonable people of good will on both sides of the table—operating in economic and political circumstances that permit the forging of fair resolution of the issues—good feelings can be shared. Far more often, even in the academy, the process becomes heated and the parties find themselves unable to reach a mutually satisfactory agreement without considerable tension and discord. Thus, it is necessary to examine two additional important areas of the collective bargaining process: pressure campaigns and impasse resolution.

Pressure Tactics

Everyone is familiar with the strike—a collective withholding of services to exert pressure on an employer to extend more favorable contract terms. But, although this "ultimate weapon" has been used with decreasing frequency in recent years, unions have increasingly recognized the importance of having their arguments at the table accompanied by activities away from the table that pressure the decision makers on the other side. Systematic pressure geared toward obtaining a favorable contract is referred to as a contract campaign. Contract campaigns have both long-term and short-term goals. Most immediately, of course, is a favorable outcome in negotiations. But contract campaigns can also strengthen the unity of the faculty organization not only during bargaining but also thereafter. Increasingly, contract campaigns link the union's bread-and-butter concerns with a broader social agenda. For academic workers, outreach to the public raises such issues as quality, access, and affordability.

The importance of examining the types of pressure campaigning that accompany the formal negotiations process is particularly critical for academic bargaining. Academics are, after all, professional truth seekers. A foundational belief for those toiling in the academy is that the best argument grounded on the best data and fortified by the most rigorous analysis will be, at the end of the day, irresistible. The flaw that often afflicts those engaged in academic collective bargaining is the ultimately ungrounded conviction that the truth will prevail. Although one's ability to grasp and articulate "the truth" is a necessary component of academic collective bargaining, by itself truth rarely ensures a just result.

Contract campaigns date back to the 1930s, when a militant style of organizing and bargaining typified the Congress of Industrial Organizations (CIO). In a departure from the American Federation of Labor's (AFL) more narrow conception of its role as delivering on wages and benefits, the CIO began to reconfigure the labor-management relationship to frame union issues as the public's issues. To put it another way, the unions' organizing and bargaining goals became a cause. After World War II, what has been called business unionism became prevalent again, as organized labor increasingly relied on lawyers and professional union staff members and full-time officers. But during the 1960s and after, the civil rights and other social movements, in conjunction with a revived AFL-CIO, revitalized grass-roots organizing and activity as a means of strengthening the union's hand.

The key to effective contract campaigns is direct involvement of the membership. The larger the members' investment in the bargaining process, the greater the members' willingness to demonstrate public support for the union's positions. When member buy-in is built from the outset, when their participation is sought in the shaping of proposals and in the bargaining agenda, and when members are educated about the logistics of the bargaining process, the outcomes of that process become more urgent to those members. A characteristic of these campaigns is that the union seeks to involve other groups whose interests may coincide with those of the academics in the bargaining unit—the student body, staff unions, administrations, the public, the legislature, and faculty governance bodies.

The tactical components in exerting pressure for a contract are determined by local conditions: what types of activities suit the temperament and style of the membership, students, and other potential supporters? The key is to determine a menu of actions that colleagues will support and participate in. The goal is to educate the campus community and the public about the issues at stake in the bargaining. Another important effect is to increase the visibility of the contract fight.

Successful academic contract campaigns draw from a variety of actions that start with the relatively simple and become increasingly ambitious. Within the institution significant features of a contract campaign may include

publicity items, like badges, petitions or pledge cards, office-door signs

frequent internal communications, like newsletters, e-mail, electronic chat rooms, op-ed pieces and other coverage in campus media

campus activity, like getting contract-negotiation news on the agenda for departmental or senate meetings, distributing handbills at appearances by upper-level administrators, gathering at bargaining sessions and at key areas of the campus, providing speakers to address campus organizations about the negotiations and their significance

Activities outside the institution may involve

media publicity, including letters to the editor and op-ed pieces, advertisements in local newspapers and other periodicals, radio spots, leafleting on issues and informational picketing at university-sponsored events

demonstrations, like attending (invited or otherwise) meetings of the board of trustees, picketing and handbilling the offices of the central administration and other visible locations, picketing and handbilling the homes of the most intransigent administrators and trustees

Conflict Resolution

When the parties find themselves unable to settle the contract in the course of the regular bargaining sessions, a variety of procedural devices may be available to assist them. This area of collective bargaining is tightly governed by the legal environment in which the parties operate. In the public sector, legislation or judicial decisions, including the legality of strikes and other tactics of economic coercion, may define or limit actions. In the private sector there are also intricate rules governing the conduct of strikes, which are legal. As a practical matter, though, these are of little consequence for full-time private-sector faculty members; since *Yeshiva*, such unions operate without legal protection anyhow. The discussion that follows offers the range of possibilities, but readers should consult with knowledgeable practitioners or labor attorneys for firm guidance.

Mediation is a relatively informal process in which a neutral third party attempts to facilitate agreement. Mediators can use a combination of separate meetings with each party and some joint sessions to serve the useful functions of enhancing communication between the parties, suggesting some creative approaches that may help break a deadlock, or doing some gentle arm-twisting. The last of these mechanisms must be restrained since mediation is a process that, by its nature, cannot compel agreement. Besides the practical component of mediation, like other possible dispute-resolution procedures, it may play an important political role in settling a contract. For example, sometimes the handwriting is on the wall: the compromises necessary to resolve a bargaining dispute may be clear, but one side or the other may need the political cover of an outside party to suggest or impose those resolutions before it can acquiesce to them publicly.

Fact-finding is a more formal procedure for resolving impasses. This assignment may be conducted by a single person or by a panel. While it is not a formal legal proceeding, fact-finding shares many of the quasi-judicial attributes of grievance arbitrations—a hearing on the record (often with a transcript), an advocate (sometimes a lawyer) for each party, witnesses, and documents formally introduced into the record. The process culminates with a written report by the fact finder. Generally, the fact finder's reports contain only advisory recommendations about settlement. But some procedures do not provide for any recommendations at all to be set forth; instead, the fact finder clarifies the issues in dispute and suggests possible resolutions for the parties to consider. Still other variations culminate in binding recommendations—sometimes triggered by a series of events that take place after issuance of the fact finder's report, such as failure of one party or the other to reject the recommendations by a supermajority vote. Sometimes a fact finder, having developed an understanding of the issues and rapport with the parties, can mediate a settlement, even after the issuance of the report.

The most formal tool available to settle deadlocked bargaining is a type of arbitration referred to as interest arbitration. This process should be distinguished from the arbitration used to resolve contract-grievance disputes. Interest arbitration serves as an alternative to the application of direct economic pressure, such as a strike by the union or a lockout by the employer. As with grievance arbitration, a relatively formal hearing is conducted in which sworn witnesses testify and documentary evidence is received, after which the parties file posthearing briefs. The subsequent ruling imposes the terms chosen by the arbitrator to settle the contract, which are essentially not subject to appeal. (There are variations in the format, most notably last-best-offer arbitration, in which the arbitrator must choose between the precise proposals presented by one or the other party at the conclusion of bargaining, either issue by issue or as a package.) Where the law permits, the threat of an imposed settlement often enables the arbitrator to facilitate a mediated agreement.

Mediators, fact finders, and arbitrators make their recommendations and decisions based on a variety of factors. These will generally include the economic and political realities, the terms prevailing at similar higher education institutions or other employers in the community ("comparables"), and the degree to which one party or the other already has compromised its position on the issues. A union entering into mediation, fact-finding, or or arbitration should keep in mind that these factors will affect the outcome, since terms agreed to by the parties directly, without recourse to a third party, are often less influenced by them.

Within the confines of the law or what is politically feasible, bargaining impasses may also be resolved by means of a strike. Although striking may be the most potent weapon available to a union, and although many academic unions have used strikes of limited duration with great success, resort to a strike must not be taken lightly. It is a high-stakes maneuver, and it should be risked only when the critical elements of success are clearly in place: broad and deep bargaining unit support; commitment to the issues remaining on the table, from union members as well as from students and the broader community; and the financial wherewithal to sustain the strike. When evaluating the efficacy of a strike, academic bargaining organizations have found that success may lie in devising creative alternatives to an all-out work stoppage, such as excluding medical schools and labs from the walkout. The mirror image of a strike is the option of a lockout imposed by the employer, in which the unilateral decision is made to shut down production until the union concedes to the settlement terms offered by the employer. This tactic is rarely, if ever, used in academic labor relations.

In the chess game that is labor relations, the union should know at the outset what paths may lead to acceptable, realistic outcomes. In many ways, the most desirable means to achieve contract settlement is direct, face-to-face meetings between the parties that yield satisfactory compromise. Such collaboration maintains collegiality and tends to produce more workable contract terms than the Solomonic solutions that may be shaped by outside parties. Good-faith negotiating can also save the parties both the time and whatever money may be needed if the resort to outside, formal proceedings were invoked. And such agreements can preserve the ability of the union membership to vote on contract ratification, a right that may be preempted by resort to one of the third-party procedures.

In many circumstances, however, it simply will not be practical to achieve an amicable resolution across the bargaining table. The obstacles may be internal to the process—negotiators who prove incapable of reaching reasonable compromises, for instance. External considerations may preclude the give-and-take needed for successful compromises as well. On the employer side, the trustees or the legislature may be too unyielding. On the union side, politics may force the union leadership to undertake a dramatic and public fight in order to satisfy the members' need to feel that the final resolution is the best that could be achieved.

As early as possible in the bargaining process, the union leadership must consider the means to be used in resolving an impasse. If the negotiations approach a deadlock, many tactics and strategies must be weighed. One practical consideration is what to present at the bargaining table when successful compromise seems unlikely, since the union will want to preserve sufficient room to modify its positions during the course of mediation, fact-finding, or arbitration. In circumstances where a strike seems likely, the union will want to hone the strike issues to those that can generate sufficient support from the union's members and key constituencies.

Timing is another key element. Union strategists need to decide the most propitious time to reach a final settlement. In public institutions, for example, it is important to keep an eye on the legislative budgeting timetable. In determining the best time for the closing stages of negotiations, one consideration might be the time when a ratification vote is feasible. Another consideration may be when a job action can most successfully be pursued. With skilled negotiators, the timing of the end point of the bargaining process is, in many ways, within the control of the union. The pace of face-to-face sessions can be adjusted, for example, and the parties may agree to an extension of the contract expiration deadline.

If a strike is to be the last resort, some campus unions try to launch it at the beginning of a semester, when it is psychologically easier to break the bond (albeit on a temporary basis) between student and educator. Others believe that mid- or end-term strikes, although possibly harder to organize, are likely to be more effective and shorter in duration. Academics often precede full strikes with informational picketing or one-day strikes; these increase pressure at the bargaining table and prepare the membership to engage in a longer term work stoppage should it be necessary.

Once final agreement is reached, unions are well advised to volunteer to write down terms that have not yet been fully worked out, in order to gain the advantage of controlling nuances in the language used. (Responsible parties will have initialed off on each tentative point of agreement during the course of negotiations.) Prudence dictates that only after the final document is reviewed and signed by the parties should a public announcement be made that a settlement has been reached. While a joint administration-union statement may be released, the union will want to communicate directly and in greater detail with its members and supporters.

Mutual-Gains Bargaining

In recent years, a distinctly different approach to collective bargaining has been developed for use in both the public and private sectors. This less adversarial approach goes by several different names: mutual-gains bargaining, interest-based bargaining, or sometimes win-win bargaining.

Traditional bargaining requires negotiators who possess some of the skills needed for successfully playing poker and chess. As in a card game, where players are expected to hold their cards close to the vest, the unwritten rules governing bargaining make it acceptable deliberately to confuse the other participants by posturing and bluffing. As in a chess game, skilled negotiators plan several moves in advance: if I trade off a particular item now, what can I get immediately in return, and what additional maneuvering will I then be free to engage in?

Mutual-gains bargaining, on the other hand, starts from different assumptions. The fundamental one is that the parties to a collective bargaining relationship have a joint interest in sharing information and in working together cooperatively to come up with mutually satisfactory resolutions to the issues before them. In this type of bargaining, all items on the table are seen as problems to be solved creatively by both parties, and the style reflects this. Participants often undergo preparatory orientation by a facilitator. They sit intermingled, rather than each team facing the other. Additionally, fewer caucuses are taken because the negotiators put more effort into brainstorming together than into crafting formal proposals and counterproposals.

When the union is dealing with an enlightened employer—one genuinely seeking to reach a fair agreement that will serve both parties' interests over time—mutual-gains bargaining can be an excellent tool. It can enable the union to get information that it might otherwise not have, and it can be efficient in leading to creative and comprehensive solutions to problems. But academic unions, like others that have tried mutual-gains bargaining, have on occasion learned the hard way of its dangers. Unlike traditional bargaining, where the union has substantial incentive to keep its members aware of what is going on at the bargaining table, the mutual-gains approach emphasizes building trust instead of staking out positions and drawing lines at the table. Consequently, too many unions have failed to do the necessary groundwork so that, if settlement is not reached using the mutual-gains approach, it is possible to shift gears on short notice and take on the employer in a contract fight.

The fundamental problem with mutual-gains bargaining, however, is that it fails to appreciate the basic political accommodations that very often are demanded by conflicting interests. Bargaining requires the threat of impasse to drive both parties to subordinate their wishes. Impasse resolution procedures, up to and including the strike, force both sides to reassess their priorities and seek the most favorable available compromise.

Bargaining is, in the end, not a game of unremitting conflict but a mode of conflict resolution. Ordinarily, it provides years of stability punctuated by relatively short periods of stress.

Making Collective Bargaining Work

DANIEL J. JULIUS

I have been involved as a scholar and largely management-side practitioner with unionization in higher education since the early 1970s. I was, therefore, intrigued when I was invited by my colleague Ernst Benjamin to write an essay designed primarily for an audience of union members or those eligible for representation rather than for employer spokespersons. Unfortunately, few forums enable us to speak freely across jurisdictional lines.

In this regard, if collective bargaining is initiated, the representatives and constituents of both parties need to ensure that the labor-relations function is managed effectively. I do not take a position on whether collective bargaining in higher education is harmful or beneficial. Simply put, large numbers of faculty and staff members have chosen to be represented by unions for purposes of collective bargaining. Of course, ensuring that relations are effective is easier said than done. This difficulty can be attributed to unique organizational features of the institutions where collective bargaining in higher education has gained a foothold.

This essay explores the following issues:

What general observations about unionization offer insight into enhancing labor-relations processes in colleges and universities?

Can we identify particular characteristics of decision-making environments in universities that enhance or impede collective bargaining? Can we identify how these characteristics influence the behavior of union and employer representatives?

Can we discern trends from industrial labor relations in industry, primarily from the perspective of craft bargaining, that elucidate similar processes in higher education? More specifically, are lessons for academe to be found in the actions of unions representing musicians, electricians, printers, or other craft-type employees?

Can we identify any salient organizational impacts associated with unionization?

The suggestions and observations that follow are pertinent for individual colleges and universities as well as for public systems, although personalities and organizational and regulatory environments vary by region, institutional affiliation, and, obviously, institutional size.

General Observations Regarding Unionization

It is difficult to isolate the effects of employee unionism from the consequences of other intellectual, political, economic, and social forces that have transformed the academy. For example, institutional transition, falling enrollments, a decline of federal and state funding, increased government regulation, the loss of public confidence in the value of a college degree, the continuing influence of state governments and coordinating boards, and the tragedy of September 11, like collective bargaining, have affected the collegiate environment. Despite many prognostications, there is simply no conclusive evidence that academic unionization, in and of itself, negatively influences institutional quality, the teacher-student mentor relationship, or professionalization of faculty members. Nor is there evidence that it positively influences overall compensation, workload, or job security. The highest paid and most secure, as well as the lowest paid and least secure, faculty and staff members (in both the public and private sectors) remain unorganized. The effect of collective bargaining on individual salaries and promotional opportunities for faculty and staff members also defies easy answers. Indeed, unionization may freeze an institution's capabilities to address these important concerns. Further, it is difficult to characterize the motive for academic unionization, or, more specifically, to identify what kind of movement the organized professoriate represents. Academic labor unions travel light ideologically and will swap goods with just about anyone. The quip that American labor is on the one hand an act of faith and on the other a thousand small movements rowing vigorously in their own directions certainly characterizes the union movement in higher education.

It is a complex task to discern what organizational strategies and behaviors are most appropriate in unionized institutions. Decision makers representing academic unions and employees have been innovative as they have adopted and adapted industrial collective bargaining processes to existing institutional structures. Unionization serves as a catalyst for continued organizational change. These changes, in turn, demand new management strategies. In this regard, the support of the institutional chief executive officer is key. In countless organizations, collective bargaining has gone awry because a president or chancellor (or union president) failed to understand either political processes attendant to collective bargaining or concomitant institutional vulnerabilities made manifest by employee negotiation tactics at state legislatures.

Those responsible for labor relations (regardless of whom is represented) need the organizational clout and autonomy to effect best practices. Of course, the notion of management is still suspect in higher education. On occasion, the dictates of collegial governance systems and cultures collide with the dictates of collective bargaining. Once unionization arrives, some decisions can no longer be consultative; collective bargaining entails that the faculty and the institution have a relationship where not all interests are shared. The labor-relations environment imposes employee and employer obligations on the parties. These facts are inescapable. Such constraints need not mean continual conflict or the end of consultative governance but a recognition that decision-making processes, legal obligations, and the individuals involved in university affairs change.

Whereas collective bargaining generates centralizing forces (revolving around campuswide or systemwide units, wherein consistency in interpretation and application of labor policies is warranted), organizational and cultural norms in most colleges and universities resist centralizing tendencies. Although we must be cautious about generalizations, the effective management of collective bargaining demands a degree of centralization in decision-making authority and requires moderate doses of conformity, consistency, and standardization.

Simply put, once a particular course of action is sanctioned, someone must hold individuals (or the institutions they represent) accountable. A similar dynamic also exists within unions themselves. In many institu-

tions or systems, however, leaders venerate institutional or school autonomy, flexibility, and delegated authority. Conflicting organizational
forces, which pull individuals in central offices (union and management)
and those on campuses (or schools) in opposite directions, are problematic. In larger unionized systems, for example, select campuses or
schools (richer, bigger, more prestigious, more autonomous) may operate on the assumption that head or system offices are unable to cen-
tralize all decision-making prerogatives or hold campus executives
(union or administrative) completely accountable. Such campuses or
schools may thus act independently to address institutional or school
concerns. These actions generate real tension between those who negotiate and those responsible for oversight of represented or administrative
employees.

The course of collective bargaining is often determined by institutional conditions in existence before bargaining. Highly adversarial relationships often predate the vote for collective bargaining. Once negotiations commence, faculty and staff unions endeavor to incorporate
existing policies and procedures into collective bargaining agreements
that reflect each party's understanding of how particular rules, regulations, and practices should have operated in more tranquil times. Precisely because collective bargaining is determined by preexisting conditions (often aggravated by inappropriate leadership practices or agendas
by those representing the administration or union), the identity of the
particular bargaining agent representing employees is less important
than the resources at the disposal of institutional or union representatives. In other words, structural variables, not the bargaining agent (i.e.,
the union), inform bargaining relationships and ultimately determine
labor-relations outcomes. For example, whether academic employees at
the California State University or the University of California are represented by the American Federation of Teachers, National Education
Association, or United Auto Workers bears little, if any, relation to the
California legislature's influence on collective bargaining through political processes.

Collective bargaining in organized systems by faculty members has
inevitably attracted the attention of, and, in some cases, stimulated action
by, academically related employees. The experience to date with recent
graduate student unions offers several clues to those who seek to profes-
sionalize the process and enhance bargaining relationships. Graduate stu-

dents ruled eligible to join unions seem somewhat less inclined to be represented by traditional faculty unions (AFT, NEA, AAUP) and have sometimes cast their lot with the UAW, Communication Workers of America, or other industrial-type unions. Administrators in institutions where graduate students are seeking or have obtained union representation (the University of California System, New York University, Yale) may not possess the labor-management experience, resources, or power to address demands of these employees (or students, depending upon the institution involved!). Even in cases where graduate assistants have been unionized for years, such as at the Universities of Michigan and Wisconsin, bargaining relationships are not always stable. In California, union negotiators have sought to influence bargaining through federal agencies, state legislators, and governor's offices. This political action, in turn, has increased institutional vulnerability and decreased the influence of university and system executives to manage negotiations. Union leaders, who promote these tactics, might bear in mind that when administrative counterparts lack necessary resources or authority to respond effectively, both sides suffer. Institutional leaders might reflect on the idea that it is easier to deal with an association of graduate students who may not yet be cynical about the intentions of the university rather than with those represented by professional negotiators who have honed their bargaining skills in industrial plants or automobile factories.

The individuals responsible for managing the collective bargaining process will continue to shape not only the process but also the perceptions of others toward unionization. For academics to be effective in bargaining, it is necessary for them to understand the technical aspects of negotiations and to grasp the essential components and rules of contract administration. The ability to manage conflict and to live with ambiguity are requirements for successful relationships. Unfortunately, mistakes made in the initial phases of collective bargaining may not become salient for at least a decade; for instance, the significance of faulty contract language may only becomes apparent when the institution initiates layoff procedures or attempts to change promotion and tenure criteria.

Labor relations conducted inappropriately are analogous to the situation where a husband and wife fail to nurture their marriage. One day, the administration and faculty wake up as strangers living in the same institution. In this respect, strong leadership is characterized by the ability to legitimize and institutionalize the labor-relations process, to ensure that labor-relations outcomes reflect desires of key organizational constituencies, to take initiative and respond to unexpected situations, to grasp power in organizations, to initiate strategic actions that neutralize organizational opponents and, lastly, to deploy the technical and experiential skills needed to select one course of action over another (when to take a strike, when to come to agreement, etc.). Of course, there is no antidote for senior leaders of unions or universities who do not support their counterparts or who allow their decisions to be determined by personal or political exigencies or, worse, who do not know what they do not know and thus fail to listen to the people who do.

Unionization enhances the influence of elected political leaders on higher education policy and outcomes. Unquestionably, the governor and top elected legislative leaders are drawn into the debate on funding, programs, workload, and even the curriculum in ways unimagined in nonunionized settings. In New York, California, several Midwestern states, and throughout New England, the collective bargaining process now routinely involves the legislature's or governor's chief labor-relations representative. In some locales, this involvement has enhanced bargaining relationships. More often, it has resulted in a decline of autonomy and flexibility for institutional systems and executives (also for union officials, particularly if local campus chapters can influence negotiations in a manner not supported by national union officers or in a manner that results in the whipsawing of campus locals in the system). Inevitably, institutional autonomy and the ability to effect policy or manage policy outcomes are eroded. In the worst-case scenario, bargaining becomes dysfunctional for both parties, particularly if legislators or national union executives are constantly drawn into the process and negotiate settlements without concern for local constituents or conditions.

Structuring decision-making processes to ensure that the system, institution, or union spokespersons effectuate strategy and policy (in areas of finance, legislative relations, and academic affairs) in alignment with collective bargaining objectives is crucial for success. Labor-relations decision processes and structures should accommodate the following:

> The position and authority of individuals who negotiate, either for the union or for the institution, must be given sufficient status and power to enable them to demand that other leaders and constituents uphold agreements made at the bargaining table and also to bring institutional or union policies into alignment with collective bargaining strategy.

Power in the labor context means more than simply positional authority. To exercise influence in colleges and universities, leaders need to demonstrate personal integrity and have the ability to articulate goals consistent with the mission of the institution. The will to influence decision-making outcomes relies also on effective performance. Performance, in turn, is contingent on personal characteristics; the perceptions of others; and an accurate understanding of external factors (state funding, enrollment trends, etc.), which ultimately circumscribe how individuals and institutions respond to labor-management dynamics.

Senior institutional leaders affiliated with labor and management must discuss and endeavor to agree on labor-relations objectives, priorities, and collective bargaining parameters before the expiration of contracts.

Information (ideas, anticipated outcomes, strategy, etc.) must flow between senior and lower-level union officers, faculty members, and administrators. In other words, constituents who raise questions in regard to labor-relations outcomes must have open informal and formal channels available to work toward appropriate organizational responses.

To understand why designing appropriate decision-making structures and exercising influence is difficult, we must understand the organizational environment in which decisions are made. While consensus does not exist on this topic, salient organizational characteristics effecting the decision-making environment are reviewed below:

Decision is by committee. Because expertise, not hierarchical office, is the organizing principle of academic institutions, committees of experts decide many critical issues. However, in many instances, committees provide the illusion of participation and involvement, whereas the real decision-making prerogatives are reserved for a small elite.

Participation is fluid. Most decision makers are amateurs in administration and management, primarily engaged in pursuing their professions. As a consequence, they wander in and out of the decision process, and power belongs to those who stay long enough to exercise it.

Issues are revolving. Issues have a way of always coming around again. Decisions are subject to pressures from outside groups, clients, and students. Other professionals push the same or similar issues full circle. Decisions are not made as much as they are pinned down temporarily.

There is a "subsidiary" process. The longer it takes to make a decision, the greater the number of issues that are piled onto the original subject. People hoping to accomplish several things at one time burden simple decisions with countless subsidiary ones.

Conflict is common. Professional groups, clients, unions, and others support divergent ideas and goals (often ambiguous) for academic organizations. As a consequence, conflict over goals and outcomes is common.

Activities are interdependent. Most leaders need the support of others to be effective, but few have formal authority over would-be supporters. Leaders thus depend on informal influence with colleagues, supervisors, and subordinates in different departments, divisions, or schools to get things accomplished. Those who seek to be effective must learn to work through others.

Power vacuums exist. Environmental vulnerability, the culture of committees, shared power, and interdependent and decentralized decision making often result in a power vacuum in academic environments. Most in leadership positions (union and administrative) are used to working with critics, few of whom will make tough decisions.

To summarize, the decision-making process in academic organizations does not resemble a normal bureaucracy or the community-of-peers model associated with the medieval guild. Decisions are neither made in a simple manner where form follows process nor is the process so chaotic as to resemble a decisional garbage can. Several images are more appropriate. First, the structure of the organization is continually challenged and highly political. Second, the decision-making environment reflects competing groups. Finally, the unsettled character of the process can be captured by using the term *decision flowing* instead of *decision making*. Decision making has a finality to it; decision flowing sounds like a never-ending process.

The implementation of an appropriate decision-making structure that accommodates organizational realities in higher-education systems is a sine qua non for the effective management of the labor-relations function. However, success entails that leaders understand that decision making is a highly circumscribed activity. Indeed, it is crucial for university or union leaders interested in making effective decisions to know not only how to influence others in order to gain support but also—and, most importantly—to know how to manage the consequences of decisions. Managing the consequences of decisions may mean that faculty members or administrators control (or at least neutralize) ever-present organizational, personal, and other competitive pressures, both internal and external, invariably focused on people and programs. Such pressures emanate from many factors: a scarcity of resources, the politicization of trustees or regents, the need for specialized workers, licensing agencies, state or federal dictates, workforce demands (part-time versus full-time employment), colleagues, senates, labor unions, and the like. Most leaders spend the greater part of their time reacting to others' agendas. In reality, decision-making prerogatives are constrained.

The Broader Industrial-Labor-Relations Context

Managing the decision-making architecture will not, in and of itself, bring about productive bargaining relationships. To respond effectively to unionization in higher education, observing the activities and behavior of craft unions in industry (e.g., electricians, plumbers, musicians, printers) is of value. Such crafts are known to be flexible within their own groups but rigid in their external relations. They can be adaptable, but adaptability is not among their prime characteristics. If craft employment conditions and rights are respected, the craft will concern itself with their administration. But if basic rights, such as tenure, are threatened, then rigid reactions can occur. When the group rises to defend its established jurisdiction or practices, a great deal of nonproductive activity can result. Crafts have the ability to participate well in the managerial process, but the relation of a craft to its management can become destructive if both parties focus on defending their respective rights and neglect solving the problem at hand.

Craft employees who work on project-type tasks usually have the freedom to run their affairs autonomously. The contractor for whom they work counts on this. However, when craftspeople work in institutions, the relationship with administrators who head those institutions can pose problems. The cause of these difficulties is frequently misstated. Observers anticipate a clash of viewpoints because the "craft orientation" is often contrasted with that of the "bureaucrat." In reality, craftspeople and bureaucrats are similar in their stress on universal standards, specialization, and evaluation of competence on the basis of performance. Conflicts arise not because of the differences but because of the similarities.

In higher education, as professional specialists appeared in the early twentieth century, they soon confronted another emerging group of specialists. Academic administrators who claimed responsibility for some of the same functions and privileges as faculty members. Inevitable jurisdictional disputes arose. As changes occurred in the academic and legal environment—enabling labor legislation, proximity of other professional and industrial unions, institutional growth and transition (brought about by enrollment-related factors), or economic downturn—academic employees organized. Faculty unionization can primarily be attributed to a craft orientation. Assertion of craft rights; control of work schedules; course content; defense of appointment, promotion, and tenure policies; protection of the faculty's role in curriculum and teaching methodology, particularly in vulnerable public systems where faculty members lack the intellectual firepower and disciplinary autonomy of colleagues in elite institutions, were, in my opinion, the most important stimuli for unionization. Economic issues remain important but were not a primary cause of unionization for full-time faculty members. Economic matters are more determinative for graduate students seeking union representation because, as employees, they lack craft prerogatives.

If the analogy to crafts is accepted as consistent with the traditional professional orientation, then the debate about professionalism versus unionism becomes less meaningful. If by unionism we mean seniority-determined work rights, uniform procedures and policies in the workplace, and guaranteed job security, unionism may conflict with professional values. However, the above analogy fits with what is thought of as the industrial, not the craft, approach to unionism.

As craft-type unionists, academic employees have negotiated provisions into contracts that reflect a professional craft orientation. For example, contracts in higher education covering academically related employees do not specify the use of standardized personnel policies, nor do they dispense with traditional academic criteria used to assess intellectual quality, and most contracts contain language protecting tenure. The traditional argument for tenure is based on its relation to and support of academic freedom. For the professional craft group, however, tenure is the keystone of the craft's existence. Through the tenuring process, traditional craft controls can be exercised. It is the equivalent of the hiring hall in the construction trades. Without the tenuring process, the professor is merely an employee with direct relations to the administration.

Other evidence of craft-type behavior among professors emerges when units of law, medicine, allied health, or other specialties endeavor to break away from university-wide bargaining units or to establish their own unions. They might do so to maintain advantageous salary differentials or to control jurisdictional and employment procedures.

What are the organizational implications of the faculty-administration or craft-bureaucrat model for those who manage these functions? The possibility that faculty associations will move away from the craft approach to a more traditional (industrial) approach is remote. Although academic unions seek the best of all worlds, including, for example, both collegial governance and binding-arbitration clauses, in the coming decades, the higher education world will be shaped by the need to be increasingly product oriented and cost conscious. Greater numbers of part-time faculty members will be hired to ensure workforce flexibility and respond to student demands. New clientele will be sought, and new programs will be initiated in a competitive search for markets and cost savings. Institutional leaders will be not only pushing hard on matters that professional employees consider to be in their jurisdictions but also negotiating cost-saving measures in health care. Given the predominantly craft style of unionism and the nature of the prospective issues in the coming years, controversies are almost certain to continue.

Salient Organizational Effects

It is exceedingly difficult to untangle the effects of employee unionism from other intellectual, social, economic, political, and organizational forces, although the few studies of the longitudinal effects of collective bargaining on college and university systems do suggest that certain organizational consequences find their roots in collective bargaining. It would, however, be difficult to substantiate direct relationships between unionism and organizational consequences. Moreover, other environmental factors, particularly evolving legal and fiscal environments in higher education, may exert similar systemic effects. With that caveat, in the remainder of this essay I identify some of the effects of collective bargaining on college and university systems and then conclude with an observation on leadership in unionized environments.

THE CENTRALIZATION OF POWER AND AUTHORITY

In unionized systems, power and influence have inevitably flowed from individual campuses to system offices and union headquarters. From there, influence accrues to external agencies, elected politicians, and others who are integral to union-management relations. These centralizing tendencies have resulted in increased bureaucracy, the codification of procedures and policies, and demands for consistent applications of university or systemwide regulations, policies, and practices.

THE NEED FOR NEW STYLES OF MANAGEMENT

One by-product of unionization has been the classification and recognition of unique responsibilities of supervisory, administrative, and academic employees. This issue is not insignificant in organizations where territorial boundaries, professional jurisdictions, and departmental autonomy have remained fluid and are considered one of the most significant organizational attributes of colleges and universities. The clarification of roles and responsibilities has, more often than not, ushered a change in personalities when unionization arrives. Managing a unionized workforce (or organizing drive) requires additional skills beyond those needed to work in nonunionized environments, although this caveat is still only grudgingly accepted in most organized institutions.

While opportunities for conflict increase once unions arrive, conflict-resolution mechanisms are also a distinctive feature of the labor-management environment. Unionism has hastened the need for managers who can administer labor agreements. Lastly, new faculty and administrative roles may contribute to organizational effectiveness by encouraging economic forecasting, strategic planning, benefits-sharing cost savings, and related policies when multiyear labor agreements are required. Unionization forces review of compensation systems and probably results in more egalitarian approaches (such as salary steps) to the distribution of compensation. Formalized compensation systems are also less common in nonunionized settings. Lastly, unionization forces organizational leaders to create a decision-making architecture to accommodate labor-management relations.

ASSESSING THE RELATION OF EMPLOYEES TO INSTITUTIONS OR SYSTEMS

In many unionized colleges and systems, relations between the organization and represented employees improve over time. Obviously exceptions exist. However, relations typically strengthen when power imbalances are reduced and when organizations act and speak with consistency. Such communication can enable groups of represented employees to gain recognition, obtain increased job security, and safeguard craft prerogatives. However, many believe academic institutions remain vibrant precisely because they are not run like motor-vehicle bureaus and because departmental and school autonomy are vigilantly defended. Some have also suggested that professional autonomy and thus academic quality will be compromised through collective bargaining. For example, in what many consider the finest institutions of higher education in the United States, professors remain nonunionized. Faculty members in elite institutions are often rugged intellectual individualists and operate in ways antithetical to values that unions promote; for example, probationary professors can be released not because of poor performance but because, in the future, more promising candidates may be found. Some contend that the least productive academic departments are those fully tenured.

Union leaders in higher education are quick to argue that these cultural norms can be accommodated. But the tensions in unions, organizations legally obligated to protect professional prerogatives and job security, are ever present. Moreover, administrators who face lengthy arbitration hearings over promotion or tenure denials are far less likely to make tough but necessary calls. In employment policy at least, unionization will cause systems to regress to a status quo. For many, this standard will be a real improvement. For others, it will be a significant disadvantage.

INCREASING SYSTEM VULNERABILITY

Future challenges to collective bargaining will probably result in the greater exposure of public systems to both internal and external pressures. Administrative leaders will find that collective bargaining is inherently cyclical; tranquil times sometimes become attenuated. The progressives of one era become the reactionaries in the next particularly when new university presidents decide to change the chemistry between "their" administration and the faculty. The skills and attributes needed to be successful, such as the ability to hold others accountable, assure standardization in contract administration, and the like, lead to the creation of internal opponents. Eventually, when the five people who hate those in charge link up with the five who are undecided, power shifts. In academe, friends come and go, but enemies remain. Collective bargaining feeds these interactions because the risk of exposure for poor decisions becomes greater in unionized organizations, where simply not making a decision is no longer an option. Unionized public systems will become more beholden to state governors and legislative leaders. Such vulnerabilities, in evidence before unionization, are now hastened as the locus of bargaining moves to legislative, not academic, offices.

Leadership

Leadership is an essential ingredient in the management of collective bargaining in colleges and universities, but not leadership in the traditional sense. The truly successful do not simply articulate a vision or engage in an elaborate planning process. They do not put great faith in rational decision making or behave as if their role is, on the one hand, to serve others or, on the other, to manipulate colleagues and subordinates through cleverness or intimidation. Leadership is impossible and certainly breaks down under conditions of goal ambiguity, professional dominance, and environmental vulnerability.

The most effective executives and faculty leaders communicate well; know their institutional culture; engage in authentic behavior; legitimize the ideas and actions of others; surround themselves with the right people; demand the bad news; continually agitate for excellence; and remain tenacious, patient, and focused on goals. They know when to react to external pressures and when not to. We can also discern cases where individuals hold important titles—union leader, president, dean, or provost—and have no effective influence, power, or leadership skills. This weakness most often besets "leaders" who handled a crisis ineffectively, who cared too much about holding onto a job, or who were put in place by those who seek to maintain the status quo—sobering thoughts for many who work in unionized organizations.

NOTE

The author wishes to thank Tom Mannix, former chief university spokesperson for the State University of New York, the University of California, and Western Michigan University, and Caesar J. Naples, former chief university spokesperson for the University of Florida and California State University systems, for their insightful comments and suggestions.

SUGGESTIONS FOR FURTHER READING

Baldridge, J. Victor. *Power and Conflict in the University*. New York: Wiley, 1979.

Baldridge, J. Victor, Frank R. Kemerer, et al. *Assessing the Impact of Faculty Collective Bargaining*. AAHE-ERIC Higher Education Research Report 8. Washington: AAHE, 1981.

Begin, James P. "Statutory Definitions of the Scope of Negotiations: The Implications for Traditional Faculty Governance." *Journal of Higher Education* 49.3 (1978): 247–60.

Bendix, Reinhard. *Work and Authority in Industry: Ideologies of Management in the Course of Industrialization*. New York: Harper, 1956.

Birnbaum, Robert M. *How Academic Leadership Works*. San Francisco: Jossey-Bass, 1992.

Blau, Peter M. *The Organization of Academic Work*. New York: Wiley, 1973.

Chandler, Margaret K. *Management Rights and Union Interests*. New York: McGraw, 1964.

Chandler, Margaret K., and Daniel J. Julius. *Faculty vs. Administration: Rights Issues in Academic Collective Bargaining*. New York: NCSCBHEP, Baruch Coll., CUNY, 1979.

Chatak, Ellen. "A Unionist's Perspective on the Future of American Unions." *Journal of Labor Research* 12.4 (1991): 327–32.

Douglas, Joel M. "The Impact of *NLRB vs. Yeshiva University* on Faculty Unionism at Public Colleges and Universities." *Journal of Collective Negotiations* 19.1 (1990): 1–28.

Etzioni, Amitai. "Authority Structure and Organizational Effectiveness." *Administrative Science Quarterly* 4 (1959): 43–67.

Freeman, Robert B., and Jeffery L. Medoff. *What Do Unions Do?* New York: Basic, 1984.

Garbarino, Joseph W. *Faculty Bargaining*. New York: McGraw, 1975.

———. "Faculty Collective Bargaining: A Status Report." *Unions in Transition*. Ed. Seymour Martin Lipset. San Francisco: Inst. of Contemporary Studies, 1986. 265–86.

———. "Faculty Unionism: The First Ten Years." *Annals of the American Academy of Political and Social Science* 448 (1980): 74–85.

Gumport, Patricia J. "Learning Academic Labor." *Comparative Social Research* 19 (2000): 1–23.

———. "Public Universities as Academic Workplaces." *Daedalus: Journal of the American Academy of Arts and Sciences* 126.4 (1997): 113–36.

Gumport, Patricia J., and John Jennings. "Graduate Student Employees: Unresolved Challenges." *Journal of the College and University Personnel Association* 48.3–4 (1998): 35–37.

Gumport, Patricia J., and Brian Puser. "Restructuring the Academic Environment." *Planning and Management for a Changing Environment: A Handbook on Redesigning Postsecondary Institutions.* Ed. M. Peterson, D. Dill, and L. Mets. San Francisco: Jossey-Bass, 1997.

Julius, Daniel J. "The Current Status of Graduate Student Unions: An Employer's Perspective." *Collective Bargaining and Accountability in Higher Education: A Report Card.* Ed. Caesar J. Naples. New York: NCSCBHEP, Baruch Coll., CUNY, 1999.

———. "The Development of Human Resources Administrators in Colleges and Universities." *Understanding the Work and Career Paths of Midlevel Administrators: Profiles and Pathways.* Ed. Linda K. Johnsrud and Vicki J. Rosser. New Directions for Higher Educ. 111 San Francisco: Jossey-Bass, 2000. 45–54.

———, ed. *Managing the Industrial Relations Process in Higher Education.* Washington: Coll. and Univ. Personnel Assn., 1993.

———. "Unionization in Higher Education: The Case of Academic Employees in Large Public Systems." *California Public Employee Relations* 161 (2003): 8–15.

———. "Will Universities Lock Out Students?" *Academe* 90.1 (2004): 34–36.

Julius, Daniel J., J. Victor Baldridge, and Jeffrey Pfeffer. "A Memo from Machiavelli," *Journal of Higher Education* 70.2 (1999): 113–33.

———. "Determinants of Influence: Why Some Faculty and Administrators in Canadian Universities are More Effective Than Others." *CSSHE Professional File* 19. Manitoba: CSSHE, 1999.

Julius, Daniel J., and Margaret K. Chandler. "Academic Bargaining Agents in Higher Education: Do Their Achievements Differ?" *Journal of Collective Negotiations* 18.1 (1989): 9–58.

Julius, Daniel J., and Patricia Gumport. "Graduate Student Unionization: Catalysts and Consequences." *Review of Higher Education* 26.2 (2002): 187–216.

Kemerer, Frank R., and J. Victor Baldridge. *Unions on Campus.* San Francisco: Jossey-Bass, 1975.

Kerr, Clark. "Industrial Relations and University Relations." *Proceedings of the Twenty-First Annual Meeting.* Madison: Industrial Relations Research Assn., 1969. 8–12.

———. "Patterns of Faculty Unionization in Higher Education." Ed. Joel. M. Douglas. *Proceedings, Twentieth Annual Conference.* NCSCBHEP. New York: Baruch Coll., CUNY, 1992.

Kochan, Ted A., Harry C. Katz, and Robert B. McKersie. *The Transformation of American Industrial Relations.* New York: Basic, 1986.

Ladd, Everett C., and Seymour M. Lipset. *The Divided Academy.* New York: McGraw, 1975.

————. *Professors, Unions, and American Higher Education*. Berkeley: Carnegie Commission on Higher Educ., 1973.

Levinstein, Aaron. "The National Center for the Study of Collective Bargaining in Higher Education: The First Ten Years." *Campus Bargaining at the Crossroads. Proceedings, Tenth Annual Conference*. NCSCBHEP. New York: Baruch Coll., CUNY, 1982. 27–33.

Meyer, Marshall W. *Bureaucratic Structure and Authority*. New York: Harper, 1972.

Mortimer, Ken P., and Terry R. McConnel. "The Context of Collective Bargaining in American Colleges and Universities." *Managing the Industrial Labor Relations Process in Higher Education*. Ed. Daniel J. Julius. Washington: Coll. and Univ. Personnel Assn., 1993.

————. *Sharing Authority Effectively*. San Francisco: Jossey-Bass, 1979.

Neal, Margaret A., and M. H. Bazerman. *Cognition and Rationality in Negotiation*. New York: Free, 1991.

NLRB v. Yeshiva University, 444 U.S. 672 (1980).

O'Reilly, Charles A., and Jennifer A. Chatman. "Culture as Social Control: Corporations, Cults, and Commitment." *Research in Organizational Behavior*. Ed. B.M. Straw and L.L. Cummings. Greenwich: JAI, 1996.

Pfeffer, Jeffrey. "Barriers to the Advance of Organizational Science: Paradigm Development as a Dependent Variable." Annual Meeting of the Academy of Management. Las Vegas. 1992.

————. *Managing with Power*. Boston: Harvard Business School P, 1992.

————. *New Directions for Organizational Theory*. New York: Oxford UP, 1997.

————. *Power in Organizations*. Marshfield: Pitman, 1981.

Posner, Gary J. "Unionization and Positive Employee Relations: The Cornell Experience—A Case Study." *Journal of the College and University Personnel Association* 32.4 (1981): 6–9.

Salancik, Gerald R., and Jeffrey Pfeffer. "The Bases and Uses of Power in Organizational Decision-Making: The Case of the University." *Administrative Science Quarterly* 19 (1974): 453–73.

————. *Organizational Dynamics: Who Gets Power and How to Hold On to It*. Washington: American Management Assn., 1977.

Sheed, Wilfred. "What Ever Happened to the Labor Movement? A Report on the State of the Unions." *Atlantic* 232 (1973): 19–29.

Stepp, John R. "Union Employment Relationships in the 1990s." *Proceedings, Eighteenth Annual Conference*. NCSCBHEP. Ed. Joel M. Douglas. New York: Baruch Coll., CUNY, 1990. 7–10.

Walton, Richard E., and Robert B. McKersie. *A Behavioral Theory of Labor Negotiations*. New York: McGraw, 1965.

Collective Bargaining Agreements: Legal and Organizational Issues

GREGG ADLER

This essay provides an overview of six basic provisions, often termed *nuts and bolts* or *boilerplate*, that appear in some form in most academic collective bargaining agreements. These include union rights; management rights; unit definition and recognition; nondiscrimination; duration of agreement, or reopeners; and dues, including checkoff and agency fee. I provide an overview of the typical characteristics and purposes of each contract provision and a brief analysis of the distinctive issues that arise in the context of academic collective bargaining. Of course, the specific content of these clauses in each collective bargaining agreement reflects local circumstances, such as the culture and history of the particular institution, the extent to which the parties historically have accommodated academic freedom and governance in the roles of labor and management, the relative bargaining strengths of academics and the administration, and the legal and political context in which the negotiations occur.

After reviewing these substantive areas of the academic collective bargaining agreement, I discuss the role of legal counsel. This discussion includes practical suggestions that locals or chapters should consider when retaining an attorney, as well as alternative models for creating an appropriate division of responsibilities among the chapter's elected leadership, staff, and outside counsel. Like the terms of the collective bargaining agreement itself, the nature of the relationship between the local chapter and its lawyer is informed by the culture of the particular institution, the relationship between the faculty and administration, and the experience and expertise of the elected leadership and the staff.

Collective Bargaining Issues

UNION RIGHTS

Most faculty contracts include a separate provision delineating the institutional rights accorded the collective bargaining agent and those engaged in its work. These range from a simple promise of freedom from discrimination and nonretaliation for exercising the legal rights of union membership to the provision of office space; access to institutional facilities and equipment; and released time for officers, staff members, and union members. Where the contract provides for multiple institutional benefits, the clause is generally entitled chapter rights or union rights. But where the union's rights are more narrow, the clause will usually be designated in accordance with the particular benefit covered, such as released time, reassigned time, access to employees, or rights of members.

Office Facilities. A well-established, longstanding bargaining relationship presupposes that faculty unions have successfully used the collective bargaining agreement to enhance their institutional effectiveness as a representative of the faculty members. First and foremost is the establishment of office space for the union within the university or college, preferably with appropriate furnishings, equipment, telephone lines, and computer access—all, if possible, at the administration's expense. Access to university services such as photocopying, printing, mail, bulletin boards, conference facilities, and audiovisual equipment is also frequently provided in the union-rights section of the contract. In most cases, however, the union is required to reimburse the administration for the actual costs associated with some of these services, such as printing and photocopying. Establishing an institutional presence through having visible office space and access to resources is not simply a convenience but provides both practical and symbolic support for the union's role in enforcing the terms of the collective bargaining agreement and in representing the membership. If the bargaining relationship is especially strained, however, some locals prefer to have phones, computers, and even offices outside institutional jurisdiction or control.

Information. Some union-rights clauses specifically require the administration to provide information relevant to collective bargaining, grievance handling, and contract administration, as well as a specific protocol for the exchange of that information (i.e., time frames, cost sharing, etc.). However, the right to such information is normally regulated by statute, and some contracts incorporate such provisions in the grievance-arbitration article. Thus the absence of such a specific requirement in the union-rights section is normally not troubling unless the contract's management-rights clause contains a waiver of the union's statutory right to information. In private-sector bargaining units including full-time faculty members, somewhat different rules apply. Because the *Yeshiva* decision impairs access to the unfair-labor practice of the National Labor Relations Board to enforce the employer's obligation to furnish relevant information, the union needs to negotiate an equivalent contractual right enforceable through the grievance and arbitration procedure.

Release Time. A key aspect of a faculty union's ability to effectively represent its members is the assignment of release time or reassigned time designated for union activities. Most academic institutions are accustomed to the concept of workload reduction for faculty research, department chair duties, and other professional activities. Many faculty contracts include a provision for release time for union activities that specifies number of hours, days, or load credits available for identified union activities. Depending on the size of the bargaining unit, contracts may provide sufficient release time to compensate a full-time chapter president, full- or part-time grievance officers, and negotiating team members at least to attend bargaining sessions and to allow delegates or officers to attend certain collective bargaining meetings or conferences.

The agreement may also provide release time for rank-and-file members to perform stafflike functions such as handling grievances, attending training and educational conferences organized by the chapter, working on special projects relating to grievances or contract administration, or attending grievance hearings. The particular type of release-time provisions a chapter should pursue depends in part on whether the model of the chapter's operation is more staff driven, providing professional services for the members, or more member-leader oriented, where the organization seeks to use and empower rank-and-file faculty members.

MANAGEMENT RIGHTS AND PAST POLICIES OR PRACTICES

Industrial-sector bargaining has developed extensive, wordy, and redundant clauses designed to protect and extend management's inherent right to make fundamental business decisions without obtaining the consent of the union. Most academic contracts contain some comparable form of management-rights clause, sometimes entitled "Management Functions," "Rights and Responsibilities of the Board of Trustees," "Administration Rights," or "Reservation of Rights," which is designed to preserve the administration's right to control certain business and academic issues.

Where the bargaining relationship between the union and the administration recognizes a history of collaborative, collegial decision making, the clauses tend to be relatively short and to the point. In those cases, the management-functions clause acknowledges the administration or governing body's authority to fulfill its statutory responsibilities (in the case of public-sector institutions), articulate and fulfill the institution's educational mission, determine staffing levels, and decide on the number and location of facilities. However, many faculty collective bargaining agreements go further and state that the administration or board has the right to establish or discontinue programs; evaluate and determine professional competence; grant tenure; promote; renew appointments; determine curriculum content; establish, modify, and enforce reasonable rules and standards; and, in some cases, determine the academic calendar.

Virtually all management-rights clauses state clearly that the rights set forth as belonging exclusively to management are limited by other provisions of the collective bargaining agreement, but the language varies significantly. Some contracts use words such as "except as otherwise provided herein," "unless expressly limited by the terms of this Agreement," or "except as specifically limited by explicit provisions of this Agreement." The purpose of these clauses is to reinforce management's right to act unilaterally without negotiating with the union in certain areas. In higher education, however, governance and academic decision making are generally shared in a much more meaningful way between the faculty and the administration than are any parallel responsibilities in manufacturing or in the service industries. So, in that respect, the significance of the management-rights clause is always dependent on the extent to which traditional management prerogatives are exercised through shared-governance procedures or have been relinquished in the rest of the contract. Nonetheless, faculty unions are generally better off with short clauses in general language than with long, detailed recitations of all the specific rights that belong exclusively to the administration.

Management will often try to strengthen its ability to act unilaterally not only by seeking a strong management-rights clause but also by broadening the zipper clause. The narrow version of this clause simply forecloses opening new issues during the term of the agreement. The broader version may also state that the contract encompasses the complete agreement between the parties or that management rights are not limited by past practices. The narrower the zipper clause, the less harmful to the union's ability to preserve valuable past practices and to fight unilateral action by the administration. To counter management erosion of shared governance and professional practices, unions seek provisions that explicitly incorporate faculty-governance policies and past practices into the collective bargaining agreement. If the agreement has an extensive management-rights clause or a broad zipper clause, only language explicitly protecting past policies or practices limits the scope of the managerial prerogatives. The limiting language should also provide that adherence to past policies and procedures is enforceable through binding arbitration.

UNIT DEFINITION / RECOGNITION

Academic contracts contain a wide variety of unit definitions. The scope of the bargaining unit is usually established on a relatively permanent basis at the time of the original organizing drive, although it can be amended subsequently by the parties at the bargaining table. The unit composition is defined in significant part by the legal landscape in which the unit was formed, since the laws of each state, as well as the National Labor Relations Act, require that certain categories of workers be excluded from certified bargaining units because they are not considered employees within the meaning of the applicable statute or regulation.

Although state collective bargaining laws vary significantly, in the academic environment the mandatory exclusions usually apply to certain managerial employees who are considered policy makers on behalf of the institution. These exclusions not only include presidents and provosts but also vice presidents, associate or assistant provosts, deans or directors and their associates or assistants, and confidential employees. However, most faculty collective bargaining units include regular full-time librarians, and many include counselors, coaches, and athletic trainers, as well as various categories of academic professionals often regarded as administrative employees. Only one, at Rutgers University, includes graduate and teaching assistants in the same unit as full-time faculty members.

Department chairs are often included in the faculty bargaining unit. This inclusion may, in keeping with academic practice, blur the traditional lines between labor and management. It may also lead management to shift power from the chairs to the deans or strain relations between the chairs and their departmental colleagues. Nonetheless, the inclusion of chairs in the bargaining unit is an important component of maintaining faculty involvement in academic decisions and may enhance the peer-review process.

A significant dividing line in faculty contracts regards adjunct or part-time faculty members. Although some faculty bargaining units encompass all part-time faculty members, including those hired as lecturers or to teach a single course on a one-time basis, most units exclude many or all categories of contingent appointees. Some contracts make distinctions based on established expectations of continuing employment or even tenure-track status rather than on part-time or full-time status, so that anyone in the category of "continuing" is in the unit whether they are part-time or full-time.

The inclusion or exclusion of contingent appointees and part-time faculty members affects the way faculty members negotiate to preserve core academic values. Although a department that maintains or increases the proportion of tenure-track full-time faculty members is more likely to promote academic freedom, academic excellence, and shared governance, academic managers often prefer to increase the proportion of adjunct faculty appointees who are far less costly and who enhance administrative flexibility. Accordingly, units composed primarily of full-time academics frequently negotiate self-protective provisions to limit the erosion of professional appointments by forbidding non-tenure-track appointments, limiting the proportion of non-tenure-track and part-time appointments, or securing pro rata compensation and job security or part-time tenure for those contingent appointees included in the bargaining unit.

Legal restrictions on the scope of bargaining generally prevent full-time tenure-track faculty members from negotiating provisions that are directly beneficial to those full-time contingent appointees or part-time appointees not included in the same bargaining unit. Hence, the representation of those contingent appointees excluded from full-time units depends primarily on their own efforts. Yet the contingent appointments of these academics, who play an increasingly important role in higher education, make them extremely vulnerable to arbitrary, unfair, and disrespectful treatment that can erode educational quality and professional standards for all. Accordingly, where full-time units are unable to negotiate directly on behalf of contingent faculty members, the full-time faculty members need not only to negotiate self-protective provisions to protect their own status and work but also to do what they can to support the organization and representation of contingent appointees.

NONDISCRIMINATION

Most agreements have some conception of nondiscrimination and contain comprehensive nondiscrimination provisions that may encompass such specific characteristics as age, race, sex, gender, sexual orientation, national origin, ethnic or cultural origin, color, creed, disability or handicap, marital status, religion, veteran status, religious or political beliefs, lawful political activities, union membership and activity (or refraining from union activity). The problem with listing specific types of discrimination is that the failure to include a type may be construed by an arbitrator as an intent to exclude it from the antidiscrimination clause's protection. A second concept avoids this danger, and some contracts use more generic language, such as "no member of the bargaining unit shall be discriminated against on the basis of any characteristic or activity protected by federal or state law." This approach incorporates all existing public-law protections but excludes those forms of discrimination that might not be covered by the applicable state or federal laws, which in a majority of jurisdictions would mean no protection against discrimination on the basis of sexual orientation or on the basis of disabilities not covered by the ADA. A third concept, one that can be used to obtain the broadest possible protection, is to combine the incorporation of public law with a list of specific types of discrimination, such as, "the university shall not discriminate against any member on the basis of race, age, sex, sexual orientation, marital status, religion, disability, national origin, political affiliation, beliefs or activities, membership in or activities on behalf of the AAUP, nor shall it violate any federal or state law applicable to the employment relationship."

Nondiscrimination clauses also vary significantly in the manner and extent to which the language is applicable to the union as well as to the employer. Although antidiscrimination laws apply to union conduct as well as to actions taken by an employer, the not-infrequent inclusion of this concept in the agreement erroneously suggests that the union has joint responsibility with the employer for employment discrimination and ignores the reality that the power to discriminate is primarily vested in the employer. The primary role of the contract in this regard is to protect faculty members from employment discrimination and to avoid the establishment of union or individual liability for discriminatory practices. Where, however, unit members engage in discriminatory actions, for example in the course of peer review, the contract should not preclude the administration from exercising its responsibility to take corrective action on behalf of the individual who has suffered discrimination.

Collective bargaining agreements also vary in how they handle the enforcement of contractual nondiscrimination commitments. Traditionally, unions have pushed for discrimination grievances to be resolved exclusively through the contract's grievance and arbitration procedure. As legal claims for state and federal employment discrimination have expanded and become more available to individual employees, the use of the collective bargaining agreement as an exclusive remedy for discrimination has become less appealing. Since it is important to academics that their collective bargaining agreements enhance rather than restrict the rights and remedies available to them, academic unions often seek not only to preserve access to the courts but also to obtain contractual protections. By the mid-1990s, management lawyers argued that the availability of arbitration under a collective bargaining agreement should be a basis for denying union-represented employees access to the courts for resolution of employment-discrimination claims.

As the law has developed, arbitration clauses in collective bargaining agreements, namely those where an arbitrator is permitted to provide the remedies available in court, have been interpreted as a waiver of an individual union member's right to go to court. Unions should, however, resist efforts by employers to use the collective agreement to preclude individual access to the courts or agencies. Unit members should have no less access to the courts than other employees. Moreover, the remedies typically available through the contract, reinstatement and lost wages, do not include the compensatory and punitive-damage awards that may be available through the courts. Consequently, unions acquiescing in these limitations may be open to claims from members alleging a failure of the duty to represent.

A number of faculty contracts have moved in the opposite direction, by including language that denies access to the grievance and arbitration mechanism when the member is pursuing the same or similar claims in an outside administrative or court proceeding. The first problem with this approach is that there may well be separate but related contractual issues that should be decided under the collective bargaining agreement's grievance procedure. The second is that, if an employee is denied access to the contractual grievance procedure simply because he or she has exercised the right to file a discrimination claim with a state or federal agency or court, then this denial may be considered discrimination or retaliation under Title VII. Consequently, both employer and union may be found liable, and the collective bargaining agreement clause illegal.

Another approach substitutes the institution's discrimination-complaint procedure for the resolution of discrimination elements of issues otherwise subject to the grievance and arbitration procedure. This substitution of the complaint procedure for the grievance process in the case of discrimination issues is lawful, provided it does not deny access to the grievance procedure for related contractual issues. For example, faculty members who alleged that their tenure denials were due to discrimination could both file for discrimination under the complaint procedure and grieve the failure to properly follow the tenure procedure under the contractual provision. This unique approach to discrimination complaints may tempt a bargaining agent seeking a way for individuals to pursue complaints of peer discrimination because it does not require the union to act as an advocate and take sides among its members. However, it risks weakening the ability of the union to safeguard the rights of both members and peers. Moreover, since the union necessarily advocates for grievants in other personnel matters, exclusion of discrimination issues from the union's responsibilities weakens its ability to safeguard personnel procedures without substantially lessening the union's need and responsibility to protect individual members against improper peer decisions.

Duration of Agreement or Reopeners. All academic collective bargaining agreements have clauses setting forth the duration of the agreement. Academic contracts are often three years in duration. Longer terms may be set where basic contract issues have been resolved, although such contracts often require salary reopeners to deal with the uncertainties of public-sector budgets. Shorter terms are often negotiated where basic issues remain in contention or the institution lacks the budgetary confidence or authority to make a longer commitment. Most AAUP faculty contracts include some form of automatic-renewal provision; some include specific dates for commencing negotiations for successor agreements.

The determination of the duration of a collective bargaining agreement requires balancing the values of stability and flexibility. Many factors affect this decision, including the maturity of the collective bargaining relationship; the level of hostility between the union and management; the legal setting; the recent history of strikes or other strife on campus; the economic condition of the institution; and the status and timing of the state budget, the political environment, and the cohesiveness of the bargaining unit members—including the actual or perceived level of support for the collective bargaining agent and its leadership. The complex variables involved do not permit a "best practice" to be identified. The specific alternatives need to be considered to achieve the most suitable combination of possible economic benefits and professional protections.

Unless the time frame and process for negotiating a successor contract is established and regulated by statute, most AAUP faculty contracts include in the duration clause a provision that the terms of the contract automatically renew for successive one-year periods. However, either party can notify the other in writing (within a set time frame before the expiration date, generally between 60–90 days or, in some cases, 120 days) of its intention to seek a modification or termination of the collective bargaining agreement. A few contracts require that this notice include a listing of the particular provisions or issues the party wishes to modify and, sometimes, the precise modifications proposed. Some contracts further state that those sections not thusly identified will automatically become part of a successor agreement. This approach is particularly desirable where the chapter has been able to establish satisfactory provisions on vital issues through previous negotiations.

Contracts often include issue-specific reopener clauses that either permit or require the parties to negotiate at a predesignated time during the term of the contract. Traditionally, reopeners have focused on wages or other economic issues. For example, where both parties are sufficiently satisfied with the contract's basic terms but economic uncertainty makes it impossible to reach agreement for more than two years, the parties may adopt a four-year agreement with a wage reopener in the third year. This arrangement can be accomplished by a four-year agreement that permits either party to reopen discussions on wages at a certain date or by a provision that leaves the last two years open for further negotiations and sets a date for the commencement of negotiations.

When negotiating such clauses, it is important to consider the applicable legal issues concerning the right to strike. In the private sector, the NLRB has held that a general no-strike clause does not waive a union's ability to strike during midterm reopener negotiations. Unions must be careful not to agree to language in the reopener that would deprive the union of its most important economic leverage to bargain effectively. In the public sector, particularly where the bargaining process includes interest arbitration, it is imperative to incorporate into the reopener specific dates for the commencement and conclusion of negotiations and a date for the arbitration in the event a negotiated agreement cannot be achieved. Additionally, where possible, a particular arbitrator should be identified, who will decide the dispute.

The reopener approach may also be effective where the administration is in transition. The current administration may be committed to achieving significant changes to noneconomic issues of importance to the faculty, which a successor administration would concede. In such instances, maintenance of the status quo as changes are pending in key leadership may be advantageous and may avoid unnecessary conflict that would impair the long-term bargaining relationship.

DUES CHECKOFF AND AGENCY FEE
Virtually all collective bargaining agreements include an article concerning the general subject of union membership that provides for checkoff authorizations and, in some cases, maintenance of membership or agency fee. The precise contours of such clauses, however, must be carefully fashioned to comply with the applicable state or federal law, and there is therefore significant variation among the institutions.

Dues Checkoff. Unions seek to negotiate an efficient and effective process whereby the institution deducts dues or fees from the salaries of those unit members who authorize deductions and transmits them to the local or chapter. The procedure ordinarily assigns the local or chapter the responsibility to establish the dues or fee rates and to resolve any disputes about these payments. However, contracts often set forth the language of the checkoff authorization forms and establish a specific annual revocation period during which members may resign and cease further payments.

To retain flexibility, the contract generally does not establish the specific amount of dues or fee payments. Instead, collective bargaining agreements use words such as, "dues and assessments as are from time to time authorized by" the union or, "any initiation fees and dues levied in accordance with the constitution and bylaws" of the local or, "the university shall deduct regular monthly dues, the amount to be deducted to be certified by the chapter treasurer." However, employers who agree to allow for such discretion increasingly require a provision by which the chapter agrees to hold harmless and indemnify the institution from any liability or damages with respect to compliance with the deduction of dues or fees.

Finally, collective bargaining agreements frequently require that the institution transmit dues that have been withheld from the paychecks of bargaining unit members at a particular time. Although the precise date for transmittal may vary depending on the institution's payroll practices, it is important to have a specific date (such as the 10th of the month) so the union will be able to effectively enforce this obligation. To monitor compliance and facilitate enforcement if necessary, it is also common for checkoff clauses to require the employer regularly to supply the chapter with lists of all bargaining unit members and new hires, as well as with statements confirming the amounts of dues that have been deducted and remitted on behalf of each employee.

Agency Fee. Although agency-fee law is a complex matter, the basic concept is not complicated: both the United States Constitution and the NLRA have been interpreted as prohibiting compulsory union membership but as allowing unions to require that nonmembers who object to joining pay an agency fee to cover the expenses of collective bargaining, grievance handling, and contract administration. Therefore, to prevent freeloading, many academic collective bargaining agreements require that each member of the bargaining unit pay either regular union dues or an appropriate agency fee as a condition of maintaining their employment with the institution. It should be noted, however, that the AAUP's "Statement on Collective Bargaining" recommends that: "In an agency shop or compulsory dues check-off arrangement, a chapter . . . should incorporate provisions designed to accommodate affirmatively asserted conscientious objection to such an arrangement with any representative."

Under the Taft-Hartley Act, which governs private-sector unions, each individual employee must sign an authorization form to allow for such deductions, and the authorizations cannot be irrevocable for more than one year or beyond the expiration date of the contract. In states like Connecticut, where deductions from the wages of state employees are required by statute, the contract may reference and incorporate the governing law. Other states have diverse specific requirements. In view of the complexity and recurrent litigation regarding agency fee, consultation of expert counsel is essential in drafting and administering these provisions.

Some contracts include language limiting the amount that the union can collect for agency fees. Although employers may think they want such restrictions because they view themselves as the protectors of the interests of nonmembers, in the end the actual amount that can be charged to nonmembers who object to paying full dues must be determined in accordance with the procedures and practices developed by the NLRB, the states, and the courts. The parties do better, therefore, to keep such language out of collective bargaining agreements to avoid creating an unnecessary additional source and forum for potential litigation over the propriety of particular agency-fee charges.

The Role of Counsel

Although procedures and practices vary considerably, virtually all bargaining agents require the assistance of experienced labor counsel to provide effective representation to their members. The specific functions that counsel is retained to perform, as well as the specific relationship between counsel and union elected leadership and staff members, are determined by several factors, including the size of the bargaining unit, the abilities of the chapter officers and staff members, the relationship between the chapter and the administration, the complexity of issues, the frequency and character of grievances and litigation, the particular legal environment, and the availability of funds.

Since selection of counsel involves fundamental decisions about how the chapter represents its members and how it conducts its internal and external affairs, it requires careful consideration and should not be deferred to a moment of crisis. Although counsel may always be found to handle a specific case, ad hoc decision making about hiring an attorney deprives the chapter of the opportunity to develop and maintain a long-term

relationship with a counsel who fully understands both the general milieu
and the academic environment in which the chapter operates. Only a lawyer with this background will be able to provide the best advice about how
to handle particular situations.

RELATIONS WITH COUNSEL

Despite the numerous factors at play in the formulation of a relationship
between the bargaining agent and legal counsel, a few fundamental principles inform the process. First and foremost, it cannot be over-
emphasized that an attorney's function is to assist and guide the chapter
officers, not to make fundamental decisions about policy. The lawyer is
an agent of the chapter who should implement the policy of the elected
leadership. Certainly the chapter's counsel may participate in a supportive or advisory capacity in the formulation of basic decisions about collective bargaining objectives, grievance resolutions, or whether to settle
or fully litigate lawsuits. But ultimately those determinations, including
decisions about litigation, must be made by the chapter's officers. A lawyer does not tell the elected leadership what to do but provides effective
legal advice to a union, which entails complete and accurate information
not only about the legal implications and likely results but also about the
risks and benefits of alternative courses of action so that a fully informed
decision can be made. Where the relationship between the chapter and
outside counsel is a longstanding one, there will of course be a greater
tendency to solicit his or her opinion on policy issues. This consultation
is appropriate as long as both the lawyer and the officers do not lose track
of who is responsible for the ultimate decision and do not engage in an
overreliance that incurs unnecessary expenditures.

Clarity regarding who exactly the chapter's counsel represents is a
second fundamental issue. The predicament faced by labor lawyers and
their union clients is that the attorneys are generally hired and fired by
the elected leadership. This structure creates a natural tendency for the
lawyer to view the officers as the client. This perspective may, however,
lead both parties to conceptualize the lawyer's role as the implementation
of the political agenda of those particular officers and the protection of
those officers from their political opponents. But at bottom the lawyer's
client is the chapter, in other words, the membership as a whole rather
than the individuals who happen to be currently in office. In most circumstances this does not create conflict, because the goals and aspirations

of the officers are consonant with the interests of the membership. None-theless, lawyers who view their responsibility broadly, by understanding that their ultimate client is the union's membership as a whole, will be more likely to provide the best possible advice on how to handle any particular situation.

The specific tasks assigned to the chapter's counsel differ dramatically from bargaining unit to bargaining unit. Some unions ask their lawyers to do everything from handling individual grievance arbitrations to acting as chief negotiator during collective bargaining sessions. Other chapters employ counsel only for actual litigation matters, or to handle particu-larly complex grievance arbitrations or to provide advice on specific legal issues relating to bargaining or contract administration or individual fac-ulty members. The exact contours of the relationship cannot be prede-termined but should encourage, not displace, leadership and membership participation in the basic aspects of contract negotiation and administra-tion. Unions become stronger when they include rank-and-file members along with officers and staff members to develop goals and plans for con-tract negotiations, participate as members of the negotiating team, handle grievances, conduct arbitrations, and engage in political and legislative activities. Experienced legal counsel facilitate this process by handling legal matters in an inclusive fashion, sharing experience and expertise with those involved, and holding training seminars on the various legal and collective bargaining issues that affect faculty members. To accom-plish this, the lawyers must be willing to view their role not simply as legal representatives but as educators.

SELECTION OF COUNSEL

The selection of a legal counsel to advise a chapter is an important process and should be conducted with the same level of seriousness we attach to the search for a new colleague. Drawing on a memo prepared for this purpose by the AAUP staff attorney Patrick Shaw, the following evalua-tive categories might be considered.

Academic and Professional Credentials. A license to practice law in the jurisdiction in which the chapter exists is important but not essential. It is more important that the attorney have significant experience in and commitment to the representation of labor organizations. Candidates should be asked about why and when attorney candidates came to practice unionside labor law—this may provide a clue as to whether the person is practicing in this area as a result of deeply held commitment or purely by circumstance. Note that labor law, which involves union-management relations, differs from employment law, which primarily involves the relationship between employers and individual employees. Although employment law includes many issues that may be pertinent to local needs, experience with labor law is essential.

Experience Related to Representation of the Chapter. Do the candidates have any experience, other than as students, with academic institutions, either as lawyers, faculty members, grievance representatives, negotiators, or educational policy makers? Examine their experience in labor negotiations, arbitration, First Amendment and academic freedom issues, employment law, representation of individual employees and faculty members, litigation, and civil-rights and employment-discrimination law. Look particularly for experience with those issues the chapter is most likely to confront.

Current Law Practice. Inquire about the candidate's law firm, including the number of lawyers, the substantive areas of the firm's practice (i.e., whether the firm primarily represents unions and employees in employment-related issues or if it engages in other possibly pertinent or conflicting areas of legal representation), the types of clients the firm represents (i.e., employees, employers, management, administrators, or academic institutions), identification of and information about specific union clients (e.g., longevity of representation, contacts for references, whether the firm has represented the union during and after changes in the elected leadership), whether the firm has had any experience dealing with academic institutions where the union is the bargaining agent, and whether the firm has had dealings with the outside counsel or firm that represents the college or university. Finally, it is prudent to inquire whether the attorney or the firm has been the subject of any disciplinary proceedings before the state bar association and, if so, about the circumstances involved.

Business Issues. Ask about the attorney's usual hourly rate, including any variations applicable to litigation as distinct from advice and counsel; about whether lower rates are charged for junior partners, associates, and paralegals; and what role the client plays in determining how particular projects will be handled. Find out the amounts charged for any administrative costs in addition to the attorney's hourly charge, such as photocopying, facsimiles, electronic legal research, and other services. Depending on the size of the chapter and the volume of legal needs, alternative billing arrangements may be explored, such as a straight retainer agreement without regard to the actual number of hours worked or a retainer-plus-hours arrangement where the chapter pays a modest monthly retainer for which the attorney agrees to provide up to a certain number of hours in return for a below-market rate for any hours worked in excess of that number.

Perspective. While each of these factors is important, they do not provide a formula for hiring legal counsel. The decision depends on weighing the candidate's training, experience, expertise, personal integrity, and overall compatibility with the needs of the chapter. In the end, the essential quality necessary for effective outside counsel is general good judgment, especially the capacity to make well-informed, reasoned, and sensible recommendations on the issues. Additionally, the lawyer needs a sound understanding of his or her role and working relationship with the union.

WORK CITED

American Association of University Professors. "Statement on Collective Bargaining." 23 Sept. 2005 <http:www.aaup.org/statements/Redbook/Rbcb.htm>.

Grievance and Arbitration

JAMES D. SEMELROTH

Collective bargaining contracts typically establish grievance procedures. These procedures provide both the means by which the union and management resolve disputes concerning the interpretation and implementation of contract provisions and the means by which the union ensures to unit members that individual rights will be protected. Without such a dispute-resolution procedure, a contract may be violated or ignored by management and, as was formerly the case, the only remedies left to the union would be protracted litigation or job actions such as walkouts. The value of even a well-constructed grievance procedure is limited if it fails to stipulate that unresolved grievances may be subject to final and binding decisions through neutral arbitration.

Grievances

The matters subject to grievance and arbitration under a collective bargaining agreement are determined by the parties' relative strength at the bargaining table and often by applicable public law or regulation. The grievance article usually includes the definition of a grievance, which often limits grievances to specific management violations or misapplications of a provision of the contract. Some contracts allow grievances for violation of campus policies that may be extensions of contract provisions or of independent policies that grant faculty members certain rights or for other disputes between the parties or involving bargaining unit members. Many agreements permit grievance of violations of past practices, and most permit the use of arguments based on past practice in interpreting and applying specific contract provisions.

Past practices may also be used to establish a right when the contract is silent on the particular issue, provided that the reliance on past practice is not precluded by the management-rights or zipper clauses. To succeed in proving a past practice, especially one not specified in the contract, well-documented evidence of the practice must be produced. Past practices are a double-edged sword. A union usually attempts to bargain into the contract the past practices it likes and bargain away or change past practices it does not like. Unions that have accepted all past practices in the contract have from time to time discovered that they have taken the bad with the good.

What Is Not a Grievance?

A dispute between members of the bargaining unit cannot be grieved. The contract is entered into between the union and the management of an institution and is consequently intended to resolve disputes between those two parties. Quite often extracontractual mechanisms—both on campus and through the judicial system—may be used to address disputes directly between unit members. In some circumstances, however, where management is responsible for resolving disputes between unit members and fails to do so, a grievance might be filed against management for failing to discharge its contractual obligation. For example, if a grievant alleges improper peer behavior in the conduct of a peer review, the grievance is not directed at the peers but at management for failing to prevent or correct the improper review.

Types of Grievances

A grievance may allege a straightforward contract violation, such as failure to provide a contractually mandated salary increase or to furnish a particular benefit. Disputes over the meaning of particular contract provisions can be less clear cut. For example, the union's use of a campus office, telephone, photocopier, and so on may be set forth in the negotiated agreement, but what are the institution's obligations when new technologies become available? Does the existing language encompass e-mail and other new technologies as they develop? In grievances requiring the interpretation of arguably ambiguous language, an arbitrator might hear evidence from the parties about their intent when they negotiated the language in question. An arbitrator in such a case might look to the generally accepted meaning of the language, past practices, bargaining notes and proposals, and the testimony of bargainers to determine what the parties intended at the bargaining table.

Personnel-decision grievances, which dispute management's decision on reappointment, promotion, or tenure of a faculty member, may be integrated with traditional academic peer procedures for review and appeal. These grievances are often treated differently in higher education contracts than in the manufacturing and service sectors. For example, arbitration is often limited to procedural questions to avoid empowering the arbitrators to substitute their academic judgment for that of the parties. Academics do seek, however, to enable the arbitrator to ensure that the administration not only has completed each required procedural step but also has done so with full and fair consideration. The common remedy for procedural violations is to remand the grievance for academic review either back to the level where the error occurred or to a previously uninvolved academic body.

Another common grievance matter concerns disciplinary procedures. Some may ask, Why have a discipline procedure in a contract that enables management to discipline faculty members? The answer is simple: since management has the legally established right to discipline employees with or without contractual procedures, a negotiated discipline article can protect members from unreasonable treatment and ensure due-process protections. Disciplinary procedures typically require an investigation stage, which may include consultation with peers; a written notice of specific charges; one or more informal reviews or hearings to discuss the allegations; an opportunity for written or oral rebuttal by the accused; and a formal hearing to determine the final decision. Other employee protections, such as the *Weingarten* right, which stipulates that employees can have a representative present when they are being questioned by an employer about an alleged disciplinary infraction, may be provided as a matter of contract or statute.

The format of disciplinary proceedings is the reverse of normal grievance processing in that at certain points the employer, rather than the grievant or union, is the moving party. Management initiates the process by issuing a notice of discipline to the employee and has the burden of production and proof in any hearing. A party bearing the burden of production must proceed in laying out its evidence before the other party responds. A party bearing the burden of proof must prove its case by whatever standard is applicable in order to prevail.

The Grievance Procedure

A contractual grievance procedure usually has several levels or steps. There is no recommended number of steps, but too many steps, especially if they have time frames that are extended or flexible, can unreasonably delay resolution. A late resolution precludes meaningful relief on many issues. For example, if one is denied a sabbatical and the grievance mechanism takes eight months, as a practical matter the opportunity for the sabbatical is lost, especially if it is tied to grants or travel or involves others in a joint-research project. The best practice, therefore, is to limit the number of internal steps to two or three.

The first step in grievance procedures is usually an attempt to solve the problem informally. A good grievance procedure provides for this informal preliminary step. Once a grievance is filed, positions can harden and settlement can become more difficult. A formal written grievance must be filed within whatever time limits are specified in the contract. The formal grievance triggers a meeting or hearing with a designated management representative. (In higher education, this representative can be the department chair, if chairs are part of management.) Frequently, the second step is at the dean's or vice-presidential level. The steps begin at lower levels of management and rise to higher levels, where ultimate authority to resolve disputes lies.

Who Can Initiate and Pursue the Grievance?

The contract-grievance article or a statutory provision usually determines who possesses the authority to initiate a grievance and process it through the various stages. The intervention of the union is not necessarily required for a bargaining unit member to file a grievance against management, to represent himself or herself, or to choose to be represented by counsel or a friend or colleague. Unions may at times prefer this autonomy because it does not require the union to act as gatekeeper, to use union resources, or to risk credibility on weak cases. But such individual access to the grievance process may also result in less-effective presentations that weaken the case on appeal or that establish bad policies. So, by virtue of statute or contract provision, the union generally maintains the right to be present and to be kept informed, and many unions insist on participation from the inception of the process. Moreover, although some unions prefer to let members pursue weak cases—even to arbitration—on their own rather than to deny members an opportunity for a hearing, most unions prefer to control access to the arbitration step on the grounds that this access is essential to the union's duty to maintain and administer the contract. The availability of expert counsel is often, of course, an important benefit of union representation. It distinguishes the circumstances of the grievant in a labor arbitration from the much less favorable circumstances of the inadequately represented consumers in the emerging commercial-arbitration procedures.

When to Grieve

If an informal attempt does not settle a dispute, the decision whether or not to grieve must be made by the individual or the union. Many factors go into these decisions. The primary criterion is, of course, whether a strong enough case that the contract has been violated can be made in the grievance process or in arbitration. If it appears that such a case can be made adequately, a formal grievance will generally be filed.

Irrespective of the strength of a grievance on the merits, a key consideration in whether or not to pursue a case may be the contractual timelines for filing. Contracts usually have a filing deadline triggered by when the grievant knew or reasonably should have known about the alleged breach. Faculty members not uncommonly come to the union after considerable time has elapsed since the event giving rise to the grievance. In such cases, there may not be time to deliberate about taking the grievance or not. Unless one can obtain an extension, filing the grievance quickly is the only available option in such a situation. One can always withdraw a grievance if the situation demands. Although arbitrators may look askance at grievances filed after the applicable deadline, often a successful argument can be made to establish an exception, so filing with the option subsequently to withdraw may be the wisest course of action.

Another consideration for deciding to file a grievance is the duty of fair representation. This legal doctrine requires the union to represent its bargaining unit members fairly, without bias, and with a certain level of competence. This duty does not mean that the union must take every grievance to arbitration but rather that the decision to take a case to arbitration or not must entail a careful consideration of the case's merits. Appropriate factors in determining whether to take a grievance or pursue it to arbitration include the resources of the union, the strength of the case, and the danger of setting a bad precedent or losing a right or past practice that faculty members enjoyed under the contract. Since failure to meet timelines by a union acting on behalf of a grievant can preclude further pursuit of a remedy and therefore a failure to represent, it is imperative that the union's internal procedures are designed to avoid such errors.

Political considerations may also affect decisions regarding which grievances to pursue. Where it is very difficult for the leadership to turn down a grievance by particular individuals or on a hot-button issue, the more prudent course may be to take the grievance to arbitration and let an outside arbitrator have the burden of denial. Or a grievance may be pursued to alert members to a contractual weakness and to build support for future negotiations. But frequent pursuit of weak cases damages the bargaining relationship and costs time and resources.

Cases involving allegedly improper termination of the employment of a unit member, sometimes referred to as the "capital punishment of labor relations," are clearly high priority. Other high-priority cases include those that have an impact on a large number of unit members, such as a pay cut; failure to pay benefits guaranteed under the contract; or layoffs. Lower-priority cases are issues that affect one person, have limited or relatively short-term impact, and no consequence for unit rights in general. Typical examples of this type of grievance are faculty promotions and annual merit increments. In these instances, the grievance process may take longer than simple reapplication the following year, although the grievance may still be necessary if the problem is repeated or the contract violation is clear or part of an emerging pattern. The relative importance of the grievance to the union and to other bargaining unit members should be considered but is less significant in deciding to file initially than to take the case to the final step. Since arbitration is costly and time consuming, unions are well advised to have an established procedure and policy for deciding whether or not to take grievances to arbitration.

Grievance Processing

The grievance process begins either when the union is contacted by a member or when the union leadership itself wishes to initiate a grievance.

THE INTERVIEW

When members initiate grievances, they are often anxious and not infrequently angry. The grievance handler should be available to listen carefully, demonstrate concern, and show respect for the seriousness of the issue but should not offer more assurance regarding the outcome than the circumstances permit.

The interview should be taken very seriously. Basic information, such as the grievant's home phone number and address, should be recorded, since communication with the grievant is essential. The grievance officer should begin building a grievance file, which should contain the necessary data on the faculty member and all grievance forms, letters, and memos as evidence about the issue. All possible relevant information should be obtained; documents may be discarded later if not needed, but one should err on the side of inclusiveness.

The most important part of the initial interview is to listen, in order to get the entire story of the incident. Members may often be emotional and confused when contemplating confronting their managers or colleagues. Emotions can easily overcome good judgment in these situations, so it is important to assess exactly what happened or did not happen to the faculty member and to distinguish facts from interpretation. The experienced grievance handler may, then, make an educated guess as to the material facts of the case but should exercise caution since this guess may affect the quality of the union's decision about whether and how far to pursue the case.

During the initial interview, the grievance officer should discuss the process with the potential grievant, going over the timelines for filing, possible outcomes, and the length of time cases normally take to wend their way through the procedure. The grievance specialist should offer a frank preliminary assessment of the case, resisting the temptation to make promises that may not be kept or to build up unrealistic hopes for a resolution of the problem.

FILING THE GRIEVANCE

Timelines. As stated earlier, the union must pay close attention to time-lines, since grievances filed late are procedurally flawed, often fatally. When the union cannot file a grievance in a timely manner because the grievant contacts the union after the deadline, the union should be careful to document this initial contact in a case file.

The Description of the Grievance. Whether the grievance is initiated with a standard grievance form or a letter, the description of the alleged contract violations must be stated clearly. Usually, the contract-grievance article describes what is required in the grievance filing. Good practice includes noting the date of the incident or when the grievant first knew of the incident, thereby establishing that the grievance is filed in a timely manner.

It is not necessary or prudent to attempt to document at the outset all arguments in support of the grievance. As the case progresses, the back-and-forth at grievance meetings may lead to revisions in the facts and theories in support of the union's case. At the same time, specificity should be sufficient to enable those reading the grievance file to understand the problem. Keep in mind also that a neutral arbitrator may not be familiar with the nuances of the academy.

Citing Contract Violations. The grievance must cite the alleged violations of the contract. The general rule is to keep the references as inclusive as possible, since adding alleged violations as the grievance progresses may be difficult. Allegations of contract violations may be withdrawn at any stage if it turns out there is insufficient evidence to support them. For example, cite an article in its entirety rather than a specific clause. If it turns out in the end that a particular sentence within a section was the only provision violated, one can narrow the allegations later. However, if one cited only the specific sentence and later discovered in the investigation and preparation phase that other contract language in the article was implicated, the union might have difficulty incorporating the additional violations in the subsequent grievance processing.

It is also prudent to cite contract provisions that may possibly be related, erring on the side of inclusion at the outset and narrowing the allegations later if necessary. Do not, however, overdo this broad-allegation strategy. To cite dozens of peripherally related contract articles when it is clear the issue is workload, for example, makes the grievant and the union grievance representative appear less certain or confident regarding the central issue in the grievance.

Stating a Remedy for the Grievance. Most contract-grievance articles require the requested remedy to be set forth in the initial grievance. The fashioning of a remedy can be tricky, since the union must be careful not to limit its options as the case progresses. If a union asks for something like "any other appropriate remedy," it signals to management and arbitrators that the remedy requested is flexible and may include expanding what was originally asked for in the initial filing.

The remedy section must be reasonable. Grievants' hurt feelings may lead them to want more than can be expected. Resist the temptation to accomodate the grievant's request for apologies, reprimands or the firing of administrators, monetary payments clearly out of line with the violation, and similarly unrealistic demands. Grievances decided by arbitrators will be limited to compensatory or "make whole" remedies and almost always exclude punitive damages. Even back-pay remedies are most often offset by outside income, including unemployment or disability payments.

Delivering the Grievance. The contract will likely describe how to deliver the grievance to management. Some contracts provide for hand delivery or certified mail. Whatever the method, proof of delivery is important for the grievance file. If the grievance is delivered by hand, a date stamp is good evidence that the grievance was filed in a timely manner by the union and received by management. Hand delivery is preferred because the post office occasionally loses mail. If the grievance is not delivered, it may be deemed untimely and ignored. With the advent of electronic mail, some contracts allow for electronic filing of grievances; more and more, grievances and arbitration procedures have come to rely on electronic communications.

Collecting Evidence and Building the File for the Grievance. As the grievance progresses, the union needs to refine its understanding of the facts and issues. One can neither rely on a single source to determine what actually happened nor assume that the grievant's account is accurate. Interviews should be sought with colleagues, administrators, payroll officers, students, or anyone who could shed light on the incidents being grieved. All relevant evidence should be placed in the grievance file along with the grievance handler's notes of interviews, assessments, recommendations, and the like.

Arguing the Grievance. Usually the grievance must be argued with management at various steps in the process. Grievance representatives disagree whether the presentation to management should be written or oral. The advocates of written submissions cite the protections of precluding management from claiming that something was not mentioned in the grievance meeting. This route is also easier for individuals who are not skilled at oral presentations.

Those who advocate oral presentations prefer not to have something in writing that would limit the grievance to what is on paper. Further, an oral exchange can be a dialogue, whereas a written presentation is a one-way communication. Of course, both formats can be used, even in the same case. What is most important is simply that the grievant's story is heard by management and that a complete understanding of the dispute is developed.

Decide beforehand who should speak at the grievance meeting. The grievance representative and the grievant should discuss this issue before meeting with management. Usually, the representative begins the meeting by outlining the dispute. If the grievant wishes to speak, both can participate in the presentation. If the grievance representative is doubtful that the grievance has merit but still wishes to provide the grievant with an opportunity to have the issue aired, the representative may allow the grievant to play a larger role in presenting the issues to management. Conversely, if the grievant is apprehensive or fearful of retaliation, the grievance representative might play a larger role in the presentation.

When the grievance meeting is over, management must respond in writing within the time frame provided in the contract. Sometimes, the parties will keep the meeting open for further discussion of possible resolution. This opportunity may require extending, by mutual consent, the contractual time frames for processing. If not, management might provide a written answer denying the grievance in whole or in part or provide a remedy in the written answer to the grievance. If the grievance is denied, the union must decide whether to proceed to the next step, to consider the issue settled and drop the grievance, or to continue negotiations at that level. Normally, in contract-grievance articles, the next higher step is to a higher level of management with the power to overrule the lower level. All too often, however, all management representatives speak with a single voice, and subsequent steps of the grievance procedure are essentially meaningless. Binding arbitration at the end of the grievance process is a particularly valuable safeguard for faculty members when this management style is utilized.

Settlements

The purpose of the grievance procedure is to resolve disputes between management and faculty. At any stage during the grievance procedure, settlement of the grievance should be the goal. Settlement is not always possible or easy, because the grievant is frequently in an all-or-nothing frame of mind, and management may never want to compromise. Nonetheless, the grievance representative should not be deterred from seeking a settlement of the grievance. Negotiating settlements is much like negotiating a contract and may be initiated by either party. Ideas are exchanged, proposals are floated, discussions of the ramifications of a settlement occur, compromises are made, and issues are worked out. Management deals directly with the union representative and communications flow from management through the grievance representative to the grievant. Proposals are tested with the grievant and countered and presented to management, just as in bargaining a contract. Good communications between the grievance representative and grievant are essential. Any compromise should be formulated in writing to avoid future disagreements on the same issue.

In negotiating settlements, review the language carefully. Management usually wants to avoid establishing a precedent, especially in cases that might broaden or strengthen contractual provisions. Unions usually want to make such settlements broadly applicable. Management may understandably want the grievant to waive any and all claims directly arising out of the specific grievance but may also overreach by seeking waiver of all future claims, known or unknown. Management may also seek to prohibit the grievant from taking action in any other forum, such as a court or state or federal agency.

Arbitration

Most higher-education contracts have an arbitration process as the final step in the grievance procedure. Arbitration of contract disputes means that the parties (the union and management) have agreed that unresolved disputes will be referred to a neutral arbitrator, who will hear evidence and issue a ruling. Arbitrators are labor-relations professionals selected by mutual agreement of the parties. The contract may call for a list of potential arbitrators to be provided by a neutral body or may include an established list of acceptable arbitrators. Generally a single individual is selected for each case. Some contracts, however, provide for a panel consisting of a neutral arbitrator and one panelist appointed by each party. This approach is sometimes viewed as a way to ensure that the panel is familiar with academic practices.

Grievance arbitration is like a minitrial. Advocates do not need to be attorneys, although they must be familiar with arbitration procedures. These procedures provide for receiving documentary and oral evidence under oath as well as for ensuring an opportunity to examine and cross-examine witnesses and to challenge proffered documents. When both sides have concluded the presentation of evidence and rest, the arbitrator may receive oral summations or require written briefs from the parties. The arbitrator or panel then has a given amount of time to render a decision. The normal standard of proof is a preponderance of the evidence, but a higher standard typically pertains to disciplinary matters.

The scope of an arbitrator's authority is set forth in the contract's grievance article (and, in some instances, in the applicable law). The hearing procedures and rules of evidence are well defined in the Voluntary Labor Arbitration Rules of the American Arbitration Association, which many contracts incorporate by reference. The rulings of the arbitrator are generally final and binding on the parties. Judicial review of arbitral decisions is rare, but arbitration awards may be overturned if an arbitrator is shown to have exceeded his or her authority or to have violated public law. By providing binding resolution of disputes, arbitration not only ensures the orderly resolution of individual disputes but also provides a foundation for stable and cooperative employment relations.

The Collective Agreement: Economic Issues

ERNST BENJAMIN

Effective representation on economic issues is essential to the academic profession and to the academy. Some academics, however, fear that bargaining contributes to the erosion of professional standards by emphasizing economic concerns and salary equity rather than merit-based salary distribution. Other academics are simply embarrassed to appear to place economics ahead of the professoriate's ideals. Academics do, nonetheless, have legitimate economic needs. Moreover, if colleges and universities are to attract and retain capable academics in a market-based economy, they need to provide salaries and benefits that are competitive with those not only at other academic institutions but in the various alternative professions to which potential academics may be drawn.

Historically, academic salaries have kept pace neither with inflation nor with salaries in other professions. The annual reports titled "On the Economic Status of the Profession," published in *Academe*, provide documentation and discussion of these problems for full-time faculty members. Although annual documentation of part-time faculty and graduate-assistant salaries is not available, periodic surveys by the National Center For Education Statistics confirm that these salaries and benefits are substantially lower than those of full-time faculty members (see United States, Dept. of Educ., *National Study and Student Financing*). Collective bargaining has certainly benefited academic compensation in some instances. Some studies find evidence that bargaining has benefited bargaining unit members overall, but most do not (Monks; Ehrenberg 212). Regardless of bargaining, academic salaries lag behind those in other sectors, and academic bargainers face an uphill struggle to successfully resolve two basic issues—how much? and to whom? Moreover, like other employees, academics have found it difficult to protect their fringe benefits in a time of escalating medical costs and corporate assaults on pension plans.

When one bargains over "how much," one bargains the estimated cost and size of the increase in salaries and benefits. The bargaining over "to whom" determines the distribution of salary-and-compensation improvements, that is, the share of the economic increase to each member (or group of members) of the bargaining unit. Administrative bargainers understand and sometimes exploit that some academics will be more concerned about their individual compensation than about that of the unit as a whole. Academics need to understand that the administration may also be divided. Budget officers may care more about absolute dollars and may focus on overall cost. Academic officers may desire to offer competitive salaries to some faculty members and departments and may thus focus on the on the narrower issues of cost to the academic budget and on which individuals, types of academics, or departments get the academic dollars. Consequently, economic bargaining may turn as much or more on the questions, to and from whom? as on, how much? Escalating medical costs further complicate these issues.

The bargaining agent generally formulates the initial economic proposal, although exceptions do occur. For example, administrators have sometimes hoped that an attractive economic offer would lead to a prompt settlement and thereby foreclose consideration of noneconomic proposals or prolonged and disruptive negotiations. Accepting such a preemptive offer is rarely advantageous, but it may be difficult to resist, particularly when it is tied to a legislative deadline or when the members have not been adequately sensitized to the importance of other outstanding issues. Academic bargainers often anticipate and avoid this scenario by submitting timely proposals, assuring that the membership understands and has a stake in key issues, and deferring the final economic settlement until other critical issues are resolved.

Most often, however, the administration awaits the bargaining agent's first move, and the agent confronts the difficult task of formulating an effective initial proposal. Although membership involvement in developing this proposal is essential, the union's presentation at the bargaining table should not be a catchall wish list. It should ordinarily be large enough to provide a better than inflationary increase overall, to encompass the diverse interests of the membership, and to permit

subsequent concessions. Yet it should not be so large as to undercut credibility with the public. Nor should it be so large as to create unrealistic
expectations that lead to membership frustration with the eventual
settlement.

How Much?

The key criteria used to establish and advocate economic targets include
the rate of inflation and thus the cost of living, comparables, previous
understandings or policies, and cost and ability to pay.

COST OF LIVING

Unit members often regard any increase less than the rate of inflation as
a salary reduction. The most common measure of inflation is the Consumer Price Index for Urban Consumers (see www.bls.gov/cpi/home
.htm). The cost of living varies by region and locality as well as over time.
So academics in expensive areas may argue that increases are required
not only because cost increases are generally greater but because their
salaries, though nominally similar to those in institutions elsewhere, are
inadequate with respect to the higher costs of living in their specific locality. Various local measures of cost of living may be obtained on the
Web, often from real estate sites. But the reliability of area-based cost-
of-living variances depends on the precision and accuracy with which the
appropriate locality can be determined. Moreover, academic agreements
rarely include cost-of-living provisions because administrators insist on a
"cap," which means that increases may be less than, but not more than,
the maximum agreed to.

COMPARABLES

Comparable institutions are those recognized as peers or trendsetters. The
administration may have a long-established peer list, or the parties may
formally agree on a list. The peers are sometimes selected because they
are perceived as similar, but institutions may designate "aspirational
peers"—those colleges or universities the administration seeks to emulate. Selection of peers frequently emphasizes such diverse factors as location, public or private control, reputation, size, degrees offered,
similarity of student or faculty recruitment pools, and program mix.

The peer comparison may be based either on salary levels or rates of increase. It may be based on overall mean salaries or increases or compensation (salary plus benefit expenditures). It may consider factors such as rank distributions and variations in program and disciplines. For example, two institutions with similar overall mean faculty salaries may differ substantially because one has a small proportion of full-time professors with unusually high salaries and the other has a large proportion of full-time professors with substantially lower salaries. Given the numerous options available for making comparisons, the selection of peer institutions and criteria of comparison shape the comparison and so often require negotiated agreement.

The best generally available peer data on salary levels and increases by institution is the AAUP salary survey. The AAUP survey is unique because it provides benefit expenditures by rank so that comparisons may include total compensation as well as salary. The AAUP data also distinguish the overall average salary increase from the increase for continuing faculty members, thereby excluding the effects of turnover and providing a more accurate indicator of actual salary improvements for those faculty members who continue at the institution from one year to the next.

Some states and institutions, however, do collect useful data through their own reports, surveys, and data-sharing agreements. Disciplinary data and salary levels for new faculty members may be obtained from the Oklahoma state survey of public land-grant universities (see Tarrant and Reichard for the 2000–01 survey) or from the public- and private-sector surveys conducted for the College and University Professional Association for Human Resources (CUPA-HR). These data are published only as median salaries by rank and not by institution, which limits their usefulness for peer analysis, but institutions may purchase special peer-based reports.

PREVIOUS UNDERSTANDINGS OR POLICIES

The parties in bargaining often have previous understandings that may include specific compensation goals. These goals may also include recapturing suspended or deferred increases or adjustments caused by difficulties in the budgetary outlook. In well-established, mature bargaining relationships, such long-term understandings can work effectively. However, economic circumstances are unpredictable, so retaining flexibility may be essential. Moreover, long-term understandings on economic issues may undercut the support and tactical flexibility necessary to achieving noneconomic objectives.

COST AND ABILITY TO PAY

Where academics commonly emphasize cost of living and comparables, administrations often emphasize cost or ability to pay. The cost of compensation increases can be difficult to estimate; if the true cost is known at all, it may be known only to the administration. Thus, the union may prefer to argue simply that the administration must find the resources to fulfill its responsibilities. But the administration counters, of course, that balancing the budget is a fundamental responsibility. So the union bargaining agent needs to have some understanding of the key factors in assessing the cost of a compensation increase.

The cost of a salary increase will include the increased salary dollars and the increased cost of purchasing fringe benefits. The administration also includes "roll up" in its estimate. Roll up ordinarily includes the increased cost of social security, workers compensation, unemployment benefits, and other insurance or taxes. The association may counter by estimating the annual recurrent savings from turnover (as highly paid staff members retire and are replaced by entry-level staff members) and from unfilled vacancies from leaves, nonrenewals, resignations, and retirements.

One-time costs, such as merit bonuses, should be clearly distinguished from increases in base pay. If the institution has some unusual nonrecurrent income, it may prefer to offer such one-time awards. Generally, such nonrecurrent awards are a problem for the bargaining agent because it is faced with trying to renegotiate this money along with new money in the next round. Conversely, in cases where the institution has a short-term budget crunch, salary increases are back-loaded, that is, agreed increases to base may not take effect until late in the academic year or in a subsequent year. This cost deferral assists the association in achieving a long-term increase in base salaries while minimizing short-term cost to the administration in a period of stringency.

ABILITY TO PAY

In especially difficult times, administrations often assert that they are unable to fund previously negotiated or prospective increases. This assertion often includes the threat that meeting or establishing the salary obligation would necessitate program elimination and reductions in bargaining unit personnel. The bargaining agent may respond by seeking access to administrative data and employing outside assistance to conduct its own budget study. Or, it may offer to accept concessions on condition that the administration demonstrates good faith by agreeing to specific noneconomic proposals, or prospective economic benefits, or some combination of these. For example, some unions have agreed to one-time salary reductions that did not reduce base salary and that were given to the administration as loans subject to repayment at a specified subsequent time. Although bargaining permits a variety of such accommodations, "concession bargaining" is always difficult and can seriously impair the bargaining relationship—especially if the union members are not persuaded of the validity of administration claims.

To Whom?

As a practical matter, the issues of "how much" and "to whom" are often closely interconnected. Among the reasons that administrators prefer selective increases is that these enable them to meet the most pressing demands with the fewest dollars. Among the reasons that academic associations favor across-the-board increases is that they require the institution to raise all unit salaries in order to raise those that it most desires to increase. Since any form of increase will be perceived to benefit some unit members disproportionately, reaching agreement on how to distribute compensation increases is often inseparable from reaching agreement on the amount of the increase.

Academic salary systems vary greatly, and collective bargaining agreements frequently rely on multiple approaches to achieve diverse objectives. For present purposes, the various approaches may be considered in four clusters: across-the-board increases, salary structures or step systems, salary-equity procedures, and selective (such as merit or market) increases.

ACROSS-THE-BOARD INCREASES

Most academics, other than those in research or research-oriented universities and departments, prefer across-the-board (a-t-b) increases. Such increases are the norm in part-time and graduate-assistant units. Many assume that a-t-b is fair because it treats everyone alike, but others complain that this approach is unfair precisely because it treats everyone, regardless of differences, alike. In fact, even if we set aside considerations of individual merit, preexisting unit-member salary differences mean that a-t-b increases don't have similar effects on all unit members. There is the difference between dollars and percentages, for example. Equal dollars a-t-b provide a higher percentage increase to lower-salaried unit members; equal percentages a-t-b provide a higher dollar increase to higher-salaried unit members. Thus, even in negotiating a-t-b approaches to salaries, collective bargaining cannot avoid making choices. What it can do is make thoughtful choices and periodically adjust the negotiated procedures to correct inequities or deficiencies.

Equal dollar increases a-t-b are most useful if the parties seek to improve the relative circumstances of lower-salaried unit members. Equal dollars may, however, foster salary compression by narrowing the percentage gap between lower- and higher-salaried unit members without leaving space for market or merit distinctions. Where faculty appointments include ranks, rank compression may be lessened and differences maintained by adjusting the dollars awarded a-t-b based on rank; in other words, each faculty member of a given rank may receive the same dollar amount, which is based on a percentage of the rank mean or median salary. In this way, those in higher ranks receive larger increments.

Percentage increases a-t-b widen the dollar gap between low- and high-salaried unit members. This method often has the effect of rewarding senior unit members and discouraging younger members. Moreover, the allocation of a large proportion of the available increase to senior appointees may leave too little for recent entries. Unless new appointees receive salaries equal to or higher than those who recently preceded them, the percentage option may create recruitment problems. Flat percentage a-t-b also results in a form of salary compression, or even inversion, that is especially demoralizing. Moreover, it may cause retention problems, since recent appointees see both long-term and new appointees doing better than themselves. Only a few of the possible permutations are explored here, but these examples show that, although no particular a-t-b formula will fit all situations, the dollar and percentage approaches of a-t-b systems may combine to meet a variety of objectives.

SALARY STRUCTURES

A salary structure may simply establish salary minima and maxima by rank or years of service. Promotion from one rank to another, which often depends on a measure of academic performance, customarily includes a special salary increment that may be included as a cost in negotiating the agreement. Minima and maxima are used to limit salary disparities. Maxima also limit costs and are especially important when increases are percentage-based. This is because, without maxima, funding increases for high-salaried unit members might prevent meeting salary objectives to lower-salaried unit members. Where salary ranges are established, however, they often permit exceptions and may have little real effect, unless they provide some annual increment tied to years of service and perhaps to qualifications such as degrees, rank, or similar criteria. Years of service and qualifications may be particularly useful criteria for establishing increments for part-time faculty members and graduate assistants who do not have promotional opportunities and who often receive no reward for the value of their continuity and experience.

STEP SYSTEMS

These more complex salary structures include recurrent step increases based on years of service, rank, or other qualifications. In academia, step systems exist primarily in public community colleges and in those public university systems where compensation practices were initially based on teacher or civil-service systems. Step systems are especially attractive to academics when they rest on legislation that creates an automatic annual entitlement requiring neither a negotiated increase nor a specific annual appropriation. This arrangement also provides some assurance of protection against inflation.

Where step systems are not already in place, they may be difficult to negotiate. Legislative authorization of recurrent annual increments that will continue beyond the life of a specific collective agreement is a matter that must be resolved outside the bargaining relationship. Absent such authorization, the step system, or at least its funding, must be renegotiated with each round of bargaining. Even so, the step system may establish mutual expectations that are useful in planning as well as bargaining. It may also include a sensible salary structure that combines elements of flat-dollar and percentage increases by rank and step in a manner that avoids compression and inversion as well as excessive disparities. Or it may not.

Depending on the formula that established the step increment in the first place, step systems may instead foster salary compression. Or the steps may become an inadequate substitute for the larger increases required to keep up with inflation or salaries in peer institutions or professions. Steps may also fail to adjust adequately for changing market differentials between academic programs. They may conceal rather than correct gender disparities based, for example, on differences due to placement at initial appointment. None of these possible deficiencies are unavoidable. Step systems, such as the one at the University of California, even accommodate substantial disciplinary market differentials and individual merit increments. The point is not that step systems are inadequate or undesirable but that they are a framework within which many of the problems with other salary systems are encountered and need to be resolved.

SALARY-EQUITY PROCEDURES

Since salary procedures do not automatically assure equity, bargaining agreements often incorporate specific equity provisions. As we have seen, considerations of equity may affect a variety of salary procedures, such as how to distribute a-t-b increases or to design a step system. But, not infrequently, academics may decide that specific equity provisions are required. These sometimes include efforts to diminish disparities that occur because of discipline, length of service, and gender.

Market Effects. Disciplinary disparities generally reflect a mix of actual and perceived market differentials. One way to assess these variances is to compare the local variations with those at comparable institutions using the differentials estimated by surveys like the Oklahoma State or CUPA-HR surveys. Since disciplinary differentials often contribute to gender disparities, the actual differences essential to recruitment and retention should be distinguished from those that are not essential. Equity procedures may need to adapt to the essential differences but might still correct any excess due to exaggerated claims.

Similarly, market pressures often lead institutions to focus increases on recruitment and retention, which disadvantages those faculty members who remain at the institution for many years, and especially those who also remain in the same rank. Danger signs include the extreme differences in full-professor salaries within a single department, which result from the star system; comparatively disproportionate numbers of associate professors because of excessive barriers to promotion; or salary compression between associate and assistant professors caused by disproportionate increases in starting salaries. The disadvantaged faculty members generally lack the individual market power to demand more equitable salaries. In seeking improvements, bargaining agents use their combined strength and the argument that the declining morale of faculty members who suffer salary inequity diminishes their contributions to the institution. Accordingly, equity provisions, such as special increases for long-term faculty members whose salaries are below the mean of their rank, are sometimes negotiated.

Gender Disparities. The disparity between the salaries of men and women is a chronic problem. AAUP has published *Paychecks,* a guide to identifying and correcting this disparity (see Haignere). To distinguish gender disparities from other sources of differences—time in rank, qualifications, duties, and discipline—it is necessary to obtain good data and to employ an appropriate multiple-regression procedure based on a conceptual model that will stand up to legal challenge. Despite these difficulties, many collective bargaining units have successfully used procedures like those described in *Paychecks* to identify and correct gender disparities. Although these procedures are too complex to describe here, four aspects of the process require mention.

First, even though rank is an obvious source of differences, it is necessary to check to see if rank is itself a result of discrimination. One sign of such discrimination may be a disproportionate number of women who are long-term associate professors. Similarly, although discipline may account for many differentials, and although gender comparisons should control for discipline, disciplinary differences may themselves be in excess of those that are required in the market and that may reflect longstanding barriers to women. Such has been the case, for example, in engineering.

Second, although the analysis of disparities and the establishment of a pool of funds for correction are statistically based, in units with substantial variations in duties and performance, the actual award of compensatory increases should not be automatic; it should be based on an academic assessment of the qualifications, assignments, and performance of each recipient.

Third, gender disparities are often founded on difference in salary or salary step at the time of initial appointment as well as differences in promotion, both of which require monitoring. Finally, even gender disparities that have been corrected tend to recur; thus, periodic review is required.

Racial and Ethnic Disparities. Because the number of disadvantaged minorities in faculty positions is generally too small to permit reliable statistical analysis, statistical analysis provides little evidence from which to determine the extent of salary discrimination based on race. The lack of adequate data also means that identification and correction depends on case-by-case monitoring and review. In addition to pursuing ordinary affirmative-action procedures, it may be appropriate to create a committee, similar to that which allocates women's equity increases, to take up the task of determining whether the salaries of minority faculty members are less than those of similarly situated nonminority faculty members and, if they are, to allocate equitable increases.

SELECTIVE INCREASES

Many comprehensive university and most doctoral-university full-time faculty bargaining units allocate a significant portion of their salary increments to selective increases. Although these increases are often termed merit increases, they generally include a mix of factors, including actual or alleged market differentials, conformity to departmental policies, the personal attitudes of evaluators, equity concerns, as well as diverse and sometimes inconsistent merit criteria. Moreover, decisional authority may be assigned to colleagues or administrators at various levels. Consequently, bargaining selective salaries is not only about rewarding merit or who gets what salary but also about who gets to decide the salaries. Any merit system must, explicitly or implicitly, fashion policies and procedures that select among or combine these alternatives.

Merit Increases. Objections to the use of merit increases include the likelihood that the evaluation of merit will be distorted by the various factors mentioned above—especially market pressures, lack of clear criteria, and conformity to administrative policy or whim (Tanguay). But proponents of merit systems offer compelling reasons to incorporate academic judgment and recognition of individual differences in the salary policies of complex institutions. Many faculty members in these institutions prefer to have their contributions individually recognized, and many faculty members, as well as administrators, seek a mechanism through which to encourage and reward accomplishments in research, teaching, and service (Sutton and Bergerson). Consequently, faculty associations have developed a variety of procedures, similar to those negotiated for other personnel decisions, to try to assure that selective increments are awarded in a manner consistent with academic standards, unit-member objectives, and fundamental fairness.

The selective increases in collective bargaining contracts are sometimes based on a general set of criteria or on factors determined at the department level and are sometimes decided by the designated decision makers. The decision makers may be departmental colleagues or chairs, college- and university-level colleagues, administrators, or some combination. Increases are more often allocated to base salary, but, depending on the availability of one-time funds, contracts sometimes agree to one-time bonuses or awards or are given in a special allocation to avoid increasing disparities in base salaries. The larger the proportion of the base increase that is selectively determined, the more important it is that the bargaining agent ensure effective faculty participation in decision making and provide an opportunity for individuals to grieve when the decisions appear unfair or contrary to the provisions of the agreement.

Market Increases. Particularly in research universities, administrators feel an intense need to accommodate market pressures. Disciplinary market differences are generally built into the salary structures; that is, faculty members in market-favored disciplines generally receive higher starting salaries and a larger dollar or even percentage share of increases than others. Individual differences within disciplines may reflect individual bargaining power based on actual or prospective outside offers. Negotiated salary pools occasionally provide a fund to meet such competing offers. More often, the contract agrees not to cap individual salaries, allowing the administration to allocate funds other than those negotiated, under specified circumstances, to provide market increases to base salaries. This kind of agreement may reduce the pressure for market-based allocation of negotiated increases but may also lead the administration to hold back funds during negotiations to ensure their availability for extra-contractual awards.

In sum, selective increases enable the administration to focus limited resources on those specific unit members whom it judges most important. The union, however, needs to leverage the market power of these individual faculty members to secure increased salaries for the entire unit, since selective raises must come at the expense of the rest of the unit. Compromise is possible where the administration recognizes that excessive salary differentials diminish overall morale and productivity. Any compromise also needs to assure that a sufficient proportion of unit members benefit from the recognition of merit differentials and share in the opportunity to shape judgments of academic policy and performance.

Additional Economic Benefits

Economic benefits include, in addition to salary, both the fringe benefits included in compensation and the professional benefits, such as grants and travel funds, that do not count as compensation.

FRINGE BENEFITS

Major fringe benefits for full-time faculty members include retirement contributions, medical and dental benefits, life insurance, dependent tuition benefits, and housing allowances. Graduate assistants have also been negotiating medical benefits. The minority of part-time faculty members whose salaries are based on a fraction of a full-time-position salary often receive pro rata benefit contributions. The vast majority of part-time faculty members are paid by the course or credit hour and lack access to benefits. Some institutions do, however, offer benefits to those part-time faculty members who teach more than an institutionally defined half-time load.

Fringe benefits are often not negotiable in whole or in part in those public institutions where benefits are established by legislation and encompass a broad range of state employees. In such cases, public-sector unions may form coalitions to lobby or negotiate with the appropriate state authorities. Even where campus or institution-level negotiations are possible, coalition bargaining may be required because the benefit policies encompass multiple bargaining units.

Comparative data on the expenditures for benefits are available from AAUP, but expenditure data may be insufficient to permit systematic comparisons among institutions. Retirement and medical and dental benefits are the most costly and important fringe benefits. The rate of retirement contributions may be compared in the case of the defined-contribution plans that are the academic norm. It is also possible, although more difficult, to compare the benefits in the case of the defined-benefit plans that still predominate in some public jurisdictions. But it is often difficult to estimate the cost of defined-benefit plans or to compare the benefits of one type of plan with the other or to estimate the costs of combined defined-benefit and defined-contribution plans. Although medical benefits are the major cause of escalating fringe-benefit costs, the actual benefits purchased are extremely difficult to ascertain or compare.

These complexities make it difficult to provide generalized observations or assistance here, but a few comments may be useful. That most benefits do not add to taxable income means that it is possible to bargain greater net economic gain for the same expenditure by improving, or at least protecting, fringe benefits. In the case of medical benefits, it may be preferable to accept increases in unit-member copayments for insurance, where these can be paid out of pretax income, than increases in unit member copays for specific medical services that are rarely large enough to be deductible. The complexity of medical benefits and their tax implications underscores the necessity of securing expert assistance either from a unit member with professional knowledge of the area or from a competent consultant. Finally, negotiators should recognize not only that the comparative benefit expenditures between institutions require consideration when establishing salary goals but also that changes in benefits will affect different unit members in different ways.

PROFESSIONAL BENEFITS

Commonly negotiated professional benefits include grants for curricular or professional development and research, travel to conferences, and paid study leaves or sabbaticals. Some of these benefits, such as travel, may be annually available to all unit members. Grants for curriculum development, summer-research grants, and paid study leaves may be based on administrative selection or competitive application and peer-review procedures similar to those used for promotion and tenure review. Some bargaining agents have secured access to such benefits for at least some part-time faculty members. The inclusion of such professional benefits in the collective agreement is an important way to establish a common commitment to improving the academic quality of the faculty and the institution.

WORKS CITED AND SUGGESTIONS FOR FURTHER READING

Ehrenberg, Ronald G. "Collective Bargaining in American Higher Education." *Governing Academia*. Ed. Ehrenberg. Ithaca: Cornell UP, 2004. 209–32.

Haignere, Lois. *Paychecks: A Guide to Conducting Salary-Equity Studies for Higher Education Faculty*. 2nd ed. Washington: AAUP, 2002.

Monks, James. "Unionization and Faculty Salaries: New Evidence from the 1990s." *Journal of Labor Research* 21 (2000): 305–14.

Sutton, Terry P., and Peter J. Bergerson. *Faculty Compensation Systems: Impact on the Quality of Higher Education Systems*. ASHE-ERIC Higher Educ. Report 28.2. San Francisco: Jossey-Bass, 2001.

Tanguay, Denise M. "Inefficient Efficiency: A Critique of Merit Pay." *Steal This University: The Rise of the Corporate University and the Academic Labor Movement*, Ed. Benjamin Johnson, Patrick Kavanagh, and Kevin Mattson. New York: Routledge, 2003. 49–60.

Tarrant, L. Lee, and Carla Reichard. *2000–2001 Faculty Salary Survey of Institutions Belonging to National Association of State Universities and Land-Grant Colleges*. Stillwater: Office of Planning, Budget, and Inst. Research Oklahoma State U, 2001.

United States. Dept. of Educ. Natl. Center for Educ. Statistics. *National Study of Postsecondary Faculty (DAS), NSOPF: 99*. CD-ROM. Washington: US Dept. of Educ., 2001.

———. *Student Financing of Graduate and First Professional Education, 1999–2000*. Washington: GPO, 2002.

The Collective Agreement: Negotiating Redbook Principles

ERNST BENJAMIN

The term *Redbook principles* refers to the academic personnel and governance practices recommended by AAUP in its compendium *Policy Documents and Reports*, commonly referred to as the Redbook. Many academic collective agreements, regardless of bargaining agent, incorporate or establish policies and practices similar to those recommended by AAUP, which illustrates two key points: that widely respected professional standards can be incorporated in bargaining agreements and that contracts that substantially depart from commonly accepted professional standards do not do so as an inherent consequence of unionization. Rather, such contracts generally continue parochial institutional practices established before bargaining.

This continuation is especially evident in community college agreements and in those of some former state teachers' colleges. Many agreements follow practices that reflect the institution's origins and those of their founding instructors, administrators, and even union staff members in the K-12 system. Some institutions and nonteaching academic staff members also retain practices originally based on state civil-service systems. In an institution where tenure resembles job security based on seniority rather than on peer evaluation or where dismissal is based on an administrative decision rather than on a peer hearing, collective bargaining has less likely imposed an industrial model than continued previous board-of-education or civil-service practices.

Contracts generally codify preexisting practices. Innovation consists primarily in finding ways to use contract language to safeguard procedures previously founded on institutional regulations or customary practices. Nonetheless, collective agreements are generally more specific and enforceable than the practices that preceded them. Consequently, administrations that previously endorsed some ideal policies because they could be set aside if found excessively constraining have resisted incorporating them in enforceable agreements. Moreover, the specificity that is often requisite to achieve enforceability of contracts may make such departures from ideal standards in bargaining institutions more evident than in those institutions where poorly enforced but idealized general policies conceal a hodgepodge of actual practices.

For example, the broad requirement that tenure candidates demonstrate excellence in scholarship or teaching has diverse meanings within and across departments. Collective agreements generally seek to establish a specific measure of excellence. Those agreements that draw on K-12 or civil-service practices may define excellence simply in terms of academic degrees or credit hours, years of service, or satisfactory scores on administrative-evaluation instruments. Those that draw on higher education practice use peer review to assess scholarly and pedagogical performance in a manner consistent with institutional and departmental missions. Contracts typically give these performance standards greater specificity than they have in noncontractual settings, but they do not contractually require a specific number of publications or precise teaching-evaluation scores. Rather, contracts typically require each department to document the types of evidence and range of achievements that will be used to determine if candidates meet expectations appropriate to the department's responsibilities. Contracts also generally provide peer-review and grievance procedures to monitor compliance with the established standards.

That contractual agreements are tailored to particular institutional settings and practices makes it difficult to recommend ideal contract language. Moreover, since each of the parties expects some give-and-take in the course of negotiation, each is likely to present initial language more in accord with its aspirations than with its realistic expectations. While negotiators often seek examples from other existing contracts, negotiations rarely begin from language that has already been shaped by the give-and-take of another institution's negotiating process. Therefore, this essay does not recommend specific language but delineates the principles and concepts that have shaped the types of collective agreements that more nearly accord with AAUP recommendations respecting ac-

ademic governance, academic freedom and tenure, and related professional issues.

Academic Governance

In its "Statement on Academic Government for Institutions Engaged in
Collective Bargaining," AAUP recommends that "bargaining should not
replace, but rather should ensure, effective traditional forms of shared
governance" (Amer. Assn. 253). Shared governance requires councils or
committees through which faculty members can engage with academic
administrators to formulate and implement academic policies. These deliberative bodies, not union-management bargaining teams, formulate
the collective academic judgments on which sound academic collective
agreements depend.

Those unfamiliar with academic bargaining often suppose that academic unions necessarily seek, and perhaps even should seek, to substitute themselves for traditional faculty governance. In fact, substitution of
bargaining for governance in academic matters is extremely rare for full-
time faculty members in four-year institutions. Shared governance is,
however, sometimes less significant in two-year institutions and for part-
time faculty members and graduate assistants, especially those that lacked
substantial governance participation before bargaining. Where shared
governance is weak, even relatively strong unions are unlikely to establish a role for faculty members in shaping an academic policy that is
commensurate with the role faculty members enjoy where bargaining
and shared governance coexist.

Scope of Bargaining

Both federal and state law generally limit collective bargaining to "terms
and conditions of employment." Matters of academic policy including not
only broad policies like curriculum, admissions standards, and graduation
requirements but also employment-related policies such as academic calendar, academic evaluation, and academic budget may not be required
or even permissible subjects of bargaining (Benjamin, "Collective Bargaining"). Yet these matters are often subject to faculty deliberation and
effective recommendation by senates and committees. The preservation

and, when possible, strengthening of traditional mechanisms of shared governance serve, therefore, to protect and extend faculty authority beyond the reach of collective bargaining.

Alternatively, some unions have relied on the meet-and-confer provisions of contracts or state labor laws to empower the union or its designees. The meet-and-confer method replaces traditional peer committees with union-management committees for the discussion of those academic policy and budget issues excluded from the scope of formal bargaining. The effectiveness of such provisions depends, like bargaining, on the strength of the union and the overall relationship between the parties. Inherently, however, meet and confer lacks not only the legal advantages afforded by the binding decisions reached through collective bargaining but the greater influence that academics often gain through participation in shared governance.

This influence rests both on the formal authority accorded to academic senates and on the legitimacy conferred by respect for academic expertise. To the extent that the union substitutes itself for shared-governance committees, the authority of the faculty is diminished. When the union appears to control or manipulate governance procedures, this appearance undercuts the legitimacy faculty members may claim based on respect for their expertise. Academic unions derive their strength from the broad support of their members—support they are unlikely to maintain if the union directly engages in the often-divisive deliberations over academic policies and resources. Frequent management complaints that the combination of unionism and shared governance provide faculty members an unfair "two bites of the apple" and violate the requirement that faculty members "not sit on both sides of the bargaining table" further illustrate why academics may prefer to preserve rather than displace traditional governance mechanisms.

Incorporating Shared Governance in the Contract

Academic contracts often contain few direct references to shared governance. This is true even in institutions where faculty participation in academic decisions is important; many such institutions have an informal agreement that preexisting shared-governance provisions are adequate or that negotiation might disturb effective ongoing relationships. Additionally, legal limitations may prevent negotiation over such matters of educational policy. In other instances, shared-governance provisions are explicitly protected. Agreements rarely include detailed governance provisions but may incorporate or refer to board, senate, and handbook policies. Other agreements include past-policy or past-practice clauses that protect existing provisions and the established mechanisms for amending them.

Agreements may codify important specific governance policies such as how faculty members are elected or appointed to peer and joint faculty and administration committees. Agreements frequently assign specific roles to departmental, college and university committees in personnel and curricular matters. They may designate peer or joint faculty-administration committees, as distinct from union-appointed committees, to administer research funds, teaching awards, or merit pay negotiated in the agreement. Union agreements and governance are thus closely interconnected but nonetheless distinct. The union negotiates roles and procedures. Faculty committees make the substantive academic recommendations.

The interdependence between academic governance and academic bargaining does require some congruence between bargaining unit membership and governance participation. Academic collective bargainers need to ensure through the agreement or governance bylaws that all unit members can participate in appropriate governance activities. Senior or full-time faculty members may have greater authority and responsibility, such as membership on promotion and tenure committees. But no category of bargaining unit members, including part-time faculty and academic staff members, should be denied representation in pertinent governance activities.

Academic Freedom and Academic Appointment Policies

Most academic agreements protect academic freedom. Some, even non-AAUP contracts, refer to or incorporate substantial parts of the "1940 Statement of Principles on Academic Freedom" (Amer. Assn. 3–10). Others refer generally to academic freedom or spell out their own definitions. Not infrequently, agreements also incorporate language requiring the prudent exercise of academic freedom, drawn not only from the "1940 Statement" but from other AAUP statements dealing with such faculty responsibilities.

Collective agreements usually strengthen academic freedom by ensuring its protection through binding arbitration rather than through relatively costly and uncertain court proceedings. In some cases, however, the contractual language may unduly limit academic expression by setting rigid rules for professorial speech based on AAUP recommendations meant as counsels of prudence rather than as absolute requirements. More commonly, collective agreements ensure the protection of academic freedom through detailed provisions respecting academic appointments, evaluation, reappointment, tenure, promotion, and dismissal.

Nondiscrimination, Equal Opportunity, and Affirmative Action

Most collective agreements contain comprehensive nondiscrimination provisions. Some contracts provide for enforcement through arbitration. Some preclude arbitration and rely on external legal remedies. Some permit both. And some require a choice between the alternatives. In view of the complex legal issues involved, these matters are discussed in Gregg Adler's essay on legal and organizational issues, in this volume. Note, however, that since discrimination may occur in the course of any personnel decision, contracts that preclude arbitration of alleged discrimination or that require the sacrifice of external legal protections in exchange for access to union representation in an arbitration proceeding plainly provide less assurance of fair decision making.

Many faculty contracts provide support for equal opportunity and affirmative action. Agreements need, however, to balance the need for administrative review with the protection of peer review to ensure equal opportunity for each. For example, many faculty members do not wish to permit appointments contrary to peer recommendations, but collegial or peer vetoes cannot be condoned if they would prevent redress of discriminatory decisions. Support for affirmative action is eroded when affirmative-action safeguards are misused to provide a pretext for administrative disregard of well-grounded peer recommendations. Sound procedures cannot be established simply though a broad statement of principle. Carefully articulated checks and balances between peer and administrative review on the one hand and departmental and college or university review on the other are the only way contracts can provide properly for each type of personnel decision.

Agreements increasingly incorporate family-friendly as well as affirmative-action policies. These include improved leave provisions that may encompass leave for childbearing, adoption, parenting, family illness, or death. Some agreements provide that the tenure clock is stopped for the duration of such leaves. Domestic-partner provisions are also increasing. Provision for subsidized campus child care, though less common, is an important and negotiable family benefit.

Appointments

Although hiring decisions are often deemed outside the scope of bargaining, many academic agreements presuppose a role for peer committees in the search for and selection of new full-time appointees. Since, however, the prospective appointees are not yet members of the bargaining unit, they do not benefit from contractual protections. Nonetheless, in this as in other personnel matters, the combination of peer and administrative participation provides some check against arbitrary or discriminatory decisions.

Peer Review

Except at some two-year institutions, faculty contracts routinely stipulate peer review in faculty evaluation, merit-based salary decisions, promotion and tenure decisions, and other personnel matters. Part-time faculty members, who are usually not included in full-time faculty units, are a serious exception.

Since appointment and even reappointment of part-time faculty members too rarely involves peer review, these faculty members lack even collegial assurance of fair consideration or protection of their academic freedom. In most cases, full-time negotiators can accomplish little for part-time faculty members unless the length of their term or the fraction of such appointments at the institution qualify them for inclusion in the full-time unit. Full-time faculty members can and often do set limits to the proportion of part-time positions on the grounds of protecting bargaining-unit work, but these provisions are of little benefit to part-time faculty members. Full-time agreements contain no provisions regarding the appointments of graduate assistants as well, and separate part-time faculty and graduate assistant units rarely negotiate a substantial role for peer review. Faculty members concerned about these matters may, however, seek remedies through academic governance.

Most full-time faculty agreements provide for peer evaluation through a system of committees working at each level of administrative review—that is, a departmental committee with the chair, a college committee with the dean, a university committee with the provost. The committees often frame specific standards to apply the general contractual criteria (such as excellence in teaching, scholarship, and service). Forms and instruments of evaluation may be departmental, college, or university-wide and are sometimes incorporated into the contract itself.

Personnel Files

Most collective bargaining agreements include provisions relating to the files prepared in the course of faculty evaluations. Generally, these provisions require that committees and administrators base their deliberations and decisions solely on material contained in the files. They often contain specifications regarding the inclusion and removal of material from the files. Most important, they usually provide for faculty members to have access to their files. Some agreements limit access to confidentially provided preemployment material by providing that such material is kept separately and is not used for postemployment evaluations. Agreements may also limit access to outside letters of evaluation by making them available to the faculty member only in summary or in the event of legal proceedings requiring disclosure.

Access to personnel files is among the more controversial policies pursued through academic bargaining (Amer. Assn. 41–46). Nevertheless, such access is a commonplace and fundamental necessity in academic collective bargaining agreements because reviewable evidence is a precondition to ensure fair evaluations. Fairness could, of course, be secured through the application of rigid standards such as degrees and seniority. Such measures are, however, inadequate substitutes for the exercise of academic judgment through peer review. Alternatively, the contract might increase the opportunity for thorough academic assessment through a substantially confidential peer evaluation. But this confidentiality would not afford adequate protection to the individual faculty member. The system of regulated and accessible personnel files is, therefore, the necessary foundation for evaluations that strike a reasonable balance between individual and peer rights and responsibilities.

Reappointment

The duration of academic appointments varies substantially between and even within institutions. Academic contracts generally provided for notice of nonreappointment at a fixed time in advance of the termination of the current appointment. The required length of notice is usually greater in the case of multiyear appointments and after reappointment.

In the absence of a tenure system, however, initial full-time appointments are often only for one academic year. The policies of institutions without tenure often state expressly that each successive reappointment is terminal; carries no expectation of reappointment; and requires, therefore, no notice of nonreappointment. The terms of subsequent appointments may also be brief but generally lengthen, or reappointment may become routine after some number of reappointments or years. In institutions without tenure (generally two-year schools), reappointment usually depends primarily on administrative evaluation. Even so, agreements typically provide that dismissal during the term of appointment and nonreappointment of unit members with seniority are subject to a grievance procedure that entails a formal evaluation and a decisional rationale.

Tenure

In institutions with tenure systems, the duration of appointments and reappointments also vary. Nonreappointment clearly differs, however, from dismissal during the term of a contract and dismissal subsequent to the award of tenure. In the case of nonreappointment, the administration need not demonstrate cause, although it may be expected to provide reasons. It will, of course, be forbidden to act for impermissible reasons, such as those that are discriminatory or violate academic freedom. Moreover, although an appellant or grievant carries the burden of proof, agreements typically offer a combination of academic appeal and grievance procedures. Further, the grounds for appeals and grievance often include not only allegation of improper motives but also alleged inadequate or erroneous academic evaluation.

Violations of academic freedom and inadequate academic evaluation are the allegations that often lead to academic appeal or to a request for reconsideration. This path—from departmental to college and university-wide committees and administrators—is similar to that normally followed in the course of a promotion or tenure review. The appeal usually includes alleged inadequate or improper consideration of academic or administrative criteria, ranging from teaching and scholarship to institutional needs, enrollment, and budget. Contracts often require that departments spell out with some precision the type of evidence that will be considered in determining whether probationary faculty members have met the required level of achievement. Contracts also provide probationary appointees regular assessments so that negative decisions are consistent with a record of previous assessments. Departures from the established practices and criteria may provide grounds for academic appeal or grievance.

In the event that nonreappointment follows full academic review, contracts generally provide limited opportunities for grievance and arbitration. These focus on procedure but, depending on the agreement, may also consider allegations of discrimination, violation of academic freedom, and failure to provide adequate or fair consideration. Thus, although arbitrators are generally barred from making academic judgments, they are often permitted to make a substantive determination about whether the academic judgments were credible, reasonable, or adequately supported. Arbitrators may also be restrained with respect to remedy. In some instances, they may not only be limited in the award of compensatory financial benefits but also be forbidden to award tenure or reappointment. Consequently, they may be confined to ordering some form of reconsideration or impartial academic review. These agreements may reflect a trade-off between the permissible breadth of arbitral review and the finality of the remedy; that is, administrations may agree to broader review where the arbitrator may only require reconsideration and may not award tenure.

Promotion

Promotion decisions are often entirely separate from reappointment and tenure decisions. The promotion procedures, however, generally correspond to those for reappointment and tenure decisions. Those two-year institutions that assign faculty ranks frequently base promotion on formal qualifications such as seniority and the attainment of advanced degrees. Most four-year bargaining agreements require demonstration of the teaching, scholarship, and service accomplishments deemed appropriate to the institution and rank of the candidate. Although the procedures are similar to those for tenure, the opportunities for grievance and arbitration may differ. On the one hand, the time and cost involved in pursuing a grievance through to arbitration leads to a preference for reapplication for promotion through the normal academic process. On the other hand, the parties may be less reluctant to permit an arbitrator to award promotion than to award tenure.

Posttenure Review

Posttenure review has become a common feature of collective agreements and of public-sector institutions generally. In practice, these reviews are often extensions of earlier systems of recurrent review for salary and other personnel awards. Some two-year agreements call for reviews with the prospect of termination in the event of unsatisfactory performance. In form, these agreements more nearly resemble systems with recurrent term appointments than tenure systems; in practice, termination of postprobationary faculty members is rare. Most four-year agreements do not permit unsatisfactory reviews to lead directly to termination but are designed to encourage and improve performance. Some systems do require specific improvements and provide for initiation of formal dismissal proceedings if unsatisfactory performance is persistent. Formal dismissals are rare, but posttenure review systems can lead to resignations that would not have occurred without them.

Dismissal

Collective bargaining agreements typically provide that administrations demonstrate just cause for dismissal, suspension, or other major disciplinary actions taken with respect to tenured appointees or term appointees during the term of their appointments. Some agreements delineate more specific criteria such as incompetence, substantial misconduct that bears directly on job performance, or failure to perform assigned duties. Many agreements respect the AAUP recommendation that the administration engage in peer consultation before pursuing disciplinary sanctions. Most agreements depart from traditional practice by providing for arbitral review of dismissal, although some continue to rely on peer-hearing recommendations and a subsequent final determination by the board of trustees. AAUP policy prefers peer hearings to arbitration in order to safeguard the right of the profession to determine professional standards of conduct but does endorse arbitration when it follows peer review (Amer. Assn. 259–60). AAUP collective bargaining units often prefer arbitration, which many believe offers both greater assurance of due process than faculty hearings and disinterested judgment, which institutional boards are unable to provide. To assure both sound consideration of academic issues and due process, some agreements incorporate both academic hearings and a subsequent opportunity for binding arbitration.

Financial Exigency and Program Discontinuance

Premature termination of tenured or term appointments may be deemed necessary for reasons unrelated to academic performance, such as institutional finances or necessary changes in academic programs. In this critical area, academic contracts often adopt, in whole or in part, nonacademic procedures rather than AAUP-recommended standards. These procedures are often referred to as "layoff and recall" rather than, as in the Redbook, "financial exigency" and "program discontinuance" (Amer. Assn. 23–25).

AAUP policy regarding institutional termination of appointments seeks to protect the academic freedom and "reasonable degree of economic security" that tenure provides. Accordingly, termination on grounds of financial exigency should be "demonstrably bona fide" (Amer. Assn. 3; 232). Where termination is based on program discontinuance, the action should reflect educational considerations recommended by the faculty and not temporary variations in enrollment. The many—especially two-year—institutions that provide for routine layoffs because of budget or enrollment shortfalls do not meet these standards. Few four-year agreements fully incorporate them.

Academic—especially four-year—contracts do, however, often provide safeguards that substantially approximate AAUP standards. Many agreements include the requirement that faculty governance or the union be consulted and that various alternative spending cuts be considered before a declaration of financial exigency that leads to terminations. Con-

tracts also require faculty involvement through shared-governance procedures before decisions eliminating academic programs.

Lengthy notice requirements extending beyond the annual budget
cycle may ensure that terminations are not expeditious solutions to temporary budgetary or enrollment shortfalls. Seniority provisions may limit
the use of finances or programmatic changes for targeting particular individuals or as a pretext for forcing retirements. Rights to consideration
for retraining, appointment to an alternative suitable position, and recall
to reopened positions for three to five years add further protections to
individual unit members and discourage frivolous claims of financial exigency. Finally, the rights of the union and the individual appointees are
often secured though binding arbitration. Accordingly, even though the
protective language in academic union contracts is often less stringent
than AAUP recommends, the enhanced enforceability means that the actual protection is often similar to or greater than that afforded in nonbargaining institutions.

Other Professional Concerns

Collective agreements include a wide range of Redbook concerns in addition to those discussed above. Rather than attempt to review them all,
I will explore several of the most common and significant. These include
professional duties, professional leaves and grants, intellectual property,
and selection and review of academic administrators.

PROFESSIONAL DUTIES

Professional duties or workload provisions generally include not only
teaching loads but also a wide range of academic responsibilities. In two-
year and baccalaureate institutions, where teaching is the preponderant
faculty responsibility, these clauses usually provide for a specific number
of instructional and office hours each term for all faculty members. Many
provide explicit, and others customary, allowances for reassigned time
for activities such as curriculum development, program administration,
and student advising. Departmental chairs or deans generally determine
specific teaching assignments. These agreements also usually provide additional compensation for teaching hours or numbers of preparations that
exceed standard requirements. Violations of precise provisions are subject
to the grievance process.

Contracts for graduate institutions may also include some definition of standard loads, although the language usually permits greater variance between departments and even among individual members of the same department. Research institutions, especially those with professional schools, are often too internally diverse to permit university-wide standardization of responsibilities. In such institutions, agreements are more likely to provide that teaching assignments will be in accordance with past practice or will be fair and reasonable. Teaching loads and research expectations vary widely. Chairs generally assign duties, but consultation with faculty committees and instructors is often expected. In view of the highly varied patterns of expectations, academic review as well as grievance procedures may be invoked when assignments are seen as excessive or professionally inappropriate. Regardless of whether professional duties are narrowly or broadly defined, however, contracts should ensure that standards for evaluation are consistent with assigned duties. (Benjamin, "Patterns").

Distance learning sometimes entails special workload considerations. The use of televised and Web-based courses means that the classroom no longer limits the number of enrollees. Further, e-mail greatly facilitates access to faculty members and the expectation that they will respond separately to each student. Accordingly, agreements increasingly provide limits on the numbers of enrollees or sections each faculty member is assigned in distance-learning courses and may require that a single course count for two or more in the event that enrollment or sections exceed specified levels.

PROFESSIONAL SUPPORT

Most two-year as well as four-year contracts make some provision for professional support. These may include grants and leaves for professional development or research as well as for necessary facilities. In two-year institutions, modest awards are often given for faculty members to develop new skills, programs, or curricula. In research-oriented institutions, awards are generally focused on research, although support may also be provided for program development. Paid leaves or sabbaticals are often available after a fixed number of years. But many research-institution agreements now permit younger faculty members to compete for summer grants and paid leaves to assist them in completing their research before consideration for tenure.

Grants and leaves, including sabbaticals, are generally awarded competitively because the number available is smaller than the number of those eligible to apply. In institutions where support is primarily provided for the development of new skills and programs, administrators frequently choose the recipients. In institutions where awards are primarily for research, peer committees usually have a major role.

Many agreements also provide smaller and more widely available funds for professional development, including travel to professional meetings and the purchase of professional journals or supplies. Major administrative expenditures for professional support, such as establishing laboratories for new appointees in the sciences or equipping workshops and studios, are not generally included in collective agreements. The health and safety regulations that are required in these environments are also seldom specified in the agreement. Some agreements do include general language requiring appropriate facilities and support services as well as a safe working environment.

INTELLECTUAL PROPERTY

Intellectual property is an increasing concern for faculty members and administrations. The possibility for lucrative patents of products and procedures has strained relations among researchers, their institutions, and outside donors or investors. Institutional policies allocating patent rights, like those allocating grant overhead, increasingly concern academic bargainers. However, patent-rights policies have not so far been included either in the Redbook or most research-university contracts. These issues are, however, frequently covered by university policies that are discussed in or established through faculty senates. As such, they are often presupposed by collective agreements or even incorporated into them through past-practices clauses.

Copyright issues, as they apply to both instructional materials and scholarly publications, are included both in the Redbook and in many collective agreements. This issue is too complex for quick summation here. Academic negotiators should definitely consult the Redbook, however, because academic practice is fundamentally different than that in typical work-for-hire situations (Amer. Assn. 182–84). The AAUP is especially concerned with the implications of copyright for academic freedom. Academics who prepare instructional materials for their classrooms or for distance learning should retain the right to control both the content and use of these materials; for example, if lecture notes were construed as works for hire, the institution could require them to be revised or even forbid their use. If courses prepared for electronic media were works for hire, the institution could require their reuse long after their content had lost academic credibility. Under AAUP policy, academics should hold the rights to works produced in the ordinary course of their instructional activities, but the administration may acquire the copyright by purchase or when they have funded projects clearly intended to result in institutionally owned materials.

SELECTION AND REVIEW OF ACADEMIC ADMINISTRATORS

Faculty members often have a primary role in the selection and review of departmental chairs or program directors and an advisory role in the selection and review of deans, provosts, and similar academic administrators (Amer. Assn. 228–29). In collective bargaining, this role is complicated by the fact that labor boards frequently rule that chairs and directors, as well as more senior administrators, are supervisors ineligible for inclusion in the bargaining unit.

Nonetheless, even though the bargaining agent may not have a direct role in the selection of supervisors, members of the unit may continue do so through traditional governance procedures. Many academic agreements incorporate specific procedures for faculty participation in the selection and review of administrators, and others incorporate or presuppose such procedures. The preservation of this important academic role is a key reason why AAUP and this essay encourage collective bargaining chapters to maintain support for more traditional academic governance procedures.

WORKS CITED

American Association of University Professors. "1940 Statement of Principles on Academic Freedom." Amer. Assn., *Policy* 3–10.

——. *Policy Documents and Reports.* 9th ed. Washington: AAUP, 2001.

——. "Statement on Academic Government for Institutions Engaged in Collective Bargaining." Amer. Assn., *Policy* 217–23.

Benjamin, Ernst. "Collective Bargaining in Public Higher Education." *Labor Law Journal* 36.8 (1985): 514–18.

——. "Patterns of Professional Evaluation and Assigned Duties in Faculty Collective Bargaining Agreements." *Higher Education Collective Bargaining during a Period of Change. Proceedings, Twenty-Second Annual Conference.* NCSCBHEP. Apr. 1994. New York: Baruch Coll., CUNY, 1994. 63–71.

PART FOUR

PERSPECTIVES

Keys to the Development of the Association of Pennsylvania State College and University Faculties (APSCUF)

MARTIN J. MORAND and RAMELLE C. MACOY

In this overview of faculty unionism in Pennsylvania's state-owned colleges and universities, we discuss how collective bargaining has contributed to improvements in both faculty compensation and individual and collective faculty rights. We also consider how these changes have affected governance at campus and state levels; institutional quality and reputation; and student access to low-cost, high-quality education.

Background

Pennsylvania public bargaining laws were enacted as a result of lobbying by the Pennsylvania AFL-CIO and its affiliates; the Pennsylvania State Education Association (PSEA); and the mobilization of public school teachers and municipal and state employees. The legal opportunity to bargain coincided with the peak years for public economic support for higher education and the growing desire of many professors for organizational power and protection. The expanded physical plants and newly enlarged faculties, together with the prospect of a seemingly inexhaustible supply of students as the baby boomers reached college age in the late 1960s, seemed to promise a golden age for higher education, its leaders, and employees.

But with these opportunities came problems. Government spending for a war on poverty and a war overseas had made clear that there was a limit to the amount of federal aid for higher education. Of more direct concern to the Association of Pennsylvania State College and University Faculties (APSCUF), state financing for the fourteen state-owned institutions was threatened by a new funding system (essentially, a voucher system) that funneled public moneys to state-related and private institutions, as well as to state-owned institutions, through grants to students. Eventually, state-college student grants declined, and the rate of increase in appropriations to the state-owned colleges diminished.

Unionization and Unit Determination:

Before unionization, APSCUF offered membership to every campus employee with professorial rank. Several of the college presidents and many administrators had emerged from APSCUF's leadership. So, when APSCUF petitioned, as an affiliate of the PSEA, to become the bargaining representative, it proposed a unit including chairs, deans, and directors. The board of presidents, with the backing of the state administration, vigorously insisted on a unit of teaching faculty members only; if a professor's union there must be, let it not undermine managerial control. In this context, the attitude of the boss became, for the first but not the last time, determinative of much in the union-management relationship. The newly elected Democratic governor, Milton Shapp, had a positive view of unionism and had received significant electoral support from the Pennsylvania AFL-CIO. Knowing Shapp's labor philosophy, APSCUF organizers succeeded in keeping chairs in the unit. They staged an end run in the form of telegrams to the governor from department chairs on several campuses asserting that if Chairs could not be part of the same unit with "their" faculty members, they would resign their chairs.

A second unit-determination issue that proved significant in the long run concerned part-time faculty members. The language of the law prohibited "overfragmentation," and the administration agreed to inclusion of part-time and temporary faculty appointees in the unit as well as librarians and counselors. This set the stage for union negotiation of salaries for temporary faculty members (i.e., adjuncts) in proportion to teaching load, a formula that has led to better wages for APSCUF temps than most other adjuncts. (As of January 2003, the minimum for teaching a three-credit course each semester is $4,783; a load of two courses a semester for the academic year triggers eligibility for health benefits.)

The vote on bargaining occurred on 11 October 1971. The governor's directive to the presidents to stay out of the contest had a significant influence on the results and long-term labor-management relations. Ninety-five percent of the eligibles voted. APSCUF won more than 55% of the votes, AAUP almost 35%, and AFT and "No Representative" each won about 5%. The APSCUF victory was followed by an immediate outreach to the "losers" on most campuses: APSCUF's first five presidents included an AAUP activist, an AFT supporter, and a professor who had chosen "No Representative."

Negotiations

A study of faculty bargaining in Pennsylvania by Walter J. Gershenfeld and Kenneth P. Mortimer found that "[t]he first agreement for the state college system yielded a substantial increase [in salaries], which led negotiated settlements . . . for other state employees. The first agreement placed average state college salaries ahead of the state-related universities" (32). This increase, which almost doubled some faculty salaries in five years, was achieved without significant increases in tuition, unlike the much smaller faculty raises at the state-related institutions, which were accompanied by much larger tuition increases. The lesser tuition increases in the state-owned institutions resulted from effective lobbying for substantial increases in state appropriations by a coalition of APSCUF, PSEA, and an APSCUF-initiated Commonwealth Association of Students (CAS). The students demonstrated on campuses and capitol steps and visited legislators in their offices. Further, CAS added legitimacy to APSCUF's lobbying; the faculty members were striving to keep student tuition down, not just to push faculty salaries up.

A less fortunate outcome, which had profoundly negative effects on governance, on the evolution of labor-management relations, and on the maturation of the faculty union (some of which were not immediately perceived), resulted from a decision announced at a prebargaining meeting to establish ground rules, namely the logistics and procedures for negotiations. APSCUF asked how the commonwealth wanted to go about implementing the previously reached agreement to conduct campus-level negotiations on matters not necessarily of a statewide nature. The Office of Administration, which represented management, responded that they had no intention of engaging in any such local negotiations. The fourteen presidents had previously initiated the concept of preserving a role for local resolution of local issues but were later persuaded that they could not possibly stand up to the professional negotiators whom the union would field, and some might "give away the store," embarrassing other presidents and so on.

The result was that the presidents had, in reality, removed themselves from the process that was to have the greatest impact on the academic world over which they presided. They and the faculty members at the campuses, apart from those who were active at the state level, were effectively removed from the learning and maturing process that collective bargaining experience nurtures and became, once again, subject to Harrisburg. Notably, it was the state, not the union, that insisted on overly centralized decision making.

Contract Administration and Governance

Problems with interpretation and administration of the first contract led to a series of grievances and, when these were not resolved, to arbitration. The union won the first seven arbitrations. These victories created an image of invincibility and persuaded management to settle other grievances before arbitration and on favorable terms. The governor convened a meeting in his office with top management and union representatives, at which he instructed management to stop quibbling about contract interpretation legalisms and go out and "run the place with common sense and common decency." At the same time, the union successfully lobbied for a supplementary appropriation that obviated the need for a threatened retrenchment of staff members and enabled the union and management to agree on a resolution of budgetary problems.

The most dramatic nonfinancial effects of collective bargaining were on governance. The new power relations on campus not only included due process and academic-freedom protections for individual faculty members but also an enhanced collegial role. Department chairs were elected. Hiring, promotion, and tenure decisions were primarily faculty-determined. But the way in which campus presidents adjusted to the new circumstances also had great bearing on how (not whether) collective bargaining changed governance.

Many campuses had faculty senates before bargaining. The fate of these senates speaks volumes to the question of whether faculty unions destroy, foster, or displace senates. In Pennsylvania, the same contract and union had several different effects. On some campuses, the president turned to the senate as a counterweight against the union. In each such instance, the union mobilized its members to dismember the senate. The smartest presidents turned the local governance body into an ally, particularly in promoting campus issues within the state system. These were campuses where the union saw great virtue in having the senate as a "respectable" faculty ally. To these senates the local unions delegated functions mandated by the collective bargaining agreement, such as implementation of the contract clause mandating a curriculum committee on each campus. Since curriculum and similar academic concerns are inherently competitive among faculty members and departments, unions are indeed better off allowing faculty committees and the senate to deliberate on these matters rather than choosing sides among their constituents.

Quality and Reputation

In the negotiations for the second contract, the union sought to consolidate economic gains while emphasizing advances in the academic quality and reputation of the schools. The contract protected staffing with a no-retrenchment clause. It also protected equitable salaries with a provision linking a reopener on salary discussions to gains won by the union representing the nonprofessional staffs. The agreement provided pay for professional development and faculty health benefits equal to those won by other state unions. It ensured the integrity of faculty participation in the areas of promotion and tenure by eliminating any financial incentive for management to reject faculty committee recommendations. Most important, the contract evidenced a more constructive approach by management toward dealings with the union. This viewpoint resulted in such academically transforming practices as the bestowal of the Distinguished Faculty Award by distinguished faculty from prominent academic institutions and faculty development, evaluation, and promotion procedures that strengthened the quality and reputation not only of the fourteen faculties but also of each institution.

The improvements have been recognized by many university administrators. For example, the state Secretary of Education, who headed the colleges at the advent of collective bargaining, was John C. Pittenger.

Although a liberal Democrat, he was against the idea of a professor's union and regarded the state colleges as intellectual backwaters. It was, therefore, particularly significant that he stated, at a press conference announcing his resignation, that "I think our collective bargaining in the colleges has worked extremely well and that we've proved you can use collective bargaining in education to improve academic quality." The president of Indiana University of Pennsylvania, Robert C. Wilburn, who later became Secretary of Education, recognized collective bargaining "as an asset to good management, largely because it is so intolerant of poor management. It exposes the incompetent administrator, forces decisions to be made without undue delay, requires rational record-keeping, demands objectivity in personnel decisions and generally substitutes accountability for vacillation between arbitrariness and popularity seeking." A dean at Slippery Rock State College explained to a conference of university administrators that "[a] written agreement is an excellent method of working out lasting compromise . . . contracts may be a very positive force in establishing . . . positive norms, expectations and standards . . . which could not have been established by one person . . . faculty/administration committees required by the union are the most serious and significant committees on our campus" (McFadden).

Organizational and Political Issues

When faculty members unionize, it is neither out of solidarity with the working class nor from a sense of community with all those of the same craft. The overwhelming support for unionization in 1971 was more defensive than ideological, as shown by APSCUF's pragmatic view regarding national affiliations. According to a taped interview in the APSCUF archives, one APSCUF president recalls:

> APSCUF had been over the course . . . of its history affiliated with all three major higher education organizations . . . the National Education Association [NEA], the American Federation of Teachers [AFT] and the American Association of University Professors [AAUP]. . . . When I came to this organization we were members of AAUP and AFT. . . . APSCUF leaders came to believe that the relationship though important, was very costly. . . . The AAUP brought a strong academic focus. . . . The AFT had brought a strong union focus. In the end it proved just too costly during

my presidency. . . . We could better use the revenues instead of sending them to the national organizations to do our own work within the state.

APSCUF's most ambitious legislative initiative arose in part from concern for strengthening the colleges. Some APSCUF leaders believed that the union's primary role was to be the praetorian guard defending the public colleges. The college presidents were not permitted to engage in lobbying; the union, however, could raise money for political action and spend it on lobbying and political campaigns. Moreover, the presidents, as public servants without benefit of a union, tenure, or due process, were relatively limited in their ability to challenge the political powers.

The faculty union's role in the state budget process has been noted. But it was most proud of its role in redefining the structure of the management. Toward this end, it spent a decade struggling to get out from under the Department of Education and to gain the autonomy, flexibility, status, and presumed clout that would come from an independent state-level governing structure. APSCUF played a leading role in organizing a coalition of students and parents, alumni, administrators, and other unions on and off campus. In 1982, APSCUF, having extracted a pledge from the governor to support legislation to create the new State System of Higher Education (SSHE), broke with other unions to support Dick Thornburgh's successful reelection campaign.

Meanwhile, CAS had irritated persons of power. As students and student organizations are wont to do, they had endorsed some controversial causes (e.g., legalizing marijuana). More significantly, they had hired staff members and retained an attorney, through whom they had successfully sued the governing board and forced the rescinding of a tuition increase on the grounds that the meeting had not had physical quorum in attendance. And contrary to APSCUF, they had endorsed (like many Pennsylvania unions with which CAS maintained a close working relationship) Thornburgh's Democratic opponent. The board of governors responded by withdrawing CAS funding from student's tuition and fees bills. Their funds cut off, CAS struggled on but eventually died. And APSCUF, which had provided moral and financial aid to CAS in its establishment, did not come to its rescue. However, the current leaders of the organization are working to assist students in resurrecting CAS.

The most stressful challenge to the independence of the SSHE and to the credibility of the union occurred during the contract negotiations in 1999. Many APSCUF leaders believed that Governor Tom Ridge had determined to intervene in the negotiations in order to strengthen his conservative credentials as a possible candidate for vice president. The faculty voted to strike. The faculty had voted strike authorization previously, but many of its members voted thusly only because they saw it as a part of the bargaining process. Thus, there was much doubt about whether they would really go out.

To strengthen their position and avert the need to strike, APSCUF leaders focused on aspects of the management proposal that would be disadvantageous to the most junior faculty members and of no harm to the most senior. Thus, its public appeal, to students and others, was that its leaders were not being self-serving. APSCUF was concerned with the rapid growth of temporary as opposed to regular faculty members and sought opportunities for regular employment for some of these longtime temporary faculty appointees. This also won sympathy from students. Further, APSCUF offered to submit all unresolved issues to binding arbitration, a process that had been used in the 1970s. Students, who did not wish to have their academic (and thus professional) careers interrupted by a strike, could not see why the management negotiators rejected this apparently reasonable option.

The union had announced its intention to strike in early fall and authorized its president, William Fulmer, to determine the date. The board of governors scheduled its September meeting on the campus at East Stroudsburg University. Upon arrival on campus, the board members were greeted by the sight of professors with their books and office materials loaded in boxes or wheelbarrows indicating a readiness to "go." Students demonstrated in support of the faculty members and condemned board members for their obstinacy. Members of the board turned to their lame-duck chairman, Fitz Eugene Dixon, and asked him to find a way of averting the strike. He conferred privately with Fulmer and asked him to postpone the strike for a couple of weeks to give the board time to reach a settlement. At this point, board member and Republican Senate Majority Leader Joseph Loeper assured Fulmer that he would block with his twenty-nine Republican members any effort by Governor Ridge to replace Dixon. Fulmer agreed to postpone the strike. A strike was averted and the contract resolved.

Subsequently, however, a newly appointed chairman and chancellor have, in the eyes of the APSCUF leadership, suffered by comparison with their predecessors. The board and chancellor have enunciated policies that, irrespective of the correctness of the particular policies, have been adopted without regard to the shared-governance practices stipulated by the contract and posited by academic-governance tradition. The union had filed legal charges, but these were preempted when a new governor, and ultimately a new board chairman, undertook to reach a better relationship with the faculty union. The current union leadership is attempting to build broader political alliances to encourage the students to reorganize a statewide union. Additionally, the leadership is reminding the faculty members that, as public employees, their union's strength rests fundamentally on its political clout and therefore on the political sophistication of the faculty members.

WORKS CITED

Gershenfeld, Walter J., and Kenneth P. Mortimer. "Faculty Collective Bargaining Activity in Pennsylvania." *Pennsylvania Journal of Collective Negotiations.* 8.2 (1979). 1–47.

McFadden, Joseph. "Are There Positive Aspects to Faculty Unionism?" Northeast Regional Conference of Academic Affairs Administrators. Drexel Univ., Philadelphia. 29 Oct. 1976.

Pittenger, John C. Press conference. Harrisburg, Pennsylvania. 1976.

Wilburn, Robert C. Telephone interview with Martin J. Morand. Sept. 2002.

A Worst-Case Scenario

BRAD ART

August 1997: Our employer launches an attack campaign. "Anybody who's connected with the system of higher education knows that tenure is a dinosaur" (Sullivan). Thus began over three years of challenging, rancorous negotiations with an intransigent management whose design was to eliminate academic freedom, close or privatize some of the state colleges, and eliminate the faculty and librarian union. After seventy-five bargaining sessions, including twenty-nine with a neutral mediator, we reached an agreement that blunted the most egregious assault on our profession and even achieved important gains for our members. This bargaining cycle was certainly the most hostile, overtly confrontational negotiation the Massachusetts State College Association (MSCA) has faced since the inception of our association some thirty years ago.

I am the Bargaining Committee chairperson for the MSCA which represents some 3,000 full-time and part-time faculty members and librarians from the nine four-year state colleges in Massachusetts. The colleges are geographically separated, each headed by its own president and board of trustees, but our faculties are united by our common union affiliation. This was my first taste of bargaining with an employer.

I would like to share some of our experience, including our disadvantageous statutory and political bargaining position and our strategies to meet these disadvantages. Our greatest strengths emanated from the moral force of our commitment to the importance of public higher education. We were willing to say no to a powerful adversary and to reject management's take-it-or-leave-it demands. We accomplished this by keeping all unit members informed and by having the conviction that we represented a constituency beyond our current membership. We understood that we were protecting our profession. Flexible and creative in formulating negotiating positions and responses, we nonetheless established a boundary beyond which we would not go.

The Setting: Management's Advantageous Position

Let me describe some of the many statutory limits placed on our association. According to our state collective bargaining law, our employer is an entity termed the Higher Education Coordinating Council in 1997 and subsequently the Massachusetts Board of Higher Education (BHE). The governor appoints members of the BHE and its chairperson. The board negotiates contracts with the MSCA through the Chancellor of Higher Education, who selects a team for the purpose of face-to-face negotiations. From 1998 through 2002, the BHE team has included attorneys, representatives of the nine college presidents, negotiators from the chancellor's office, and on occasion the BHE chairperson. This layered structure, which required that we conduct negotiations not only indirectly with a governor, the governor's advisers, the Board of Higher Education, its chairperson, a chancellor, and nine college presidents but also directly with the management team, entailed dealing with an unpredictable, hydra-headed monster. Unlike direct negotiations with a college-based board of trustees accessible to faculty members and librarians, this multi-layered decision making confounds bargaining even in good times. Each inaccessible layer has its own political and educational agenda as well as its own understanding of what a college does and what purpose it serves.

Another statutory limitation in Massachusetts is the prohibition on public-employee strikes. This prohibition extends to withholding of certain services. In Massachusetts, public employees can legally engage in some kinds of work to rule, a job action where employees do no more than the minimum of their job requirements to cause a slowdown. For example, members of the bargaining unit stopped participating on governance committees on the theory that this was individual, voluntary activity that could be suspended without crossing the line into an illegal work stoppage. Exactly where the line gets crossed has not been litigated with regard to state college employees. However, the courts have found that tasks not specifically enumerated in the collective bargaining agreement may be so essential that they are implied in the collective bargaining agreement. So, if employees refuse to perform them, they would be in violation of the law. The penalties for violating the no-strike provisions of the collective bargaining law can include termination, fines, and damages.

There are two other restrictions on workers negotiating in the Massachusetts public sector. First, management can impose its position on the union if the negotiations reach impasse. The formal process requires both parties to go through a stage of mediation. If mediation brings no resolution, the parties proceed to fact finding. However, public-sector employee unions do not enjoy binding arbitration. So, no matter what the fact finder decides, management can impose its position unilaterally. This power discourages management from modifying its positions.

Second, the nonfinancial and financial elements of agreements between the parties are sundered by statute. When the parties reach agreement, the entire package goes to each group's constituency for ratification. If both principals agree, the law requires that certain cost estimates be provided to the governor, who is then free to submit the financial package to the legislature for funding or to decline to submit it. If the legislature passes the necessary funding legislation, the bill then goes to the governor for signature or veto. Even if the financial provisions of the contract fail to get funded, the nonfinancial language changes are still binding. This is good for employees where language establishes or enhances employee rights, but it is dangerous for employees where the contract grants concessions to management. We were careful to put contingency language in the agreement so that our language concessions would not be put into effect if the economic benefits were not realized. Unfortunately, several of our sister higher education unions did not employ this protection. The governor reneged on their raises by vetoing them, and the legislature has not thus far overridden the vetoes or fully funded the contracts, but the unions are stuck with the language concessions they made.

The legal prohibitions on striking and the legal limitations on work to rule, combined with the absence of binding arbitration, mean that the impasse-resolution procedures do not establish a bargaining process consistent with a fair exchange between legally equal parties. Although the union must be prepared with reasonable, creative proposals and is constantly under pressure to give in, management's hydra-headed monster may be only minimally constrained or motivated.

An Immovable Object

In November 1997, as part of the BHE's prebargaining campaign leading up to negotiations in March 1998, James Carlin, chairperson of the Board of Higher Education, delivered a speech to the Boston Chamber of Commerce. In it, he called tenure "an absolute scam." He ridiculed academic freedom and the teaching profession. He claimed that "at least 50% of all non-hard sciences research on American campuses is a lot of foolishness." He asserted that faculty are given "every fringe benefit God ever invented" and bemoaned the "fact" that most college presidents "have very little to say about the educational side of their institution" ("I Know"). While Carlin attacked these elements in all public and private institutions of higher education, he promised to correct the problem in the nine state colleges of Massachusetts.

Carlin, an insurance and real estate tycoon, imagined himself a pioneer leading a revolution against the "ineffective and inefficient" industry of American higher education. He represented the proprivatization position of the Pioneer Institute, a Massachusetts policy group, of which he was an active board member (www.pioneerinstitute.org). The state colleges were to be his first victory in a national campaign to promote a crude corporate model, which would accord the chief executive officer, formerly known as the college president, absolute power to hire and fire personnel without cause and to set course assignments and content. Carlin adamantly opposed labor unions, portraying them as protectors of the incompetent and nothing more. To give a sense of his rhetoric, depending on the speech and his mood, Carlin estimated the incompetent at 1%, 3%, 5%, 7%, or 33% of faculty members (see "Taking Higher Education"). He admitted his statistics were anecdotal estimates, but he did not see a problem with that. The print press quoted, but did not challenge, his numbers (see Sullivan; Miller; Pressley; "Bad Teachers"). No one in the political arena took exception to his statements.

Carlin's speeches, interviews, and face-to-face confrontational style made him the willing lightening rod for controversy. Although we did not hesitate to challenge his vision and assumptions, we avoided identifying him as the problem. We believed it was crucial to stay fixed on the policies and proposals, and their potentially damaging consequences. Carlin's strategy of confrontational one-liners was well received by the *Chronicle of Higher Education* (Healy). Nonetheless, our persistence led to his dramatic downfall, though not the end of the policies he espoused.

Management Proposals

Reflecting Carlin's Boston Chamber of Commerce speech, management's proposals were straightforward. They included the elimination of tenure, shared governance, and across-the-board salary increases. In place of tenure, and its attendant protection for academic freedom, we were offered one-, three-, and five-year renewable-term contracts. In place of autonomous governance, we were offered governance orchestrated by college presidents. Salary increases, if any, would be called merit increases and would be awarded at the sole discretion of the college president without any stated criteria or standards. During one stage in the negotiations, management proposed that, for at least 25% of unit members, no salary increases would be possible. Additionally, variable workloads would be determined solely by the college president. Reduction of one member's workload would be balanced by increases in the workload of colleagues. Increased workloads could be imposed without uniformity and without limitation. A professor could be required to teach as many courses as the president demanded. Department chairs would be removed from the bargaining unit. A wide range of other prerogatives would grant college presidents nearly unchecked powers.

Carlin threatened to make at least one of the state colleges into a charter college. His threat to privatize at least one of the state colleges was reflected in the governor's House 1 budget some months later. It was also the theme of a policy paper produced by the Pioneer Institute.

The employer was serious about these proposals. In the guise of improving the state's public higher education, the BHE set out to make an example of our unit. Unlike negotiations where initial postures may be exaggerated, then softened, these management-rights proposals remained on the table, in various extreme incarnations, for more than a year. Even those faculty members and librarians who would have liked to take the money and run could find nowhere to go. The financial package was a 0% increase for each of the three years of the agreement. This management proposal occurred during times of record state revenues and budget surpluses.

An Unstoppable Force

Our bargaining committee consists of nine members (each representing one of the nine colleges), the association president (as an ex officio and nonvoting member), and one consultant provided by the Massachusetts Teachers Association (MTA-NEA). We first met as a new team in February 1997, and our initial challenge was to overcome our lack of familiarity with one another, and then, more importantly, to protect the diverse academic cultures at each of the colleges. Each representative's constituency had its own academic culture. It was necessary to merge the committee into an effective unit.

The danger of a committee of nine representatives serving nine different campus cultures is that one or more of the representatives can be out-voted on issues vital to its constituency. Simply not understanding the culture of a sister campus made us run the risk of dismissing as unimportant an issue of local importance. To be effective, we had to protect each campus, as well as the many other constituencies in the association. From the beginning, we established a committee practice of discussing each issue until each member was satisfied with the proposal or response to management. In practice, we restricted voting in the committee to that legally required when a settlement was to be transmitted to the bargaining unit for a vote. Any other request for a vote was understood as a warning that we were not acting in concert and effectively brought us together. In their sweeping attacks on all of us and on our profession, management's proposals helped us stay united by minimizing our differences.

Despite external pressures and internal union politics, the bargaining committee worked as a cohesive team. We also kept the membership of the unit informed in detail about the progress of negotiations. We decided that keeping management's proposals under wraps would diminish trust between our bargaining committee and our membership. We took pains to explain the dangerous import of management's proposals, for example, how its tenure proposals would undermine academic freedom, how its posttenure review threatened institutional academic integrity and quality, and so forth.

Our tactics ran the full legal route. Our affiliated organization, the MTA, began by conducting an opinion poll, and then ran a series of radio ads promoting public higher education and challenging Carlin. We also gave formal speeches before the Board of Higher Education, picketed its meetings, suspended campus governance, and placed ads in the *Chronicle* warning future colleagues to think twice before working in this system.

The key to our success was the bargaining unit members' resolve.

This resolve was exemplified repeatedly, but it was never firmer than when we rejected management's proposal that current tenured faculty members would retain tenure but new hires would not be offered the same protection of academic freedom. Rather than succumb to this temptation, the membership did not yield. Our bargaining team felt consistently supported by the membership at large. I cannot praise my colleagues enough for their steadfast willingness to protect the profession for all of us and for those who come after us.

And what happened to chairman Carlin? His confrontational style coupled with our unwavering commitment to represent our profession with integrity seemed to cause him to unravel. After a year of escalating tension and grueling negotiations, which he only occasionally attended, there was one BHE meeting in particular that stands out. Some two dozen MSCA members were present, but no MSCA representative was permitted to address the board. Faculty members remained seated or stood quietly in the back of the room with signs; the BHE meeting proceeded without incident or interruption to its end.

As the attendees dispersed, a colleague of mine, Gerald Tetrault, and I exited the building into the crisp New England spring air. We saw Carlin with another board member about ten yards away. Appreciating the first really beautiful day of spring, I called, "Mr. Carlin, did you bring this beautiful weather from [your winter home in] Florida?" Carlin looked in our direction. Noting the next day was St. Patrick's Day, and that the chairman wore a bright green tie, my colleague added with genuine good nature, "Have a happy St. Patrick's Day, Mr. Carlin."

Carlin exploded into a tirade of profanity (this is verbatim as I remember it), "Fuck you! You don't wish me a good anything. You wish I would have another heart attack and die right here on the sidewalk." After several minutes more of this kind of talk, and our efforts to calm him, we walked away. Within days, the state legislators, college presidents, and apparently the governor had heard of the incident.

Two months later, Carlin announced his resignation from the BHE (Zernike). Who knows how many factors like this one contributed to his decision? Shortly thereafter, his lead counsel was gone. The battle continued, prolonged by the untimely death of the chancellor, then the resignation and replacement of the governor. Through differing circumstances, three prominent architects of the BHE positions were gone. We successfully met the confrontational style with determination. The proposals persisted, however, driven by a momentum established by a political ideology of privatization still endorsed by the libertarian Pioneer Institute and yet another governor.

In the end, we protected tenure, academic freedom, and shared governance. We accepted a revised posttenure review process that contained a full just-cause standard of protection. We limited inherently unfair "merit" pay to off-base bonuses. We recouped the monies that did not roll over, adding the monies as on-base, in-rank adjustments to salaries for all unit members. Despite the highly publicized antifaculty posture of our employer at the outset of bargaining, by the time we settled, we not only protected the rights of our members but also were able to make substantial economic gains, for which even today I receive thanks from our members.

Perseverance and integrity paid off. As Carlin said in his diatribe of November 1997, "What's right will ultimately prevail and what's wrong will ultimately fail."

NOTE

I want to thank Donna Sirutis, our MTA-NEA consultant, for her research and editorial aid in the preparation of this paper.

WORKS CITED

"Bad Teachers Don't Deserve Protection." Editorial. *Boston Herald*. 30 Apr. 1999: 38.

Carlin, James F. "I Know My Campus Is Broken, but If I Try to Fix It, I'll Lose My Job." Greater Boston Chamber of Commerce. Boston. 4 Nov. 1997.

———. "Taking Higher Education to the Head of the Class." Unpublished essay, 1998.

Healy, Patrick. "A Take-No-Prisoners Approach to Changing Public Higher Education in Massachusetts." *Chronicle of Higher Education* 5 Dec. 1997: A41.

Miller, Leslie. "Bay State Panel to Target Tenure in Negotiations." *Springfield Union* 27 Aug. 1999: A6.

Pressley, Darrell S. "Board: Power to Fire Bad Profs Should Be Part of Reviews." 29 Apr. 1999. <http.//www.bostonherald.com>.

Sullivan, Jack. "Carlin Seeks End to Higher-Ed Tenure." *Boston Herald* 27 Aug. 1997: 21.

Zernike, Kate. "Carlin to Resign As State Higher Education Chief." *Boston Globe* 30 Apr. 1999: A01.

Professionalism, Inclusiveness, and Accountability in Collective Bargaining

RICHARD KATZ and DEAN CASALE

Collective bargaining in higher education, as in the United States at large, has historically been constrained by the contradiction between collective action and individualism. In academe, this contradiction is heightened by the solitary nature of academic work, both in research and in the class-room. Collective bargaining in higher education has also been constrained by the perceived contradiction between academe as a profession and organized labor as the domain of trade unions. Another crucial constraint is organized labor's delayed appeal to the senior members of the higher education workforce. Tenure-track and tenured professors take on collective bargaining leadership roles only after they have earned a doctorate and achieved tenure. Most first-time leaders of collective bargaining locals and associations are already in their early forties. Despite these constraints, there has been a resurgence of collective bargaining in higher education.

In this essay, we will first show how the current resurgence in collective bargaining in higher education differs from past surges. To do so, we examine membership trends in the American Federation of Teachers and argue that current market conditions are transforming both how higher education professionals perceive themselves as intellectual workers and how organized labor perceives higher education professionals. Second, we are tenured associate professors of English at Kean University and leaders of AFT local 2187, generally referred to as the Kean Federation of Teachers (KFT). We will recount our recent success in gaining leadership positions in the campus union as an exemplary case for new approaches and practices in collective bargaining in higher education.

The Changing Implications of Professionalism

AFT has encouraged higher education locals since its inception in the 1960s. Now, another AFT resurgence is underway, led not only by higher educators but also new professional sectors, such as nurses, doctors, dentists, and technicians. At the AFT's Higher Education Conference in San Diego in 2000, we were energized when we heard AFL-CIO President John J. Sweeney state that "higher education is the fastest growing sector of organized labor in the United States." This growth reflects in part a new awareness among academics that they are viewed by higher education managers more as a commodity whose cost is to be controlled than as professionals with qualitative value.

Professionalism requires adequate compensation; adequate numbers of full-time tenure-track faculty members, librarians, and professional staff members; and adequate classroom and research resources. But sufficient resources were not channeled into higher education in the 1990s, especially in the state-funded public sector, as they had been in the late 1950s and the 1960s. The shortfall in state funding in the 1990s drove up the cost of tuition, especially at public higher education institutions, where support for public higher education as a percentage of the state budget fell 29% from 1988 to 2000 (Council, "What Happened").[1] But even escalating tuition has failed to replace the declines in state funding. Universities have adapted by increasing class size, by hiring less-well-qualified and poorly compensated adjunct instructors, and by increasing workloads for graduate assistants.[2] Public higher education hears calls not for adequate state funding but for accountability, more regulation, and fewer tenure-track full-time faculty members.

At the same time, the self-regulation of academic faculty members is eroded by increased grafting of the private-sector corporate model onto colleges and universities, even in the public sector, where increasingly autonomous local boards of trustees manage their underfunded institutions as if they were profit-making enterprises. As state and local legislative bodies cut their shares of public funds for institutional operating budgets, boards of trustees allocate a larger proportion of resources to administration and a smaller proportion to classroom instruction. University and college policy making is reserved more and more to boards of trustees, undermining traditional academic structures of shared governance. So, professors and other higher education professionals who want to protect and secure the daily conditions that support their professional work increasingly look to unionism.

Certain features of academic professionalism are especially salient for organizing professional labor in a shrinking full-time tenure-track academic job market. First, many young professors still believe that, despite the shrinking job market that took hold in the early 1980s and the scarcity of tenure-track jobs, they can still get a desirable appointment. Further, they still aspire to become major critics or scholars, even one of the few stars securing a six-figure salary or at least a light teaching load. In other words, they believe they can reach the quality of academic life enjoyed by the top 5% or so of the profession. But most professors today work in the midst of deteriorating daily conditions of employment and earn flat salaries. Contrary to the belief that burgeoning faculty salaries are driving up student tuition, faculty salaries adjusted for inflation remain as they were in the 1970s (Winter). The widening divide between hopeful perception and reality, between a few stars and everyone else in the profession, makes it easier for organized labor to interest higher education workers. Organized labor appeals not only to those most vulnerable and least compensated in higher education—part-time and adjunct professors and graduate assistants—but also to many tenured professors whose experience has diminished their illusions but not their aspirations.

Moreover, when unions organize graduate assistants and adjuncts and win for them rights, power, and better terms and conditions, they are perceived by tenure-track faculty members to do so at the expense of full-time professionals. This perception is reinforced by the reality of shrinking resources for higher education. Underfunding of higher education at a time of increasing student enrollments means that more and more underpaid part-time workers will do more and more work to serve more and more students. Tenured professors are better paid and better protected but, proportionally a smaller and besieged class, see their working conditions deteriorate, job mobility disappear and their retirement savings dwindle.

In fact, higher educators, from graduate assistants to adjunct instructors to tenured professors, are all in the same sinking boat, with more and more of them in steerage. The full-time academic job market, which has been severely tight since the early 1980s, constrains faculty job mobility, tying academic career prospects to the fortunes of the institution. Collective bargaining in higher education needs to improve and enhance the economic terms and professional conditions of employment of graduate assistants, adjunct instructors, and part-time faculty members at the bottom rung of the academic ladder even while protecting and enhancing the terms and conditions that ensure the professionalism of tenured full-time faculty members. At the same time, collective bargaining must work to assure the academic and economic well-being of the local institution.

AFT State University Bargaining in New Jersey

Our home institution, Kean University, is part of a nine-institution sector of New Jersey state public higher education, which shares in a statewide master contract between the State of New Jersey and the AFT-affiliated Council of New Jersey State College Locals. Adjunct faculty members are also represented by the Council of New Jersey State College Locals and work under their own statewide master contract. At Kean University, adjunct faculty members, who in the 2002–03 academic year numbered 660, operate locally under a separate association, the Kean University Adjunct Faculty Federation. The other New Jersey public universities (Rutgers University, The University of Medicine and Dentistry of New Jersey, and the New Jersey Institute of Technology) do not participate in the master contract. They are represented by AAUP chapters that each bargain separate contracts with the administrations of their respective institutions.

Like the other eight institutions in its sector, the Kean Federation of Teachers is a local institutional member of an AFT statewide bargaining council. KFT members include full-time faculty members, librarians, and professional support staff who contribute 0.95% of their salaries in dues to the AFT, with slightly more than 33% of those dues going to the state council and roughly 20% going to the national AFT. As these revenue allocations suggest, local AFT campuses in New Jersey retain the largest portion of members' dues. Each local, such as the KFT, is able to negotiate local letters of agreement and memoranda of understanding with the campus administration, which serve as addenda and modifiers to the statewide master contract.

A significant dimension, then, of the local-dominated AFT collective bargaining structure is its responsiveness to the local institution and its place in the state structure. Each local's relationship with its members, its home administration and board of trustees, its student population, and its surrounding community is distinct. Local negotiations, therefore, take on different forms from institution to institution. The distinct missions and histories of each of the nine campuses come very much into play in the character of campus locals and, therefore, in local negotiations with home institutions.

Both local and statewide bargaining in public higher education are often mistakenly categorized with other forms of collective bargaining. In the public sector, although unions and administrations sit across from each other at the bargaining table, both are state employees. From the institution's president to the newly employed professional staff member or adjunct instructor, each is a servant of the state, paid by the state, and accountable to the taxpaying citizenry. When state employees sit on both sides of the bargaining table and negotiate over state-allocated resources rather than corporate revenues, the classic labor-management hierarchy and the profit motive become a budget struggle between what Pierre Bourdieu terms the "right" and "left hands of the State"(2-3). Having a finite, predetermined budget—one directly indexed to tax revenues and student tuition—renders negotiations, which are undertaken in a complex, multilayered interplay of constituencies, indelibly political. Full-time faculty members, librarians, and professional staff members, each with their varying needs, all belong to the same union, as is the case at Kean. The local administrations and the boards of trustees have varying relations with one another and with the state, although all are management. In the form of state appropriations and tuition and fees, taxpayers and students provide revenues to the institutional budgets and thereby have the first and final stakes in collective bargaining.

Collective bargaining in higher education entails both the practical politics of negotiating terms and conditions of employment for specific constituencies and the ideological politics of ideas and beliefs that affect the local institution. In higher education, collective bargaining has foundered when, in Bourdieu's terms, the right hand of the state, which represents and buttresses the free-market preference for deregulation, overwhelms the left hand of the state, which represents the public commonweal of services to the citizenry, including public higher education. In *Acts of Resistance: Against the Tyranny of the Market*, Bourdieu asserts that the right hand of the state has dominated and that there has been "a return of individualism," which undermines the left hand of the state and makes possible a "blame the victim" ideology (7). This enables the state to cut funding for common functions such as public education and to lower taxes or to increase funding for the business sector through subsidies, outsourcing, and privatization.

Making Bargaining Responsive to Professional Concerns

In the deteriorating climate for public higher education in New Jersey in 1995, we began a successful challenge to the union leadership at Kean by appealing to the members' professionalism and collective responsibility for themselves, the university, and its students. The union leadership, which had been in power for more than twenty years, had come to dominate all aspects of campus life by taking control of the faculty senate and determining who was tenured and promoted and who received professional support. That leadership was increasingly at odds with the junior faculty, especially newly hired women and minorities whose professional credentials and research interests were perceived by the union leadership to be a threat. Furthermore, the union was swept into the downward spiral of decreasing state funding and unable to cope with the right wing's privatizing, deregulating "Contract with America" agenda. To further this agenda, Governor Christine Todd Whitman abolished the Department of Higher Education in her first week in office in 1995 and made local boards of trustees at all public New Jersey campuses autonomous, independent of central state authority. The union leadership at Kean buckled. Acquiescing to dwindling numbers of full-time faculty members and decreasing numbers of promotions and declining professional resources, the union leadership circled its wagons and rewarded only those whom they deemed loyal to the union leadership. And supporting the Republican appointees on Kean's now locally powerful board of trustees, the union gave its endorsement for president of the university to one of the few nonunion faculty members on campus, an assistant professor whom the board of trustees promoted two ranks to full professor in violation of existing negotiated campus agreements and past practice (Council, Agreement 30–31). Finally, the statewide council settled an abysmal master contract with Governor Whitman's administration in 1996 that gave 0% salary increases for two years and further eroded conditions of employment. The discontent with the union's leadership, which had been brewing for a decade, boiled over.

Challenging the union's retreat from professionalism and accountability to its membership, we ran on a platform of openness and inclusiveness, professional responsibility and reward. We called for a democratic reform of the promotion process, leadership positions and rewards more inclusive of women and minorities, annual budgets and audits of the union's finances, and an end to union domination of the faculty senate and of academic governance of the university.

In large measure because of the new collective activism of younger faculty members, women, and minorities spurred by our campaign to challenge the existing union leadership, the former union leadership's endorsed presidential candidate failed to become university president. In 1996, Richard Katz was elected to the union leadership as president and Dean Casale as secretary of the Kean local. We then worked to establish a more inclusive union and instituted professional reforms of the tenure and promotion process that benefited the younger faculty appointees, professional staff members, and librarians.

Through new letters of agreement, we negotiated expanded and more representative retention, tenure, and promotion committee structures to include participation by all academic departments on retention and tenure committees. In the past, only four departments were represented on each of four retention and tenure committees. We expanded representation on the University Promotion Committee from six departments to twelve, ensuring that each of the university's four colleges was represented by three departments, and also limited faculty and academic departments from succeeding themselves. Previously, the University Promotion Committee, whose members are elected, had been dominated year after year by a small cadre of faculty members from the same departments.

In short, we found that at Kean an inclusive and more open democratic union was consistent with the professionalism of its members. As the new inclusive promotion structure gained legitimacy across campus and with the administration, faculty promotions increased from 6 or 7 a year to an average of 17 a year and included many more for women and minorities. We joined the administration in lobbying the state government for more operating funds for Kean and succeeded in helping Kean move up sharply from the least-funded institution in its sector. We advocated for and won an increase in full-time faculty size, which went from 336 to 376 in five years. We secured policies that made travel funds for research and professional development available to all faculty members at Kean for the first time and provided computers to each full-time faculty member. The KFT also led efforts to establish a new faculty mentoring program that paired newly appointed faculty with veteran mentors and reduced the required teaching load from 8 to 7 courses for the first year. For professional staff and librarians, we negotiated access to travel funds for professional development and a promotion structure where none existed before. Finally, the KFT stopped running a slate of candidates for the university senate, thereby removing the union from matters of academic policy.

The change in leadership at the KFT contributed substantially to the election in 1997 of a new, more professionally oriented leadership for the Council of New Jersey State College Locals. In 1999, this leadership negotiated an excellent master contract with the state that provided salary increases of nearly 16% over four years for senior faculty members and up to 38% for junior faculty members. The KFT saw its membership increase from 400 to 475 and had the highest percentage of union membership in the state—93%. Moreover, voluntary contributions to the KFT's political treasury went from nearly zero to over $5,000 each year. Both of these achievements earned awards for the KFT from the national AFT.

The KFT, the state council, the AFT, and collective bargaining in higher education generally can now strategize from a position of collective strength based on an agenda no longer at odds with itself. We can defend accountable, inclusive professionalism in public education against unaccountable private interests that have repeatedly failed to show that they can either turn education into a profit-making enterprise or demonstrate that corporate practices improve educational performance.

Successful collective bargaining in a state higher education institution is largely dependent on two key factors: calling on and emphasizing members' individual and shared commitments to professionalism and negotiating with a broadened perspective that appeals to key constituencies not seated at the bargaining table, especially students and taxpayers. Taken together, an emphasis on professionalism and enlightened service to the commonweal helps undercut the hegemonic logic of the market. Negotiation is no longer limited to salary demands and bettering individuals' terms and conditions. Also important is organized labor's commitment to social justice, a commitment not only to the professional interests of its women and minority members but also to institutional needs, students, the community, taxpayers, and the state.

Organized labor has always insisted that when its members prosper, so do their communities. American higher education has been slow to align itself meaningfully and enduringly with working-class labor, despite the fact that the work of higher education is intellectual labor. Academic collective bargaining sensitive both to professional service and to social justice returns academe to its best self—certainly to its best future.

NOTES

1. New Jersey state college enrollment increased 13.3% as state support per student increased 7.6% and tuition and fees rose 169.5% from 1988 to 2000 ("What Happened").

2. In New Jersey, adjuncts are not required to have doctorates and receive less than $2,500 a course and no health benefits, as specified in their master contract.

WORKS CITED

Bourdieu, Pierre. *Acts of Resistance: Against the Tyranny of the Market.* Trans. Richard Nice. New York: New, 1998.

Council of New Jersey State College Locals. Collective Bargaining Agreement with the State of New Jersey. 1 July 1992–30 June 1995.

———. "What Happened to Excellence? Funding Higher Education in New Jersey." Mar. 2002.

Sweeney, John J. Address. AFT Higher Education Conference. Hilton Hotel, San Diego. 22 Apr. 2000.

Winter, Greg. "Why the Cost of College Keeps Going Up." *New York Times* 26 Oct. 2003, late ed., sec. 4: 2.

After the Contract: Vigilance

ROGER HATCH and JOHN PFEIFFER

Once a contract has been bargained, the principal work of a faculty union is to secure due process in the university administration's daily governance of the faculty. Never before has the role of a faculty union been so important as it now is in a commercial and academic environment that is increasingly impersonal, unregulated, and entrepreneurial. Administration presentations of university budgets, for example, often seem to amount to smoke-and-mirror scripts. Increasing numbers of administrators are not drawn from the faculty, but rather have been bureaucrats for most of their careers; thus they are not always attuned to the best interests of the faculty. Administrators are also more transient, especially at the higher levels of administration, where a stay of more than five years is unusual. As a result, they know less about the history of the institution and faculty working conditions. They may in fact have an interest in substantially erasing that history to avoid the restrictions of precedent. Because their security and advancement usually depend directly on their supervisors, they often manage defensively and in self-interested ways.

At Central Michigan University (CMU), more than twenty years ago, the union secured a vital provision that required the administration to gain union approval for all relatively significant changes in working conditions, even when those conditions had not been formally stated in the contract. This protection currently rests on two clauses. The first requires that management rights "shall be exercised so as not to substantially expand responsibilities of bargaining unit members" (paragraph 3, article 3). The second states that "CMU agrees that the conditions of employment shall be maintained at not less than the standards in existence at the time of this agreement" (paragraph 4, article 4).

In recent years, these provisions have given the faculty union the opportunity to challenge not only the wording on the university's form for student evaluation of teaching but also the way this form is to be administered, the times that classes are scheduled, and the scheduling by deans of faculty meetings on the days before classes have begun. These provisions are also vital in the faculty's ongoing battle to resist increases in class size, the upward creep of standards for published research, and the erosion of the number of tenure-track faculty teaching positions through the substitution of temporary faculty teaching positions.

Our experience is that for these maintenance-of-standards protections to be effective, the faculty union must monitor administrative acts with daily vigilance. Every administrative act is potentially a serious change in working conditions. Protecting working conditions requires an informed, persistent union leadership and membership. Otherwise, the union wins less in its contracts, and its previous gains are eroded. In what follows, we wish to describe three areas of vigilant practice that illustrate how the union at CMU has succeeded in ensuring that the provisions of the contract are fully implemented and that the administration remains conscious that the union will require all the administration's other actions to adhere to established procedures.

Informal Meetings Between Union and Management

Our contract requires regular informal meetings between union and administration leaders for the purpose of maintaining and improving relationships. These meetings occur at least monthly. They allow the union to raise objections to management failures to abide by the contract and to management acts that are prohibited by the contract, long before these matters would rise to the level of a formal grievance. Regular attendees are two officers of the provost's office, both of whom are members of the administration's bargaining team; the union president; the president-elect; and the grievance-committee chair and professional union representative. The grievance-committee chair is usually the chief historian and archivist of the union's practices and policies in dealing with the administration. The professional advises union leaders on applicable labor statutes.

In such informal meetings, sometimes we have been able to resolve formal grievances. One grievance demanded that the administration provide pay stubs with wording easily intelligible to all faculty members. Although the campus community had complained for several years about the confusing, almost misleading wording on earlier pay stubs, nothing was done until the union filed a formal grievance. Once it was filed, however, the matter was resolved promptly through discussions at these contractually required meetings rather than through the far more lengthy formal grievance process. Two other cases also started as grievances but were settled in an expanded format of the monthly informal meetings. In the first, a dean ordered that each faculty member in her school submit a written professional development plan, including specific performance goals. After the union filed a grievance, the administration, in the informal monthly-meeting format, agreed that such a topic affects detailed duties and conditions of employment that must be bargained in the master contract. Another case involved posttenure reviews, which were permitted by the contract. There was, however, no language describing the process for these reviews. When administrators required tenured faculty to give written descriptions of goals as part of an updated resume, the union filed a grievance. In the informal meeting format, the union got the administration to understand that the written individual goals were dangerous to the faculty members because they amounted to special contracts which, if not met, would be grounds for discipline or dismissal. The administration agreed it had no power to order such special contracts.

These meetings also provide a context for dealing with problems that have not yet become formal grievances. For example, our contract requires deans to conduct annual conferences with all untenured faculty members so that they may know how well they are proceeding toward tenure. After each conference, deans are required to write a postconference letter describing what was said. The contract, however, did not mandate a time frame for sending these letters. After several faculty members reported delays, the union began monitoring the timeliness of the letters. Union leaders discussed this matter in these regular informal meetings. Some letters were not sent until a year after the conference had occurred. In one instance, this delay allowed the union to prevent the administration from terminating the employment of an untenured faculty member. The result of this kind of vigilance is that in our recent contract negotiations, the administration, rather than the union, proposed establishing reasonable timelines for issuing these letters.

At these meetings, we have also often obtained Freedom of Information Act information without actually having to file the legal paperwork. In this exchange, the union regularly receives substantial information about nonunion, temporary and lecturer faculty members. This helps us monitor whether the numbers of cheaply compensated instructors are creeping up, which is crucial because a large number of such contingent appointments would have a possible proportionate reduction in numbers of unionized faculty members. In addition, at each of these meetings, we review all unresolved grievances, noting the progress on them and taking immediate advantage of new dispositions by the union or the administration that may lead to direct, informal resolutions of these grievances.

Grievance Procedures

A second area of vigilance in monitoring the contract involves the work of the grievance committee, which consists of six to ten members and includes both experienced and newer faculty members. The committee deals with each new problem presented on behalf of an individual or the union itself in the light of the entire history of the union's relationship with the administration. Simultaneously, it must advise the union board of directors in monitoring everything the administration does that might affect faculty working conditions (and this is a lot). For example, it watches the actions of the university senate. Although the senate usually has union leaders as part of its leadership, the senate sometimes takes actions or creates policies that require formal union approval. Recent senate actions have included, for example, a proposal to change the length of daily class meetings and a project to change the questions on the university's form for student evaluation of teaching. The class meeting length was finally addressed in bargaining. The university's change in the form for student evaluation of teaching was approved in ad hoc negotiations. The grievance committee also monitors the actions of deans. It is assisted in this by department chairs, who at CMU are part of the faculty union. This monitoring has led to the requirement that deans of all colleges follow uniform personnel practices in a wide variety of areas. The grievance committee also meets periodically to devise strategy and tactics respecting all unresolved grievances, as well as to discuss all individual faculty cases that have not reached formal grievance status. Such cases might include faculty members who are having difficulties in the early stages of the tenure or promotion processes or who have been charged with some kind of impropriety, such as sexual harassment, racial discrimination, or professional indiscretion (i.e., misrepresentation in a grant application, especially one that is funded).

For special cases, the grievance committee involves faculty specialists. For example, the advent of Internet courses poses a special set of problems that require specialized technological and legal knowledge to address adequately. Presently, these courses are whirled in a blizzard of varying regulations and certification authorities across the hundreds of institutions that have them. They are legal and technological quicksand for unadvised and unsupported faculty members. At Central Michigan University, the grievance committee has succeeded in enlisting several faculty members with expertise in computer technology, media and copyright law, and the logistics of virtual pedagogy to assist in pursuing grievances that have successfully prevented the administration from denying faculty members the appropriate rights and compensation for their work.

Informed Members

The third area for vigilance involves rank-and-file faculty members. Unfortunately, most faculty members have not read the contract and have imprecise, often self-injuring understandings of the institutional working rules and the protections afforded to faculty. To counteract this, the union engages in a variety of educational activities. It publishes a newsletter designed to inform the members, reporting the most important new management actions and explaining the implications for members. The union also conducts annual workshops to provide advice to those applying for reappointment, tenure, and promotion. It maintains a Web site with information and advice for both current and prospective faculty members.

In contract years, the union hosts forums for the faculty to discuss important bargaining issues. The bargaining team also devises a detailed survey on all subjects to be addressed in bargaining. While both the pre-bargaining forums and the survey seek to obtain faculty opinions, they also are designed to educate the faculty members, often helping them ask questions some did not know they should be asking.

The most important advice we offer to individual faculty members is to get as much as possible in writing, particularly with respect to specific understandings regarding their duties, compensation, and benefits. E-mail communications are often viewed as acceptable. When presented with errors or misrepresentations in a letter from a dean or department chair, a faculty member is foolish not to send a rebuttal letter. Sometimes there is no written communication from a dean or chair when it would be to the advantage of the faculty member to have one. In these instances, it may make sense for the faculty member to put her or his understanding of things in a memo to the department chair or dean. The recipient's silence then has some of the force of consent, making the faculty member's letter the last word in the formal communication and thus potentially determinative.

Resisting Takeaways

One of the ironic rewards of vigilance for effective enforcement of the contract by union leaders at CMU has been that the administration has sought in bargaining to take back some of the union's achievements secured over the years. We point quickly to four recent instances. First is the administration's effort to change what had been an all-faculty committee to resolve disputes over changes in department bylaws to a joint faculty-administration committee. Second was the attempt by the administration to force departments to submit modifications to bylaws with which administrators disagreed; earlier, the initiative had rested entirely with departments. Third is the administration's effort to change the constitution of the review committee for appeals of denial of tenure from a body consisting entirely of faculty members to a joint body of administrators and faculty members. Fourth is the administration's proposal of a merit-pay program, which contained standards that abrogated the contractualized authority of departments to have the primary power to describe these standards. This proposal also provided no means for review or appeal and came despite overwhelmingly negative faculty reaction to a merit-pay scheme in the prior contract, which had led virtually all the faculty members, including those who got the merit pay, to denounce the program.

———

In sum, we urge faculty unions to be vigilant at all times. Establish ways to discuss and resolve problems without relying entirely on a formal grievance process. Establish a knowledgeable, broadly based grievance committee, and carefully monitor all new practices and policies. Educate and inform rank-and-file members. Encourage faculty members to get as much as possible in writing. And, finally, be ready for administrative efforts to try to take back these earlier faculty gains in subsequent bargaining.

WORK CITED

Central Michigan University Faculty Association. Collective Bargaining Agreement with Central Michigan University. 2005–08.

We Want a New Deal: Reflections on Organizing and Bargaining at Roosevelt University

LIESL ORENIC

While teaching part time at Roosevelt University in Chicago, I worked with other adjunct faculty members to organize the Roosevelt Adjunct Faculty Organization (RAFO), affiliated with the Illinois Education Association-National Education Association (IEA-NEA). This process began in March 1999 and ended, for me, shortly after we settled our first contract in April 2001. Over the course of these two years, I completed my dissertation in American labor history at Carnegie Mellon University, cared for my first child, who was an infant when organizing began, had a second child, taught at several other universities, and bargained RAFO's first contract. The intent of this essay is twofold. First, the essay recounts my experience juggling many responsibilities and concerns about long-term employment during a union-organizing campaign. Second, it provides some insight into RAFO's success in organizing a lasting union and bargaining a good first contract.

The days of organizing and especially bargaining were hectic, fulfilling, meaningful, and exasperating. In the beginning, I was concerned about rocking the boat. I had a good relationship with the program director and assistant dean and mostly received the course assignments I requested. On the other hand, the magic of entering the classroom for the first time had worn off, and I was frustrated by the low wages and temporary status. I was not alone; about sixty percent of Roosevelt University's classes are taught by adjunct faculty members.

Organizing and bargaining significantly chipped away at my already scarce free time. My husband and I did a good bit of "passing the baby" as he came home from work and I left to teach, meet, or bargain at least three evenings a week—a stressful situation. During the day, I crammed dissertation revisions, grading, class preparation, and union work into predawn hours and nap times while being a "stay-at-home mom." My husband, an active unionist at his own workplace, was tremendously supportive, but exhausted too, especially when our second child, born halfway through bargaining, was colicky. On a professional level, I was scared that my active and public participation in organizing and bargaining would leave me blacklisted from the tenure-track world, but at the same time the experience opened my eyes to new opportunities in labor education and the labor movement more generally.

At times, I could hardly bear to hear another word about RAFO; it seemed to consume so much of my time and energy. However, on most days I felt very invested in our efforts and their place in the larger movement to change working conditions in higher education and the "part-timing" of America. The good days outnumbered the bad, thanks to the intelligence, creativity, and dedication of my colleagues and the exhilaration I felt as we made steady progress in building a union and then bargaining our contract.

Organizing

In March 1999, a flyer appeared in my campus mailbox highlighting the recent organizing success of adjunct faculty at Columbia College, an institution just blocks away. Intrigued by the information and challenged by the invitation to start something at Roosevelt, I attended the first meeting with an IEA organizer who had worked on the Columbia campaign. Working on a dissertation in labor history, this situation provided me the opportunity to put my money where my mouth was. If I believed in collective action, here was my chance to prove it.

A core group of adjunct activists grew from this first meeting. We initially worked closely with our IEA organizer. Through his subtle insistence that we build our own organizing strategy, our growing self-confidence, and our collective decades of experience at the university, we constructed an organizing campaign. Our campaign took into consideration the independent nature of the colleges in the university; the fact that the university was a private institution and thus covered under the

National Labor Relations Act, not Illinois education law; and, most importantly, the unique progressive history of the institution.

After World War II, a group of faculty members founded the university with the goal of providing equal access to higher education for Chicago's returning GIs, particularly Jewish and African American soldiers turned away from other institutions. Roosevelt University was named for Franklin Delano Roosevelt and Eleanor Roosevelt, and over the years it has played an important role in offering higher education to Chicago's working-class and African American communities. Throughout the organizing campaign, our literature included quotes by both of the Roosevelts, often the same as those found prominently displayed throughout the university.

The first step in organizing was figuring out who we were and what we wanted. As adjuncts often teaching one or two evening courses a week at Roosevelt and other institutions, most of us had little or no idea of who other adjuncts were, but without the right to request this information through the Illinois Freedom of Information Act, we needed to find other ways to find the names and departments of adjunct faculty members. To build our database, we copied names off of mailboxes and asked for help from office staff members throughout the university. We succeeded in getting a working list of adjunct faculty members and, at the same time, we built a relationship with the clerical workers and their union.

Our first campus mailing was a survey designed to introduce RAFO to the adjunct faculty members and to gauge their dissatisfaction with wages and working conditions. We anticipated that nearly 90% of adjunct faculty respondents would be unhappy with their wages but were somewhat surprised to find that many of them felt that having a role in university governance was important too. From this survey and others, we focused our campaign on wages, working conditions, and governance.

Staking out the moral high ground was critical to our success. We stuck to the issues and highlighted the years of dedicated service many adjuncts had given to the university. One of our first flyers asked adjuncts if they thought they were worth 11 cents, the amount per tuition dollar we earned for our teaching. To find this figure, we multiplied the cost per course by the average class size, and then divided our salary for each course by that number. The result was that 11% of the tuition received by this computation actually went for teaching. We were careful never to attack any person in the institution, even when intense conflicts in departments arose. Most important, we built our campaign on Franklin Roosevelt's heritage, symbolized by our slogan, "we want a new deal."

By December 1999, we had collected enough authorization cards to file for an election. I had the opportunity to announce this fact to a room full of people participating in a panel discussion on adjunct faculty issues at the American Historical Association conference in January 2000. The news was met with applause, and this recognition—that full-time and part-time faculty members in my own discipline were supportive—was heartening. For the first eleven months, the university administration took a wait-and-see attitude in terms of responding publicly to our campaign. They did respond in the weeks before the representation election, when the president of the university sent letters to all adjunct faculty members explaining all the progress made over the years in improving adjunct faculty wages and working conditions. His letters mentioned a $300 increase in salary, which brought most adjuncts up to $2,000 for each three-hour course, as well as the availability to adjuncts of voicemail, e-mail, and shared office space. A response signed by the organizing committee stated that what the president called "amenities" were actually fundamental to our ability to do our jobs and that, in the light of the high salary the president himself received, the $2,000 a course was hardly a dignified wage.

Bargaining

We won the election by a substantial margin and quickly set out to develop a bargaining strategy. We again surveyed adjunct faculty members to see what they wanted in the contract. Wages, benefits, some system for course assignment, and a voice in governance topped the list. For five months the bargaining committee met several times a month to craft a contract proposal.

By August 2000, we had constructed a contract proposal and chosen a table team, a team of bargaining-committee members who would actually do the bargaining. We held a general meeting for all RAFO members and other adjuncts to meet and vote on the contract proposal. Meetings such as these were important for keeping less-active members involved and informed and for building the union in the most transparent and democratic way possible.

Scheduling meetings for adjunct faculty members is tremendously difficult because so many teach in the evenings and on Saturdays and often work day jobs as well. We quickly realized that a Web site would become our most powerful communication tool. The RAFO Web site (www.rafo.org) was fundamental to our success. Thanks to our fantastic Web master, an adjunct professor in political science, this Web site became a forum for our press releases and copies of our press coverage, a link to other adjunct faculty Web sites, a meeting announcement board, and a place for those interested to ask questions and receive answers. During bargaining it became an even more important tool. Much to the surprise of the administration and many RAFO members, we posted our initial contract proposal before the first meeting with the administration.

Over the course of contract negotiations, we posted brief but specific updates after every bargaining session. We also sent these updates directly to our growing e-mail list. These communications provided our members an opportunity to see what we were negotiating and when. After each update, we received both supportive and critical feedback from members. Some people questioned the order of the issues being bargained at the table and wanted us to get right to salary. The bargaining team felt strongly that if we bargained salary first, then it would be much harder to achieve our other goals.

Posting updates also let the administration know that the bargaining team was in constant conversation with anyone and everyone in RAFO who wanted to participate. Indeed, university administrators told us they checked in on our Web site regularly to read the updates. In lighter moments, the university's lawyer sometimes referred to what he read on the Web site as we convened for a new bargaining session.

Gains

After seven months of bargaining, we settled the first collective bargaining contract for the faculty at Roosevelt University. The contract included a salary schedule that reflected length of service and, from our perspective, was based on 60% of what assistant professors earned at the university. Starting with the average assistant professor salary and job duties, we estimated that 40% of their work was in service and scholarship. We then divided the remaining 60% by 7 (the Roosevelt course load) and came up with our top salary figure. The administration did not acknowledge this formulation, which would have set a precedent in bargaining they did not want. However, they agreed to the dollar amount as the top figure of the salary scale.

Because nonrenewal without explanation is a significant concern for adjunct faculty members, we bargained a remediation process for instructors needing to improve their classroom skills. The contract also included other important nonwage issues: an academic-freedom clause, a grievance procedure with binding arbitration, representation on the faculty senate, participation in college councils, and a system for course assignment that considered both qualifications and seniority. We felt these reflected our professional interests and the desire of many adjuncts to participate more fully in university life.

With a contract ratified and a solid and growing membership, I left RAFO for a new job as a higher education organizer for the IEA-NEA. The opportunity to use my new skills in organizing was a welcome one. For a year I worked with adjunct faculty members at several universities around the state and in the Chicago community-college system to organize unions on their own campuses. Organizing, like teaching and researching, was a relatively autonomous pursuit that required both creativity and self-discipline. Besides the crazy hours that sometimes conflicted with the day-to-day schedule of family life, organizing was the second best job I could ever imagine holding.

The best job I hoped for was a tenure-track position teaching history. I apprehensively applied for positions in the Chicago area, concerned that my role in RAFO might pigeonhole me as a troublemaker. My name and face had appeared in several local news stories about RAFO, and I did not omit my organizing experience from my c.v.

My fears were realistic but, in this case, unfounded. In September 2002, I joined the history and American studies department at Dominican University in suburban Chicago, in a tenure-track position. My previous adjunct experience proved to be an asset, and my organizing activities complemented the university's mission that includes the promotion of social justice.

Without question, working with other adjunct faculty members at Roosevelt University was one of the most meaningful things I have ever done in my life. The effort it took to balance family life, teaching and research, and union activities was difficult. However, the union we made and the contract we bargained were worth it. I know that RAFO improved the wages and working conditions of adjunct faculty members at Roosevelt University, and I believe it made Roosevelt a better institution because it now includes most of its faculty members in a much more significant way. In the bigger picture, the success of RAFO inspired other adjuncts to begin organizing around Chicago and, I hope, even further afield.

From Cynicism to Commitment: The Impact of Collective Bargaining and Campus Climate on Contingent Faculty Members

ELIZABETH HOFFMAN

As in much of the labor force, the use of temporary employees has increased dramatically in higher education during the last two decades. At the twenty-three campuses of the California State University (CSU) system in fall 2002, over half of the faculty members (54%) were full- or part-time temporary employees. Even more disturbing, these 12,365 temporary faculty members represented 36% of the full-time equivalent faculty. These data provide an indication of how much teaching the temporary faculty members were doing. But, in some departments, temporary faculty members were responsible for as much as 75% of the actual student contact hours.[1] Contrary to the common misconception that temporary faculty members generally have full-time positions elsewhere and drop by the campus to teach a class in the evening, 41% of the temporary faculty in the CSU taught at or above a half-time load. Another misconception is that temporary faculty members teach for a year or so on their way to permanent positions; in fact, about 37% of the CSU temporary faculty members had taught in the CSU system for six or more years. Every year, the CSU has retirees who leave the system after a career of twenty or more years of faithful service as what one temporary faculty member cynically called a "perma-temp." Clearly, temporary faculty members constitute a workforce that, despite the contingent nature of their employment contracts, is central rather than peripheral to the needs of the students.

The Role of Lecturers

Because temporary faculty members—called lecturers in the CSU system—do so much of the teaching, they are important to the success of

CSU students. Students deserve faculty members who are well supported by the institution. No student should be disadvantaged because he or she picks out of the course schedule a section that happens to by taught by the ubiquitous "staff." Staff, of course, translates into whichever lecturer happens to be assigned to that section. During the 2001 Campus Equity Week, an event highlighting the work of contingent faculty members across the United States and Canada, lecturers at the San Bernardino campus of the CSU wore name tags saying, "Hi, I'm Dr. Staff." As a lecturer myself at the Cal State, Long Beach, campus, I once had a student come to the classroom door earnestly inquiring for "Professor Staff." It actually took me a minute to figure out that the student meant me.

It is important to remember that the problems associated with overreliance on temporary faculty members are not the fault of the individual temporary faculty members. Lecturers in the CSU system are dedicated, committed teachers who bring a wealth of experience and expertise to the classroom. But because of the conditions of employment, the lecturers often feel marginalized and isolated from their colleagues. They are seldom part of faculty governance structures and are generally excluded from curriculum and policy decisions. The contingent nature of their contracts makes lecturers think twice about speaking out on controversial issues and undermines the academic freedom that is the essence of a university.

Lecturers often are concerned that if they set rigorous class standards, they risk low evaluations from the students and might not be rehired. With heavy teaching loads, often at more than one campus, lecturers struggle to maintain currency in their discipline. They persevere—a recent CSU-system workload study showed that over half of the lecturers participated in professional, scholarly, and creative activities, even though they themselves funded most of the cost of these activities.[2] But commitment to teaching and disciplines can be difficult to maintain when lecturers are part of a system from which they are often structurally and systematically excluded. Constant anxiety about getting work saps temporary faculty members. Lack of institutional support and professional respect leads to anger and, even worse, cynicism.

Representing Lecturers

I have seen this anger, and unfortunately the cynicism, in my role as Lecturer Representative in the California Faculty Association (CFA), the exclusive bargaining agent for all the faculty members (tenure-track and temporary), librarians, coaches, and counselors in the CSU. I have seen discouraged and dispirited faculty members in my assignment as a Lecturer Project Leader at the Faculty Center for Professional Development at Cal State, Long Beach. However, my experience as a union representative and as a member of the CFA bargaining team has taught me that collective bargaining can bring significant and concrete improvements in the job security, benefits, and working conditions of temporary faculty members. And my teaching and faculty-center work at Cal State, Long Beach, have shown me if a campus can establish a collegial atmosphere and enlightened policies—policies that go beyond the mandates of the bargaining agreement—then temporary faculty members will feel more supported in their teaching and more connected to the university community. Strong contract protections and inclusive campus policies make lecturers feel less like faceless cogs who are part of a cheap, flexible workforce and more like respected members of the academy, with individual rights and commensurate professional responsibilities.

From the first collective bargaining agreement with the CSU in 1983 to the agreement ratified in spring of 2002, the CFA has sought to support the teaching effectiveness of lecturers by improving their working conditions and encouraging stable appointments and fair reappointment policies.[3] Lecturers in the CSU are on the same salary schedule as tenure-track faculty members and receive salary increases at the same percentage level. Being paid on a pro rata basis (as AAUP recommends) instead of by course is a major achievement for temporary faculty members. Although, on average, lecturers with a full-time course load earn less than tenure-track faculty members, lecturers have the same right as their other faculty colleagues to earn service salary-step increases after teaching twenty-four weighted teaching units (which are equivalent to eight semester-long courses). And, although they remain temporary faculty members, lecturers can advance through faculty ranks by earning what is called a range elevation.

Further protections include the requirement that lecturers receive formal written notification of their classification, salary, conditions of employment, and evaluation criteria. Lecturers who apply for subsequent employment have careful-consideration rights, which, after a number of arbitrations, has come to mean that the employment decision cannot be capricious or arbitrary and that the departments must carefully review the information in a lecturer's personnel file. In short, these rights acknowledge the lecturer as a professional with individual rights. A lecturer appointed to a similar assignment in the same department in consecutive academic years must receive the same or higher salary as previously earned. The similar-assignment language gives lecturers, if they are reappointed, an entitlement to at least the same time base and salary as they had received during a previous academic appointment. For most lecturers, this entitlement is contingent on work availability; however, about 10% of the temporary faculty members are appointed to full-time noncontingent lecturerships.

Lecturers have sick leave and paid maternity or paternity leave. They may take a leave of absence while maintaining assignment rights and salary level. In the most recent contract, lecturers have enhanced benefits eligibility: with six weighted teaching units (two courses) and a one-semester appointment, they have full medical benefits. This eligibility was made possible by legislation sponsored by CFA, and further legislation was just signed into law permitting CFA to bargain lecturer benefits based on the same eligibility criteria in the California Public Employees' Retirement System.

These contract rights—enforced by lecturers' grievance rights—help create decent working conditions. The 2002 contract also has significant job-security provisions. Now employed lecturers have preference for work, allowing them to increase their time base and potentially get enough work on one campus to earn a living. Eligible lecturers have had one-year appointment rights; now lecturers employed for at least one semester for each of six consecutive years receive an automatic three-year appointment. These appointments have presumption of reappointment for subsequent three-year appointments with satisfactory evaluations, giving lecturers due-process rights that help ensure true academic freedom. Finally, the contract calls for stable department funding to cover lecturer pay raises so that experienced temporary faculty members are not disadvantaged by becoming too expensive. Winning these rights took organization, discipline, and a unified bargaining unit willing to hang tough through a long, arduous process of contract development, bargaining, mediation, impasse, and fact-finding.

The collective bargaining agreement has laid a foundation at the Cal State, Long Beach, campus for what has developed into an institutional model of good practice in the employment of temporary faculty members. The contractually mandated improvements in working conditions and job security make lecturers more likely to have the courage and commitment to speak out and become involved in the campus community. For example, the Long Beach Academic Senate now has eight lecturer academic senators, as well as lecturer representation on almost every senate committee, including the executive committee. The campus also has an administration committed to this model of good practice and willing to put resources into supporting that model. One example of administrative commitment is the collaborative work of the Labor-Management Committee. The committee is mandated to meet once a term to discuss contract implementation. At Long Beach, the committee meets every month and has become a venue not only for problem solving but also for planning ways to build a better campus environment. The administration has also provided resources for two lecturer project leaders in the Faculty Center for Professional Development. As a result of these resources, which include flyers, e-mail, a Web site, a handbook, orientation meetings, and workshops about campus policies and events, lecturers are much better informed. Lecturers are more involved in faculty development activities; for example, half of the faculty members attending last summer's sessions of the annual General Education Summer Institute at our campus were lecturers. In a somewhat ironic twist on inclusiveness, the PEN Project, a peer-mentoring and coaching-partnership program started and directed by lecturers in the faculty center, is open to all faculty members on campus and has increasingly had tenure-track faculty members ask to be part of the program.

An examination of the lecturer-evaluation and range-elevation processes shows how the collaborative atmosphere at the Long Beach campus can work to the benefit of lecturers. The basic structure of the two processes is outlined in the collective bargaining agreement. Lecturers on the Labor-Management Committee and on the Academic Senate worked with the administration to develop fair policies with clear procedures. The evaluation policy, so crucial to lecturer reappointment, requires evaluation in accordance with the lecturer's job description. However, the Long Beach campus allows, at the lecturer's option, evaluation of scholarly and creative activities or professional contributions outside the scope of the job description. The range-elevation policy at Long Beach, developed with input from lecturer academic senators, presents a long list of different activities that can be used to demonstrate professional growth and development, thereby acknowledging and rewarding the many different ways lecturers give to the students and to the intellectual life of the campus.

Every term the faculty center offers informational workshops on the evaluation process; the workshops held this past term were attended by part-time and full-time temporary faculty members, department chairs, and administrators from Employee Relations and Academic Affairs, including the Associate Vice President for Academic Personnel. The workshops are cochaired by two lecturers, the atmosphere is informal, people are on a first-name basis, and the discussion is a chance for lecturers to share their concerns about the process and for both administrators and lecturers to provide input into how evaluation could be a more effective and helpful part of their academic lives. Previous input from lecturers helped shape a recent revision of the campus standard-evaluation form. Moreover, to take the process full circle, ideas from these workshops are included in CFA's draft of proposals for our next round of contract bargaining.

Perspective

The collegial and collaborative spirit at Cal State, Long Beach, is encouraging, and credit for this positive spirit goes to an administration that is supportive of all the faculty members on campus. As a lecturer at this campus, I am not cynical but neither am I naive about the continuing vulnerabilities and difficulties inherent in temporary faculty appointments. The real solution, of course, is fewer temporary appointments and more tenure-track appointments, and there is currently reason to hope that such change will happen. The CFA-sponsored ACR-73 is a legislative mandate for the CSU administration, the statewide academic senate, and CFA to jointly develop a plan to raise the percentage of tenured and tenure-track faculty members to a 75-25 ratio, with the provisions that qualified lecturers are seriously considered for these positions and that no currently employed lecturers lose their jobs as a result of implementing the plan.[4]

Unfortunately, the actual implementation of the plan has been delayed by the current budget crisis in California, but the plan is moving in the right direction: there are more permanent faculty members and appropriate institutional support for them, professional respect for temporary members is flourishing, and job security for the remaining temporary faculty members is in place. Commitment to equitable support of all faculty members is in fact a commitment to equitable support of all students, and such equity can only occur with adequate resources, protective contract language, and a campus climate of collegiality and respect.

NOTES

1. The data in this and the next paragraph were obtained from the CSU administration by the CFA research specialist Andrew Lyons in June 2003.

2. This report is available at the Web site of the statewide academic senate (www.cs.csustan.edu/~john/Postings/SWAS/ACR_73/).

3. The current collective bargaining agreement between the California Faculty Association and the California State University is available at www.calfac .org. Also available at this Web site is the *California Faculty Association Lecturers' Handbook*.

4. The ACR-73 report is available at the Web site of the statewide academic senate (www.cs.csustan.edu/~john/Postings/SWAS/ACR_73/).

Balancing Act: Challenges of Administering the Contractual Rights of Temporary Faculty Members

GARY W. REICHARD

Several years ago, I collaborated with three colleagues (two of whom were temporary faculty members, or lecturers, as they are called in the California State University) on a panel entitled Contracts and Common Sense at a national conference. The focus of that session was on how, by applying simple common sense to contract language, faculty members and administrators could work together to improve the human condition of temporary faculty appointees. This focus remains a strong commitment on our campus. When a round of negotiations between the CSU and the California Faculty Association (CFA) is completed, administrators at CSU, Long Beach, try to humanize the provisions of the resulting agreement—not only for lecturers but also for all who are affected by those provisions. My emphasis in this piece, however, is somewhat different: it explores the constraints and challenges that confront campus-level administrators who want to support the rights of temporary faculty members but who must also be attentive to the effect such support has on institutional flexibility and on the variety of constituencies that make up the institution.

Three significant challenges face administrators in their efforts to support temporary faculty members: first, with respect to lecturers themselves, there is the complexity of defining appropriate rules and criteria for evaluation that will inform reappointment and range-elevation decisions. Second, administrators must ensure that department chairs (who, in the CSU, are members of the same bargaining unit as lecturers) have the flexibility to make the necessary subjective judgments and staffing decisions to meet student needs while upholding the contractual entitlements of individual lecturers. Third, in an overarching sense, administrators must—especially in difficult financial times—maintain institutional agility in order to be able to make desirable and necessary programmatic changes (including, for example, providing for the possibility of committing greater resources for the use of teaching associates). Other challenges certainly exist for administrators in the CSU collective bargaining environment, but these three areas provide a sense of the complexity of issues with which campus administrations contend.

Lecturer Evaluation: What Should Be Evaluated?

For years, the collective bargaining agreement between the CSU and the CFA has required regular evaluation of all lecturers appointed for a full academic year. Sections 15.21 through 15.24 of the agreement require that faculty evaluations include consideration of student evaluations of teaching performance; for full-time lecturers, evaluation is conducted by a peer committee, as well as by the "appropriate administrator" (30); for part-time lecturers, there is at least "opportunity for peer input" (31); and for all lecturers, evaluations become part of the personnel file. For lecturers appointed for only one semester (or, on quarter campuses, for only one or two quarters), evaluation is at the discretion of the department, but a lecturer may request evaluation if she or he wishes. These requirements provide important protections against arbitrary decisions about reappointment and are generally consistent with "best practices" that have been suggested by national advocacy groups for temporary faculty members (see, for example, Amer. Assn. 86; Baldwin and Chronister 149–50). Although the agreement requires evaluation of lecturers, however, it does not provide specific guidelines concerning criteria and documentation for such evaluations; this is left to the individual campus to determine.

In his 1998 study *Managed Professionals: Unionized Faculty and Restructuring Academic Labor*, Gary Rhoades notes that most collective bargaining agreements that require evaluation of temporary faculty members cast such evaluation as "a duty—or professional responsibility [of temporary faculty]—rather than a right because the provisions do not offer part-timers the right of evaluation as a means to ensure salary increases or reappointment" (159). In the CSU system, I believe that most campuses tend to see evaluation more as a right of lecturers, even as it serves as a useful instrument for chairs and administrators. Moreover, in contrast to Rhoades's generalization, evaluation of CSU lecturers is directly connected to reappointment decisions and, more significantly, to consideration of lecturers for the equivalent of promotion—termed range elevation in the CSU-CFA environment.

The concept of range elevation originated with the 1998 agreement, which provided that lecturers who have been continuously employed in a range (or salary tier) for five years and who have no further eligibility for regular service-based salary increases are entitled to request consideration for movement to the next higher salary tier, with renewed rights to service-based salary increases and with a higher salary ceiling. All campuses were required to adopt written procedures governing range elevation, but the development of specific criteria was left to local control by each campus. Once again, the question of what to evaluate was left to faculty members and administrators to determine—this time, by means of the shared-governance process.

The absence of specific criteria for lecturer evaluation in the CSU-CFA bargaining agreement allows for—and produces—unevenness in the nature and quality of evaluation across the CSU system. But where there is a will to make evaluation as fair and effective as possible, campus autonomy can have very positive results, and the evaluation process can be designed to benefit both lecturers and the departments that they serve. At CSU, Long Beach, we have utilized our campus Labor-Management Committee to develop a useful standardized evaluation form that seems to serve both Lecturers and evaluators very well (Division). Campus labor-management committees were first required by the collective bargaining agreement in 1995. Specifically, a new section, 8.2, provided in part that "each campus shall establish a joint labor/management committee, which shall be composed of three (3) representatives employed at the campus from each party. The committee shall meet at least once during each academic term." Implementation of this provision across CSU campuses has been uneven. At Long Beach, the Labor-Management Committee initially met two to four times a semester—and now meets once a month—and has taken up a wide range of issues. On some campuses, meetings are held much less frequently and with less-productive results.

Development of the lecturer evaluation form at CSU, Long Beach, was a complex task. Even with considerable input from lecturers themselves, it has been difficult to reach consensus as to how much of a lecturer's performance should be evaluated in terms of both documentation and scope of activities. The issue is how to recognize in the evaluation process the generally instruction-only nature of lecturers' appointments while at the same time permitting lecturers to put on record professional activities and achievements that transcend their instructional assignment. To deal with this issue, the Labor-Management Committee decided to include the following statement in the introductory section of the standard evaluation form:

> If the Lecturer has submitted a curriculum vitae, a description of the year's professional accomplishments and contributions, a reflective narrative and/or a written peer evaluation, that information must remain attached when this evaluation is forwarded to the Dean and to the Office of Academic Personnel.

The introduction to sections 2 and 3 ("Professional Growth and Development and University / Community Service") of the standard evaluation form provides:

> Lecturers without specific assignments in addition to instruction are not expected to, but may choose to, submit evidence of their Professional Growth and Development and Community Service. If such materials are submitted, departments must evaluate the materials even though these areas are not part of the Lecturer's assignment.

As reinforcement, the administrative memorandum that Academic Affairs sends to department chairs each fall semester reiterates these guidelines: "additional documentation, if submitted by a Lecturer . . . must be considered in the Lecturer's periodic evaluation" (Division, Lecturer).[1]

The provisions that allow lecturers to include additional documentation with their evaluations have helped produce a balance for the lecturer. On the one hand, there is respect for the boundaries of the differentiated assignment; on the other, allowance for consideration of activities that go above and beyond the formal assignment. However, the provisions also add to the work of department chairs and the peer committees (which are composed of tenured faculty members) who conduct the evaluations. This problem was obvious when the Labor-Management Committee was working on the standard form. Consequently, chairs (and associate deans) have been fully consulted in the process of developing and revising the form, and their suggestions and input taken into account. At the same time, in an effort to minimize opposition to the new form on the part of chairs who have legitimate complaints about their escalating workload, Academic Affairs engaged in a persuasion campaign, emphasizing the value to the departments of having full and accurate information about the range of contributions by lecturers. It is a measure of the shared values on our campus that such persuasive techniques were largely successful and that there has been a minimum of resistance to instituting the more extensive evaluation process that results when lecturers choose to submit additional documentation. It also seems that individual lecturers are satisfied with the balance that has been struck.

In essence, the same formula was followed in the shared-governance process that produced the campus policy on range elevation for lecturers. section 3 ("Evaluation Criteria") of the CSU, Long Beach, policy statement, entitled *Range Elevation for Lecturers*, stipulates a list of thirty-one different sorts of activities and achievements "that may be used to demonstrate appropriate professional growth and development." The introduction to this section states that the list "is neither exhaustive nor minimal, but simply a listing" and that "no weighting shall be inferred from the order." Again, department chairs had input in the development of this policy. It, too, has been largely effective in allowing for balance in the ways that lecturers can present their individual cases for range elevation.

The role of the campus administration in resolving the lecturer evaluation conundrum has been important but not all-controlling. Indeed, in the context of collective bargaining, an administration does not have complete latitude in shaping the evaluation process on a campus. However, administrators can always choose to facilitate or to resist. Specifically, whether to participate constructively in the Labor-Management Committee is a matter of choice for campus administrations throughout the CSU. The choice at CSU, Long Beach, has been to facilitate. Results, I think, have borne out the wisdom of that choice.

Preserving Freedom of Action for Department Chairs

Of all the balancing acts that are required of campuses by the lecturers' rights and entitlements in the CSU-CFA bargaining agreement, preservation of legitimate authority and flexibility for department chairs is one of the most challenging. As already noted, department chairs in the CSU are members of the faculty bargaining unit (CFA). At the same time, they are quasi-administrators in that they serve as "the dean's designees" for many purposes—most notably in scheduling and assigning workload. Not surprisingly, chairs are often frustrated by their lack of authority in contrast to their responsibilities. In such circumstances, it is particularly important for administrators—deans and provosts, especially—to empower chairs or, at least, to reduce obstacles that impair their ability to carry out their scheduling and class-assignment responsibilities.

Because bargaining in 2000–01 between the CSU and the CFA resulted in a salary provision that afforded a 7.0% salary increase for department chairs on academic-year (i.e., nine-month) contracts but no such increase for those scores of department chairs throughout the CSU who serve on twelve-month contracts, it had become especially important for administrators to show consideration for the difficulties that chairs face in administering new and quite complicated provisions concerning lecturers. The 2001 agreement also included new provisions (sections 12.12–12.15) that created three-year contracts for lecturers who had served continuously for the preceding six years and that established an explicit presumption of reappointment to succeeding three-year contracts. This was a revolutionary concept in CSU lecturer-appointment practices. Section 12.13 specified that lecturers on three-year appointments "shall have the expectation of appointment to subsequent three-year appointments except in instances of documented unsatisfactory performance or serious conduct problems." This represented a reversal of past practice, whereby it was always stated that a lecturer could have "no presumption of reappointment." Identification of lecturers who are eligible for such extended and renewable appointments on a campus is a task that must be handled by Academic Affairs, but the implementation of such contracts, in terms of assigning workload in the department and planning across academic years, falls to the department chair. The presumption of future employment afforded by the new provision has rendered the lecturer-evaluation process—also a responsibility of department chairs—even more important.

Another new provision of the agreement posed an initial problem for chairs as they worked through their scheduling responsibilities. This provision, section 12.29, laid out a complex formulation of "preference for available temporary work" that called on departments to ensure, among other things, that any "new or additional work" in the department is offered first to qualified incumbent temporary faculty members rather than to nonincumbents. The provision included a number of criteria that must be satisfied before the department may hire from outside the ranks of incumbents. This complicated set of provisions was eventually clarified not through further systemwide discussion and negotiation but by a 2003 arbitration decision (see *California State*). The arbitrator defined "new work" as including not only "new courses or sections" but also classes that were previously taught by faculty members currently on leave, by faculty members who have been separated (including recently retired) from the institution, and by faculty members who are no longer available to teach a given class. He also instituted a priority order for providing work to incumbent lecturers, beginning with three-year full-time appointees and ranging down to part-time lecturers with no entitlement. Before that resolution, however, department chairs in the CSU were faced with extremely complicated constraints as they attempted to establish their department schedules.

During the two years preceding the arbitrator's decision, administrators on CSU campuses had to decide how far to press for a broad interpretation of "new or additional work" that would redound to the benefit of incumbent lecturers, as opposed to defining such work more narrowly and thereby permitting considerable flexibility in making staffing decisions. For example, if "new or additional work" were defined narrowly—to include only completely new courses—then departments could, in theory, hire nonincumbents for all other unassigned new sections (see California). However, if additional sections of existing courses were included in the definition, then incumbent lecturers would have priority for appointment to teach many more of a department's available sections. The approach taken on our campus was to follow the model that we had used successfully in the past, working within the Labor-Management Committee—with input from both department chairs and lecturers—to develop ground rules for departments to follow. Although the December 2003 arbitration decision overtook this process, this episode serves as a good example of how collective bargaining can produce—sometimes intentionally—ambiguities where administrators have considerable interpretive discretion.

Maintaining Necessary Institutional Agility

As the burgeoning literature on temporary faculty employment practices consistently emphasizes, the need for institutional flexibility (or *agility*, as I have termed it here) is primarily responsible for the rapid growth in the numbers of temporary faculty nationwide. The CSU is no exception in this regard and indeed may have been a pacesetter of sorts in the institutionalization of part-time faculty members before it became a nationwide trend. (As a result, when collective bargaining came to the CSU in the mid-eighties, lecturers—already a standard part of the CSU landscape—were included in the faculty bargaining unit.) As noted at the outset, on the one hand, the administration at CSU, Long Beach, has chosen to take a consistently supportive approach in dealing with lecturer issues and has encouraged the integration of lecturers into department life and into faculty professional development activities of all types. On the other hand, campus administrators have a responsibility to preserve enough agility to permit institutional decisions that may run counter to the protection of lecturers vis-à-vis other constituencies and interests at the department level. One of the best examples of such a potential conflict involves the use of teaching associates (TAs) by academic departments.

The basic constraint facing departments and campus administrators in the use of TAs is embodied in a 1991 CSU-CFA memorandum of understanding that includes the following statement:

> It is intended that the decision to use graduate students to perform instruction, and the portion of instruction performed by such persons, be decisions based upon the needs of the program and the stated mission of the university. The California Faculty Association agrees that should it believe that graduate students are being used in an inappropriate manner, the California Faculty Association will seek resolution of the issue by a meeting of the parties to discuss administrative action prior to taking action through other agencies or forums. (California Faculty Association 218)

At the campus level, this constraint has never been easy to manage. At CSU, Long Beach, departments that wish to expand their TA programs are apt to encounter CFA suspicion that they are motivated by a desire to replace lecturers with an even less expensive form of instructional labor: graduate students. Since ours is a campus that has aspirations for strengthening key graduate programs, the administration has generally taken the side of the departments in this debate, attempting to help chairs to develop persuasive programmatic reasons for expansion of their TA programs (while also insisting on regular and effective supervision and evaluation of TAs). This is an important area of unresolved difference between our local CFA chapter and campus administration. It too will likely be negotiated and, I hope, resolved through consultation and discussion in the campus Labor-Management Committee. Moreover, the certification of the United Auto Workers union as the bargaining agent for TAs in the California State University system may now turn this into a three-way negotiation.

———

In the uncertain economic climate in which the CSU is currently operating, there will inevitably be strong pressures for agility at the campus level, and administrators will have to make judgments that will require negotiation and discussion with CFA leadership. As these challenges arise, the administration at CSU, Long Beach, is committed to respecting the letter of the CSU-CFA bargaining agreement. At the same time, however, it may become difficult to take a consistently generous interpretation of the agreement's provisions, in view of countervailing pressures. If circumstances arise where this balancing act leads to disagreements with the local CFA leadership as to whether the spirit of the agreement is being respected, we are fortunate that we have an effective Labor-Management Committee that can serve as a forum for discussion. In the meantime, academic administrators at CSU, Long Beach, will continue to take seriously the responsibility that Roger G. Baldwin and Jay L. Chronister place on "senior administrative leaders" to ensure "fair and equitable treatment of faculty in non-tenure-eligible positions as well as consistent administration of policies and procedures" (188). Thereby, the interests of students, faculty members, and institutional quality will be best served.

NOTE

1. This language is no longer used on the most recent (2004–05) version of the standard evaluation form for lecturers. Instead, evaluators are referred to the procedures and instructional memo on lecturer evaluation that is issued annually by academic affairs. The relevant statement in that memo reads: "Part-time lecturers *may* submit additional materials such as a current curriculum

vitae, a reflective narrative, and/or a peer evaluation of teaching. If such additional documentation is submitted by a lecturer, it must be considered in the lecturer's periodic evaluation. Lecturers may submit materials from the previous semester if not yet reviewed due to evaluation timelines" (see Division).

WORKS CITED

American Association of University Professors. "The Status of Non-Tenure-Track Faculty." *Policy Documents and Reports.* 9th ed. Washington: AAUP, 2001.

Baldwin, Roger G., and Jay L. Chronister. *Teaching without Tenure: Policies and Practices for a New Era.* Baltimore: Johns Hopkins UP, 2001.

California Faculty Association. Collective Bargaining Agreement with California State University. 14 May 2002–15 Mar. 2006.

California State University v. California Faculty Association. Arbitration agreement. 1998–2001.

Division of Academic Affairs, California State University, Long Beach. Lecturer Evaluation Form. 22 Dec. 2005. <www.csulb.edu/divisions/aa/>. Path: Academic Personnel; Evaluations-Lecturers; New Lecturer Evaluation Form.

Range Elevation for Lecturers. Academic Senate, Division of Academic Affairs. California State University, Long Beach. 18 Mar. 2002. 23 June 2005 <www .csulb.edu/divisions/aa/grad_undergrad/senate>. Path: Policy Statements; Range Elevation for Lecturers.

Rhoades, Gary. *Managed Professionals: Unionized Faculty and Restructuring Academic Labor.* Albany: State U of New York P, 1998.

GRADUATE ASSISTANTS

Campus Union Coalitions and the Corporate University: Organizing at the University of California

ANDREW GROSS

When I began this article—14 and 15 October 2002—the American Federation of Teachers (AFT), representing lecturers, was on strike at all nine campuses at the University of California (UC), and the Coalition of University Employees (CUE), representing clerical workers, was on strike at five. These strikes followed others throughout the UC system; they were sanctioned by the Sacramento Central Labor Council and were strongly supported by various student, professional, and employee organizations, including the union for academic student employees (ASEs), the Association of Graduate Student Employees (AGSE-UAW, Local 2865), which had staged its own systemwide strikes in 1999 and 2000 and, in 2002, encouraged its members to respect the lecturers' and clericals' picket lines (Lawson). The clericals ratified their contract in May 2003, the lecturers in July of the same year. (For CUE see Wittmeyer; for AFT see www .cft.org/councils/uc/index.html.) While the contracts did not win everything the unions were after, the struggles leading up to them convinced campus labor activists that the problems facing various employee groups are collective in nature and therefore best addressed through collaborative action (see CUE at www.cueunion.org/events/email-050103.php3). Strikes are disruptive, and necessarily so, for they occur when employees feel it is no longer possible to communicate with management through institutional channels. However, strikes and the organizing leading up to them can also mark a resurgence of campus community, as witnessed by the coalitions that emerged among lecturers, clerical workers, academic student employees, and other campus workers throughout the UC system.

Corporatization

I was a graduate student during the drive for ASE unionization and a postdoctoral teaching fellow during the lecturer and clerical strikes, so I directly experienced both the conditions leading to the various job actions and the coalitions emerging from them. I helped organize the ASE strikes, helped negotiate the first systemwide UC-UAW contract, and served as AGSE-UAW's first campus-unit chair at UC, Davis. As a postdoc in 2001–02, I worked with lecturers who, because of the precariousness of their positions, could only look at graduate student gains with envy and trepidation. This was not the fault of the lecturers but of a series of corporate-style restructurings that pitted graduate students, postdocs, and lecturers against one another for the same low-paying academic jobs. This essay argues that campus labor coalitions offer an effective means to counter the corporate restructuring of the university, often simply referred to as *corporatization*.

What is corporatization? As universities become more dependent on corporate funding, they begin to mimic corporate business practices by increasing their reliance on cheap student and adjunct labor; outsourcing remedial teaching, food preparation, and janitorial services; increasing class size; and expanding untested distance-learning technologies to free resources for prestige hires, which have the cultural capital to attract money capital (for lists of the corporate-business tactics being appropriated by many universities, along with arguments about what corporatization means in a university setting, see Nelson, "Between"; Aronowitz, *Knowledge*; and Moser). It is this perceived correlation between cultural capital and money capital that poses the most direct threat to lower-paying university jobs. This is made clear by Ronald Ehrenburg, professor of economics and director of the Cornell University Higher Education Research Institute: "If you are a university, what is the most important thing? Do you want your staff's compensation to be as high relative to its peers, or your faculty's? It is actually the reputation of the faculty that makes the reputation of the university, and to get that faculty, you have to pay them well" (qtd. in van der Werf A28).

This essay focuses on the most pressing consequence of corporatization for campus employees: the "casualization" of work, or the conversion of full-time into part-time jobs. The final report of the 1997 MLA Committee on Professional Employment notes that "those who advocate downsizing and streamlining the university along corporate lines acquiesce in or even promote the replacement of tenure-track faculty members with less expensive part-timers and adjuncts." A recent AAUP report on faculty appointments describes the extent to which academic employment has changed since 1975: "The number of non-tenure-track faculty has increased by 92% while the number of probationary (tenure-track) faculty has actually declined by 12%" (Moser 5). Richard Moser labels this employment structure, weighted toward a rapidly expanding class of part-time and adjunct instructors, the "multi-tiered" system, tracing its official sanction back to the government bailout of Chrysler in the 1970s (1).

The multitiered system as such is not the result of corporatization, since American universities have traditionally employed both tenure-track and non-tenure-track faculty members. What is new, and characteristic, of corporate restructuring is the increasingly impermeable nature of the border between classifications, separating not so much work, since lecturers and professors often teach similar courses, but levels of compensation. It is increasingly difficult to move from a lecturer's to a professor's job, at least within the same institution, and this difficulty has everything to do with the fact that the two employee groups receive vastly different salaries and benefits packages (Coalition 4). The institutional benefits of the multitiered system are primarily economic, not educational; as universities expand, they are able to drive down the cost of labor by paying more teachers less money. The money saved by this arrangement favors the growth of a permanent bureaucracy of administrators who manage expenses while occupying the top rungs of the salary ladder. As Stanley Aronowitz explains:

> The formation of a permanent administrative bureaucracy in education was the crucial internal precondition for the gulf that now separates faculty and students from educational leaders, leading to the development of the corporate university. The decline of academic life represents, in part, the degree to which the faculty has surrendered autonomy, that is, a governance and curriculum system that is largely self-generating and self-reproducing. Instead, as we have seen, the learning enterprise has become subject to the growing power of administration, which more and more responds not to faculty and students,

except at the margins, but to political and corporate forces that claim sovereignty over higher education. (*Knowledge* 164)

The UC system has come under fire for both its employment practices and its administrative salaries. In 1998, the UC Board of Regents boosted the pay of top administrators, increasing the UC president Richard Atkinson's salary from $263,500 to $310,900. An article in the UC Berkeley student paper, the *Daily Californian*, ran this subtitle: "Board gives UC Berkeley chancellor bigger salary than President Clinton, Gov. Pete Wilson" (Ng 1). The article was relatively positive about the raises because administrators argued that faculty members would get proportional compensation, a promise that, according to the *UCLA Faculty Association Newsletter* of January 2003, has never materialized: "In 1998–99 chancellors got a 17.9% increase and other executives an average of 5.9%, while faculty got 4.5%. In 1999–00, chancellors got 7.8%, other executives 8.5%, and faculty got 2.9%" (UCLA 7). In 1999, Michelle Pannor, the UC student regent, voted against administrative salary increases on the grounds that education, not administration, should be UC's top priority. In 2001, California State Assembly member Jenny Oropeza (D-55th district) voiced concerns over the administrative costs of the university: "In spite of the University's agreement to increase the quality of undergraduate education, one of its fastest rising costs is academic administration. . . . We need to ensure that the University's priorities are in the right place—on educating students" (Tavares 1). The AFT publishes a list of top UC administrative salaries on its Web site (www.cft.org/councils/uc/pdfs/adm.pdf; see also Shevitz A22).

During the recent strikes at the University of California, Flo Hatcher, chair of the AAUP's committee on part-time and non-tenure-track appointments, addressed an open letter to the UC community summing up both issues: "The proliferation of new types of contingent appointments makes administrators less accountable and the university community as a whole less cohesive." Hatcher's reference to university community gets at the heart of the issue: at stake in the recent UC strikes are two competing models of community. I shall polemically label these two models the corporate and the collaborative to distinguish them from the tradition of campus collegiality, which both union members and administrators invoke as an ideal, but to very different ends.

The Basis for Student-Employee Organization

Although this article was written on the occasion of the clericals' and lecturers' strikes, it will deal with conflicting visions of university community as they relate to AGSE-UAW's nineteen-year struggle for recognition and a first contract. The situation of ASEs is relevant to the present context because AGSE-UAW developed many of the aggressive tactics, like the systemwide strike, recently deployed by the AFT. More important, lecturers and ASEs are realizing that they not only have common tactics but a common cause. Recent university employment practices have increasingly placed ASEs and lecturers in competition for the same low-paying, lower-division jobs. Both groups are now trying to protect their jobs and preserve the quality of undergraduate education by working together instead of at loggerheads. I first explore how ASEs organized at the University of California, then examine to what extent organizing improved ASE working conditions; finally, I provide a brief sketch of how ASEs and lectureres can team up to promote a collaborative model of campus community.

While UC administrators probably opposed the student employee union on economic grounds, they argued publicly and in court that a union would disrupt the campus community in three ways: by interfering with the mentoring relationship between professors and students, by involving "big union" and outside arbitrators in decisions over educational matters, and by destroying the nature of graduate student apprenticeship. The UCLA chancellor, Charles Young, for instance, mobilizes all three arguments in the following statement, typical of the official line taken by UC spokespersons during the unionization drive: "unionization would seriously harm the flexibility, collegiality, and harmony the university strives to foster between our students and their academic mentors" (Wallace). This standard rhetoric for institutions trying to discredit student employee organizing campaigns is also found, for example, in an editorial by Thomas Appelquist, dean of the Yale University Graduate School: "The defining relationship between faculty members and graduate students is the educational one that brought them together, not the relationship of employer and employee."

This rhetoric attempts to draw a sharp line between collective bargaining, presented as an antagonistic relation between employer and employee, and the campus community, embodied in the collegial relation between mentor and apprentice. The completely inaccurate distinction depends on the sleight-of-hand suggestion that employment is a form of education in the university community and, therefore, that employers are actually educators. One of the distinguishing characteristics of the corporate university is, however, the structural separation of education and management. When AGSE-UAW was struggling to achieve its first contract, many professors would have given student employees health care and cost-of-living raises had it been in their power to do so. However, the decision lay with the business side of the house, not with individual faculty members. Indeed, there is a growing concern at some universities that committees do not provide faculty members with enough input into institutional decision-making procedures (Tierney). The faculty members could, in principle, exercise a great deal of authority at UC, but some hold they are not doing so (Hollinger).

The administrative version of campus community has two public-relations advantages: it obscures the administration's central role in establishing the terms and conditions of ASE employment and portrays the labor struggle as a generational conflict, something that is expected to happen at a university. Unsurprisingly, the utopian model of campus employment (work as education) often collapses into the rhetoric of pure paternalism. One dean went so far as to state that since he didn't bargain with his children over their allowance, he didn't see why he had to bargain with TAs over wages (Quigley; Singer).

More important than the public-relations battle is the fight in the courtroom. The UC administration resisted unionization for 18 years, pouring its considerable resources into a court battle aimed at proving that ASEs were apprentices, not workers, despite the fact that student employees earned wages for their labor and did and still do provide a significant percentage of the contact hours with UC undergraduates. The union calculates 60% but the UC administration has maintained that ASEs were responsible for a much lower percentage of student contact. To the best of my knowledge, the debate over the exact figures has never been resolved. That student employees would be responsible for so much work at a major research institution is uncommon but not unprecedented. The Coalition on the Academic Workforce reports that "graduate students taught anywhere from 25 to 60 percent of the undergraduate classes in Ph.D. programs in all of the reporting disciplines" (2).

A series of important rulings in 1996 and 1998 rejected the administration's position. In 1996, Judge James W. Tamm of the Public

Employment Relations Board (PERB) ruled that ASEs at UCLA were not teaching undergraduates primarily for their own (the ASE's) education: "the evidence is clear that there are simply too many undergraduate students and too few faculty to provide a first class education without the services of teaching assistants." He also found that "After 71 days of formal hearing, involving approximately 200 witnesses, there is simply no credible evidence in this record to support a finding that mentor relationships will deteriorate if the students in question are found to be employees" (qtd. in Khadjavi).[1] The findings affirmed what ASEs had been saying all along about the structure of higher education: that ASE labor is central to the functioning of the modern university and that the mentoring relationship between academic adviser and graduate student is distinct from the employment relationship between manager and worker.

Achieving a Contract

The struggle for recognition was followed by the struggle for a first contract. This is one of the most frustrating obstacles for student activists: management has the money and time to drag out negotiations, knowing full well that the union loses seasoned activists to burnout and graduation. UC employs dilatory tactics with all its unions, stalling negotiations until employees give in or go on strike. After a year of negotiating with no results, AGSE-UAW decided to engage in another systemwide strike over what it claimed were unfair labor practices involving, among other things, the university's refusal to bargain at the table. This scenario has played out again and again, most recently with CUE and AFT, who went on strike over UC's refusal to bargain.

Experience shows, however, that strikes alone are insufficient to win recognition or a contract. They have to be planned in conjunction with legal and legislative strategies, which depend on the involvement of union legal teams and professional organizers. The administration would probably not have responded to the strikes had it not been for pressure from PERB and the state legislature, which, thanks to active lobbying, was largely sympathetic to our cause. In terms of the strikes themselves, AGSE-UAW experimented with different tactics, including strikes on individual campuses, rolling strikes that began on one campus and then extended to others, and finally systemwide strikes—which are the hardest to organize but prove the most effective at attracting the attention of the administration and the press. We went on strike during finals week, when demand for TA labor is at its highest. We were careful, however, not to hold onto student work, since this might be construed as theft, but instead handed in all course material to our advisers in an orderly way. (Because ASEs do so much of the grading, it was impossible to hire replacement workers.) We learned to hold our strikes at the end of the fall quarter or semester, since the long summer vacation, when students are away from campus, dissipates the publicity and therefore the impact of spring job actions.

We also decided to form informational or permeable picket lines, which aim to educate students about the reasons for a strike rather than keep them off of campus. (Most campuses are so sprawling that closing them down, as in a traditional industrial job action, would be impossible anyway.) In preparing our membership for the strikes, we relied on traditional models of person-to-person organizing, namely, canvassing the campus, visiting ASEs in their offices, and calling them at home. E-mail is never as effective as a personal conversation, and campus e-mail can be read by administrators. Finally, we tried to include other unions and student organizations on campus. I will return to the issue of collaboration later.

Contract Gains

The contract AGSE-UAW finally ratified in December 2000 marked important gains in rights and benefits for TAs, readers, and tutors. These include increases in wages (a 4.5% compound increase over the life of the contract) and fee remissions (which reached 100% to become a full tuition waiver by the third year of the contract). The fee remission alone approximates a $1,500 yearly benefit, the equivalent of a 12% to 13% raise. Other benefits include workload protection and protection against sexual harassment and discrimination. Having learned from other UC unions that an internal grievance procedure was inadequate to solve serious problems, we held out for third-party arbitration—one of the biggest fights of the contract, especially when it came to workload issues. (Although we considered arbitration a major victory at the time, it is unclear if this provision has succeeded in reducing workload in areas like composition and foreign language instruction, where there are serious problems.) The contract also contains language guaranteeing health benefits for ASEs employed at 25% time or higher. By the end of the contract, these benefits included provisions for vision and dental insurance on all campuses (see www.uaw2865.org).

While most union members were satisfied with this first contract, it did not accomplish everything we hoped it would. Recent research indicates that our bargaining experiences were fairly typical of graduate assistant unions, which have proved better at bargaining reductions in tuition and fees than reductions in workload or increases in salary (Ehrenberg et al. 9, 12n14). In fact, the union's first defeat occurred before we even began to negotiate the contract, when PERB ruled that research assistants are not employees for the purposes of state labor law. Nevertheless, we found we were able to leverage research assistant benefits through bargaining, mainly because the administration did not want to provide an economic disincentive for the kind of work they perform, which is also essential to the running of a research institution. One major point of internal contention during negotiations was the no-strike clause, which prohibits the union from endorsing strikes by other UC unions during the duration of the contract. This does not mean that the union leadership cannot encourage members to respect other picket lines, as happened during the recent AFT and CUE strikes, or that individual members cannot decide to walk out on their own. However, there is a higher degree of risk involved in such unprotected actions, and union members could be subject to the disciplinary procedures also outlined in the contract. After a great deal of internal debate, the bargaining team— and then the rank-and-file members—accepted the no-strike clause, reasoning that the trade-off was grievance and arbitration, which is a more effective way to enforce a contract than trying to organize a job action for every violation. Nevertheless, we worried about how the clause would affect our ability to support other unions. UC has recently insisted on including a similar clause in the AFT contract.

The struggle to win the contract was divisive, but only insofar as it exposed already existing divisions between labor and management. Contrary to management's claim, the contract has not disturbed the mentoring relationship between faculty members and graduate students. Judge Tamm was correct in predicting that collective bargaining would not harm individual mentoring. This prediction has been borne out by recent studies suggesting that unionization does not significantly influence faculty-student relations (see Rabban and Euben) as well as by anecdotal evidence at the University of California. Why would professors find it more difficult to work with students who have clearly defined rights and benefits like health care?

Continuing Issues

Unionization has also improved relations between academic student employees and lecturers; in the most recent struggle, many ASEs followed their union's recommendation to respect the lecturers' picket lines, and the AFT borrowed some of the tactics developed by AGSE, including the systemwide strike and permeable picket lines. But the relations between lecturers and graduate students have not always been harmonious, especially in recent years. Several departments are being restructured in ways that put these two groups of employees—and a rapidly expanding pool of postdoctoral teaching fellows—into competition for the same jobs. The number of jobs is not decreasing; UC is growing so quickly that it is building a new campus in Merced. Rather, the jobs that used to go to lecturers, who were not tenured but who did have long-term employment possibilities, are now being awarded to graduate students who leave in six years or postdocs who leave in two (see Laurence; Leatherman).

One major source of conflict leading up to the recent AFT strike was the status of lecturers in the UC, Davis, English department. Previously, lecturers typically received performance evaluations after their first six years. When they were deemed to have demonstrated excellence in teaching, they were rewarded with longer-term, renewable contracts. This policy made it possible to have a career in the English department without holding tenure. Recently, a number of lecturers have been "let go" before the six-year review—not because they received poor job evaluations but because their contracts were simply not renewed. At the same time, the number of graduate students and postdocs in the department has been increasing. On 9 August 2004, PERB ruled that the lecturers unfairly dismissed at UC, Davis, be given their contractually guaranteed performance reviews, and, in the event of favorable reviews, be reinstated in their jobs (for the AFT account of the ruling, see Seyman and Roddy; Jacobson).

The balance between graduate assistants and lecturers is not easily resolved. The department has clearly failed to follow the MLA Committee on Professional Employment's advice to reduce program size, despite the fact that the committee was chaired by a member of our department, former MLA president Sandra Gilbert. Contrary to the MLA recommendation, the dean of humanities is encouraging the department to increase the size of the graduate program while decreasing the number of lecturers. But is this dean's action a bad thing? On the surface, at least, it looks like non-tenure-track jobs are being converted to tenure-track—another MLA recommendation (Jacobson). Moreover, more graduate students need more academic advisers—and the department has, in fact, expanded its tenure-track faculty in recent years. Another possible explanation, not incompatible with the previous one, is that the composition jobs, already the assignment of lecturers, are now being pushed from the second tier to the third, in other words, from lecturers to postdocs and graduate students. The number of competing interests and interpretations has made it difficult for various employee groups—professors, lecturers, postdocs, and graduate students—to cooperate in finding a solution to the growing tension, although most of them have the department's best interest in mind, and many genuinely sympathize with one another as individuals.

One way to bring competing parties together is to consider structural problems from a community perspective, cutting across the lines of competing job classifications. Graduate students have a unique outlook here both because their career trajectories are supposed to span job classifications and because today, more often than not, career advancement is a dream rather than a reality. Ideally, graduate students move from graduate programs to postdocs to professorships. Recent studies indicate, however, that the graduate students of today are likely to be the adjuncts and part-timers of tomorrow. In 1997, the MLA predicted that *"fewer than half the seven or eight thousand graduate students likely to earn Ph.D.s in English and foreign languages between 1996 and 2000 can expect to obtain full-time tenure-track positions within a year of receiving their degrees"* (italics in original). Recent surveys seem to confirm these predictions. According to a study completed in 1999, "less than 59% of new Ph.D.[s] in the humanities who received their degrees in 1998, reported having definite commitments of employment or plans for future study at the time they received their Ph.D.s" (Ehrenberg et al. 5). The predictions for graduates in the sciences are dire as well (Lee; Lok).

These findings suggest that graduate students and postdocs are in the precarious position of receiving excellent training for jobs that are, for one reason or another, harder to get. Nevertheless, numbers often fail to influence university policy or, for that matter, personal perspectives. Leaving policy aside for a moment—and the institutional means of addressing the conflicting interests of graduate students and lecturers—I will briefly turn to the matter of perspective. Many graduate students and postdocs are sustained by dreams of making it. In fact, academics at all levels, who are committed to the American ideal of personal achievement, turn a blind eye to the horrendous employment conditions that are standard in most colleges and universities. The CAW report observes, "Most [part-time teachers with master's degrees or PhDs] could earn comparable salaries as fast food workers, baggage porters, or theater lobby attendants" (Coalition 3). Once teachers get stuck in low-paying jobs, it is difficult to move out. A history of lengthy and recurrent part-time employment often disqualifies PhDs for tenure-track jobs, even when part-time employment reflects a structural problem, not a lack of professional qualifications.

This is the Ivory Tower's dirty little secret, our "madwoman in the attic." We talk about the social significance of teaching, often marketing ourselves as progressives and radicals, but we approach the job market like free-market fundamentalists, trying to beat out our opponents in a war of all against all. If the academy was ever a community of scholars, it is quickly becoming an arena of competitors. Aronowitz describes the transition from community to competition as a process of "proletarianization" and links it to, among other things, the way postsecondary education has been restructured to meet the needs of the corporate job market (Aronowitz, "Academic Unionism" 204).

While it might be an exaggeration to describe academic workers as the proletarians of the knowledge industry, it should be clear by now that universities are not the collegial communities antiunion administrators make them out to be. It is essential that unions provide employees with the resources to get beyond university rhetoric and change university policy. Contract negotiations and the binding agreements that come out of them offer a collective way of addressing what are clearly common problems. In fact, it often takes collective action and collaboration to make common problems visible in the first place. While it might seem to be in the self-interest of graduate students to advocate ASE over lecturer positions, the broader graduate student position, the one activated by collective action, insists that the lecturers doing a valuable job now should be treated fairly precisely because many graduate students will work as lecturers in the future. Organizing with lecturers shows graduate students where they might be going, and organizing with graduate students reminds lecturers where they have been. This cross-classification perspective offers a necessary corrective to the free-market narrative of personal success and failure. Once different employee groups learn to see problems in common, they can begin to develop common strategies. For instance, if graduate students bargain for higher wages and better benefits, it becomes less tempting to use them to replace lecturers. Whatever long-term strategies the graduate students and the lecturers develop, they will have to aim not at protecting low-paying jobs but at reversing the university's growing reliance on all forms of part-time and adjunct employment.

If common action helps employees see beyond the narrow interests of their job classifications, it also brings education to the fore—a perspective that is sometimes lost in the conflict surrounding departmental restructuring. When I began my graduate studies at UC, Davis, incoming composition TAs spent a quarter team teaching with more experienced instructors, many of whom were lecturers. This practice worked well, but it has been abandoned. One of the reasons seems to be the job classification system. Teaching graduate students lies outside the lecturers' job description, although few would deny that they were doing a good job of teaching us how to teach. This is a perfect issue for collaborative organizing. Because lecturers were able to articulate arguments about the collaborative nature of education, they were able to rally large numbers of graduate students and postdocs to their cause.

The current AFT contract has not managed to expand the lecturers' job descriptions. More seriously, it might not even succeed in protecting lecturers' jobs. Nevertheless, those interested in making UC a fair place to work have some grounds to be optimistic. The labor coalitions forming at UC have helped shift the campus discourse from profit and prestige to community and education. California is currently facing a severe budget crisis that will put these coalitions—and the values they stand for—to the test. UC President Richard Atkinson has made it clear that employee salaries and positions are on the chopping block. Nevertheless, the union movement is growing in strength, and it might be able to resist some of the staff-directed cost-cutting measures that the administration will try to put in place.

The university's aggressive restructuring has produced a new series of coalitions and alliances made up of student and employee organizations that previously had little contact with one another. Collective action makes a campus community possible in what is otherwise a disjointed, multitiered workspace: students in the humanities wind up organizing with engineers, undergraduates support their TAs, graduate students stand with lecturers and clericals during job actions, and all these groups rally around sweatshop issues. One example of cross-interest collaboration is the three-week student sit-in (April–May 2001) in the president's office at Harvard, demanding the university pay its staff members a living wage. According to the *Nation*, many of the students involved in this action were trained at Union Summer, John Sweeney's initiative to get university students involved with the AFL-CIO (Manners 16). Another example is the Teamster-Turtle coalition that emerged in the Seattle protests. This coalition probably resulted from labor's new approach to activism: when unions like the UAW began organizing college campuses, many leftist students, inclined to be environmentalists, began to see how labor issues intersect with environmental issues in areas like sustainable growth. Recently, AGSE-UAW has begun using the grievance procedure it won through a year of negotiation to protect international students put at risk after 9/11 (Bunn; Rayfield). Unions and the collaborative strategies they enable are important tools for bringing the campus community together and for protecting the members of the campus community most at risk.

Campus Community

What model of campus community emerges out of collective bargaining? The community is antagonistic, as the administrators say, but because the antagonism is already built into the multitiered system, which tends to play employee groups against one another. Collective bargaining places the antagonism where it should be, not between competing classifications, which in a collegial community should not exist at all, but between management and labor. Bargaining also provides an institutionalized procedure that can transform generalized antagonism into specific problems that can be addressed, and sometimes solved, through recurrent, binding agreements. It is important not to romanticize contract negotiations. Bad practice does become ratified, and bad contracts do become standard.

Some feel that this is precisely what happened with the no-strike clauses at UC. But if there are risks, there are also benefits, such as grievance procedures, fee and tuition reductions, and health care.

A cooperative model of labor-management relations is possible. Barry Bluestone and Irving Bluestone's *Negotiating for the Future* endorses a joint-action model whereby unions and management work together to make tough decisions (207). While the joint-action model might work at institutions committed to maintaining a fair and cooperative university community, it will not work at the University of California as long as administrators insist on running the campus like a corporation.

NOTE

The case cited by Khadjavi is *Regents of the University of California*, 20 PERC A27129 (1996).

WORKS CITED

Appelquist, Thomas. "Graduate Students Are Not Employees." *Chronicle of Higher Education* 18 Apr. 1997: B6.

Aronowitz, Stanley. "Academic Unionism and the Future of Higher Education." Nelson, *Will Teach* 181–215.

———. *The Knowledge Factory: Dismantling the Corporate University and Creating True Higher Learning.* Boston: Beacon, 2001.

Atkinson, Richard. A Budget Update from the University of California President for UC Faculty and Staff. 4 Aug. 2003. 7 Aug. 2003 <http://www.ucop.edu/news/budget/issue9.html>.

Bluestone, Barry, and Irving Bluestone. *Negotiating the Future: A Labor Perspective on American Business.* New York: Basic, 1992.

Buck, Jane. "The President's Report: Successes, Setbacks, and Contingent Labor." *Academe Online* 87.5 (2001). 17 July 2003 <http://www.aaup.org/publications/Academe/01SO/So01toc.htm>.

Bunn, Elizabeth. "Letter to UC President Richard Atkinson." 29 Nov. 2001. UAW Local 2865 home page. 4 Dec. 2002. 30 June 2005 <http://www.uaw2865.org.html>. Path: Media and Press; November 29, 2001.

Coalition on the Academic Workforce. "Summary of Data from Surveys by the Coalition on the Academic Workforce." 22 Nov. 2000. American Historical Association home page. 11 Mar. 2002. <http://www.theaha.org/caw/>.

Ehrenberg, Ronald, Daniel Klaff, Adam Kezsbom, and Matthew Nagowski. "Collective Bargaining in American Higher Education." Cornell Higher Educ. Research Institute Conference, Governance of Higher Educ. Institutions and Systems. 4–5 June 2002 Ithaca. 15 June 2003 <http://web.cornell.edu/UniversityFaculty/OnLineForum/GradForum/EhrenbergExc.pdf>.

Hatcher, Flo. "Open Letter to the UC-Davis Community." E-mail to UC, Davis, faculty and staff. 8 Oct. 2002.

Hollinger, David. "Faculty Governance, The University of California, and the Future of Academe." *Academe* 87.3 (2001). 17 July 2003 <http://www.aaup .org/publications/Academe/01mj/mj01holl.htm>.

Jacobson, Jennifer. "Letting Lecturers Go to Expand the Tenure Track." *Chronicle of Higher Education* 11 Apr. 2002. 9 Sept. 2005 <http://chronicle.com/jobs/ 2002/04/2002041101c.htm>.

Khadjavi, Lily. "Should Graduate Student Employees Have Collective Bargaining Rights?" *Bad Subjects* 29 (1996). 10 Sept. 2005 <http://bad.eserver.org/ issues/1996/29>. Path: *STRIKE!*.

Lawson, Dan. Letter to members of UAW Local 2865. Aug. 2002. 4 Dec. 2002 <http://www.uaw2865.org/announcements.html#strikenews>.

Laurence, David. "The 1999 MLA Survey of Staffing in English and Foreign Language Departments." *ADE Bulletin* 129 (2001): 53–62. 23 July 2003 <http:// www.mla.org/staffing_survey99>.

Leatherman, Courtney. "Part-Timers Continue to Replace Full-Timers on College Faculties." *Chronicle of Higher Education* 28 Jan. 2000: A18–19.

Lee, Jennifer. "Postdoc Trail: Long and Filled with Pitfalls." *New York Times* 21 Aug. 2001: F3.

Lok, Corie. "Postdocs Call for Better Pay and Conditions." *Nature* 8 Mar. 2001: 137.

Manners, Jane. "Joe Hill Goes to Harvard: A Growing Student-Labor Alliance Is Bringing Victories on Campus and Beyond." *Nation* 2 July 2001: 16–18.

MLA Committee on Professional Employment. Final Report. New York: MLA, 1997. 28 June 2005 <http://www.mla.org/prof_employment>. Path: Preface.

Moser, Richard. "The New Academic Labor System, Corporatization, and the Renewal of Academic Citizenship." 6 Dec. 2001. 17 July 2003 <http://www .aaup.org/Issues/part-time/cewmose.htm>.

Ng, Bernice. "UC Regents Hike Pay for Officials, Faculty." *Daily Californian* 21 Sept. 1998. 17 July 2003 <http://archive.dailycal.org/archive/98/9/21/salaries .html>.

Nelson, Cary. "Between Crisis and Opportunity: The Future of the Academic Workplace." Nelson, *Will Teach* 3–31.

———, ed. *Will Teach for Food: Academic Labor in Crisis.* Minneapolis: U of Minnesota P, 1997.

Pannor, Michelle. "Student Regent Speaks Out on Administrative Salary Increases." *New University Newspaper* 17 July 2003 <http://www.newuniversity .org/archive/1999-2000/fall/991011/n-991011-regent.html>.

Quigley, Mark. "Organizing over the Long Haul: The SAGE/UAW Campaign at the University of California." *Workplace: A Journal for Academic Labor* 4.1 (2001). 4 Mar. 2002 <www.louisville.edu/journal/workplace/issue7/quigley.html>.

Rabban, David, and Donna Euben. Brief of Amicus Curiae American Association of University Professors in support of Petitioner United Automobile Workers, AFL-CIO. NYU v. UAW, 332 NLRB 1205 (2000) (No. 2-RC-22082). 10 July 2003 <http://members.aol.com/gsocuaw/amicus_aaup.html>.

Rayfield, Elizabeth. "Local 2865 Opposes Efforts to Scapegoat and Discriminate against International Students in Wake of the September 11th Tragedy." 1 Nov. 2001. 4 Mar. 2002 <http://www.uaw2865.org/press.html>.

Seyman, Richard, and Kevin Roddy. "PERB Rules UCD Lecturers Improperly Denied Review." *UC-AFT Perspective* 17.1 (2004): 3. 30 June 2005 <http://www.cft.org/councils/uc/pdfs/ucpersfo4.pdf>.

Shevitz, Tanya. "UC May Raise Pay for Top Positions: Increases Would Dwarf Those for Faculty, Staff." *San Francisco Chronicle* 9 Nov. 2001: A22.

Singer, Jonathan. "Striking in Unexpected Places." *Workplace* 2.1 (2001). 10 July 2003 <http://www.workplace-gsc.com/workplace2-1/singer.html#5>.

Tavares, Stephanie. "State Conducts UC Audit." *Daily Nexus* 29 Oct. 2001. 17 July 2003 <http://www.ucsbdailynexus.com/news/1969/1590.html>.

Tierney, William. "Why Committees Don't Work: Creating a Structure for Change." *Academe* 87.3 (2001). 17 July 2003 <http://www.aaup.org/publications/Academe/01mj/mj01tier.htm>.

UCLA Faculty Association. "The UC Faculty Salary Puzzle." *UCLA Faculty Association Newsletter* Jan. 2003. 4 May 2003 <http://www.uclafacultyassociation.info/newsletters/salary_puzzle.htm>.

van der Werf, Martin. "How Much Should Colleges Pay Their Janitors? *Chronicle of Higher Education* 3 Aug. 2001: A27.

Wallace, Amy. "Teaching Assistants Call Strike at UCLA." *Los Angeles Times* 18 Nov. 1996: B1.

Wittmeyer, Alicia. "Clerical Workers Vote to Accept UC-Proposed Contract." *Daily Californian* 1 May 2003. 7 June 2003 <http://www.dailycal.org/article.asp?id=11435>.

Observations on an Unsuccessful Organizing Drive at Cornell University

JACLYN MARIE JANESK

Since John Sweeney's election in 1995 as president of the AFL-CIO, unions have more vigorously organized groups of employees who previously had low rates of unionization. Some of the greatest activity has been by graduate students in institutions of higher learning. This stepped-up organizing activity took place during a period of uncertainty over the legal status of private-sector graduate-employee unionization and before the National Labor Relations Board decision in the 2004 *Brown University* case to revert to its earlier position that graduate employees are not covered by the federal statute.

Graduate-employee unionization efforts frequently met strong opposition from administrations that pursued the available legal opportunities to resist recognition. This resistance occurred at such private institutions as Columbia University, the University of Pennsylvania, and Brown University and also, less successfully, at such public institutions as the University of California and the University of Illinois. At Cornell University, graduate students thought that they had the key to overcoming this type of opposition: an agreement with the administration precluding any challenge to the election and further pledging to abide by the union contract for its term, even if the NLRB found graduate unionization illegal during the interim. Yet the campaign failed because persuading graduate students to vote yes proved harder than anticipated.

The purpose of this paper is not to place blame for a failed organizing drive but instead to look at the unionization effort from the perspective of a Cornell student, to see what went wrong. Did the union mostly do everything right to win the election and still come up short? Or did the organizers run an inadequate campaign? Taking into account the internal and external pressures that affect voters, organizers, and opposing groups, each particular organizing effort must be examined on its own terms.

Formation of the Cornell Association of Student Employees (CASE)

The unionization effort of graduate students at Cornell dates back to early 2001. Not surprising, the idea took shape in the Industrial and Labor Relations School, one of Cornell's less-well-funded public colleges, where several students felt that many of their needs with respect to office space, pay, hours, and other conditions of employment were not being met. These students of labor believed that the best way to achieve change was through collective bargaining. At first, they considered organizing just the ILR school but soon discovered through informal conversations that students in other schools shared many of the same concerns. A core group of about four students in ILR spent approximately six months researching the various local graduate student unions and the key national unions involved in the effort. The group that formed was known as CASE, the Cornell Association of Student Employees.

The students contacted the four national unions that they felt most comfortable with and that might be willing to take on their organizing campaign. The Communications Workers of America (CWA) and the United Electrical Workers (UE) were immediately dismissed because they did not have a strong presence in the field of higher education and could not commit adequate resources. The final two unions in contention were the American Federation of Teachers (AFT) and the United Auto Workers (UAW), both of which have a strong presence on campuses (among adjuncts and graduate employees in the latter case) and both of which pledged to provide whatever was needed to win. What eventually proved decisive was one student's past interaction with an AFT organizing effort. This particular graduate student argued strongly that an AFT failure at the University of Minnesota marked it as incapable of succeeding with Cornell graduate students. The UAW's willingness to provide resources and to have a strong presence on the Cornell campus proved decisive, and that organization was selected as the vehicle for the organizing drive.

CASE-UAW reached an agreement with the University administration in July 2001 that defined a bargaining unit, set dates for the NLRB-administered election, and acknowledged that certain academic issues were outside the scope of bargaining. Soon after, CASE-UAW began its organizing drive with an effort to collect cards.

The Outcome

On 23 and 24 October 2002, the CASE organizing effort came to an end with a 1,351 to 580 vote against union representation. The 2,049 ballots cast (118 votes were challenged) represented 88.4% of those eligible to vote. This represented the UAW's largest voter turnout, in terms of percentage, in over five years.

CASE supporters certainly were disappointed with the outcome, and the Cornell community generally was shocked by the overwhelming disparity of the vote; most had expected a close election. Many attributed the large gap to the high voter turnout. Often in union elections, the union succeeds in getting "yes" voters to the polls far more effectively than any antiunion forces succeed in urging "no" voters to cast ballots. Yet in this election, both the administration and groups not associated with CASE were apparently quite successful in urging all those eligible to vote to do so, making the turnout highly representative of the graduate assistant body. Perhaps also contributing to the result was the general tendency of voters who are undecided as the election draws near to vote against the union.

Research Methods

In the aftermath of the election, I sought to analyze the results by conducting firsthand interviews of graduate students both in and out of the bargaining unit. I included those not in the bargaining unit because the actual composition of the unit was a source of contention throughout the campaign; information regarding the choices made was not widely disseminated, and many graduate students wanted to know the reasoning for the unit being defined as it was, requiring, for example, at least 25% tuition remission to be able to vote in the election. The union failed to answer this question adequately, and the opposition gave voice to many outside the bargaining unit.

The research was opinion-based for the most part, which cannot be indicative of absolutes; however, the views conveyed surely were representative of the major strains on campus and of the concerns surrounding the campaign. Those interviewed were promised confidentiality because it became apparent that most students did not feel comfortable being completely frank unless this anonymity applied. My research was supplemented by a review of documents sent out by the Cornell administration and of the Web sites of several student groups such as At What Cost?, a graduate assistant group that emerged in August of 2002, relatively late in the campaign.

CASE Organizing Strategy

CASE's most vociferous arguments centered on broad concepts such as democracy, a seat at the table, and a stronger voice and were conveyed with grassroots rhetoric. Although CASE launched the campaign intending to present a range of educational forums, their efforts became overwhelmingly tied up with card collecting. CASE began collecting cards in the fall of 2001 and continued through the spring, but voting did not take place until the next academic year. Thus, one factor determining the outcome may have been that a significant number of the students who signed cards graduated before the election. Graduation rates, however, were accounted for as well as they could be; CASE organizers—a combination of the one full-time organizer furnished by the UAW, the four graduate students paid by the UAW for part-time work, and graduate student volunteers—knew from whom they were collecting cards and ensured that the graduate students subject to the solicitation were not graduating.

The length of the time period spent collecting cards is indicative of weak support. It would have been most effective to collect cards in the fall semester and to vote in the spring. But when CASE organizers found themselves coming up short in the fall of 2001, they needed to continue to collect cards and to delay the eventual filing with the labor board. Another factor to keep in mind is that cards signed with a promise of confidentiality may be a weak indicator of actual balloting for several reasons. Not only are signatures on authorization cards not binding but also some students later reported signing cards simply to get organizers to leave them alone. The students generally were not being invited to rallies or discussions or debates, where turnout would be much more indicative of firm support for the union.

CASE was described by many students as having a very in-your-face approach. The perceived aggression served to turn voters against the union and motivated some to get out and vote out of sheer anger. Potential voters on CASE's contact list were approached multiple times and often felt bothered and intruded on. Undeniably, commendable eagerness and persistence were present in large measure, but the organizers' actions were perceived by many as overdone and alienating. This made voters think about what it would be like to be part of such an aggressive union, since there was no distinction made in voters' minds between what to expect in organizing and then later in bargaining. In many ways, CASE did nothing fundamentally wrong; they may simply have done too much. CASE was structurally sound but strategically flawed.

Graduate Students or Graduate Employees?

The question of identity—and of corresponding legal status—was of substantial concern to many voters. CASE did not adequately convey the need for a union to graduate students who saw unions as strictly for blue-collar employees such as the autoworkers who were at the core of the UAW's membership. CASE preached about a seat at the table and other issues of democracy, but most voters thought that they had this voice already—as students—in the form of the Graduate and Professional Student Assembly.

Graduate students in large numbers saw themselves primarily as students at Cornell, their presence on campus explained by educational opportunities offered rather than by the pay or health benefits they received. As one student put it, "the notion that a bunch of overprivileged eggheads getting their PhD's at an Ivy League institution needs a union to protect them is ridiculous and beyond my ability to express in words." Although this viewpoint stood at one extreme, it is obvious that variations of this opinion pervaded much of the student body. That many of the students in the bargaining unit were receiving lucrative financial packages was a further obstacle for CASE: about 95% had half or more of their tuition expenses covered. CASE might have been better served had it focused on specifics of how students would have benefited from a union, emphasizing professional issues of the academy rather than pay and benefits.

The initial decision to select the UAW as the organizational vehicle for the union drive may have gone a long way toward sealing the fate of the drive. Aside and apart from general misgivings about being union-represented, one strongly held view of those who voted against the union was an uneasiness about affiliation with the UAW in particular. This was exacerbated by a perception that the UAW, rather than CASE, was calling the shots in the campaign. This viewpoint was summed up by one anonymous student thusly: "there are appropriate places for unions and appropriate unions for places." Many who perused the UAW Web site found it off-putting, carrying an air of militancy out of sync with campus life. Those who did not already agree that unionization was necessarily beneficial found their concerns inadequately addressed.

In keeping with this, many of those interviewed indicated that they would have voted for the union had it been affiliated with the AFT, an organization that they believed would have been more in touch with academic concerns. (Ironically, a primary reason for selecting the UAW cited by those who launched the drive was its strong presence on campuses.) Even after the defeat, CASE organizers did not accept that they failed to communicate the utility of the UAW adequately and instead argued that those who voted no not only used this as an excuse but also would not have voted yes even if the AFT had been the designated bargaining agent.

CASE organizers' failure to educate their peers on the issues did not result from a lack of zeal or commitment. Rather, they simply failed to recognize whom they were organizing. All industries are different, and no single unionization method can be used in all workplaces. As a whole, graduate students are very intelligent and eager to learn, and in this instance many wanted information that CASE just did not give them. This was perceived as an issue of respect; students felt that CASE did not credit the voters with having the ability to sort through the relevant facts and to make informed decisions. CASE organizers were working long hours and often became impatient as a result. Consequently, the communications problem was compounded by CASE organizers' occasional perception of honest questions as attacks, when in fact many students were merely eager to learn both sides of the issues.

CASE transplanted many of the tactics used in the New York University and Columbia University organizing drives, failing to distinguish among the student bodies. Cornell is located in a very different area than NYU and Columbia. What works in liberal New York City may not be at all effective in Ithaca, a mainly rural area. And Cornell's emphasis in the hard sciences generated opposition because, traditionally, students in these disciplines are much more conservative and resistant to unionization. Students in the sciences value facts, tending to examine everything. They think micro, not macro, unlike their liberal arts colleagues.

The group At What Cost? presented itself as being open to free inquiry. It formed late in the campaign, barely two months before the balloting took place. But it gained a voice quickly because it served a need: it functioned as a sounding board for students to discuss the issues. Although most of those involved in the group undoubtedly were opposed to a graduate assistant union, At What Cost? presented itself as promoting exploration of the union issue rather than as directly opposing unionization. Accordingly, it didn't run an overtly negative campaign and was content with drawing many students into an open discussion they felt was not taking place elsewhere. Had CASE been more open to answering questions on the role of the UAW—questions about how academic issues would be dealt with by the union and so on—perhaps more voters would have been persuaded to vote for the union.

The H1B visa issue is a case in point. An H1B visa is a nonimmigrant employment-based visa for workers coming to the United States to work in specialty occupations. The types of jobs covered correspond to those in areas of study favored by Cornell graduate students: engineering, computers, and general math and sciences. These visas became a major issue in the campaign because of the high population of international students in such programs. Just before the election, wide publicity was given to a charge that the UAW was against expanding the H1B visa program, in keeping with that union's long history of advocating for American jobs for American workers. Just days before the election, CASE successfully limited the damage to the UAW's image by explaining that the UAW opposed H1B expansion but only because of its temporary status and that the union in fact supported more lenient policies for issuance of the visa and even the expansion of nonexploitative visa programs, such as green cards. In the end, although this controversy was very public, postelection interviews revealed that many international students did not in fact find it determinative when they cast their votes on the union question.

Although the most frequently vocalized theme of CASE's campaign was the need for a seat at the table and democracy for graduate assistants, there was also some public debate on such nuts-and-bolts matters as office space, workload, and intellectual property. Some of that discussion worked to CASE's disadvantage, however, since it triggered some students to think about why they chose Cornell, an elite institution, in the first place. As one student put it, "we're going to rescind on the opportunity that most never receive and tell an Ivy League school that they're not good enough?" Most respondents, revealing the value they placed on unionization compared with the quality and reputation of a school, stated in postelection interviews that they would rather be enrolled at a non-unionized Cornell than attend a lower-tier school that was unionized. In addition, some expressed concern (and complained that these concerns were inadequately addressed during the campaign) about what would happen to Cornell's selectivity rating if it were unionized.

Were CASE Organizers Isolated?

A person who feels passionately about a cause may not be entirely rational about it and can become irritated when others do not come to the same conclusion. To many of the organizers, unionization was nothing but beneficial. Coming from the ILR school, organizers were not sensitive to the fact that the knowledge they had of the labor movement and their attraction to it were not universally shared. But chemistry students, engineers, and many other students often know little about unionization other than what they see on television or read in the newspaper. The CASE organizers failed to make critical connections with their peers.

Another of the cultural disconnects was that many felt that those at the core of CASE were motivated primarily by their desire to be part of the labor movement. As some put it, quite harshly, the union drive was seen as a valuable addition to the student organizers' resumes. Although these accusations were exaggerated, at the very least, these perceptions were real and cost CASE votes.

Antiunion Campaign by Cornell Administration

Some professors and administrators did publicly denounce the union, but for the most part the administration took a neutral stance, and the faculty did not get directly involved. The Cornell administration apparently calculated that overt opposition to the unionization effort simply would have driven students to the union side. (Officially, Cornell commented only that they wanted students to educate themselves on both sides of the issues and vote what they thought was best for themselves and the future of the institution.) Indeed, it might be said that the Cornell administration knew their students better than CASE did.

The sole exception to the administration's restraint was a widely disseminated electronic message to the Cornell community by President Hunter Rawlings late in the campaign. On 12 September 2002, Rawlings welcomed students back to campus and informed them of the upcoming union election. He expressed Cornell's commitment to labor and long-standing relationship with the labor movement before going on to question the need for a graduate assistant union. Calling into question the union's ability to represent the best interests of the university and its tradition of research and teaching, Rawlings stated that the existence of a single bargaining unit would preclude the option of students negotiating individual financial packages and would prohibit accommodations for individual circumstances.

Although Rawlings's message refrained from outright antiunion sentiments, the underlying negative sentiment toward CASE was communicated quite effectively. The approach was shrewd, serving to alienate only those who were already committed to voting for the union. For undecided voters, his communication was perceived as addressing their real concerns without being strident. "He simply stated what could happen," as many students commented.

———

In the end, most graduate assistants simply were not convinced of the need for a union. There was no clear-cut or heated issue for CASE to rally behind, and the administration wisely did not forcefully intervene. The core of ILR students who originated the idea of a union proved unable to connect their solutions with the problems as perceived by the rest of the campus.

Getting a Contract versus Gaining a Voice: Some Obstacles to Forming Effective Graduate-Student-Employee Unions

ANNA GERONIMO HAUSMANN

Graduate-student-employee unions are a relatively new phenomenon in higher education, the first such union being founded at the University of Wisconsin, Madison, more than thirty years ago. In fact, the formation of graduate student unions can be seen as a product of and as a response to the profound changes that higher education has gone through in those same years. It's not hard to see how the financial squeeze on universities, both public and private, has resulted in dramatic changes in the way graduate education is conducted, from the use of graduate student employees to teach large percentages of undergraduate courses to the downsizing and even elimination of some graduate degree programs. The increasing pace of organizing on campuses in the last several years, and especially the advent of unions at private institutions, suggests that unionization provides a remedy to these fundamental changes. The question remains, however, whether unionization is the most effective remedy.

From my experience as a graduate student who organized the Graduate Student Employees Union (GSEU) at the State University of New York, I have identified four issues that can become obstacles to forming effective graduate-student-employee unions. I don't want to suggest, however, that these obstacles should stop graduate students from organizing. Rather, I believe that we in the academic community who support graduate student unions need to recognize and discuss these potential limitations if we are to correct them.

How Do We See Ourselves?

In unionizing graduate student employees, the first step is to prove to a state or federal labor board that insofar as graduate students are doing their work—teaching, working in the lab—the students are functioning primarily as employees and not as students. It is getting more difficult to prove this point, since the National Labor Relations Board has now reversed its 2000 ruling that graduate students who work are employees.

But the point that graduate students are workers rests on a false premise, since their status as employees is contingent on their status as students. To be a graduate student employee, one has to be a graduate student; this precondition is not merely semantic but the crux of the issue. The definition of graduate students' labor as separate from their academic programs may sometimes be true and sometimes not, but in any case, as any graduate student employee will tell you, it can be confusing. Even in the most extreme of circumstances, such as in English departments where TAs run their courses completely on their own, their work is interwoven with getting their degrees. If this sense persists even for those TAs teaching autonomously, imagine how confusing this definition is for graduate students who as employees work in labs on research that may also become part of their dissertations.

This is not to say that graduate student employment is not work: it most certainly is work, as anyone who has ever graded piles of student papers or endlessly filled a pipette from one container and emptied it into another will tell you. But the recurrent slippage between employment and student status makes it difficult for graduate student employees to access the inherent democratizing principle of unionization—the idea that workers should be fairly paid for their work. More important, the persistence of their student status makes it difficult for graduate student employees to organize around the most fundamental of union issues, such as job security or advancement. Their work, after all, is designed to put them out of work. One of the primary goals of most unions is job security and longevity. But for graduate students, their main goal almost from the moment they step on campus is to finish their job and move on. This essential transitory status severely undermines the development of leadership and organizing skills that will strengthen and perpetuate the union.

Reinventing the Wheel Every Four Years

When I began organizing with the GSEU, I didn't understand the important role played by institutional memory that comes from years in the workplace. But the fact is that the unique circumstances of graduate student employment, specifically the high turnover rate of the employees and the cyclical nature of their employment, impede the creation of a strong, member-driven organization. All unions struggle with the issue of member involvement outside contract negotiations. Unions strive to keep their membership engaged. Mobilizing members means keeping them aware of their role not just in keeping the union functioning by performing necessary tasks like serving as shop stewards but also in making the union a vital and powerful presence in the workplace.

But this picture of union mobilizing is also a dream, and turning it into reality takes years of united effort. The mobilizing model relies on trained, experienced members to recruit and educate other members. Mobilization means the union must disseminate information and empower the membership so that every member knows the contract, knows her or his rights, and brings the full power of the union on the job with her or him every day. But this type of education takes time. Graduate students may spend an average of nine years in graduate school, but few will spend all that time as graduate student employees. Graduate students cycle through their programs as employees for four or five years but then often drift out of the bargaining unit to write their dissertations, which does not afford them the time necessary to establish the institutional memory and structural support necessary for a member-driven, rather than staff-dependent, union.

That graduate students often don't become activists until several years into their programs complicates the problem of turnover. New graduate students are at the height of their potential and value to the institution and have yet to experience the radicalizing job conditions or reappointment problems that would lead them to look to a union as a remedy. This view of new graduate students is founded on Gloria Steinem's analysis of the conservatism of college-age women in her essay, "The Good News Is: These Are Not the Best Years of Your Life," in which she claims that young women are more conservative because they have not yet experienced the life events that are most radicalizing for women—among them, entering the paid workforce, marriage, parenthood, and aging (364). I see a close parallel between Steinem's description of young women in general and the circumstances of beginning graduate students in particular.

I do not mean to say that turnover is a problem unique to graduate-student-employee unions. In fact, after organizing at GSEU, I worked for a health-care union representing nursing-home staff, a category of workers with an enormous turnover rate. One very significant difference between nursing-home workers and graduate student employees is that, although there is turnover among health-care workers, they are generally not cycling out of the profession but rather tend to move from one facility to another. It's actually very easy to get fired from a nursing home because they have strict attendance policies; but because of the shortage of workers in the industry, it's also easy to get another job at a different facility. Thus, although a large percentage of workers may be new to a facility, they aren't new to the field or unaware of the exploitative practices in the industry.

Structure without Substance

While I see turnover of the membership as the biggest potential problem for graduate-employee unions, this problem can be mitigated by a strong organizational structure in the form of a paid professional staff. But having a paid staff doesn't necessarily mean one will have a strong union. In his essay on graduate-employee unions, William Vaughn notes the problem posed by turnover and concludes "that's why you have to build a formal, permanent structure" (46). But a union dependent on a paid staff without the active involvement of members has its own problems, one of which is organization building. For one thing, dependence on paid professional-staff leadership hinders the union from developing into an active political force and undermines its collaboration with other political entities on campus. In addition, a union run by its staff can be a less effective bargaining agent because of lack of member support. Paid staff members can do the administrative work necessary to run a union; they can train stewards and print newsletters. But they aren't members. Members need to define and take ownership of the union's issues; they can only do this through their active engagement in the organization. Member engagement, not staff efficiency, makes a strong union.

The Obstacle of Competition

Finally, another equally knotty obstacle to building the long-term, empowered relationship among workers that is necessary for a strong union structure is the culture of competition in graduate school, which separates graduate employees from one another and thus from effective collectivity. This culture of competition derives support from the belief that social distinctions represent a genuine meritocracy. In academia, many in the professoriate promote this myth to justify their own privileges in disregard of the arbitrary and capricious effects of an academic job market shaped more by economic and political constraints than academic values. As Vaughn notes, graduate students as well as professors are invested in the notion of academia as a meritocracy (47). And as long as graduate students still participate in the myth that academic labor differs in kind from other types of labor, as long as they fail to see how graduate education has been transformed, perhaps compromised, by the more prosaic goal of staffing undergraduate classes, graduate students will remain alienated from the nature of their labor. This alienation will substantially aid in the perpetuation of their exploitation and impede the efforts of unions to organize.

The nature of academia has changed so profoundly over the last thirty years as universities have come to be managed like corporations with an eye to the bottom line and graduate programs have been forsaken for professional-degree programs. One major argument made by those against unions for graduate students is that they may damage and make adversarial the student-teacher relationship. This argument has not been borne out in studies. Gordon Hewitt concludes that "No evidence suggests that such graduate student unionization interferes with the graduate student mentor-mentee relationship" (qtd. in Rabban and Euben).

In fact, one could argue that it is the changes in academia, not unionization, that have created an adversarial relationship between student and adviser. The mentoring relationship between student and adviser and the apprenticeship nature of the graduate studies are undermined, if not completely obliterated, by the exploitation of graduate student labor necessitated by budget cuts and the professionalization of graduate school. The apprentice experience is diminished when graduate student work is excessive, repetitive, and ceases to afford new learning opportunities. The mentoring relationship is impaired when graduate students and faculty members lack time and opportunity to interact or interact only through a relationship based not on advanced learning but on the faculty member's supervisory and excessive demands on the graduate assistant for routine work. These changes reveal clearly the graduate student's role as worker but underscore the difficulty of using unionization as a remedy. As the role of graduate students—once clearly educational, if also clearly indentured—becomes increasingly employment-focused, unionization may do more to institutionalize the employment relationship than to restore the educational relationship.

Having outlined these potential problems with graduate-employee unions, I do have something positive to say about them. The simple fact is that life is better for graduate student employees with a union than it is without one. With a union, you're going to get regular wage increases. With a union, you and likely your family will get health insurance paid for by the employer—often the same insurance offered to faculty members. You may get other monetary benefits, such as child care and fees remission, and you will also receive equally important nonmonetary benefits, such as job descriptions, standardized appointment letters, and a stepped grievance procedure. These important benefits do significantly improve the lives and working conditions of graduate students. By pointing out the challenges facing graduate student unions, I don't mean to minimize their accomplishments or the importance of the power of collective action.

If, however, you are expecting by forming a union to have some influence on the root causes of graduate-student-employee exploitation, if you're looking to change universities' views of graduate employees as the answer to their financial problems, that's not going to happen. Unions can immeasurably improve the terms and conditions of graduate student *employment*, but in their present form they are not addressing the inequities and exploitation of graduate *education*. Only those members of the academy who already have a seat at the table can do that.

WORKS CITED

Rabban, David, and Euben, Donna. Brief of Amicus Curiae American Association of University Professors in Support of Petitioner United Automobile Workers, AFL-CIO. *NYU v. UAW*, 332 NLRB 1205 (2000) (No. 2-RC-22082). 29 July 2005. <http://members.aol.com/gsocuaw/amicus_aaup.html>.

Steinem, Gloria. "The Good News Is: These Are Not the Best Years of Your Life." *Ms* Sept. 1979: 64–68. Rpt. in *The Norton Reader*. New York: Norton, 2000. 363–68.

Vaughn, William. "Apprentice or Employee? Graduate Students and Their Unions." *Academe* 84.6 (1998): 43–49.

What I Learned in a Bargaining Year

ALYSSA PICARD

> I seem to be unstable, chameleon-like, yielding one after another to many diverse
> and even incompatible influences; struggling to assimilate something from each and
> yet striving to carry it forward. . . . Upon the whole, the forces that have influenced
> me have come from persons and from situations more than from books—not that
> I have not, I hope, learned a great deal from philosophical writings, but that what I
> have learned from them has been technical in comparison with what I have been
> forced to think upon and about because of some experience in which I found myself
> entangled.
>
> —John Dewey, "From Absolutism to Experimentalism"

Until recently, you couldn't have paid me enough to be anything but an
academic. I sped through college in three years and wrote graduate
school applications while hunched excitedly over a typewriter balanced
on a footlocker in my college dormitory room. For months, I fell asleep
thinking of the words that I imagined my adviser would whisper in my
ear when I finally received my doctoral hood (I had read of this ritual
incantation in the catalog of an elite East Coast university): "I welcome
you to the ancient and venerable company of scholars." When I received
my first acceptance—which came in an answering-machine message one
rainy March night—I fell to my knees and wept. There was going to be
a place for me—for my curiosity, for my geekiness, for my interest in the
past and my passion for teaching—in the world.

I enrolled in, and graduated from, one of the best United States history programs in the country, at what I still believe is one of the greatest
public universities on the face of the earth. I read every word of every
book and article assigned to me in my first years of graduate school,
published original work in a peer-reviewed journal, and collaborated on
a well-received article about teaching in the premier journal in my field.
But throughout my years in graduate school, I was also a student of a
hidden curriculum: the lessons my institution and my discipline taught
about what kinds of work were valued, how those who worked were to

be treated, and how mightily those workers would have to struggle to improve the conditions of their lives.

Like John Dewey, I was subject to "diverse and incompatible influences": what follows is the story of how the strongest of those pushed me out of the academy, probably for good.

Lessons about My University

I stumbled into my role as the lead negotiator for the Graduate Employees Organization at the University of Michigan in 2001–02. Because they thought I was conscientious and detail-minded, progressive friends of mine had cajoled me into working on the union's grievance committee in the fall of 1999; I agreed mostly because I felt guilty saying no. Two years of grievance work organized me for life. A woman came to the union office in tears after being stalked by an armed undergraduate student—her department's response to the fact that she had worked over double her allotted hours for the semester, with much of that time spent filing police reports, was that she had filed her claim for extra pay one day too late. A second woman, who was not a United States citizen, was being sexually harassed by her adviser, who threatened her with deportation if she reported him. She was afraid even to give us her name. A third woman, who was being sexually harassed by a male professor who was not her supervisor (and who was later discharged from the university for cause), arrived at work one day to find that the lock on her office door had been changed—and that she had been permanently separated from years of collected data—because her adviser didn't like the "ruckus" the harasser caused when he showed up and banged on their shared office door.

Sometimes the grievance process helped these employees, and sometimes it did not. With other union members, I gathered a sheaf of proposed changes to the collective bargaining agreement between my union and my university, many of them aimed at addressing the very abuses we spent so much time futilely trying to redress. There were other problems, too: inadequate child care for graduate student parents, poor training for new teachers, lack of health insurance for people with low appointment levels, and—surprisingly—the absence of affirmative-action language in our contract.

We thought of these as multiple aspects of the same problem: higher education is inaccessible to many people, particularly those whose identities or experiences put them in the margins. Affirmative action, whose direct beneficiaries are women and people of color, addresses part of this need. But child care, more widely available health care, and a better grievance procedure for dealing with cases of harassment would address other needs, making graduate school a living possibility for parents, for those from low-income families, for students with chronic illnesses, and for those (primarily women) who might have been driven away by the cumbersome and lengthy process of proving a harassment claim if not by the harassment itself. By 2001, our institution was in the midst of an epic legal defense of affirmative action, arguing the novel claim that diversity of all sorts provided educational benefits for the entire university community. We took their legal strategy seriously—and that was a mistake.

I came to several depressing conclusions about the University of Michigan in 2002. One of the most depressing was that, despite the millions of dollars they directed to the high-profile (and, mercifully, successful) defense of the institution's law school and undergraduate affirmative-action policies, the managers of the University of Michigan cared far less about affirmative action than they did about the ability to make the choices they wanted to make when and how they wanted to make them.

People of color have always been underrepresented in the ranks of Michigan's teaching staff, and increasing their representation has been a formal goal of the Graduate Employees Organization since we won recognition in 1975. To visualize how long we have been struggling toward this end, I need look no further than the wall of the union office, where a photo from the historic month-long recognition strike features two men in Afros holding a sign that reads, "More Black TAs." (Arguing for the euphemistic "affirmative action" today seems a pallid imitation of their radicalism: what I mean is, more black TAs.)

Twenty-one years after those two men walked the picket line, and after strenuous resistance, negotiators for the administration agreed to the establishment of a joint labor-management committee for the review of the procedures used in the hiring of graduate students. In 1999, that joint committee urged the appointment of a permanent monitor of data on the employment policies and practices in each academic department. The committee had found problems: students of color did not get to teach as often as white students and, as a result, were disadvantaged on the academic job market. A hiring monitor, working with the committee, could help solve those problems: labor and management would examine the hiring practices in each department and try to figure out which practices (of posting and circulation of job notices, etc.) yielded the most equitable results in hiring. What—particularly in contrast to such a brazen demand as "More Black TAs"—could be less objectionable?

At the bargaining table in 1999—midway through the affirmative-action cases that would later be decided in the United States Supreme Court—the university's bargaining team refused to make any contractual hiring or graduate-admissions commitments to affirmative action. In both 1999 and 2002, when union negotiators proposed the creation of the monitoring position suggested by the labor-management group, the university negotiator first denied the need for such monitoring and then argued that the monitoring could be fairly done by an officer of the Human Resources and Affirmative Action Department of the university. Yet this was the very department whose associate director (also the university's chief negotiator) had just denied that an affirmative-action monitor was even necessary.

Members of my union were deeply skeptical of the ability of university human resources personnel to police their own implementation of affirmative action. This skepticism was one reason we organized to strike. Late in the marathon bargaining session that took place the day before our scheduled walkout, the university's negotiator finally signed affirmative-action language, and provision for a hiring monitor is now a permanent feature of our contract. In public, the University of Michigan continues to insist on—and is now the object of both pride and scorn for—its principled commitment to affirmative action. But the institution's leaders were willing to authorize a bargaining posture that suggested that everything necessary to improve the climate for people of color at Michigan had already been done. They resisted our proposed improvements in the presence of many students of color who came to watch bargaining, thereby fostering a hostile climate by implying that these observers' concerns were imaginary ones. The lesson I learned was that my university's managers match their behavior as employers to their rhetoric in court only under threat of labor unrest.

Another thing I learned is that a deep fissure is emerging between the administration and the faculty of the University of Michigan—a gap that reflects not only the age-old antipathy between administrators and academics but also fundamental and perhaps irreconcilable differences in their beliefs about the nature and characteristics of the university. The university's negotiating team was made up of five faculty members, one administrator, and two human resources employees, but the lead negotiator is the only person who can make statements binding on a bargaining team: it is his or her statements that can be used to support labor-board charges of regressive or "bad faith" bargaining, in which one of the parties to negotiations initially offers deal X and later replaces it with deal X-1. Charges of bad faith are easier to substantiate on economic issues, when the value of the employer's or the union's total economic package is at issue. Exploration of noneconomic issues permits somewhat broader latitude—and therefore presents less reason for someone who is working to resolve them to stay silent.

That lead negotiator—a human resources officer—barely spoke in each bargaining session until the last few nights of negotiations. In his stead, faculty members were assigned to rake through each of our proposals and accompanying presentations, asking questions in a style our team came to think of as a protracted dissertation-defense format. For academics, the idea that reasoned discourse will result in a consensus founded in the evidence seems self-evident; management's strategy also cleverly maximized the effects of the customary power differential between graduate students and faculty members and graduate students' instinctive impulse to justify themselves by providing intelligent answers to knotty problems. However, because our contract negotiations are customarily open to our members, this approach meant that many, many people personally experienced (and were angered by) the university team's reluctance to actually negotiate. For almost five months, the only person empowered to make meaningful statements of position for the university sat mute, and very few counterproposals dribbled back across the table.

The university's lead negotiator sometimes seemed dismayed to hear the kinds of things that came out of the mouths of his team members while he was observing his months of silence. One of our key platform issues was modifying the process of English language testing and training that international graduate students had to undergo before they were allowed to enter the classroom. Individual departments made decisions about who needed to be trained and who did not, which in practice meant that brown-skinned native speakers of English from countries like

India (where English is an official language) were asked to come to the United States to be "trained" in the English language weeks before classes began, whereas white native English speakers from Ireland (where English is also an official language and is spoken in every bit as distinctive an accent as English in India is) were not. In the process of discussing the English testing requirement, an economics professor on the management team admitted that it was designed as a sop to nativist Reagan-era state officeholders; that three weeks of English training were completely inadequate for graduate students who were truly not fluent in English, that departments supported the training not because they thought it worked but because they needed something to tell parents who called to complain about the accented but perfectly fluent English of Michigan instructors, and that it was certainly true that the testing and evaluation process failed to identify United States citizens whose language (not to mention teaching) skills needed improvement. One member of our team asked what the members of the university's bargaining team thought of the racial disparity in testing practices. "It sounds racist to me," an Indian professor of engineering volunteered. The university's chief negotiator rolled his eyes.

The contract we subsequently signed says that all prospective graduate student teachers, regardless of citizenship, must have their English skills evaluated. What we really wanted was a uniform process of training and evaluation of all teaching skills for everyone, but administration negotiators resisted our proposals about such a process with uncommon vigor. Our original proposal, spurred by reports that the School of Education provided no training to its graduate student instructors at all, was that the institution provide eight hours of pedagogical training to all new graduate student teachers. (The School of Education reportedly reasoned that since most of its graduate students had already taught K-12, they therefore required no additional training to teach undergraduates. My observation that my years of instructing Michigan undergraduates had left me completely unequipped to teach second graders drew no response from the university's chief negotiator.) After five months of negotiations and on the eve of a strike, university management finally signed an agreement to provide four hours of training for each new employee.

The reactions of the men and women who represented the university to these proposals highlighted the institution's corporate bent and made me question whether I had not, in attempting to escape the craven profit motivations of industry, accidentally bungled into a work environment all the more offensive for its hypocrisy. How could people representing a university nominally committed to affirmative action, to equal treatment without regard for citizenship, and to training world-class teachers react with listlessness, if not outright hostility, to our attempts to discuss how we might advance those aims? I did not know, and neither did the union members who came out in throngs every night to watch negotiating sessions.

At times, forty or more people (including the union and university teams) filled the bargaining room, and more gathered in the lobby outside. The presence of so many people was chaotic, but the value to the union was incalculable. Every time the university's chief negotiator repeated that he did not want to put something into writing because he trusted (and thought we should trust) the word of the associate dean, to whom he referred as a man of honor, fifty or a hundred observers went out the next day and told people in their departments what they had seen and heard. More people started turning up at rallies, at membership meetings, and at negotiating sessions themselves.

In the end, more than a thousand members walked off the job on 11 March 2002 for the one-day walkout we called when negotiations over economic issues (principally child care and wages) stalled. Construction workers at the university's much-heralded Life Sciences Center, which will serve in part as a pipeline for pricey biotechnology drugs, refused to cross our picket lines at their work sites, and construction on our campus ground to a halt for the day, costing management untold amounts of money. Representatives of the administration, suddenly much more willing to negotiate, settled less than a week later; we won major concessions on all our strike-platform issues. At the membership meeting where we announced our win, another member of the bargaining team told three hundred excited graduate students, "Power concedes nothing that is not taken from it. And we took lots." (He was, of course, paraphrasing Frederick Douglass: "Power concedes nothing without a demand. It never did and it never will" [204].)

We received a great deal of support from faculty members during negotiations and when negotiations failed; one social science professor even provided doughnuts and coffee for the graduate students who walked the picket lines. But amazingly, after the negotiations ended, even the faculty members on the university's bargaining team—whom we had come to think of as conscienceless tools of the administration, if not as our actual ideological enemies—publicly expressed their admiration for our focus on making graduate education at Michigan more accessible to a wide range of people, many of whom were numerically in the minority of our membership. Our final strike package had included the language-testing issue, as well as demands on affirmative action, child care, health care for employees with low appointments, pay equity for the university's eight graduate student librarians (who had previously made two-thirds of what the rest of us did), a revised and expedited harassment grievance procedure, and modest pay raises for everyone. (Agreements on several of these proposals, like our proposal on affirmative action, were achieved late in the evening before the walkout.) The only issue that affected most members was the wage increase. The engineering professor who had described the language-testing policy as "racist" later told the student newspaper, "In a democracy, it's the majority that rules and the minority is out, and here the majority was trying to lift the minority, and I wasn't expecting that. That was admirable" (Sprow, "Bargaining").

Lessons about Unions

There is, in the union world, a tendency to fetishize contract negotiations.[1] Bargaining is simultaneously the time when the relative positions of labor and management are most clear and (especially when a contractual no-strike clause expires) when there is the most potential for them to be inverted. Negotiators themselves are often credited with the success or blamed for the failure of negotiations; a "skilled negotiator," in this analysis, wins things an "unskilled" one cannot. But my skill, or lack thereof, had little to do with the quality of the contract we signed: although we could have lost a lot at the bargaining table, we didn't win anything until we were in the streets. Our successes at Michigan and the successes of graduate unions in general spring almost entirely from incessant organizing and from a type of militancy that is perhaps uniquely possible for unions with rapid turnover of leaders and members.

The idea that a union with high membership turnover might not be a bad thing—might, in fact, be a good thing—is not uncontroversial. Management and some unionists argue that bargaining units made up of casual or itinerant labor are weaker, more prone to excessive reliance on staff members, and incapable of establishing the long-term relationships of trust that characterize successful collective bargaining. From the unionist's perspective, a high-turnover workplace may be more difficult to organize, or at least less susceptible to traditional organizing tactics. Savvy union organizers use the existing social networks of a workplace to plan an organizing campaign, and those networks are difficult to map when everyone changes jobs each semester.

But, as the recent wins of casualized laborers suggest, these problems can be overcome. Those who nevertheless choose to emphasize the difficulty (or undesirability) of organizing in high-turnover industries are underrating these wins—or are guilty of a far more insidious disingenuousness. Employers turn over their labor forces the way they do partly because they *want* to make it difficult for us to organize. University employers refer to the high turnover of their graduate employees to argue before state and federal labor boards that these employees are too itinerant a group to deserve union representation. At low points in labor history, unions themselves have capitulated to the argument that high-turnover workforces don't need—or, more ominously, can't be organized into—unions. High turnover was one of the arguments that an elitist, craft-focused American Federation of Labor used against organizing industrial workers in the late nineteenth and early twentieth centuries, and it's an argument used today by those who oppose unionization of immigrant farm workers and other contingent workers, including non-tenure-track faculty members.

It is difficult to organize a high-turnover industry. The insurance-model and service-union approaches that prevail in some parts of the union movement, in which an established pool of members receive services from paid union staffers in exchange for dues or fees, is not cost effective for low-paid contingent workers. But efforts to meet the challenges of organizing in this environment can inspire an enormously powerful style of unionism. Where service unions solve problems for members by flying in lawyers, negotiating contracts, collecting dues, and going home, unions that organize internally, and depend more on their members, can be sites of a vibrant democracy. In organizing unions, members solve their own problems and forge coalitions that stay together until everyone's concerns are resolved. In the best organizing unions, members are involved in decision making at all levels. They learn how to organize other members and how to cultivate leadership qualities in one another. The union guys never go home, because the members *are* the union.

Rapid turnover in membership usually entails—and should entail—rapid turnover in leadership. The knowledge that the management-leadership relationship doesn't have to last forever can free union leaders to stake out whatever position (or disposition) seems necessary in confronting the employer. The chief negotiator who bangs his shoes on the negotiating table like Nikita Khrushchev one year (as my immediate predecessor did) will be gone in the next contract cycle. The officers who organize a strike will step down before the contract expires again: in my own local's thirty-year history, no individual has served as president for longer than two years. Leaders who know that they will hold positions of power for a limited time are free to make the decisions that are best for all the members, rather than the decisions that make their own long-standing relationships with management more comfortable. If loyalty to the members erodes the trust between management and the union, that might not be a bad thing. When the managers of the University of Michigan can argue without embarrassment for paying librarians two-thirds of what everyone else gets because "that's the way it's always been" (in a profession that is historically dominated by economically undervalued women and at an institution that is home to several major research projects on gendered pay inequities in the workplace), there shouldn't be too much trust between those managers and the union. Great unionists have always understood that labor relations run on power, not affection.

The importance of militancy to graduate unions' successes is clear to university managers, who gesture frequently to leadership turnover and the militancy that can result when they argue against unionization of their student employees. In a recent *Chronicle of Higher Education* article, for example, the University of Massachusetts chancellor Marcellette Williams commented that while the university (which hosts one of the few labor-side labor-relations programs in the country) did not oppose unionization in principle, it had found the United Auto Workers (which was seeking to organize badly undercompensated residence-hall advisers) difficult to work with. She specifically cited a history of "contentious negotiations" with members of the existing UAW-affiliated graduate-employee union, as well as their insistence on filing a high number of grievances. Williams complained that because of the rapid turnover of leadership in the union, "We devote overwhelmingly more administrative time, much of it responding to confrontation, to dealing with this union than with any of our other bargaining units."

Leaders of universities are going to need to spend more time cleaning up the mess that results from the massive failure of the higher education labor market: graduate employees teach up to half of all class hours at many institutions, and many of us have no reasonable prospect of obtaining full-time academic employment after five or even ten years in our universities' graduate programs (Lafer). Budget cuts and the focus of university managers on cost cutting, often without regard to academic quality, have led to the virtual evaporation of the tenure-track jobs that every generation of graduate students is assured will materialize "any year now." (Recently, the chair of the English department at the University of Michigan admitted to a group of non-tenure-track department faculty members that only 50% of the department's PhDs *ever* secure tenure-track employment.) The emperor of academic life is wearing no clothes, and I have yet to organize another graduate student who isn't acutely aware of that fact. On some level, turnover in our organizations, and the militancy that results from the potent combination of disillusionment and organizing skill, is a function of the way universities turn over their teaching staff. For that turnover, they have themselves primarily to blame.

Finally, and perhaps most important, militancy sets an essential example for undergraduate students. On the eve of our work action, the provost of the University of Michigan told the student newspaper, "A work stoppage of any length would be extremely disruptive to our educational effort, and would seriously shortchange our undergraduate students" (Sprow "Students"). But we all teach by example, and I think that my students can learn to meekly accept whatever their bosses offer almost anywhere—I didn't want them to learn that lesson at one of the greatest public universities in the world, and I certainly don't want them learning it from me. What finally drove me out of the academy was my fear that, in years of currying favor with search and tenure committees, this would be the most lasting lesson my lived example would manage to convey. Weeks after our strike, one student in my class on the civil rights movement wrote to me and said, "Although I had read about it in books, the sad fact is that I had never before seen a group of ordinary people come together to solve problems in their own lives."

What will I ever teach that will be more important than that?

NOTE

1. In 1975, the University of Michigan graduate students Gayle Rubin and Ann Bobroff coauthored an article titled "On the Fetishization of Bargaining" for a newsletter published by the Graduate Employees Organization. I am indebted to them for the terminology and some of the ideas I am using here.

WORKS CITED

Douglass, Frederick. "The Significance of Emancipation in the West Indies." *The Frederick Douglass Papers. Ser. 1: Speeches, Debates, and Interviews.* Ed. John W. Blassingame. Vol. 3. New Haven: Yale UP, 1979–92. 204.

Lafer, Gordon. "Graduate Student Unions Fight the Corporate University." *Dissent* (2001): 65.

Rubin, Gayle, and Ann Bobroff. "On the Fetishization of Bargaining." 1975.

Sprow, Maria. "Students Question Impact of GEO Strike." *Michigan Daily* 5 Mar. 2002: 3.

———. "Bargaining Team Talks about GEO Negotiations." *Michigan Daily* 10 Apr. 2002: 7.

Williams, Marcellette G. "Why a Union for RAs Makes No Sense." *Chronicle of Higher Education* 26 Apr. 2002. 5 July 2005 <http://www.umass.edu/pastchancellors/williams/announcements/chronicle020426.html>.

PART FIVE

REFLECTIONS AND PROSPECTS

Reflections

ERNST BENJAMIN

Although the foregoing perspectives in section four generally support academic bargaining, the analyses and arguments differ in important respects. The variations do not depend only on the specific topics or viewpoints of the authors. Although there are elements common to collective bargaining, these essays illustrate that time and circumstance arrange and rearrange bargaining relationships in ways that fracture the dichotomies often employed to characterize them. It is true that these authors, and the editors, view bargaining through lenses we have each ground to our unique specifications, but it is also true that, as one adjusts the lenses, the image of the elements of the bargaining relationship, like the bits of colored glass seen through a kaleidoscope, form diverse, complex, and changing patterns. The comments that follow are intended to encourage an appreciation of this complexity.

The dichotomous terms employed by labor-relations professionals to describe the bargaining relationship include pejorative *immature* and *mature* and *adversarial* and *mutual gains* or *win-lose* and *win-win*, and *contentious* and *problem solving*. Observers also distinguish at times between bargaining as a process that goes on at the bargaining table and the larger conflict between employees and employers that may take place in the workplace and the public arena. In the academic context, observers may debate whether academics are regarded as employees or professionals and whether academics should seek to achieve their objectives through unionization or shared governance. Various of the preceding essays have emphasized one of these alternatives, sometimes to the exclusion of another, although it is not always clear whether this is attributable to to the point of view of the author or to the specific time and circumstances described, for some situations do indeed confirm the conventional wisdom just as some do not. The exploration of the conventional alternatives that follows is not, therefore, aimed at assessing the validity of specific accounts but at using these accounts to illustrate the diversity and complexity that sometimes confirms and sometimes defies conventional, or unconventional, wisdom.

The Bargaining Relationship

Labor-relations professionals often distinguish between immature and mature bargaining relationships. The former relationships are thought more contentious, volatile, and ineffectual; the latter more cooperative, orderly, and problem solving. The struggle of graduate students to achieve bargaining rights in California in the face of university intransigence described by Andrew Gross certainly fits the immature bargaining-relationship pattern. As other essays show, however, the quality of a bargaining relationship does not inevitably mature but may fluctuate and, unfortunately, worsen rather than improve over time. Indeed, the relationship described by Martin J. Morand and Ramelle C. MaCoy was, at least from their viewpoint, relatively productive or mature in the early days and more rather than less difficult in later years. Similarly, Brad Art's "worst case" erupts after many years of less-contentious bargaining.

This worsening has occurred in part because in the public sector, unlike the private, employers were often initially reluctant to take an adversarial stance or pursue their own agendas while the unions rode the wave of support that brought about protective legislation. Then, because of various factors, including budgetary constraints, competing priorities, changing views of the role of public management, and political reversals, public managers often became more assertive and unions more defensive.

New participants, as distinct from new institutional relationships, may heighten conflict as Dan Julius suggests and as Alyssa Picard seems to confirm in the case of graduate student bargaining. So, where Picard finds turnover a source of energy and innovation, Anna Geronimo Hausmann suggests that leadership turnover makes graduate assistant unions weaker and creates the risk that they may become excessively staff-dependent. Of course, many bargaining relationships do also improve over time in some respects. Richard Katz and Dean Casale describe how new union leadership promoted effective bargaining. The cooperative contract implementation described by both Elizabeth Hoffman and Gary W. Reichard, and even by Roger Hatch and John Pfeiffer (although they stress the need for vigilance), reflects an effective working relationship developed over many years.

Although collective bargaining, almost by definition, is an adversarial process, it is even harder to assess the extent to which the quality of bargaining relationships should be described as adversarial or cooperative. To take an extreme example, the contentious bargaining in public view described by Picard actually led to a rather quick settlement that she regards as a union win following a one-day walkout. The unusually contentious management rhetoric Art relates actually had little impact on the collective agreement; certainly less than the scarcely remarked long-term budgetary stringency.

Conversely, Hoffman and Reichard carefully circumscribe their accounts of cooperative campus efforts to avoid contentious issues, apart from Hoffman's brief and understated allusion to the fact that "[w]inning these rights took organization, discipline, and a unified bargaining unit willing to hang tough through a long arduous process of contract development, bargaining, mediation, impasse, and fact-finding." Even this list ignores the substantial changes in union leadership and the union's political efforts, which have enhanced the influence of lecturers within the union as well as the effectiveness of the union itself.

Several essays emphasize that each side has its own internal complexities. Julius outlines the need for and difficulty of achieving a consistent management leadership. This complexity is clearly reflected in the different attitudes of the human resources staff and the faculty management representatives described in the graduate assistant bargaining by Picard. Academic bargainers may at times exploit these differences by, for example, seeking money from the provost and academic authority from the chief financial officer. But internal administration differences may also protract and frustrate negotiations, reinforce the common union complaint that the administration representative lacks authority to bargain, and even lead to regressive bargaining. Conversely, Art notes the challenge of coordinating diverse locals in Massachusetts. Unions too may find it difficult to maintain credibility and reach agreement with management because of internal differences among their members, especially where management seeks to exploit these differences (see, for example, Morand and MaCoy on faculty governance).

It is notable, finally, that Julius attributes excessive centralization to the needs of bargaining, whereas Morand and MaCoy argue that it is a management option, not a necessity. The New Jersey and California examples also indicate that there is substantial room for local initiative and variation in large systems where union and management agree to facilitative relationships.

The Bargaining Process

If the authors vary in their characterization of the bargaining relationship, they manifest broad agreement on the key feature of the bargaining process: it is best viewed not simply as a negotiating process but rather in the context of the broad range of interactions within and between the employee and management organizations. Although this broader perspective also shapes the structure of this volume, it is important to emphasize two substantial qualifications.

NEGOTIATIONS

First, preparation for and conduct and skill at the negotiating table does matter. It is true that academic agreements, unlike some agreements in the trades, are seldom resolved based on pattern bargaining at lunch between an experienced business agent and a management representative. The one faculty negotiation of this nature with which I'm familiar contributed to a substantial subsequent change in union leadership. It is also true that table tactics vary and have limited impact, though in the real world of negotiations, I know that getting a group of firefighters a percent more than the cops through table tactics mattered a lot to the firefighters.

Each side at the table seeks clues about what it will really take to get an agreement, and presentation and argument can shape perceptions and outcomes. Thus, even as Picard warns against "fetishizing" bargaining, she notes that her arguments did get through to some members of the management team. Most experienced negotiators would probably agree, moreover, that the administrative recalcitrance she describes at the bargaining table was in significant part a consequence of negotiations performed for a public audience. The perspectives presented here generally do not adequately reflect that experienced negotiators do get things done at the table and, not infrequently, in the sidebar discussions held by key participants away from the table. This may require experienced negotiators or fast learners. It may also require the privacy in which conflict resolution, as well as most political deals, such as those alluded to by Morand and MaCoy, take place.

Second, even if one believes that pressure tactics matter far more than discussions at the table—as in many cases they do—preparation for and conduct of negotiations are crucial to problem solving and, especially, to working out the specific language in which agreements are expressed. The sort of vigilant or facilitative contract implementation that the essays by Hatch and Pfeiffer, by Hoffman, and by Reichard emphasize presupposes and contributes to the development of carefully constructed agreements.

SUPPORTING NEGOTIATIONS

Nonetheless, academic unions generally depend on organizational and political support to achieve their negotiating objectives. All the essays recognize the importance of effective member involvement and support. Note that this support often requires not only ascertaining membership concerns but also involving members in the development of proposals and the conduct of union activities and, as Katz and Casale emphasize, even enhancing their role in shared governance. Similarly most of the essays recognize the need to keep members informed. Mechanisms include publications, Web sites, and meetings. Some associations use e-mail alerts and phone trees for crucial information or as aids to organization.

Effective organizing also involves reaching beyond the membership to the university community, the public, and the relevant political authorities. Julius warns, and many academics are well aware, that it can be risky to invite public scrutiny or legislative involvement in university matters. Morand and MaCoy describe how a union may benefit from such involvement and, then, how first students and then faculty members paid a price for this involvement when the political winds changed. Massachusetts provides another example of unwelcome political intervention. But public colleges and universities do often attract community concern and political interest. Unions do better if they plan how best to shape that concern and interest than if they merely seek to avoid it. Liesl Orenic offers a particularly good example of early planning to shape an appropriate and effective message in a private institution.

Gross emphasizes the value of campus coalition building, which not only broadens campus support but also provides a better foundation for community outreach and legislative activity. It may also, as he indicates, require some adjustments and compromises when unit-member interests diverge. Resolution of coalition differences often depends, however, not only on specific policy adjustments but also on the extent to which academics identify primarily as professionals or as employees or find a way to satisfactorily integrate these two perspectives.

Academic Employees and Academic Professionals

Two essays by scholars-participants of long-term labor relations, Morand and MaCoy on the union side and Julius on the management side, note that academics are generally not ideologically committed to the labor movement but rather are pragmatically concerned to improve their own terms of employment and professional standing. Of course, a similarly pragmatic view can be and typically is attributed to American workers in general. Conversely, as the several essays by graduate student activists show most clearly, new recruits to academic union leadership are often motivated by larger political concerns, including identification with the labor movement. Morand and MaCoy, as well as the editors and several other authors of this volume, illustrate that many faculty union leaders have also shared that political identification.

Those academic activists who have attempted to articulate a theory to explain or inspire academic unionism have typically wrestled with two sometimes contending, but more often closely intertwined, perspectives. In the first, academics are employees; in the second, they are professionals. The essays on graduate assistant bargaining show that graduate assistants need to establish that they are indeed employees as well as students; and Jaclyn Marie Janesk's description of the unsuccessful campaign at Cornell illustrates what happens when graduate students perceive themselves primarily as students. The other graduate assistant essays integrate the student and employee perspectives like Katz and Casale do in their essay on faculty members, by arguing that the distinctively professional characteristics of academic work are threatened and eroding because of the corporatization of the university. Unionization, they reason, is a necessary though not always sufficient response.

This view that unionization is the antidote to corporatization is most clearly articulated here by the graduate assistant and younger faculty authors. This is not because it is new. The essay on graduate employees by Marcus Harvey traces it back to Upton Sinclair. Although this view is also discussed, especially in the essays that focus on contingent faculty members, it is not confined to these faculty members. Many faculty unionists, including myself, shared this "new left" perspective in the early seventies. Justice Brennan articulated it clearly in his 1980 *Yeshiva* dissent: "Education has become 'big business,' and the task of operating the university enterprise has been transferred from the faculty to an autonomous administration, which faces the same pressures to cut cost and increase efficiencies that confront any large industrial organization" (703–04). What is new, and rightly emphasized by these authors, is that corporatization has proceeded to the point of developing a two-tiered academic labor market in which a critical mass of academics may lose hope of attaining or preserving their professional status.

The danger of relegation to the second tier has increased the pressures on the personal as well as the professional lives of academics. Women who seek to combine family and a first-tier career confront particularly intense demands. Orenic's essay reminds us that this concern is not only important in shaping bargaining objectives but in recruiting and sustaining union participation. Unions dependent on the voluntary participation of academics already overburdened with professional and family responsibilities need effective responses. These may range from seeking to broaden member participation to negotiating the child-care facilities and released time that many academics require as a condition of ongoing participation. Effective unions protect the personal as well as the professional lives of their members.

In the past, proponents of academic unions had to explain that by following the craft-union rather than the industrial-union example, faculty members could use unions to advance professional standards. Now, as Hausmann emphasizes, corporatization has gone so far that unions may be limited to preserving only the basic terms and conditions of employment. Yet, as Gross observes, unions can bring in a broader social perspective. Fundamentally, all the essays on part-time faculty and graduate assistant unions show that even these disadvantaged groups can in some measure protect and enhance their professional opportunities through collective bargaining. Although Katz and Casale address this issue more directly than others, all of the full-time faculty essays also offer examples of the successful defense or promotion of professional standards.

The professional practice that most distinguishes faculty members from other workers or employees, even in the crafts, is participation in shared governance. It is also the most endangered. Even Justice Brennan, writing in 1980, observed in his *Yeshiva* dissent the "erosion of the faculty role in the institution's decision-making process" (704). These essays confirm that the danger to shared governance arises from the unchecked growth of "autonomous administration" and not, as critics feared, from the growth of unionization. Hausmann is right to warn that the corporatization of the university cannot be reversed by collective bargaining alone. But each of the essays has offered evidence that bargaining does provide some checks on autonomous administration. Bargaining can, as many of the essays document, serve not only to defend professional autonomy but also to advance professional standards and to reinforce shared governance.

WORK CITED

NLRB v. Yeshiva University, 444 U.S. 672 (1980).

Prospects

MICHAEL MAUER

Those engaged in academic organizing and representation divide into two groups: those who see substantial grounds for optimism in the process and those whose vision is unremittingly bleak. The "glass is half empty" proponents have plenty of powerful arguments to bolster their case that the prospects are grim for the future of unions in higher education. The legal landscape and the political realities outlined in previous essays in this volume paint a picture of obstacles that are formidable by any measure.

In the public sector, the challenges begin with the stark reality that a substantial number of states simply have no legislative framework under which faculty members or other professionals in the academy can unionize, even though this right is considered fundamental in the rest of the developed world. In many instances, what legislation there is does not accord due recognition to the right of the academic workers to determine for themselves under which particular group they wish to unionize. Rather, the law itself mandates a bargaining unit, thereby taking political choices out of the hands of those whose professional livelihoods are at stake in managing their own relationships. Thus, insurmountable legal restrictions may be brought to bear on the possibility of full-time faculty members and their adjunct colleagues making common cause and unionizing together. Other statutorily mandated or judicially established unit determinations can make a virtual mockery of a legislature's granting of the right to unionize. Perhaps the most salient example is in Washington state, where the legislative imprimatur on the right to unionize at the University of Washington was accompanied by a statutory dictate that medical-school professors—a group that has, unfortunately, a well-deserved reputation for being more resistant than other faculty members to the lure of unionism—must be included in any faculty union at that flagship institution.

Those seeking to erect legal obstacles to the organizing aspirations of academic workers in private institutions to unionize have had a good run as well. Since the 1980 *Yeshiva* ruling, the National Labor Relations Act's nominal coverage of full-time faculty members in private-sector colleges and universities has become almost invisible. The legal barriers were raised even higher by the post-*Yeshiva* legal decisions that drew on *Catholic Bishop*'s doctrine to disable ever-larger numbers of academic workers in religiously affiliated institutions from having the option of unionizing. The legal threats to define *supervisor* in ways that will further restrict faculty organizing also lurk. And always present is the employer's practical ability to delay for many years the day of reckoning on the right to unionize and to force union proponents to spend many tens of thousands of dollars on legal proceedings.

Even when a union is successfully established, legal obstacles can impede the union's effectiveness in representing its members. Many bargaining laws, for example, set forth overly restrictive limits on what unions may bring to the bargaining table, and many fail to provide meaningful dispute-resolution procedures when the parties have difficulty reaching a contract settlement. Quite often, when the parties are at loggerheads on the terms of an initial or a new collective bargaining agreement, the law forbids the union to strike or to pursue any reasonable alternative, such as binding arbitration.

Pessimists will add the significant political impediments to campus organizing discussed in this volume's essay to this grim mix. These include the creation of more and more non-tenure-eligible positions, which thus combine numbers of those most vulnerable faculty members with the pool of unorganized faculty members. Furthermore, both increased corporate funding and control over academic research and curriculum and authoritarian management practices are increasing. And—to pile the negatives on—campus organizing takes place in the context of decreasing union density among American workers generally. Throughout the country, we have seen for many years now a growing unfriendly climate for organizing efforts. The weak position of organized labor off campuses—arising out of outright hostility in its various forms in addition to the widespread perception that unions are simply powerless—surely contributes to the weak position of academic unions.

The academic "glass half full" folks reply that there certainly are grounds for considerable optimism about a future for academic unionism. For starters, the legal landscape is not unremittingly bleak. Part-time and many contingent faculty appointees in the private sector are not enmeshed by *Yeshiva*, nor have public-sector administrations succeeded in applying the *Yeshiva* holding to full-time faculty members in their jurisdictions. In fact, the public-sector trend—although there has been some movement toward greater restrictions—is toward new enabling legislation. On the political front, despite the *Brown University* setback, graduate student employees are not abandoning their efforts to claim their right to unionize as legitimate academic workers. Creative approaches by academic organizers generally, with or without legislative protection, are continuing to produce results, as increasing numbers of adjunct faculty members and other academic workers are drawing critical support for their union efforts through rank-and-file mobilization and coalition work. On a broader scale, there are hopeful shifts outside the academy, including a revived political push by organized labor and its allies to expand the right to unionize, a dramatic increase in political engagement by unions and workers, and a recommitment by labor leaders to a wide-reaching social agenda. Some of these developments play into academic organizing perfectly, since the exposure and condemnation of corporate outlaws helps shine light on the damage caused by academic corporate managers who push casualization of the academic labor force and the corporatization of the academy as a whole.

Whither the future for academic organizing? Much depends, of course, on how the winds blow in the larger society in which academics exist and work. But it is the conviction of contributors to this volume that much of our destiny is in our control. Key to the degree of success will be whether academic unionists can understand and articulate the threats posed by corporate control, such as its suspicion of tenure and academic freedom, in a way that persuades colleagues to understand organized solidarity as the most powerful way to advance their agenda.

In assessing the prospects for successful organizing by academics, it is important to remember the powerful hold that the culture of shop-floor control by workers still has in the academy. In workplaces outside college campuses, there is a generally accepted compact that the boss makes decisions about production and the workers are free to agitate or organize in order to improve their working conditions. In sharp contrast stands the long-standing assumptions about shared governance that still occupy a place of prominence on our campuses. In most academic institutions—unionized or not—academics continue to see their work as central to the institution and expect accordingly that they will occupy a prominent place in institutional decision making. How else to explain the widespread existence and continued vitality of faculty governance mechanisms, as well as the many hundreds of active AAUP advocacy chapters on campuses of all types? No comparable level of nonunion-worker organization can be found in any other sector of the American workforce. The essential ideal of faculty governance has created a reality in higher education, whereby unionization is not so much an either-or proposition as a continuum in the ways a group of academics may exercise self-governance. Surely the assumptions of faculty control over colleges and universities will continue to serve as a springboard for academic workers when they decide to forge ahead and pursue formal unionization. In any event, this is the last chapter in this volume, but the last chapter in the advance of academic unionism surely is yet to be written.

NOTES ON CONTRIBUTORS

GREGG ADLER is a partner in the Hartford labor and employment firm of Livingston, Adler, Pulda, Meiklejohn and Kelly, P.C., which represents a number of private- and public-sector labor organizations, as well as individual workers in various types of employment disputes, negotiations, and litigation matters.

BRAD ART is professor and chair of the Department of Philosophy at Westfield State College. Since 1997, he has served as chairperson of the bargaining committee of the Massachusetts State College Association / Massachusetts Teachers Association. He has published two books, *What Is The Best Life? An Introduction to Ethics* and *Ethics and the Good Life* and is currently writing a philosophical analysis of the Bible.

ERNST BENJAMIN has retired from the AAUP, where he served as director of research and general secretary. He taught political science, interdisciplinary studies, and labor relations at Wayne State University (WSU). There he served as coordinator of labor studies in the College of Liberal Arts, director of the Weekend College Program, and interim dean of the College of Lifelong Learning. For WSU-AAUP he served as executive committee member, chief negotiator, and president. For AAUP he served as chair of the Collective Bargaining Congress, council member, executive committee member, and is a consultant member of Committee A. He has published widely on higher education policy and faculty issues.

DEAN CASALE is associate professor of English at Kean University. He served as president, vice president, chief local negotiator, and secretary of the Kean Federation of Teachers. He represented the Kean Federation of Teachers in successful negotiations for the statewide master contract in 2003.

ANDREW GROSS helped unionize student employees at the University of California while earning his PhD in English at UC, Davis. After graduation, he served as a postdoctoral teaching fellow, was active in the union representing lecturers (AFT), and volunteered for a college program at San Quentin prison. He has published on labor issues, consumer culture, prison literature, and representations of the Holocaust. He is an assistant professor in American literature at the John F. Kennedy Institute of the Free University Berlin.

PATRICIA J. GUMPORT is director of the Stanford Institute for Higher Education Research and professor of education at Stanford University. She has studied the institutionalization of new knowledge, professional socialization in graduate education, and the tensions between management and governance in organizational restructuring. Her forthcoming book on academic restructuring portrays the ascendance of industry logic and its consequences in public higher education during the last quarter of the twentieth century.

MARCUS HARVEY is the national AAUP's West Coast staff representative. He found a calling in the academic labor movement while pursuing graduate studies at the University of Florida in American history and has served in a number of positions in the Graduate Assistants United and the United Faculty of Florida. As a systemwide chief negotiator, he bargained the 1999–2001 contract for the three GAU chapters (UF, USF, and FAMU) in Florida's state university system.

ROGER D. HATCH has taught at Indiana University and Central Michigan University and specializes in the relation of religion and politics in America. He has been involved for about thirty years with the Central Michigan University Faculty Association, where he served on its board of directors, on multiple bargaining teams, as president of the association, and as chair of the grievance committee.

ANNA GERONIMO HAUSMANN worked as an organizer for the Graduate Students Employees Union, served as president of GSEU, and was on the union's bargaining committee that secured its first contract—the first contract in the nation to cover graduate students at multiple state university campuses. She has worked as an organizer for Service Employees International Union (SEIU) representing health-care workers and has been a part-time instructor at State University of New York, Buffalo.

ELIZABETH HOFFMAN is Associate Vice President-Lecturers of the California Faculty Association and serves on the bargaining team and the board of directors, on AAUP's Committee on Contingent Faculty and the Profession, and on the AAUP National Council. At California State University, Long Beach, she is a lecturer in English and Lecturer Project Leader in the Faculty Center for Professional Development. Her publications include "Galileo, Campus Equity Week, and the Future of the University" and "Lecturers in the CSU: Making a Commitment in Uncertain Times."

JACLYN MARIE JANESK holds a BS in industrial and labor relations from Cornell University. She has worked on both sides in the labor-relations field, with a union representing nurses in New Jersey and in human resources departments for several retail firms.

DANIEL J. JULIUS is provost and vice president for academic affairs at Benedictine University. He previously served as the senior administrator responsible for employee relations and collective bargaining for state college and university systems in Vermont and California and for the University of San Francisco, a private institution. He is a past president of the College and University Personnel Association and the Academy of Academic Personnel Administrators and is on the advisory board of the National Center for the Study of Collective Bargaining in Higher Education at Hunter College, City University of New York. He has been a consultant to over sixty institutions and systems and taught at the University of Toronto; University of California, Berkeley; and Stanford University.

RICHARD KATZ is associate professor of English at Kean University. He served as president of the Kean Federation of Teachers, AFL-CIO Local 2187, and now serves on the executive council of the federation and as delegate to the Council of New Jersey State College Locals. He represented the Kean Federation of Teachers in successful negotiations for the statewide master contract in 1999 and 2003.

RAMELLE C. MACOY has retired from his position as associate professor, industrial and labor relations, Indiana University of Pennsylvania. He served as director of the Association of Pennsylvania State College and University Faculties.

MICHAEL MAUER is director of organizing and services for the AAUP. A labor lawyer, he has worked in labor-management relations, predominantly in the education sector. He has worked for the National Labor Relations Board, for the overseas affiliate of the National Education Association, as the assistant administrative officer of the Washington-Baltimore Newspaper Guild (TNG-CWA), and as director of collective bargaining for the Service Employees International Union (SEIU). He is a long-standing member of the National Writers Union, Local 1981 of the United Auto Workers, AFL-CIO and author of *The Union Member's Complete Guide*.

IRIS MOLOTSKY served as director of membership development for the AAUP for eighteen years, helping faculty members develop advocacy chapters. She also headed the association's public information office, conducting communication workshops for faculty members nationwide.

MARTIN J. MORAND has retired from his position as professor, industrial and labor relations, Indiana University of Pennsylvania. He served as executive director of the Association of Pennsylvania State College and University Faculties.

LIESL ORENIC is associate professor of history and director of American Studies at Dominican University. She was a founding member of the Roosevelt Adjunct Faculty Organization (RAFO), Illinois Education Association–National Education Association at Roosevelt University and worked as a higher education organizer for the Illinois Education Association. She is completing a book, "On the Ramp: Ground Service Workers in the American Airline Industry, 1930–1970." Her publications include "Rethinking Workplace Culture: Fleet Service Clerks in the American Airlines Industry, 1945–1970." She serves on the board of directors of the Labor and Working-Class History Association and is cochair of the Chicago Center for Working-Class Studies.

JOHN R. PFEIFFER has taught at the University of Detroit, University of Kentucky, United States Air Force Academy, and Central Michigan University. His fields include nineteenth-century British literature, African American studies, bibliography and research, history and analysis of speculative literature, rhetoric, composition, and legal writing. He has been involved for about thirty years with the Central Michigan University Faculty Association, where he served on its board of directors, on multiple bargaining teams, as president of the association, and as chair of the grievance committee.

ALYSSA PICARD served on the grievance committee and as lead negotiator for the Graduate Employees Organization as a graduate student at the University of Michigan. As a field staffer for the AFT-Michigan (AFL-

CIO), she organizes local unions and bargains contracts for a wide range of educational employees.

GARY W. REICHARD is provost and senior vice president for academic affairs at California State University, Long Beach. He served as associate vice president for academic personnel, working regularly with the campus chapter of the California Faculty Association, and as a member of the CSU systemwide collective bargaining team. He presents on faculty staffing practices, conditions facing temporary faculty members, tenure and posttenure review processes, and shared governance in higher education.

JAMES D. SEMELROTH served on the regional staff of the California Faculty Association, where he also served as arbitration specialist and interim general manager. He served as a national AAUP special officer, and Collective Bargaining Congress vice chair. He taught at Western Michigan University, where he was grievance officer and chief faculty negotiator. He also served as president of the Michigan AAUP conference (1977–82).

PATRICK SHAW is an associate secretary on the staff of the AAUP. He worked at the National Labor Relations Board, served as general counsel for the Indiana Conference of Teamsters, and worked in private practice in Washington, DC, representing unions. Before joining the AAUP staff, Shaw was a business agent for Teamsters Local 364 in South Bend, Indiana.

INDEX

private institutions, 13, 67–77
  boards of trustees, 102–03
  compensation, 41–43
  contingent faculty members, 125–26
  graduate student organizing, 138
  impact of *NLRB v. Yeshiva University*,
    78–79, 80–93
  membership in bargaining units, 34–37
professional ethics. *See* academic
  values
professionalism, 14, 19, 25, 27–30, 49,
  292–95, 299–300, 384–86
  contingent faculty members, 318
  professional ethics, 2
  Redbook principles, 257–72
Proskauer Rose LLP, 140
Public Employment Relations Board
  (PERB), 337–38, 340, 341
public institutions, 78–79
  boards of trustees, 102–03, 293–94,
    297
  compensation, 41–43
  contingent faculty, 114–18
  economic resources, 293
  enabling legislation, 23–25, 67, 78–79, 138, 386–87
  faculty specialization, 114
  membership in bargaining units, 34–37
  professional-standards bargaining,
    257
  research institutions, 121
  See also two-year institutions
public relations. *See* communication
  and information sharing

Quigley, Mark, 337

Rabban, David, 340
Radical Caucus in English and the
  Modern Languages, 138
Rawling, Hunter, 357
Rayfield, Elizabeth, 345
Reagan administration, 82–83
Redbook principles (AAUP), 102, 257–72
Reichard, Carla, 245
Reichard, Gary W., 17, 381, 383
representation hearings, 72
research assistants. *See* graduate
  employees

retrenchment (layoff) policies, 46–47,
  103, 268–69
Rhoades, Gary
  on compensation, 44
  on contingent faculty members, 112,
    115, 123, 125, 134
  on graduate employees, 134
  on retrenchment policies, 46–47
  on shared governance, 47–49
  on strikes, 40
Rhoads, Robert A., 134
Ridge, Tom, 282
rights of academic workers. *See* personnel policies
Robin, Corey, 141, 145
Roddy, Kevin, 341
Roosevelt Adjunct Faculty Organization (RAFO), 308–14
Roosevelt University, 17, 125, 308–14
Rubin, Gayle, 375n1
Rutgers University, 125, 143, 151, 217–18

sabbaticals, 270–71
Saint John's University, 28–29, 32
Saint Thomas University case, 92
salaries. *See* compensation
San Francisco State University, 28–29
Schell, Eileen E., 124, 125
Schmid, Julie M., 134
Schuster, Jack H., 1, 117
scope of bargaining, 14–15, 68–69,
  259–60, 387
Seeger, Pete, 13
Semelroth, James, 14
Service Employees International
  Union (SEIU), 34, 125, 137
Seyman, Richard, 341
Shaman, Susan, 5
Shapp, Milton, 276
shared governance, 7–8, 164–65,
  390
  contingent faculty members, 316,
    319
  employer perspectives, 198
  enhancement by advocacy organizing, 110
  enhancement by bargaining, 9–12,
    15, 18–19, 47–49, 259–61, 386
  graduate students, 137
  institutional growth, 29
  intellectual property protections, 48,
    271–72